501
MUST-SEE
MOVIES

501 MUST-SEE MOVIES

Bounty
Books

An Hachette UK Company
www.hachette.co.uk

First published in Great Britain in 2004 by Bounty Books,
a division of Octopus Publishing Group Ltd
Carmelite House
50 Victoria Embankment
London EC4Y 0DZ
www.octopusbooks.co.uk

Revised edition 2010
First published in paperback in 2013
This revised edition published in 2016

ISBN: 978-0-7537-2976-2

A CIP catalogue record is available from the British Library

Printed and bound in China

10 9 8 7 6 5 4 3 2

Publisher: Samantha Warrington
Art Director: Miranda Snow
Managing Editor: Karen Rigden
Senior Production Manager: Peter Hunt
Packaged by The Urban Ant Ltd

Photographs courtesy of the Kobal Collection

CONTENTS

INTRODUCTION

501 Must-see Movies – 'Define "must-see"'! I hear you exclaim through gritted teeth. Cinephiles are notoriously opinionated – passionate about auteur, actors, directors, cinematographers, or cameramen. They know their genres; they know their plots, subplots, subtexts, homage and allusions, the context and the history, the perfectionist care that has gone into each angle and frame. They know too who was in the frame to star, who backed out, who failed to show, which directors gave the studio bosses grey hair prematurely, as their schedules and budgets skyrocketed into the stratosphere, and which low-budget gems have made cinema history. They have plotted the career paths and listed the achievements of the most influential players. They can define and defend German Expressionism, French New Wave, Italian Modernism, Postmodernism and Film Noir and predict next year's box-office blockbusters and 'sleepers' from the 'best boy' credits. Are you that cinephile?

If so, there is no doubt that you will take issue with some of the 501 movies described in these pages. Of necessity the selection is subjective to some degree. However, before you slam this (beautifully illustrated) book down in disgust because your favourite isn't included, or raise your blood pressure as you disagree with the opinions of our five expert contributors, consider. For every expert there is a novice, someone who has not seen every movie on the planet but who would like to make an informed choice at their local video store or art-house cinema; someone who is starting a film club or aspires to be a director or cinematographer. That someone will be fascinated by the wealth of background detail, the pithy plot outlines, the Academy Awards for which each movie was nominated and which of those it actually won –

who will learn the career development of directors, actors, screenplay writers and then sit down and enjoy, maybe for the first time, one of the extraordinary, groundbreaking, beautiful, avant-garde, memorable, startling, shocking or amusing films described here. Don't you envy those movie virgins? Then, of course, there are the many of us who just enjoy the entertainment and magic of a movie masterpiece, in the quiet and dark of our local cinema, or who long for just such a reference work as this to check our failing memories against the facts.

So how did we define 'must see'? Well first we made selections from the genres Action/Adventure & Epic, Comedy, Drama, Horror, Musical, Mystery & Thriller, Romance, Science Fiction & Fantasy, War and Western, then consulted the many lists of 'favourite' or 'best' movies that have been compiled. Our expert critics had their own views of course. Then we looked at the body of work each director, actor, cameraman and crew contributed to the decade or decades featured in the chronology of this book. We looked at films which complemented or contrasted with one another within their genre or which reflected the era in which they were made.

Here you will find astonishing achievements in special effects before and after CGI, brave cinematographical experiments, courageous social commentary, staggering performances, debuts and swansongs. With this book at your elbow you can start and stop angry debates, be stimulated, informed and amused and all before the lights go down and the credits roll. But then, please watch the films described here and form your own opinions. Enjoy!

ACTION/ADVENTURE & EPIC

NAPOLÉON

Abel Gance, France, 1927

Beginning in his schooldays, the film charts the life of Napoléon, from his flight from Corsica, through the French Revolution and the Terror, culminating in his invasion of Italy in 1797. Abel Gance's biopic of Napoléon is one of silent cinema's monumental achievements. But this six-hour account of the Emperor's life was intended by Gance as merely the first of a five-part account. The requisite list of statistics can be trotted out regarding the film's epic ambition: three years' worth of research and writing, thousands of extras, a dozen or so cameramen employed, not to mention the millions of francs spent in production. But these statistics pale in the face of the sheer range of techniques Gance used to tell his story, especially in thée innovative use of camera movement to render a storm-tossed ship, a galloping horse, even a snowball in flight. Perhaps the most celebrated of all Gance's technical coups is the final 20-minute triptych sequence, which alternates widescreen panoramic shots with multiple-image montages projected simultaneously on three screens, a process named 'Polyvision'. Gance's *Napoléon* endures not only for the epic scale of the story and its treatment, but also as an outstanding example of cinema in its early years being explored for its experimental possibilities as a still new visual medium.

CAST INCLUDES:
Albert Dieudonné, Vladimir Roudenko, Edmond Van Daële, Alexandre Koubitzky
SCREENPLAY:
Abel Gance
CINEMATOGRAPHY:
Léonce-Henri Burel, Jules Kruger, Joseph-Louis Mundwiller, Torpkoff

CLEOPATRA

Cecil B. DeMille, USA, 1934

48 BC. Cleopatra, Queen of Egypt (Colbert), is facing a palace revolt and welcomes the arrival of Julius Caesar (William) as a way of securing her power under Roman rule. When Caesar, whom she has led astray, is killed, Cleopatra transfers her attentions to Marc Antony (Wilcoxon), whom she attempts to seduce and manipulate. The characteristic opulence of DeMille's take on the story of the legendary Egyptian asp-clasper is well encapsulated by its poster tagline: 'A love affair that shook the world set in a spectacle of thrilling magnificence'. For which read, 'campy', 'grandiose' and 'ludicrous historically'. The sets, designed by Hans Dreier, are strikingly opulent, and the costumes revealing. All the key qualities, in short, that one expects of one of classical Hollywood's masters of spectacle.

CAST INCLUDES:
Claudette Colbert, Warren William, Henry Wilcoxon, Joseph Schildkraut, Ian Keith
SCREENPLAY:
Bartlett Cormack, Waldemar Young, Vincent Lawrence
CINEMATOGRAPHY:
Victor Milner

ACADEMY AWARD
Best Cinematography:
Victor Milner

THE ADVENTURES OF ROBIN HOOD

Michael Curtiz & William Keighley, USA, 1938

Sir Robin of Locksley (Flynn) falls foul of the Norman authorities and turns outlaw when Prince John (Rains) usurps his brother's succession to the throne. Fleeing to Sherwood Forest, Sir Robin becomes Robin Hood, gathering around him a band of Merry Men. Robin woos and wins Lady Marian (de Havilland), who feeds him news of John's plots. When Marian is captured, Robin and his men storm Nottingham Castle to rescue her.

CAST INCLUDES:
Errol Flynn, Olivia de Havilland, Basil Rathbone, Claude Rains, Patric Knowles
SCREENPLAY:
Norman Reilly Raine, Seton I Miller
CINEMATOGRAPHY:
Tony Gaudio, Sol Polito

ACADEMY AWARDS
Best Art Direction: Carl Jules Weyl,
Best Film Editing: Ralph Dawson
Best Music, Original Score: Erich Wolfgang Korngold

The film that set the all-action standard by which other screen swashbucklers would be judged, Curtiz's take on the Sherwood Forest saga of 'robbing from the rich to give to the poor' is distinguished by Flynn's thrusting charisma as the film's lead (having pipped James Cagney, who was the director's original first choice, to the role). Flynn plays Sir Robin of Locksley the renegade aristo who, with his merry band of forest-dwelling marauders, confronts the corrupt ruling class of the day. Graced with a brilliantly choreographed, climactic sword fight between Flynn and Basil Rathbone as the villainous Sir Guy of Gisbourne, during which the action cuts between the men and their shadows, *The Adventures of Robin Hood* is graced with an Oscar-winning score by Erich Korngold and still sparkling Technicolor cinematography (an innovation in the 1930s) which was digitally enhanced for Warner's 2003 rerelease of the film.

GONE WITH THE WIND

Victor Fleming, USA, 1939

CAST INCLUDES:
Clark Gable, Vivien Leigh,
Olivia de Havilland,
Hattie McDaniel,
Thomas Mitchell, Leslie
Howard, George Reeves
SCREENPLAY:
Sidney Howard from the
novel by Margaret Mitchell
CINEMATOGRAPHY:
Ernest Haller

ACADEMY AWARDS

Best Actress in a Leading
Role: Vivien Leigh
Best Actress in a Supporting
Role: Hattie McDaniel
Best Art Direction:
Lyle Wheeler
Best Cinematography:
Ernest Haller, Ray Rennahan
Best Director:
Victor Fleming
Best Film Editing:
Hal C. Kern,
James E. Newcom
Outstanding Production:
Selznick International Pictures
Best Writing, Screenplay:
Sidney Howard, Technical
Achievement Award

Adapted from Margaret Mitchell's best-selling novel of the American South during the years of the Civil War and Reconstruction, *Gone with the Wind* was a monumental piece of Hollywood filmmaking in every conceivable respect. Costing $4.25 million (roughly equivalent to $50 million today) and lasting over three and a half hours, the film won ten Oscars, a record that stood until 1959 when *Ben-Hur* won 11. Director Victor Fleming – who was brought in after three weeks by producer David O. Selznick to replace the original director, George Cukor – presided over a number of technical innovations and cinematic firsts on the film. These included staging, for the burning of Atlanta, what was then the largest fire scene ever shot; the use of matte paintings to complete partially constructed sets (only the second use of this technique with Technicolor film); establishing the unknown actress Vivien Leigh, who had been cast as Scarlett O'Hara through a talent search (Katharine Hepburn and Paulette Goddard had both been considered for the role); and securing the first Academy Award for a black person (Hattie McDaniel, winning Best Supporting Actress for her role as 'Mammy'). *Gone with the Wind* can be properly considered as the prototype of the Hollywood 'blockbuster'.

THE SEA HAWK

Michael Curtiz, USA, 1940

CAST INCLUDES:
Errol Flynn, Brenda Marshall,
Claude Rains, Alan Hale,
Flora Robson
SCREENPLAY:
Howard Koch, Seton I. Miller
CINEMATOGRAPHY:
Sol Polito

Geoffrey Thorpe (Flynn), a buccaneer, is hired by Queen Elizabeth I (Robson) to harass the Spanish Armada which is waiting to attack England. Thorpe surprises them with attacks on their galleons. For *The Sea Hawk*, Warners reunited the team that had made *The Adventures of Robin Hood* (1938) a successful production: director Michael Curtiz, composer Erich Wolfgang Korngold and actors Errol Flynn, Claude Rains and Alan Hale. Flynn is energetically charming as the roguish Thorpe, secret lover of the Queen and a privateer against Spain, and Claude Rains is the villainous Spanish envoy, Don José. Shot in black-and-white rather than Technicolor, this high-seas swashbuckler was in part intended to be a morale-boosting exercise that would encourage the British in their fight against Germany.

THE TREASURE OF THE SIERRA MADRE

John Huston, USA, 1948

CAST INCLUDES:
Humphrey Bogart,
Walter Huston,
Tim Holt, Bruce Bennett
SCREENPLAY:
John Huston from the novel
by B. Traven
CINEMATOGRAPHY:
Ted D. McCord

Having been swindled by a crooked contractor, Dobbs (Bogart) and Curtin (Holt), a couple of adventurers, meet up with Howard (Huston), an old prospector, who tells them the hills are full of gold. The trio set off to hunt for the bounty but greed gradually gets the better of them. Director John Huston cast Humphrey Bogart in one of the most noxious roles of the actor's career. As Fred C. Dobbs, Bogart is the epitome of paranoid venality who, despite having his life saved twice by his fellow treasure-hunters, spirals into greed-induced madness. Having developed a taste and facility for location shooting while making propaganda films during the Second World War, Huston convinced Warners to let him shoot for ten weeks in Mexico, and the film gains much from the sun-bleached mountainside settings. This is an adventure film in which the quest is not an end in itself but the alibi for a fatalistic character study in which the moral differences between an older, wiser man and the mistrustful, middle-aged Dobbs become starkly apparent, and between which Curtin, the younger man, must choose.

ACADEMY AWARDS
Best Actor in a Supporting
Role: Walter Huston
Best Director:
John Huston

THE WAGES OF FEAR
LE SALAIRE DE LA PEUR

Henri-Georges Clouzot, France/Italy, 1953

In the South American jungle, an American oil company pays four men to deliver supplies of highly sensitive nitroglycerene to a remote oil field. A hostile rivalry develops between the two sets of drivers: the slightest jolt to either of their trucks will result in death. *The Wages of Fear* is a 'road movie' with only one possible destination: hell. Henri-Georges Clouzot's bleakly pessimistic, black-and-white thriller was a huge international success on its release, thanks to the unerring skill with which the director builds the tension to breaking point. The film's four main characters together represent a vision of the 'international adventurer' not as charming, risk-taking rogue, but as corrupt and cynical mercenary. The first half of the film is devoted to establishing the squalid and oppressive conditions in which this group of junk-town dogs find themselves, holed up in a poor part of Venezuela. A fire in an oil well gives them the chance to break out of their dead-end lives when an American petrochemical company hires them for the nearly suicidal job of transporting the explosives to the well. On the pitted and perilous roads, the two trucks they drive are virtual time bombs primed to detonate at any moment, and their unbearably tense journey occupies the latter half of the film.

THE SEVEN SAMURAI
SHICHININ NO SAMURAI

Akira Kurosawa, Japan, 1954

A veteran samurai (Shimura) answers a village's request for protection from marauding bandits. He assembles a team of six other samurai and they teach the townspeople how to defend themselves. When 40 bandits attack the village, a fight to the death ensues. Although set in 16th-century Japan, *The Seven Samurai*, as Kurosawa readily acknowledged, was heavily indebted to Hollywood westerns and particularly to John Ford. From its opening shot of galloping horsemen silhouetted against the horizon to its story of an elite team of warriors being assembled to protect a threatened village, the film was innovative with its influences – it would eventually be remade by John Sturges as *The Magnificent Seven*. The film takes time establishing the individual characters of the team of samurai and detailing their ambiguous relations with the villagers they are hired to protect. Kurosawa's genius for pictorial composition and choreographed movement made *The Seven Samurai* a perfect example of epic, bravura filmmaking.

THE TEN COMMANDMENTS

Cecil B. DeMille, USA, 1956

CAST INCLUDES:
Charlton Heston, Yul Brynner, Anne Baxter
SCREENPLAY:
Æneas MacKenzie, Jesse Lasky Jr., Jack Gariss, Fredric M. Frank (screenplay)
CINEMATOGRAPHY:
Loyal Griggs

ACADEMY AWARD
Best Effects, Special Effects: John P. Fulton

Moses (Heston) leads the slaves from the tyranny of the Egyptian pharaoh (Brynner) and into the desert where he receives the Word of God. Moses attracts the attentions of Queen Nefertiti (Baxter) until he rebels and is sent into exile. DeMille had already made an earlier version of *The Ten Commandments* in 1923, before this epic 1956 reprise of the biblical story. Shot in widescreen Technicolor and lasting nearly four hours, *The Ten Commandments* set the standard by which many epics, biblical or otherwise, would be measured. DeMille pulled out all the stops in terms of special effects: the images of Moses turning his staff into a snake and the Nile into blood were unprecedented visual innovations at the time, and the parting of the Red Sea remains one of Hollywood's most treasured 'miracles' of special effects.

WAR AND PEACE

King Vidor, Italy/USA, 1956

Focused around Napoléon's 1812 invasion of Russia, the film follows the lives of three aristocratic Russians, Natasha (Hepburn), Pierre (Fonda) and Bolkonsky (Ferrer), over the course of 15 years. Another epic Dino D. Laurentiis/Carlo Ponti co-production, this $6 million costume-drama adaptation of Leo Tolstoy's equally epic novel of the same name was Paramount's second big production of 1956, the other being DeMille's *The Ten Commandments*. Moving from lavish ballroom scenes to huge battle reconstructions, Vidor pulled out all the stops in the film's three hours, making the most of Jack Cardiff's sumptuous colour cinematography and the VistaVision widescreen format to create some opulent compositions of movement and colour.

CAST INCLUDES:
Audrey Hepburn, Henry Fonda, Mel Ferrer, Vittorio Gassman, Herbert Lom
SCREENPLAY:
Bridget Boland, Mario Camerini, Robert Westerby from the novel by Leo Tolstoy
CINEMATOGRAPHY:
Jack Cardiff

NORTH BY NORTHWEST

Alfred Hitchcock, USA, 1959

CAST INCLUDES:
Cary Grant, Eva Marie Saint,
James Mason,
Jessie Royce Landis
SCREENPLAY:
Ernest Lehman
CINEMATOGRAPHY:
Robert Burks

An advertising executive, Roger O. Thornhill (Grant), is mistaken for a government agent by a gang of spies and is pursued across the US, while being helped by the beautiful Eve Kendall (Saint). One of Hitchcock's best-loved classics, *North by Northwest* is a mistaken-identity caper movie in which the master of suspense puts the ever-suave Cary Grant through his paces (it would be the fourth and final collaboration between the actor and director) as a man on the run in a mystifying game of cat and mouse. Or perhaps that should be cropduster and quarry. The film features two of cinema's most famous set pieces: the chase scene in which Grant is terrorized by a biplane that harries him across empty fields; and the equally famous climactic scene in which Grant and Saint are chased across the monumental presidential sculptures of Mount Rushmore. In between the pursuit sequences the two leads engage in frisky thrust-and-parry dialogue, as though they'd somehow wandered out of a romantic comedy into a big-budget thriller and can't quite get their bearings. For all its set-piece action, *North by Northwest* is Hitchcock in light, likeable mode. The fearsome and intimate malevolence of *Psycho* was only a year away.

CAST INCLUDES: Charlton Heston, Jack Hawkins, Haya Harareet, Stephen Boyd, Hugh Griffith
SCREENPLAY: Karl Turnberg from the novel by Lew Wallace
CINEMATOGRAPHY: Robert L. Surtees

BEN-HUR

William Wyler, USA, 1959

Jerusalem at the beginning of the first century. Judah Ben-Hur (Heston) is a rich Jewish prince and merchant who welcomes his old friend Messala (Boyd) when he arrives as commanding officer of the Roman legions. But tensions develop between them and Messala contrives to have Judah framed and condemned to life as a galley slave. Judah swears to seek his revenge. Winning 11 Oscars and still legendary, this vast biblical epic remains the grandest of the widescreen Hollywood blockbusters of the 1950s. Subtitled 'A Tale of the Christ', and opening with an overture playing against a shot of Michelangelo's Sistine Chapel, the grandiose nature of the film's ambitions is asserted right from the start. An adaptation of a 1926 film of the same name, Wyler's 1959 version was the most expensive film ever made at the time, costing $15 million and almost bankrupting a financially unstable MGM, and involving six years of preproduction and six months of location shooting in Italy. The film's scenes of chariot racing remain one of the iconic moments of all-out Hollywood spectacle, taking up 20 minutes of the film's nearly four hours. They took three months to film on what was then the largest single set ever constructed.

SPARTACUS

Stanley Kubrick, USA, 1960

CAST INCLUDES:
Tony Curtis, Kirk Douglas,
Laurence Olivier, Jean
Simmons, Charles Laughton
SCREENPLAY:
Dalton Trumbo from the
novel by Howard Fast
CINEMATOGRAPHY:
Russell Metty

Spartacus (Douglas) was born and raised a slave. After being trained as a gladiator, he turns on his masters and leads the other slaves in rebellion. Under Spartacus, the rebels travel to southern Italy, where they intend to cross the sea to return to their homes. Two Roman statesmen, the republican Gracchus (Laughton) and the militarist Crassus (Olivier), attempt to manipulate the rebels for their own political benefit. In the 1960s, *Spartacus* was seen as being the first 'intellectual epic' since the days of silent cinema, in which the ideas were as central as the action sequences. And *Spartacus* indeed combines both the cerebral and the spectacular in its concentration on the political machinations taking place around the slave rebellion. With its stellar international cast, an intelligent screenplay (by then blacklisted writer, Dalton Trumbo), the film was produced by its lead actor Kirk Douglas and is reputed to have definitively put its director, Stanley Kubrick, off working on a big-budget Hollywood picture ever again without complete independence. Today, elements of the film inevitably appear dated but it remains a rousing, immensely confident piece of epic filmmaking, and worthy of its five Oscars.

LAWRENCE OF ARABIA

David Lean, GB, 1962

CAST INCLUDES:
Peter O'Toole, Alec Guinness,
Anthony Quinn, Jack Hawkins,
Omar Sharif, Arthur Kennedy
SCREENPLAY:
T.E. Lawrence (writings),
Robert Bolt, Michael Wilson (sc.)
CINEMATOGRAPHY:
Freddie Young

During the First World War, young lieutenant T.E. Lawrence is seconded to act as an observer with Prince Feisal, the leader of an Arab tribal army. Lawrence decides to stay and help the prince and to keep him on the side of the Allies against the Turks. 'Four hours long, with no stars, and no women, and no love story, and not much action either': Omar Sharif's description of David Lean's epic would hardly make a ringing poster endorsement, yet the film was a great success, not least at the 1963 Academy Awards where it took seven Oscars. The film's subject is the First World War exploits of T.E Lawrence, who played a crucial role in enlisting Arab tribes to fight alongside the British against Turkey. Lawrence was a complicated historical figure, a social and sexual nonconformist whose own legendary self-image he was happy to help construct, and the film doesn't entirely skirt these issues.

ZULU

Cy Endfield, GB, 1964

CAST INCLUDES: Michael Caine, Stanley Baker, Jack Hawkins, Ulla Jacobsson, James Booth
SCREENPLAY: Cy Endfield from the article by John Prebble
CINEMATOGRAPHY: Stephen Dade

On 22 January 1879, the British Army suffers one of its worst defeats when Zulu forces massacre 1,500 of its troops. After the battle, a Zulu force of over 4,000 advances on a small British outpost at Rorke's Drift guarded by 139 Welsh infantrymen. The film focuses on the ensuing 12-hour battle. Making his name in an uncharacteristic role, Michael Caine plays Lt. Gonville Bromhead, a young aristocrat with no combat experience. With some memorable set pieces, *Zulu* is a 'Boy's Own' tale of military honour and derring-do. The troops' expectation of an inevitable Zulu attack leads to a steady ratcheting-up of tension, enlivened by the interplay of the characters. The budget of $2 million was relatively small, and the production had to deal with location-based adversity: the first 11 days of the shoot were lost to bad weather which, nevertheless, allowed for intense rehearsals so that when shooting started, the pace was so rapid that all the lost time was made up. Only 500 Zulus were available to work on the film, with 4,000 required for the battle scenes, so artificial figures were created: watch carefully as they gather on the hilltops and look out for the legless, pre-digital Zulus.

DR ZHIVAGO

David Lean, GB, 1965

Told in flashback, *Dr Zhivago* follows the life of surgeon-poet Yuri Zhivago (Sharif) through the days of the Russian Revolution, the First World War, the Russian Civil War and the years of Stalin's Terror. How can Zhivago's love for Lara (Christie) survive such upheavals? Adapted from Boris Pasternak's novel, Lean's epic is a three-hour-long panorama of 50 years' worth of Russian history told through the lens of the love affair between Zhivago, a humanist, artist and medic, and Lara, the young woman who becomes his muse. Robert Bolt's heavily abridged adaptation of Pasternak's novel retained its central theme of the individual's place in history but Lean was criticized for using the epochal upheavals of war and revolution as the backdrop to a love story, creating a 'picture postcard' view of history. Lean re-created revolution-era Russia on sets built in Spain and Canada, shooting most of the scenes during winter. The director's much-vaunted attention to detail and stunning period set pieces made the film a huge success, and it won five Oscars.

CAST INCLUDES:
Omar Sharif, Julie Christie, Rod Steiger, Alec Guiness, Tom Courtney, Ralph Richardson
SCREENPLAY:
Robert Bolt from the novel by Boris Pasternak
CINEMATOGRAPHY:
Freddie Young, Nicolas Roeg

THE LION IN WINTER

Anthony Harvey, GB, 1968

CAST INCLUDES:
Katharine Hepburn,
Peter O'Toole, Nigel Terry,
Anthony Hopkins
SCREENPLAY:
James Goldman from his play
CINEMATOGRAPHY:
Douglas Slocombe

1183. Court intrigues develop around which of Henry II's (O'Toole) four sons will succeed him. Henry favours his youngest son (Terry), while his wife, Eleanor of Aquitaine (Hepburn), has other plans for the oldest (Hopkins), Richard the Lionhearted.

The action in *The Lion in Winter* is less violent than verbal, a matter more of royal skullduggery than set-piece sword fights. The battlefield here is the English court of King Henry II at Christmas where, in the company of his sons and wife, Eleanor of Aquitaine (who lives imprisoned in a French tower), the 50-year-old King is deciding on his successor.

Adapted from James Goldman's play, the film's emphasis is on the intrigues, schemes and power plays between the royal family and, in keeping with his theatrical source, director Harvey opted to cast leading stage performers for the supporting roles; the film saw the screen debuts of Anthony Hopkins, Nigel Terry and Timothy Dalton as the child king of France. Restricting the action largely to the castle confines, this is a Waspish depiction of dynastic struggles where the themes of love, honour and loyalty are explored through poisonous repartee and cunning stratagems.

ACADEMY AWARDS
Best Actress in
a Leading Role:
Katharine Hepburn
Best Music, Original Score
for a Motion Picture Not a
Musical: John Barry
Best Writing, Screenplay
Based on Material
From Another Medium:
James Goldman.

WATERLOO

Sergei Bondarchuk, Italy/Russia, 1970

CAST INCLUDES:
Rod Steiger, Christopher Plummer, Virginia McKenna, Jack Hawkins, Orson Welles
SCREENPLAY:
Sergei Bondarchuk, Vittorio Bonicelli, H.A.L. Craig
CINEMATOGRAPHY:
Armando Nannuzzi

Napoléon (Steiger) escapes from imprisonment on Elba, causing the French Army to defect from the king back to him. The Duke of Wellington (Plummer) faces Napoléon with a ragtag army of Britons, Belgians, Prussians and mercenaries. The two meet at Waterloo, where the fate of Europe will be decided. *Waterloo* was one of the many elephantine international co-productions that the Italian producer Dino De Laurentiis specialized in making throughout the 1960s and 1970s and was a commercial disaster on its release. Director Sergei Bondarchuk, having already cut his teeth on the mammoth Soviet film version of *War and Peace* (1956), which was reputed to have cost around $100 million, worked with an international cast of big-name actors and called on cohorts of the Red Army for kinetic re-creations of the battle scenes. Lasting for four hours in its Russian version, the Americans slashed two hours off the film's running time, making an already sprawling story almost incomprehensible in places.

AGUIRRE: THE WRATH OF GOD
AGUIRRE, DER ZORN GOTTES

Werner Herzog, Germany/Peru/Mexico, 1972

CAST INCLUDES:
Klaus Kinski, Alejandro Repulles, Cecilia Rivera, Helena Rojo, Dan Ades, Peter Berling
SCREENPLAY:
Werner Herzog
CINEMATOGRAPHY:
Thomas Mauch

In 16th-century South America, a group of Spanish conquistadors descend the Amazon River in search of El Dorado, the legendary 'City of Gold'. As the expedition party falls foul of the local Indians and suffers disease and hunger, it slowly falls apart. The megalomaniac second-in-command, Don Lope de Aguirre (Kinski), seizes control. Described as 'one of the great river films', Herzog's Amazonian epic charts the descent into disillusionment, despair and self-destruction of the group seeking the ever-elusive city and the riches it promises. This is cinema of primal savagery, as much in its aesthetic minimalism of handheld cameras aboard lurching rafts as for its portrayal of civilization succumbing to murderous atavism, at the centre of which is the explosive, gargoyle-like presence of Klaus Kinski as the messianic adventurer. Herzog's insistent concentration on the power of place – the river, its swamps and forests – and the emphasis on filth, disease and brutality produce an environment of unforgiving cruelty in which he grounds the film's allegory of the human capacity for self-delusion.

THE POSEIDON ADVENTURE

Ronald Neame, USA, 1972

It's New Year's Eve, and a luxury cruise liner, the SS *Poseidon*, is on its final voyage before being dismantled. An undersea earthquake unleashes a flood of tidal waves that capsize the ship, turning it upside down. A small crew of survivors trapped on board must fight their way to safety. Along with *The Towering Inferno* (1974), *The Poseidon Adventure* is one of the best of Hollywood's crop of 1970s' disaster movies. Which is not to say that it hasn't acquired a certain camp patina over time, thanks largely to the now dated special effects and the countless *Airplane* send-ups of the genre. Despite this, the race-against-time narrative in which characters develop under extreme duress makes for a satisfying depiction of ship-bound peril. The motley bunch of survivors includes Gene Hackman as a tough-minded, liberal preacher, Ernest Borgnine as a blowhard cop constantly competing with Hackman for leadership of the group, the cop's ex-prostitute wife (Stevens) and an assortment of others whose chief function is to gain our sympathy only to perish tragically.

CAST INCLUDES:
Gene Hackman, Ernest Borgnine, Red Buttons, Roddy McDowall, Shelley Winters, Stella Stevens
SCREENPLAY:
Wendell Mayes, Stirling Silliphant from the novel by Paul Gallico
CINEMATOGRAPHY:
Harold E. Stine

ENTER THE DRAGON

Robert Clouse, USA, 1973

CAST INCLUDES:
Bruce Lee, John Saxton, Kien Shih, Jim Kelly
SCREENPLAY:
Michael Allin
CINEMATOGRAPHY:
Gilbert Hubbs

A martial arts expert (Lee) is hired by an intelligence agency to uncover the criminal activities of Mr Han (Shih), who sponsors a martial arts competition set on an island near Hong Kong. Lee infiltrates the competition and teams up with two other agents to avenge his sister's death and to destroy Han's drugs and prostitution ring. *Enter the Dragon* is a lurid '70s' spectacle that succeeded in adapting elements of the hugely popular Bond films – Lee's infiltration of an island fortress, the manic supervillain Mr Han – to the grindhouse genres of exploitation and kung fu movies, bringing Hong Kong action cinema to an international audience. With several tournament fight scenes, a cat burglar sequence and a climactic showdown set in a hall of mirrors between Lee and Mr Han, this was the work that made Lee a legend, largely because it was his last completed film. Lee died, aged 32, before the film was released, but *Enter the Dragon* remains a highly influential cult precursor of the recent renaissance of martial arts films.

PAPILLON

Franklin J. Schaffner, USA, 1973

1931: Henri 'Papillon' Charrière is a petty criminal wrongly convicted of murder and sentenced to life imprisonment in a penal colony in French Guiana, South America. Dega (Hoffman) is also a resident of the colony. Papillon makes repeated attempts to escape but is always recaptured and thrown into solitary confinement. Based on the 'true story' of Henri Charrière, whose nickname 'Papillon' (French for 'butterfly') was the title of his best-selling account of escape from a penal colony, Schaffner's film version cast Steve McQueen as the dogged escapee. The film strives for grimy authenticity in its depiction of the penal colony as a brutal hellhole. With each escape attempt, Papillon is set on an endurance course of blood, sweat and leprosy that the spectator goes through with him. The film marked the end of a run of highly successful films for McQueen, including *The Great Escape*, *Bullitt* and *The Getaway*, in which he established his screen persona as a rugged, impassive survivor.

CAST INCLUDES:
Steve McQueen,
Dustin Hoffman,
Victor Jory, Don Gordon,
Anthony Zerbe
SCREENPLAY:
Dalton Trumbo, Lorenzo
Semple Jr. from the novel by
Henri Charrière
CINEMATOGRAPHY:
Fred J. Koenekamp

ACADEMY AWARD
Best Music,
Original Dramatic Score:
Jerry Goldsmith

THE TOWERING INFERNO

Irwin Allen, John Guillermin, USA, 1974

CAST INCLUDES:
Steve McQueen, Paul
Newman, William Holden,
Fred Astaire, Faye Dunaway
SCREENPLAY:
Stirling Silliphant from the
novels *The Tower* by Richard
Martin Stern and *The Glass
Inferno* by Thomas N.
Scortia & Frank M. Robinson
CINEMATOGRAPHY:
Fred Koenekamp, Joseph Biroc

During a celebratory party, a newly built skyscraper bursts into flames. A courageous fire captain (McQueen) on the outside and the desperate architect (Newman) trapped inside struggle to save the guests. Directed by Irwin Allen, who produced *The Poseidon Adventure*, *The Towering Inferno* replaces the former film's stricken ship with a 130-storey skyscraper wreathed in flames and fills the structure with a similarly ill-assorted group. *Earthquake*, another popular big-budget disaster movie, was released in the same year, but *Inferno* came top at the US box office helped, no doubt, by Steve McQueen and Paul Newman. Running at over two and a half hours long, the film drains every last bit of tension from the initial premise and makes great play with its ever more spectacular effects and stunts.

RAIDERS OF THE LOST ARK

Steven Spielberg, USA, 1981

CAST INCLUDES:
Harrison Ford, Karen Allen,
Paul Freeman, Ronald Lacey,
Denholm Elliott
SCREENPLAY:
George Lucas &
Philip Kaufman (story),
Lawrence Kasdan
CINEMATOGRAPHY:
Douglas Slocombe

ACADEMY AWARDS
Best Art Direction-Set
Decoration:
Norman Reynolds,
Leslie Dilley, Michael Ford
Best Film Editing:
Michael Kahn
Best Sound: Bill Varney,
Steve Maslow, Gregg
Landaker, Roy Charman
Best Visual Effects: Richard
Edlund, Kit West, Bruce
Nicholson, Joe Johnston
Special Achievement Award
(Sound Effects Editing):
Ben Burtt,
Richard L. Anderson

A highly entertaining romp of an action film that throws in everything from giant spiders to Nazi villains, biblical and Egyptian mythology, thrills, spills and special effects. *Raiders of the Lost Ark* marked the first collaboration between Spielberg and George Lucas, the two most commercially successful American filmmakers. This was the first of Spielberg's all-action Indiana Jones films, followed by *Indiana Jones and the Temple of Doom* (1984) and *Indiana Jones and the Last Crusade* (1989). While *Raiders* was acknowledged by the director to be a tribute to the action serials of his youth, it's a truly postmodern cornucopia of cinematic styles and genres, drawing on westerns, horror films, war and Bond movies. Spielberg also described his vision of Harrison Ford's character as a combination of Errol Flynn in *The Adventures of Don Juan* and Humphrey Bogart in *The Treasure of the Sierra Madre*; an American critic summed up his appeal nicely when he described Indiana Jones as being as 'indestructible as a cartoon coyote'.

FITZCARRALDO

Werner Herzog, Germany/Peru, 1982

CAST INCLUDES:
Klaus Kinski, Claudia Cardinale, José Lewgoy, Miguel Angel Fuentes, Paul Hittscher
SCREENPLAY:
Werner Herzog
CINEMATOGRAPHY:
Thomas Mauch

An obsessive Irish opera enthusiast (Kinski) plans to build an opera house in the Peruvian jungle. First he has to make his fortune, and decides on a rubber plantation on an inhospitable stretch of the river. Fitzgerald recruits local Indians to haul his riverboat over the mountain that stands between him and the realization of his dreams. With its central image of a ship being hauled over a mountain, Herzog's epic account of Irish adventurer Brian Sweeney Fitzgerald's vision is a film about the costs of obsession. Fitzgerald is dismissed as 'conquistador of the useless' after his plans to build a trans-Andean railroad and to sell ice in the area have both foundered. But his monomaniac dedication to realizing his vision finds unlikely allies, including the seemingly hostile native Indians, who name him 'Fitzcarraldo'. Made before the days of digital effects, Herzog took his crew down the Amazon and it's hard not to see the character of Fitzcarraldo, the risk-taking visionary, as the director's alter ego. Given the extraordinarily chaotic nature of the film's production, which involved the loss of the two previously cast leads and Herzog having to start over again after a year's worth of filming, plus injuries and deaths among the crew, not to mention Kinski's legendary volatility, it's clear that there were equal degrees of obsession at work on either side of the camera.

GANDHI

Richard Attenborough, USA/GB/India, 1982

CAST INCLUDES:
Ben Kingsley, Candice Bergen, Roshan Seth, Edward Fox, John Gielgud
SCREENPLAY:
John Briley
CINEMATOGRAPHY:
Ronnie Taylor, Billy Williams

The story of the life of Mohandas K. 'Mahatma' Gandhi, from his days as a struggling anti-racist lawyer in apartheid-era South Africa to becoming Indian leader. Returning to India, Gandhi sees the British treating Indians as second-class citizens. He inspires his countrymen to rise against the British through nonviolent means. Attenborough's film is truly epic in both scope and scale. Covering five decades of Indian history, the film follows the blueprint of David Lean's *Lawrence of Arabia*: beginning with the death of the protagonist, following with his funeral and flashing back to his life's achievements. Attenborough's commitment to the project was itself epic – the director had begun researching the project 20 years earlier and had been planning it for the best part of four decades. Before CGI allowed filmmakers to create digital crowd scenes, Gandhi set the record for the sheer number of extras: a quarter of a million extras were employed for a single scene. Kingsley's extraordinary chameleon-like performance won him an Academy Award; one of the nine that the film earned.

THE RIGHT STUFF

Philip Kaufman, USA, 1983

CAST INCLUDES:
Sam Shepard, Scott Glenn,
Ed Harris, Dennis Quaid,
Fred Ward
SCREENPLAY:
Philip Kaufman from the
book by Tom Wolfe
CINEMATOGRAPHY:
Caleb Deschanel

During the early days of the American space programme, seven test pilots are selected to become astronauts in Project Mercury. They must undergo gruelling training if the Americans are going to win the race against the Soviets and be the first to send a manned mission into space. *The Right Stuff* is based on Tom Wolfe's 1979 bestseller about the early days of the US space programme, when test pilots were pushing planes towards MACH speeds that would pull them beyond Earth, and when debates were still active over whether spaceflights should go unmanned or carry 'Spam in a can', as ace test pilot Chuck Yeager described manned missions. A study of daredevil heroism derived from the real-life exploits of Yeager (Shepard), John Glenn (Ed Harris) and the first astronauts, Philip Kaufman's gripping epic features striking special effects and stunning aerial cinematography that won it three Oscars. Refreshingly, it doesn't shy away from the political and media machinations at work in the American desire to send the first man into space.

A PASSAGE TO INDIA

David Lean, GB/USA, 1984

India, the 1920s: tensions develop between Indians and colonial Britons when a young Englishwoman, Adela Quested (Davis), who has travelled to India to visit her fiancé, accuses the young Muslim doctor Aziz H. Ahmed (Banerjee) of rape. It had been 14 years since his last feature film, *Ryan's Daughter*, when David Lean returned to filmmaking with his 1984 adaptation of E.M. Forster's celebrated novel, *A Passage to India*. It explores the barely suppressed resentment and racism existing between the British Raj and its Indians, and its poisonous effects when Adela presses the charge and the doctor goes on trial. Lean treats the subject matter on a characteristically grand scale and this historical costume drama was one of the key films of the 'heritage cinema' genre that was so popular in 1980s British filmmaking.

ACADEMY AWARDS
Best Actress in a Supporting
Role: Peggy Ashcroft
Best Music, Original Score:
Maurice Jarre

CAST INCLUDES: Judy Davis, Victor Banerjee, Peggy Ashcroft, James Fox, Alec Guinness
SCREENPLAY: David Lean from the novel by E.M. Forster
CINEMATOGRAPHY: Ernest Day

RAN

Akira Kurosawa, Japan/France, 1985

Lord Hidetora (Nakadai) is an ageing Japanese warlord who intends to divide his kingdom between his three sons. The elder two are satisfied while the youngest believes his father has gone mad and predicts conflict between his older brothers. Made when Kurosawa was 75, *Ran* (meaning 'chaos') was the venerable director's version of Shakespeare's *King Lear*, a project that took ten years to reach the screen. The film is less a straightforward stage-to-screen adaptation (Lear's daughters are gender-swapped to sons) than an examination of greed, betrayal and disloyalty to the codes of personal honour placed within a dynastic power struggle that finds bloody expression on the battlefield. Kurosawa had amply demonstrated his mastery of staging epic action scenes in films, such as *The Seven Samurai* (1954), *Yojimbo* (1961) and *Kagemusha* (1980), and *Ran* was proof that his ability to orchestrate epic slices of movement and colour remained that of a cinematic virtuoso.

CAST INCLUDES:
Tatsuya Nakadai, Akira Terao, Jinpachi Nezu, Daisuke Ryu, Mieko Harada
SCREENPLAY:
Masato Ide, Akira Kurosawa, Hideo Oguni based on *King Lear* by William Shakespeare
CINEMATOGRAPHY:
Takao Saito, Masaharu Ueda, Asakazu Nakai

ACADEMY AWARD
Best Costume Design:
Emi Wada

TOP GUN

Tony Scott, USA, 1986

CAST INCLUDES:
Tom Cruise, Kelly McGillis, Val Kilmer, Anthony Edwards, Tom Skerritt
SCREENPLAY:
Jim Cash, Jack Epps Jr. from an article by Ehud Yonay
CINEMATOGRAPHY:
Jeffrey L. Kimball

ACADEMY AWARD
Best Music, Original Song:
Giorgio Moroder,
Tom Whitlock

Lt Pete 'Maverick' Mitchell (Cruise), a fighter pilot, is sent to the Top Gun Naval Flying School, where he strives to be the best pilot and is attracted to Charlotte Blackwood (McGillis), a civilian tutor. Although, in essence, a barely disguised recruitment film for the US Air Force, *Top Gun* features some breathtaking aerial sequences in which Cruise and colleagues engage in all manner of dogfighting daredevilry. As the ultra-competitive yet conflicted 'Maverick', Cruise has a rival in another 'top gun' airman known as 'Iceman' (Kilmer), an air-ace Dad whose mysterious death still troubles him and a love interest in the shape of earthbound instructor Charlie (McGillis). It's clearly not the emotional and psychological aspects of the story that interest director Tony Scott but the gung-ho airborne action, which is riveting.

THE LAST EMPEROR

Bernardo Bertolucci, France/Italy/GB, 1987

At the age of three, Pu-yi is named emperor of China. The film follows his life through his brief reign, his abdication and decline into a dissolute lifestyle to his final days as a humble gardener in the Peking Botanical Gardens. *The Last Emperor* was the film with which Bernardo Bertolucci went beyond his self-proclaimed status as one of the 'sons' of Jean-Luc Godard and a leading light of 1960s' and 1970s' European art cinema, reaching out to the widest possible international audience. While *The Last Emperor* retains certain conventions of the 'historical epic', especially in the way that the life of a single individual – in this case, Pu-yi, the child emperor – is used as a prism through which to address a nation's history, Bertolucci's approach is that of a director who has fully absorbed the refinements of cinematic modernism. Pu-yi is a paradoxically passive character to be at the heart of such an epic; sealed within an opulent, hermetic court and occupying a position that represents only ceremonial significance, he is dubbed 'the emperor of nothing', whose story is told in an intricately interwoven tapestry of flashforward and flashback. As well as using authentic costumes and thousands of extras, Bertolucci shot entirely on location in the People's Republic of China and was given permission to film inside the Forbidden City, the vast imperial complex of 250 acres and 9,999 rooms. With this combination of real locations and his strange, dreamlike use of space and colour, Bertolucci fashioned an epic spectacle that managed to be both sumptuously grand and psychologically intimate. His triumph would pay off in terms of public, critical and Academy Award acclaim and lead to him making two subsequent 'intimate epics': *The Sheltering Sky* (1990) and *Little Buddha* (1994).

CAST INCLUDES:
John Lone, Joan Chen, Peter O'Toole, Tao Wu
SCREENPLAY:
Henry Pu-yi, Mark Peploe, Bernardo Bertolucci from the book by Henry Pu-yi
CINEMATOGRAPHY:
Vittorio Storaro

DID YOU KNOW?
The Last Emperor won nine Oscars at the 1988 Academy Awards.

DIE HARD

John McTiernan, USA, 1988

CAST INCLUDES:
Bruce Willis, Allan Rickman,
Bonnie Bedelia,
Reginald Veljohsnon
SCREENPLAY:
Jeb Stuart, Steven E de Souza
from the novel by
Roderick Thorp
CINEMATOGRAPHY:
Jan de Bont

During a Christmas trip to Los Angeles, New York cop John McClane (Willis) is trapped in a skyscraper when a group of terrorists occupy the building. His wife (Bedelia) is among the group captured by the charismatic terrorist leader (Rickman). McClane is all that stands between the hostages and their captors. In the language of the 'high-concept' pitch beloved of '80s' Hollywood, *Die Hard*, with its combination of gung-ho action and skyscraper-set peril, could be described as '*Rambo* meets *The Towering Inferno*'. This was the first of the Die Hard films, in which Willis established himself as one of Hollywood's principal vest-wearing, gun-toting action men, having previously been best known for playing a smirking private eye in the US television series *Moonlighting*. But alongside the cat-and-mouse interplay between Willis's resourceful, wisecracking cop and Rickman's suave and ruthless terrorist, it's the building that's the star. The lift shafts, heating ducts and sheer glass façades of the Nakatomi Corporation's high-rise HQ become the setting for a catalogue of violent confrontations, high-adrenalin stunts and huge explosions.

TRUE LIES

James Cameron, USA, 1994

CAST INCLUDES:
Arnold Schwarzenegger,
Jamie Lee Curtis,
Tom Arnold, Art Malik,
Bill Paxton, Tia Carrere
SCREENPLAY:
James Cameron,
Claude Zidi, Simon Michael,
Didier Kaminka
CINEMATOGRAPHY:
Russell Carpenter

Harry Tasker (Schwarzenegger) works for a top-secret organization and is investigating a group of Arab terrorists involved in smuggling nuclear weapons. His wife, Helen (Curtis), who believes Harry to be a computer salesman, feels neglected by her husband and begins a flirtation with a man who pretends to be a spy (Paxton). When Harry and Helen are kidnapped by the terrorists, Harry is forced to reveal his true identity to his wife. *True Lies* has Schwarzenegger playing a semi-parodic version of his well-established action-hero role, and this allows director James Cameron to attempt an unlikely fusion of two seemingly incompatible genres – the action-adventure film and the screwball comedy. Whether it was conceived to broaden the actor's range and humanize his *Terminator* persona, the film's concentration on the husband-and-wife relationship lacks the conviction of the action sequences which, as one would expect from Cameron, come thick, fast and increasingly spectacularly.

SPEED

Jan de Bont, USA, 1994

ACADEMY AWARD
Best Sound:
Gregg Landaker,
Steve Maslow, Bob Beemer,
David R.B. MacMillan

CAST INCLUDES:
Keanu Reeves,
Dennis Hopper,
Sandra Bullock,
Joe Morton, Jeff Daniels
SCREENPLAY:
Graham Yost
CINEMATOGRAPHY:
Andrzej Bartkowiak

Jack Traven (Reeves), a young cop, must save the passengers of a bus that has a bomb set to explode if the bus goes below 50 miles per hour. *Speed* is one of those films that does exactly what it says in the title; it tears along with the machine-tooled precision of a big-budget action film intent on dispensing wall-to-wall thrills, stunts and special effects. An inventive thriller that starts with hostages trapped in an elevator and continues with two chases, one on a bus, another on a subway train, *Speed* pits a resourceful bomb-disposal expert (Reeves) against a maniac ex-cop with a grudge (Hopper) who is orchestrating the mayhem. Featuring Sandra Bullock as the woman who must keep her foot to the pedal on the bomb-primed bus, the film also revealed Keanu Reeves to be a compelling action hero – next stop: *The Matrix*. Director Jan de Bont, who had worked as a cinematographer on action movies such as *Total Recall* and *Die Hard*, delivers a compelling white-knuckle ride all the way to the subway station.

BRAVEHEART

Mel Gibson, USA, 1995

CAST INCLUDES:
Mel Gibson, Sophie Marceau, Brian Cox, Patrick McGoohan, Catherine McCormack, Angus MacFadyen
SCREENPLAY:
Randall Wallace
CINEMATOGRAPHY:
John Toll

13th-century Scotland. A Scottish rebel, William Wallace (Gibson), leads an uprising against the cruel English reign of Edward Longshanks (McGoohan) who plans to take the Scottish crown for himself. His father died trying to bring freedom to the Scots when he was a young boy, so Wallace, with the support of Robert the Bruce (MacFadyen), takes on the invader. Hardly the last word in historical accuracy, Gibson's directorial debut, an account of 13th-century Scots taking on their evil English oppressors, is a wattle-and-daub epic of muddy, bloody battles. Gibson plays freedom fighter William Wallace as an ultra-macho mythical warrior, a resourceful military strategist and a martyr-in-the-making (dying on the rack, his last word is 'Freedom!'), while also enjoying dalliances with a French princess (Marceau) and an old flame (McCormack). Given an R rating for its scenes of 'brutal medieval warfare', *Braveheart* bagged six Academy Awards including Best Director. While the battle scenes are something to behold, the real interest lies in the way Gibson ups the ante in Hollywood cinema's enduring fascination with the spectacle of broken, bloodied male bodies, where narcissism and masochism combine to create the image of warrior-star. The next stop for Gibson would be obvious: *The Passion of the Christ*, the ultimate in celluloid bloodletting.

THE MUMMY

Stephen Sommers, USA, 1999

CAST INCLUDES:
Brendan Fraser,
Rachel Weisz, John Hannah,
Arnold Vosloo
SCREENPLAY:
Stephen Sommers
CINEMATOGRAPHY:
Adrian Biddle

In ancient Egypt, the powerful priest Imhotep (Vosloo) is cursed and mummified alive after an affair with his pharoah's mistress. Fast-forward to 1923 and a group of explorers, including American adventurer Rick O'Connell (Fraser), accidentally resurrect the mummy. It's bad news all round as Imhotep wants to destroy the world, but it's a particular calamity for Rick's new love, Evelyn (Weisz), who has been chosen as the substitute for Imhotep's lost love. Director Stephen Sommers' intention was to make a rollicking, period adventure in the Indiana Jones mould, and like *Temple of Doom*, he has laced the film liberally with supernatural scares. The characters are pretty stock, but unavoidably likeable. With a never-ending supply of one-liners, the dashing but egotistical Rick is a superb roguish hero, and the chemistry between him and the capricious scholar Evelyn is one of the film's great joys. But without a doubt the star of the show is the mummy itself. Although undeniably slick and modern, *The Mummy* also has an enchanting old-fashioned innocence.

CROUCHING TIGER, HIDDEN DRAGON WO HU CANG LONG

Ang Lee, Hong Kong/USA, 2000

CAST INCLUDES:
Yun Fat Chow, Michelle Yeoh,
Pei-Pei Chang, Ziyi Zhang
SCREENPLAY:
Hui-Ling Wang, James
Schamus, Kua Jung Tsai from
the novel by Du Lu Wang
CINEMATOGRAPHY:
Peter Pau

Li Mu Bai (Fat) is a warrior whose sword, the magic Green Destiny, is stolen. Li must recover it while also avenging the death of his father at the hands of the evil Jade Fox (Chang). He is joined in his quest by Yu Shu Lien (Yeoh), the unacknowledged love of his life. 'Sense and Sensibility with sword fights' was how screenwriter and stalwart Ang Lee collaborator James Schamus described the Hong Kong–born director's foray into martial arts action cinema. Lee's reputation as a master of finessed psychological dramas (*Eat, Drink, Man, Woman; The Ice Storm*) and period-costume dramas (*Sense and Sensibility*) did not appear to make him the obvious contender to deliver a kung fu epic, least of all one in Mandarin Chinese which was to make it to the multiplexes and multi-Oscar acclaim. Set in the mythical Chinese past, *Crouching Tiger* is a film about honour, betrayal and supernaturally gifted warriors who are able to effortlessly defy gravity. The fight sequences are breathtaking, with the actors scaling walls, leaping from roof to roof and, in one memorable scene, literally fighting it out in the treetops courtesy of Yuen Wo-Ping's 'wire fu' choreography (which also featured in *The Matrix*). The action adds to the film's richly romantic epic sweep, further enhanced by the commanding presences of Fat and Yeoh and a swooning score performed by cellist Yo Yo Ma.

GLADIATOR

Ridley Scott, USA/GB, 2000

CAST INCLUDES:
Russell Crowe, Joaquin Phoenix, Connie Nielsen, Oliver Reed, Richard Harris
SCREENPLAY:
David Franzoni (story), David Franzoni, John Logan, William Nicholson (screenplay)
CINEMATOGRAPHY:
John Mathieson

AD 180. General Maximus Decimus Meridius (Crowe) is named 'Keeper of Rome' by the dying Emperor Marcus Aurelius (Harris) after successfully vanquishing the Barbarian hordes. But the emperor's son, Commodus (Phoenix), has other ideas. Following a foiled execution, Maximus flees to his Spanish home to discover his wife and son have been murdered. Enslaved and trained as a gladiator, Maximus is one of a troupe of warriors called to Rome for the gladiatorial games where he is soon involved in plots to overthrow the emperor. With a mammoth budget and a four-month shoot in four countries, director Ridley Scott aimed, with *Gladiator*, to revive the genre of the 'ancient epic', which had not proved to be much of a crowd-puller since the international vogue in the 1960s for 'swords and sandals' spectaculars such as *Spartacus* (1960). Today, the thousands of extras mandatory in such epic undertakings may be multiplied thanks to CGI, and *Gladiator* is one of the prime examples of the new cinematic fashion for 'pixellated antiquity'. As well as using CGI to re-create the Colosseum in Rome, there was another, unexpected use found for Scott's special effects team: the death, during filming, of Oliver Reed, called for a stealthy dose of digital reanimation. The film deservedly won six Oscars.

CAST INCLUDES:
Elijah Wood, Orlando Bloom, Ian McKellen, Liv Tyler, Christopher Lee, Cate Blanchett, Sala Baker
SCREENPLAY:
Fran Walsh, Philippa Boyens, Peter Jackson from the novel by J.R.R. Tolkien
CINEMATOGRAPHY:
Andrew Lesnie

THE LORD OF THE RINGS: THE FELLOWSHIP OF THE RING

Peter Jackson, New Zealand/USA, 2001

An ancient ring thought lost for centuries has been found, and given to a Hobbit named Frodo (Wood). When Gandalf (McKellen) discovers that this is the One Ring of the Dark Lord Sauron (Baker), Frodo must make an epic quest to the Cracks of Doom to destroy it. Director Peter Jackson's screen adaptation of J.R.R. Tolkien's mammoth Middle Earth trilogy is an epic feat in itself: three films – *The Fellowship of the Ring* (2001), *The Two Towers* (2002) and *The Return of the King* (2003) – filmed over an 18-month production period at a cost of $300 million. Jackson's combination of the landscape of his native New Zealand and extensive use of CGI have served to make his 'Ring Cycle' the standard not only for fantasy cinema, but also for modern epic cinema in general. Taken all together, Jackson's epic vision of Tolkien's Middle Earth is a landscape of final battles, mythical monsters and age-old quests that is rendered throughout with spectacular panache.

MASTER AND COMMANDER: THE FAR SIDE OF THE WORLD

Peter Weir, USA, 2003

CAST INCLUDES:
Russell Crowe, Paul Bettany, James D'Arcy, Edward Woodall, Chris Larkin
SCREENPLAY:
Peter Weir, John Collee from the novels by Patrick O'Brien
CINEMATOGRAPHY:
Russell Boyd; Producer: Samuel Goldwyn Jr., Peter Weir, Duncan Henderson

During the Napoléonic Wars, HMS *Surprise*, a British frigate, and a larger French warship, the *Acheron*, hunt one another off the South American coast. Peter Weir's film brings to the screen characters from Patrick O'Brien's highly regarded series of seafaring novels and centres on the relationship between naval officer Capt Jack Aubrey, whose crew call him 'Lucky Jack', and the ship's surgeon, Stephen Maturin, a pair of firm friends and conversational sparring partners. Opening with a prolonged, bravura battle scene set in the foggy South Atlantic, the film takes time to establish the characters of the crew, their everyday onboard relations and their reactions to the fierce weather and violent skirmishes with the French battleship that stalks them. The film's core lies in the relationship between Capt Aubrey and Maturin, who find frequent respite from the violence of their lives by playing string duets together. Where one is a military traditionalist, the other tends to a more rationalist, scientific world-view.

PIRATES OF THE CARIBBEAN: THE CURSE OF THE BLACK PEARL

Gore Verbinski, USA, 2003

CAST INCLUDES:
Johnny Depp, Geoffrey Rush, Orlando Bloom, Keira Knightley, Jack Davenport
SCREENPLAY:
Ted Elliott (screenplay & story), Terry Rossio, (screenplay & story), Stuart Beattie (story), Jay Wolpert (story)
CINEMATOGRAPHY:
Dariusz Wolski

Jack Sparrow (Depp) is an inept pirate who rescues Elizabeth Swann (Knightley), who is then kidnapped by Barbossa (Rush), captain of the pirate ship the *Black Pearl*. Barbossa and crew are cursed to sail the seas as the living dead unless they make a sacrifice to restore them to life. Jack and Will Turner (Bloom), a heroic blacksmith, set off to rescue Elizabeth. *Pirates of the Caribbean* is a special effects swashbuckler for kids, an action-adventure film as theme-park ride. Literally so: at a budget of $100 million, Disney adapted for the screen one of its most popular theme park attractions. It is unabashedly scary fun, in which Johnny Depp's roguishly incompetent brigand and Orlando Bloom's capable blacksmith take on sword-wielding hordes of undead pirates. The film runs through all the possible variations of high-seas skulduggery in a nonstop carnival of chases and fight scenes. As Elizabeth, Keira Knightley is no tremulous damsel, battling with the best of them in this tongue-in-cheek romp.

KILL BILL: VOL. 1 & VOL. 2

Quentin Tarantino, USA, 2003 & 2004

After going AWOL from the Deadly Viper Assassination Squad, The Bride (Thurman) is tracked down, shot and left for dead by former boss and lover Bill (Carradine). Four years later she wakes from a coma and immediately sets out on a revenge rampage that starts with her old colleagues and builds inexorably towards Bill himself. After six years without a release, Tarantino looked to be taking a big risk by splitting *Kill Bill* into two parts. We needn't have worried, as each 'volume' is bursting with the rich detail and smart ideas with which Tarantino made his name. What's more, by splitting the film in two he has been able to take different but complementary approaches to each part in order to wring out every last drop of drama. *Volume 1* is a no-holds-barred, demented revenge actioner, all enormous set pieces and snappy one-liners, whilst *Volume 2* slows the pace, calms the madness and really gets under the skin of the two main characters. In either case this is seriously bravura filmmaking. At times we're almost swamped by the swirling primary colours and beautifully rich scenery, but it never pushes you over the top and Tarantino is always ready to temper the chaos with a perfectly timed slow-motion close-up to diffuse the action.

CAST INCLUDES:
Uma Thurman, Lucy Liu,
Vivica A. Fox, Daryl Hannah,
David Carradine
SCREENPLAY:
Quentin Tarantino
CINEMATOGRAPHY:
Robert Richardson

300

Zack Snyder, USA, 2006

In 480 BC the Battle of Thermopylae sees 300 Spartan warriors face off against a 100,000-strong Persian army. The Spartans' incredible confidence and potency surprises the invading King Xerxes (Santoro) and intimidates his soldiers. One of the most celebrated legends of ancient history, the enigmatic story of a small band of heroes defending their country from an overwhelming invasion is highly inspirational by anyone's standards, and a no-brainer for Hollywood. An outline of actual events is the launching point, but imagination soon takes over and the world is gradually revealed to be an almost dreamlike version of reality. A suitable 'look' was achieved by shooting everything in front of green screens, which allows the filmmakers to create any environment they can imagine and simply place the action over it. The otherworldly feel extends to the characters. The Spartan army is a vision of bronzed Adonis-like perfection, while the Persians are a medley of slaves, wizards, fantastic beasts and exotic warriors.

CAST INCLUDES:
Gerard Butler, Lena Headey,
David Wenham, Dominic
West, Rodrigo Santoro
SCREENPLAY:
Zack Snyder, Kurt Johnstad,
Michael Gordon, Frank Miller
(graphic novel), Lynn Varley
(graphic novel)
CINEMATOGRAPHY:
Larry Fong

CASINO ROYALE

Martin Campbell, GB/Czech Rep/USA/Germany, 2006

Recently promoted to '00' status, British spy James Bond (Craig) embarks on his first mission. Terrorist banker Le Chiffre (Mikkelsen) is to participate in a high-stakes poker tournament in order to cripple various disreputable organizations, and Bond must ensure he doesn't win. Returning to the screen after a four-year hiatus, Bond probably had more to fear from Jason Bourne than any traditional villain. In between the lackluster *Die Another Day* (Pierce Brosnan's last outing as Bond) and triumphant *Casino Royale*, *The Bourne Identity*

and *Supremacy* came along and completely changed expectations of what films like this are capable of. Thankfully Bond producers sensed the impending revolution and retooled the world's most famous secret agent. Craig is a far more physical Bond than has hitherto been seen and is probably the closest yet to creator Ian Fleming's vision. He combines the brute power of Sean Connery with the suave charm of Roger Moore in a way that few expected when the controversial casting was announced. The film itself stands head and shoulders above recent Bond offerings, with a stunning vitality not seen since the early days of the franchise. Director Martin Campbell has perfectly judged the balance between Bond's traditional style and the more immediate, hyper-kinetic approach that now dominates action cinema.

CAST INCLUDES:
Daniel Craig, Judi Dench, Eva Green, Mads Mikkelsen, Jeffrey Wright, Giancarlo Giannini
SCREENPLAY:
Neal Purvis, Robert Wade, Paul Haggis
CINEMATOGRAPHY:
Phil Meheux

IRON MAN

Jon Favereau, USA, 2008

Tony Stark (Robert Downey Jr.), head of a successful weapons company, is kidnapped whilst demonstrating a new missile in Afghanistan. Although under instructions to build a missile for his terrorist captors, Stark instead uses the materials to construct a suit of flying armour that will not only help him escape, but also keep the shrapnel now embedded in his chest from killing him. Once back home in America his ordeal forces him to examine the morality of his career and make some altruistic changes. After witnessing Hollywood studios fumble in adapting some of their lesser-known superheroes for the big screen, Marvel (the comic book company responsible for *Spider-Man* and *The Incredible Hulk*, amongst others) decided to set up their own production company and do things 'properly'. By handling things in-house, they were able to control everything from scripting to marketing, which results in a feeling of organic authenticity not usually found in films of this scale. But whilst Marvel has succeeded in harnessing the benefits of a DIY approach, they seem to have completely avoided the pitfalls. The visual effects and action sequences are as huge and impressive as we've come to expect from a film like this, but there is a dollop of wit to them that is highly refreshing. Likewise, Tony Stark himself is every inch the superhero when in the Iron Man suit, but in 'human form' he projects a flawed, sardonic personality that is far more charming and interesting than Bruce Wayne and Clark Kent combined.

CAST INCLUDES:
Robert Downey Jr., Gwyneth Paltrow, Terrence Howard, Jeff Bridges
SCREENPLAY:
Mark Fergus, Hawk Ostby, Art Marcum, Matt Holloway
CINEMATOGRAPHY:
Matthew Libatique

WATCHMEN

Zack Snyder, USA, 2009

In an alternate 1985, the Watchmen, a disparate band of masked heroes, have been forced into retirement by an ungrateful and litigious public. When nuclear war threatens and one of their own is murdered, they must unite again to confront a supervillain with a terrible plan.

For two decades this expansive and convoluted graphic novel was considered unfilmable. Fêted by comic fans as the ultimate example of their medium, anyone taking on an adaptation seemed doomed to disaster. But director Zack Snyder has successfully crafted an exuberant, Technicolor adventure, rich in both compelling action and provocative themes. Unlike most costumed avengers, the Watchmen fight crime and uphold (a version of) the law without the aid of superpowers. This key conceit allows the film to address issues such as the nature of identity and altruism, whilst political and social themes are also examined via the depiction of an alternative America on the brink of Armageddon. But at its heart, *Watchmen* is a popcorn action movie, and there's no danger of the more cerebral aspirations cramping its gaudy and exuberant style. After the opening titles convey the relevant backstory, we're launched into a typically bravura fight scene, the first of numerous breathtaking action sequences taking in settings from Mars to the Vietnam War. As the Watchmen are thrown together for the first time in years (resentments and rivalries intact), they're each afforded the time required to develop their characters amidst all the action. From a cast of relative unknowns, Jackie Earle Haley's Rorschach is the clear standout. A shadowy, raincoated figure, Rorschach resembles Bogart's Sam Spade in both physical presence and temperament, his uncompromising search for answers driving the narrative.

The film was tagged 'the *Citizen Kane* of comic book movies' before cameras even rolled. But with themes of emasculation, a foundering society and an abundance of brash violence and casual sexism, this is surely the *Fight Club* of comic book movies.

CAST INCLUDES:
Matthew Goode, Patrick Wilson, Billy Crudup, Jackie Earle Haley, Malin Akerman, Jeffrey Dean Morgan
SCREENPLAY:
David Hayter, Alex Tse
CINEMATOGRAPHY:
Larry Fong

THE AVENGERS

Joss Whedon, USA, 2012

CAST INCLUDES:
Robert Downey Jr., Chris Evans, Mark Ruffalo, Chris Hemsworth, Samuel L. Jackson, Tom Hiddleston
SCREENPLAY:
Joss Whedon, Zak Penn
CINEMATOGRAPHY:
Seamus McGarvey

Loki (Hiddleston), the adoptive brother and nemesis of Norse god Thor (Hemsworth), travels to Earth in order to steal a mysterious device of unimaginable power known as the tesseract. As it becomes clear global domination is also part of Loki's plan, S.H.I.E.L.D. agent Nick Fury (Jackson) charges an eclectic group of superheroes and eccentrics with defending mankind. Thanks to a string of stand-alone movies introducing audiences to the key Avengers, their first outing together is freed from the need for time-consuming origin stories. Instead Tony Stark/Iron Man (Downey Jr.), Steve Rogers/Captain America (Evans), Thor (Hemsworth) and Bruce Banner/The Hulk (Ruffalo) arrive fully fledged and ready to rumble. Director Joss Whedon makes great use of his impressive cast, helping them slip smoothly between the humorous and dramatic performances that are central to the movie's broad appeal. He also allows room for moments of emotional turmoil amongst the more conflicted characters, a risky choice in a film of this nature, but one that, largely thanks to the casting, pays off handsomely. We can see how Rogers struggles to understand a future in which his Second World War–era morality is seen as quaintly anachronistic, and we begin to learn that Stark's bravado masks a self-doubt that could become crippling. But such character subtleties never take precedent as the movie ticks off several entries on the typical comic book fan's ultimate wish list. The Helicarrier (S.H.I.E.L.D.'s enormous and aerodynamically improbable flying ship) is present and correct, 'minor' Avengers such as Hawkeye and Black Widow feature prominently, and even fan-favourite über villain Thanos crops up in a post-credits teaser. Gods, superheroes, aliens, chases, battles, and even good acting – there really is something for everyone.

SKYFALL

Sam Mendes, GB/USA, 2012

CAST INCLUDES:
Daniel Craig, Judi Dench,
Javier Bardem, Ralph Fiennes,
Naomie Harris, Albert Finney
SCREENPLAY:
Neal Purvis, Robert Wade,
John Logan
CINEMATOGRAPHY:
Roger Deakins

ACADEMY AWARDS
Best Achievement in Music,
Original Song:
Adele, Paul Epworth
Best Achievement
in Sound Editing:
Per Hallenberg,
Karen Baker Landers

After failing to recover a computer hard drive containing the secret identities of undercover NATO agents, Bond (Craig) is seriously injured and chooses to go underground. But when MI6 itself is targeted by mysterious cyberterrorist Silva (Bardem), Bond returns to duty to protect M (Dench) from a personal vendetta that threatens her life. Although *Casino Royale*, Craig's 2006 debut as Britain's favourite womanizing superspy, was a huge commercial and critical success, the lacklustre follow-up (2008's *Quantum of Solace*) took the wind out of the franchise's sails somewhat. So news that Bond 23 would be helmed by accomplished art-house filmmaker Sam Mendes (*American Beauty*, *Revolutionary Road*) was as welcome as it was unexpected. Not only was the critical response to his film overwhelmingly positive, but the decision to disregard certain aspects of the usual formula appeared to instigate a crossover into hitherto uninterested markets, leading to a box-office haul that dwarfs all other entries in the series. Not that the Bond DNA is entirely absent — there proved to be enough to keep loyal fans more than happy.

Where recent villains have been the bland executives of secret international criminal organizations, *Skyfall* gets us back on track with a traditional maniacal lunatic at the centre of an improbable plot. Bardem is gloriously hammy as the disfigured, sexually ambiguous and clearly unhinged Silva, but can muster a genuinely chilling presence when the need for tension demands it. Craig again proves himself more than capable of accessing the nuances of modern Bond, a character in which we've come to expect flaws. After sinking into a state of almost masochistic self-pity following an early disaster, it's a fallible and uncertain Bond who emerges, and that's an inherently fascinating character.

COMEDY

SAFETY LAST

Fred C. Newmeyer, Sam Taylor, USA, 1923

The Boy wants to better himself in order to marry the Girl, so he leaves his home town for the big city and becomes a salesman in a large department store. He shares an apartment with the Pal, who is a 'human fly' – an expert in scaling high buildings. The Boy gets into all kinds of trouble at work, but hides this from the Girl who believes he's already been promoted. She follows him to the city where the Boy manages to fool her by 'borrowing' the general manager's office. The Boy then persuades his bosses to pay him a large sum for arranging a publicity stunt whereby the Pal will climb up the building – attracting huge crowds. However, when the Pal is chased off by a policeman, the Boy has to do the climb himself. After defeating a host of life-threatening hazards, he reaches the top to find the Girl waiting for him.

Safety Last was the best known of Lloyd's feature films. The story line is merely the route to the great final climb, one of the classic sequences of silent cinema, and Lloyd never revealed how he did it. Various stunt men were, indeed, employed, but close and medium shots without back projection show that he climbed to a goodly height himself, negotiating such obstacles as pigeons, nervous spectators, a dog, a net, a malicious plank of wood, a photographer's flash and a collapsing clock. Each of these obstacles is a comic scene in itself, and the whole sequence takes up a good third of the film.

CAST INCLUDES: Harold Lloyd, Mildred David, Bill Strothers, Noah Young
SCREENPLAY: Story by Jean C. Havez, Hal Roach, Sam Taylor; titles by H.M. Walker, Tim Whelan
CINEMATOGRAPHY (B/W): Walter Lundin

THE GENERAL

Clyde Bruckman, Buster Keaton, USA, 1926

CAST INCLUDES:
Buster Keaton, Marion Mack, Charles Henry Smith, Richard Allen
SCREENPLAY:
Al Boasberg, Charles Smith, Buster Keaton, Clyde Bruckman, Paul Gerard Smith
CINEMATOGRAPHY (B/W):
Bert Haines, Dev Jennings

When the American Civil War breaks out, Johnnie Gray (Keaton) tries to enlist with the Confederates; however, the army feel he's of more use in his job as the engineer on 'his' locomotive 'The General'. His girlfriend, Annabelle (Mack), leaves him, believing he's too much of a coward to fight. A year later, Annabelle is kidnapped. Johnnie rescues her and returns to the South with valuable battle information and a Union general whom he finds hiding in the cab of his train. He is rewarded with a commission and the now adoring attention of Annabelle. For many this is Keaton's masterpiece, although critical and audience response was lukewarm at the time. *The General* is a visual treasure-trove. Apart from the glorious location shooting and the great attention to historical detail, Keaton did all his own very risky train stunts. He even managed to arrange for a real train to crash off a burning bridge into a deep ravine. The engine is still believed to be down there, somewhere.

DUCK SOUP

Leo McCarey, USA, 1933

CAST INCLUDES:
Groucho Marx, Harpo Marx, Chico Marx, Zeppo Marx, Margaret Dumont, Louis Calhern
SCREENPLAY:
Bert Kalmar, Harry Ruby, with additional dialogue by Arthur Sheekman and Nat Perrin
CINEMATOGRAPHY (B/W):
Henry Sharp

Mrs Teasdale (Dumont), a wealthy citizen of Freedonia, offers to donate $20 million to save that little country from bankruptcy, but only if her candidate, Rufus T. Firefly (Groucho), is installed as the new president. Firefly, an unsympathetic and undiplomatic character, decides that he wishes to be married to Mrs Teasdale's money. However Ambassador Trentino (Calhern) of Sylvania (the little country next door) also intends to wed Mrs Teasdale, both for her money and as the first step in his plot to take over Freedonia. Although the mass public didn't warm to the Marx Brothers' firecracker humour until their next film, *A Night at the Opera* (1934), Marx buffs count it as one of their best. Director Leo McCarey already had a fine comedy record. It was he who suggested the famous mirror routine in which Groucho is pretty sure that the moustachioed face looking back at him is not his reflection, but can't quite catch it out. *Duck Soup*'s script, dialogue, jokes and one-liners were all also superb. Furthermore, this was a Marx Brothers' film with a message. It has many harsh things to say about war, government and dictators, but as this was done Marx-style, with buffoonery and sarcasm, many just found it disrespectful (including Mussolini, who banned it).

IT'S A GIFT

Norman Z. McLeod, USA, 1934

CAST INCLUDES:
W.C. Fields,
Kathleen Howard,
Jean Rouverol,
Julian Madison,
Tommy Bupp, Baby LeRoy,
Tammany Young
SCREENPLAY:
Jack Cunningham plus
contributions from
uncredited others
CINEMATOGRAPHY (B/W):
Henry Sharp

After leaving Mrs Bisonette (Howard) to her endless grievances, Harold Bisonette (Fields) goes to his store to find that his inept assistant, Everett (Young), has agreed to mind Baby Dunk (LeRoy), and now the store is covered in molasses while an angry customer yells for kumquats and a blind one destroys half his merchandise while looking for a stick of chewing gum. Suddenly, however, he comes into enough money to purchase, by mail-order, his dream of a ranch in an orange grove. He sets off for California, only to discover that he's bought one dead tree and a tumbledown shack. Things take an upswing, however, when his family leave him and a rich man appears who wants to buy his land. *It's a Gift* is Fields at his most side-splitting. The classic set pieces include his attempt to get a quiet wife-free night's sleep on the porch, hindered by everyman and his milk bottles, coconuts, garbage cans and babies. As so often, Fields' character is alone with only his bumbling ineptness to protect him from an appalling family and a cruel world. Yet we can only admire a man with such an astute judgement of character ('Anyone who hates dogs and children can't be all bad').

CAST INCLUDES:
Charlie Chaplin, Paulette
Goddard, Henry Bergman,
Tiny Sandford,
Chester Conklin
SCREENPLAY:
Charlie Chaplin
CINEMATOGRAPHY (B/W):
Rollie Tothero

MODERN TIMES

Charlie Chaplin, USA, 1936

The Little Tramp (Chaplin) is a factory worker whose conveyor belt job is to tighten the nuts on pieces of machinery. He is used as a guinea pig in tests on the 'Billows Feeding Machine', a practical device that automatically feeds your men while at work: 'Don't stop for lunch; be ahead of your competitor'. After a hilarious 'disagreement' with this machine, he cracks under the strain, goes berserk and is sent to a lunatic asylum. On his release, he is arrested and jailed for supposedly being a Communist. Once released, he finds life so tough that he tries unsuccessfully to get rearrested. Chaplin's rearguard action against sound continued in *Modern Times*. Even though the film is billed as his first sound film, in fact the spoken word only comes through machines such as the prison warden's radio. Charlie does sing a song, but in gibberish – albeit explained by his hand gestures. It was this attack on the grinding life of the worker that enabled the House of Un-American Activities to pronounce Chaplin a Communist and force him to leave the country.

NOTHING SACRED

William A. Wellman, USA, 1937

Reporter Wally Cook (March) is in the black books of editor Oliver Stone (Connolly), over a hoax that backfired, and is relegated to obituaries. He hears of Hazel Flagg (Lombard), a typist in Vermont who has contracted radium poisoning and only has a few months to live. Sensing a front-page sob story, he finds Hazel and persuades her that, if he takes her to New York, its sympathetic citizens will give her a wonderful time. Indeed, the Mayor of New York hands her the key to the city. However, it now transpires that Hazel isn't sick; she, too was hoaxing and the two hoaxers now fall in love. When doctors confirm that Hazel is in perfect health, the couple slip away but, to avoid scandal, they announce Hazel's death in the papers first. This kind of black comedy was new in 1937, and some critics were troubled by their amusement at such a nasty little story about such bad behaviour. However, they concluded that comedy was perhaps better concerned with hypocrisy and humbug than with silly social intrigues and marital squabbles. *Nothing Sacred* is a superb amalgamation of talent. Val Lewton, then in Selznick's story department, found the original tale and sent it to Ben Hecht in New York. Hecht and his co-writers turned it into a slick smart satire with simmering dialogue. William Wellman brought the passion and technical mastery he'd hitherto invested in action and adventure films; and Selznick was, as ever, an involved and creative producer.

CAST INCLUDES:
Carole Lombard, Fredric March, Charles Winninger, Walter Connolly, Sig Ruman
SCREENPLAY:
Ben Hecht, Ring Lardner Jr. (uncredited), Budd Schulberg (uncredited) from the story by James H. Street
CINEMATOGRAPHY (B/W):
W. Howard Greene

DID YOU KNOW?

This was Carole Lombard's only Technicolor film.

WAY OUT WEST

James W. Horne, USA, 1937

CAST INCLUDES:
Stan Laurel, Oliver Hardy,
Sharon Lynn,
James Finlayson,
Rosina Lawrence,
Stanley Fields
SCREENPLAY:
Charles Rogers, Felix Adler,
James Parrott,
James W. Horne (uncredited),
Arthur V. Jones (uncredited)
from a story by Jack Jevne,
Charles Rogers
CINEMATOGRAPHY (B/W):
Art Lloyd, Walter Lundin

Stanley (Laurel) and Ollie (Hardy) travel to Brushwood Gulch to fulfil their promise of delivering a dead prospector's gold mine deeds to his daughter Mary (Lawrence). The saloon owner, Mickey Finn (Finlayson), is Mary's guardian, but he wants the deeds for himself. He tells his wife, Lola Marcel (Lynn), to pretend to be Mary, and Stan and Ollie give the deeds to her. Lola then gets Mary to sign the lease over to her as guardian. Then Stan and Ollie discover the real Mary, and the battle is on to get the deeds back for her.

Way Out West contains the most delightful pieces of Stan & Ollie business. They do an exquisite soft-shoe shuffle and sing a still sought-after version of 'Trail of the Lonesome Pine'. Their attempt to rescue Mary from her wicked guardians involves a rope, a pulley, and Ollie as a counterbalance being pulled up by Stan, who lets go for a moment so that he can 'spit on me hands'. There's the grand tickling scene, and the one where Stan lights a lamp with his flaming thumb, plus the scene where he gets a lift on a stagecoach by showing a leg. They have as many ideas in one scene as most directors can produce for a whole film, and at least as many laughs.

BRINGING UP BABY

Howard Hawks, USA, 1938

CAST INCLUDES:
Cary Grant, Katharine Hepburn, Charles Ruggles, May Robson
SCREENPLAY:
Dudley Nichols and Hagar Wilde from a story by Hagar Wilde
CINEMATOGRAPHY (B/W):
Russell Metty

Dr David Huxley (Grant), a stuffy young palaeontologist due to be married in two days, and only one bone short of a priceless dinosaur skeleton, hopes that, during a game of golf, he can persuade a potential donor to give him the money he needs to acquire the final bone. There he meets Susan Vance (Hepburn), a scatty young socialite with a hyperactive dog who steals first his golf ball and then his car. On reaching her home, they are greeted by Baby, a young leopard that Susan's brother in Brazil has posted to her for safekeeping. Smitten Susan's subsequent chaotic actions revolve around her efforts to keep David with her and away from his fiancée. In the end, everyone lives happily ever after – except the dinosaur, which didn't make it. For many, *Bringing Up Baby* is the definitive screwball comedy, but on its release it was a commercial and critical flop. Hepburn and Hawks both parted company with RKO, but each went on to greater things while, in the course of time, *Bringing Up Baby*, too, gained the recognition it had always deserved.

HIS GIRL FRIDAY

Howard Hawks, USA, 1949

Ace reporter Hildy Johnson (Russell) goes to the quickwitted, self-serving managing editor Walter Burns (Grant) – who is also her boss and ex-husband – to tell him that she's leaving the paper and is about to marry Bruce Baldwin (Bellamy), an insurance salesman. Burns realizes he wants Hildy back both as wife and crack reporter. He uses every trick in the book to discredit Baldwin, and tempts Hildy with a front-page story about Earl Williams (Qualen), a possibly innocent man who has been convicted of murder. Williams escapes from prison and, with the police on his tail, heads for the newspaper where the staff hide him in a roll-top desk. In the thick of the excitement, Hildy becomes aware that she doesn't want to leave her job and that the man she really loves is Burns. With overlapping dialogue, rapid-fire delivery and sarcastic insults, the film has all the ingredients of a screwball masterpiece.

CAST INCLUDES: Cary Grant, Rosalind Russell, Ralph Bellamy, Gene Lockhart, Porter Hall. John Qualen
SCREENPLAY: Charles Lederer from the play *The Front Page* by Ben Hecht and Charles MacArthur
CINEMATOGRAPHY (B/W): Joseph Walker

SULLIVAN'S TRAVELS

Preston Sturges, USA, 1941

CAST INCLUDES:
Joel McCrea, Veronica Lake,
Robert Warwick, William
Demarest, Franklin Pangborn,
Porter Hall, Byron Foulger,
Margaret Hayes
SCREENPLAY:
Preston Sturges
CINEMATOGRAPHY (B/W):
John (F.) Seitz

John L. Sullivan (McCrea) is a Hollywood director who wishes to stop making 'fluffy' comedies and direct a significant film about human suffering. When it is pointed out to him that he knows nothing of suffering, given his background and upbringing, he dresses as a hobo and sets off to find out. To begin with, the quest is very difficult because his privileged world – in the shape of studio publicists – won't leave him alone. He meets up with a young woman (Lake), disillusioned with Hollywood, who decides to join him. Eventually, the pair do meet with and share the suffering of the homeless and the hopeless. He witnesses chain gang convicts laughing at a Mickey Mouse cartoon and finally realizes the true value of laughter – that it can be, if only for a moment, a lifeline of escape and a ray of hope. Preston Sturges had been writing sought-after scripts for nearly a decade but, come the forties, he thought it time to direct them himself. *Sullivan's Travels* was his third, and already he was beginning to frighten the studio. Here was a film by a comedy director about a comedy director and a beautiful woman wandering around in filthy clothes looking for poverty. Eventually, Paramount sidestepped the problem by coming up with the tagline: 'Veronica Lake's on the take'. To lovers of comedy, this movie offers a banquet of brilliant dialogue and one-liners.

TO BE OR NOT TO BE

Ernst Lubitsch , USA, 1942

CAST INCLUDES:
Carole Lombard,
Jack Benny,
Robert Stack,
Felix Bressart
SCREENPLAY:
Edwin Justus Mayer,
Melchior Lengyel
CINEMATOGRAPHY (B/W):
Rudolph Maté

Joseph Tura (Benny) and his wife Maria (Lombard) lead a troupe of actors in Poland before and during the Nazi occupation. Maria is having a liaison with bomber pilot Lt Sobinski (Stack). Every night, Sobinski waits in the audience until Tura begins 'To be or not to be...' and then leaves the auditorium for Maria's dressing room, knowing that her husband is safely stuck on the stage for some time. Sobinski, who is part of a Polish squadron based in England, suspects Professor Siletsky of being a Nazi spy. Siletsky is indeed a double agent. He has been collecting names of members of the Warsaw underground to give to the Nazis and the Tura troupe is recruited to intercept these incriminating lists. The whole cast meld their different strands of this classic comedy into a seamless whole.

KIND HEARTS AND CORONETS

Robert Hamer, GB, 1949

CAST INCLUDES:
Alec Guinness, Dennis
Price, Valerie Hobson,
Joan Greenwood
SCREENPLAY:
Robert Hamer and
John Dighton
CINEMATOGRAPHY (B/W):
Douglas Slocombe

Louis Manzzini's mother was the youngest daughter of Ethelred d'Ascoyne, Duke of Chalfont – until she ran off with a penniless opera singer and her family disowned her. Louis (Price) grows up having to work in a draper's shop. After his mother's death, an embittered Louis determines to avenge them both and reclaim the Chalfont title, to which end he murders his way though the d'Ascoyne family – and rounds things off by marrying Edith (Hobson), the widow of one of his murdered cousins. At all times both narrative and dialogue are counterpointed by exquisite visual touches, but the element of the film most readily remembered is the extraordinary acting feat of (Sir) Alec Guinness who plays all eight of the remaining d'Ascoynes (other than Louis) including Lady Agatha, his suffragette aunt.

BORN YESTERDAY

ACADEMY AWARD
Best Actress in a Leading
Role: Judy Holliday

George Cukor, USA, 1950

Harry Brock (Crawford), a self-made junk-metal tycoon, arrives in Washington to establish an illegal business cartel – with the assistance of grateful Washington politicians whose ambitions he will finance. However, he wants his mistress, Billie (Holliday) – an ex-chorus-line 'dumb broad' who regularly beats him at gin rummy – to grace his arm on social occasions. To this end, he hires journalist Paul Verrall (Holden) to put some ideas into her head and to get her to talk 'nice'. The not-so-dumb Billie learns fast, and soon both men have a great deal more to handle than they ever expected. *Born Yesterday* is more than a screwball comedy. Kanin enriches the script with an acute awareness of the political and social post-war situation in America. However, Holliday's Billie is the classic screen example of tough cookie gets an education, makes good – and gets the guy.

CAST INCLUDES:
Judy Holliday, William
Holden, Broderick Crawford,
Howard St John
SCREENPLAY:
Albert Mannheimer, based
on the play by Garson Kanin
CINEMATOGRAPHY (B/W):
Joseph Walker

LES VAÇANCES DE M. HULOT

Jacques Tati, France, 1953

The accident-prone Monsieur Hulot (Tati) is on his way to a vacation in a normally quiet seaside town in Brittany, spluttering and backfiring in his Archaic Amilcar. Decked out in his holiday gear – hat, trousers pulled up too high, stripey socks and smoking his pipe – Hulot sets out, with his bouncing stride, to become a friendly vacationer with the others in the hotel and at the beach. He is polite, considerate and well meaning. However, wherever he goes and whatever he does, chaos follows. Tati doesn't need a plot for his films; neither does he focus on himself as the central character. His films are, however, structured and preplanned in minute detail. He fills his scenes with people and objects and leaves the viewer to decide where to look. Sometimes he is at the centre, as in *Monsieur Hulot's Holiday*, when his tiny kayak folds up around him, panicking the vacationers who think he's a shark. At other times he is irrelevant, as when a station full of people, unable to understand the announcements, career from one platform to another. Tati is able to be both satirical and kind, awkward and graceful. He is the gentle genius of comedy who produced a handful of masterpieces – and this is one.

CAST INCLUDES:
Jacques Tati, Nathalie Pascaud, Michèle Rolla, Valentine Camax
SCREENPLAY:
Jacques Tati, Henri Marquet
CINEMATOGRAPHY (B/W):
Jacques Mercanton, Jean Mousselle

SOME LIKE IT HOT

Billy Wilder, USA, 1959

CAST INCLUDES:
Marilyn Monroe, Tony Curtis, Jack Lemmon, George Raft, Pat O'Brien
SCREENPLAY:
Billy Wilder and I.A.L Diamond
CINEMATOGRAPHY (B/W):
Charles Lang Jr.

Chicago, 1929. Joe (Curtis) and Jerry (Lemmon), two unemployed musicians, have just landed a speakeasy job when a police raid means the boys must scram to avoid arrest. Minutes later they witness the St Valentine's Day Massacre – and are themselves seen by the mobsters. To get out of town, they dress up and join – as Josephine and Daphne – an all-women's orchestra on its way to Florida. Joe falls for the band's singer, Sugar Kane (Monroe), and invents another persona, Junior, in order to win her. Elderly millionaire Osgood Fielding III (Brown) falls in love with Daphne. The mobsters turn up again, and have to be eluded. After that, Joe and Osgood propose – and Sugar and Daphne accept. Nothing in *Some Like It Hot* – an all-time favourite film – fails. Despite all the reported problems of working with a 'dazed and confused' Marilyn, the outcome is superb. Wilder even manages to get Shakespearean, playing Sugar and Junior as high comedy, and Daphne and Osgood as the clowns. The best drag movie till *Tootsie* (1982) – and maybe then some.

MOVE OVER, DARLING

Michael Gordon, USA, 1963

Ellen, aka Eve (Day), missing and legally dead for five years, returns to her husband, Nick (Garner), just after Nick has got remarried – to the sexy Bianca (Bergen). Ellen had survived a plane crash over the Pacific Ocean and had been on a desert island, with no phone or sun cream, albeit with fellow survivor Stephen, aka Adam (Conners), until rescued by a US submarine. Ellen realizes that she must take things slowly – even her children don't recognize her – but her mother-in-law (Ritter) decides to take out a bigamy order against her son. A sojourn in jail gives Nick time to sort out which wife he really wants to keep. This giddy tale, first filmed as *My Favourite Wife* (1940), was being remade as *Something's Got To Give*, with Marilyn Monnroe – but Marilyn died. Doris Day and James Garner then stepped in, and the confluence of their comedic talents created this bright, funny, sixties' marital comedy. Life on set was often hard for Day. On this occasion she was working with two cracked ribs, after an overenthusiastic move by Garner, and was later put through a car wash, although the producers did, thoughtfully, leave this scene till the last day in case the car wash detergents gave them any problems with her complexion.

CAST INCLUDES:
Doris Day, James Garner,
Polly Bergen, Thelma Ritter,
Fred Clark, Chuck Connors
SCREENPLAY:
Hal Kanter and Jack Sher
from the 1940 story
My Favourite Wife, and the
1940 screenplay *My Favourite
Wife*, both by Bella Spewack,
Sam Spewack; also story
Move Over Darling by
Leo McCarey
CINEMATOGRAPHY:
Daniel L. Fapp

DID YOU KNOW?

Doris Day wrote in her 1975 autobiography that it was difficult to breathe and painful to laugh because she was so mummified with tape and bandages under her costumes after cracking her ribs.

THE PINK PANTHER

Blake Edwards, GB/USA, 1963

· ·

The Pink Panther, the largest diamond in the world, belongs to Dala, an Indian Princess, who takes it with her on holiday to an exclusive Swiss ski resort. It is no coincidence that at the resort is also Sir Charles Lytton, an infamous jewel thief known as 'The Phantom'. Hot on the heels of The Phantom is the French detective Inspector Clouseau. Unfortunately, Clouseau doesn't know whose heels he's looking for, nor that his beautiful wife, Simone (Capucine), is The Phantom's lover and accomplice...

Peter Sellers deserves the credit for the success of *The Pink Panther*, and its sequels. Inspector Clouseau is his inspiration. He created an astoundingly inept character: bumbling, fumbling, maladroit, clueless, clumsy, ineffectual and very bad at French. Fortunately, Clouseau was also loveable, and his international fan base blossomed. The suave, elegant David Niven, as the gentleman jewel thief, was a further piece of admirable casting. The animated Pink Panther of the credit sequence, accessorized by Henry Mancini's 'Pink Panther' theme, also went on to become its own series.

CAST INCLUDES:
David Niven, Peter Sellers,
Robert Wagner, Capucine,
Brenda De Banzie,
Colin Gordon,
John LeMesurier,
James Lanphier,
Claudia Cardinale
SCREENPLAY:
Maurice Richlin,
Blake Edwards
CINEMATOGRAPHY:
Philip (H.) Lathrop

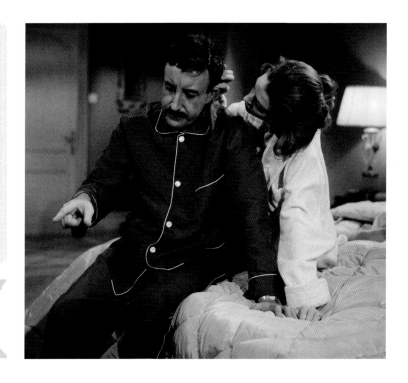

DID YOU KNOW?
In 1965 the film
was given an Academy
Award nominatation for
Best Music, Score.

THE PRODUCERS

(AKA *Springtime for Hitler*), Mel Brooks, USA, 1968

CAST INCLUDES:
Zero Mostel, Gene Wilder, Kenneth Mars, Estelle Winwood, Renée Taylor, Christopher Hewett, Lee Meredith
SCREENPLAY:
Mel Brooks
CINEMATOGRAPHY:
Joseph (F.) Coffey

ACADEMY AWARD
Best Writing, Story and Screenplay –Written Directly for the Screen: Mel Brooks

Accountant Leo Bloom (Wilder) tells down-on-his-luck producer Max Bialystock (Mostel), who has to charm wealthy widows to raise money for his plays, that he could make far more money from an outright flop. None of his 'angels' would expect anything back from a flop. Their formula for failure is a musical called *Springtime for Hitler*. It boasts a dance line of jackbooted chorus girls and such catchy lyrics as 'Don't be stupid, be a smarty! Come and join the Nazi Party'. The reactions on the audience's faces during the first act register complete horror, but by the end of the evening the house is in raptures. Bialystock is ruined – his flop is a hit! Mel Brooks is unquestionably the monarch of the worst possible taste, but the nerve of a man who could manifest such an idea, in any shape or form, is awesome.

THE ODD COUPLE

Gene Saks, USA, 1968

CAST INCLUDES:
Jack Lemmon, Walter Matthau, John Fiedler, Herb (Herbert) Edelman, (as Herbert Edelman), David Sheiner, Larry Haines, Monica Evans, Carole Shelley
SCREENPLAY:
Neil Simon (also play)
CINEMATOGRAPHY:
Robert B. Hauser

Felix (Lemmon) has broken up with his wife and she's thrown him out. He paces the streets of New York trying to commit suicide, but doesn't succeed. He goes round to the flat of his poker mate, Oscar (Matthau), a writer, who offers to let Felix share his apartment. Unfortunately, Felix is neurotically house proud, while Oscar (already divorced) is a normally contented slob who is being tidied towards a murderous breakdown. Oscar sets up a double date for them both, but even that fails as the girls merely end up weeping in sympathy with a sobbing Felix. Finally, Oscar throws Felix out, but the neatnik comes up with a surprising solution to his housing problems.

Neil Simon's play (based, he says, on the experiences of his brother Danny when he got divorced) was a smash on Broadway and in cities all over the USA prior to being filmed. However, for the movie version, Lemmon and Matthau encapsulated so perfectly Simon's unforgettable characters in their polarized roles, and radiated such a powerful love-hate magnetism, that a piece of movie-comedy magic was born.

HAROLD AND MAUDE

Hal Ashby, USA, 1971

CAST INCLUDES:
Ruth Gordon, Bud Cort,
Vivian Pickles, Cyril Cusack,
Charles Tyner, Ellen Greer
SCREENPLAY:
Colin Higgins
CINEMATOGRAPHY:
John Alonzo

Harold Chasen (Cort), nearly 20 years old, walks slowly and dramatically down the staircase of his manorial home, lights some candles and then attempts to hang himself. His mother (Pickles) is mildly irritated; she's seen it all before. Shortly afterwards, while attending a stranger's funeral, Harold realizes someone is trying to attract his attention, and thus he meets nearly 80-year-old Maude; she likes strangers' funerals too. Maude, a bundle of energy, takes Harold, a bundle of gloom, back to her railway-car home. She teaches him to dance, sing, rescue sad trees and 'borrow' cars and motorbikes. She includes him in her life and her lunatic adventures until he is ready to open up to love. A young man deeply damaged by his refrigerated, upper-class upbringing; an elderly lady dancing and twirling to Cat Stevens; is it all too dated? In 2003, the American magazine *Entertainment Weekly* did a poll of the Top 50 Cult Movies, and *Harold and Maude* is there at number four, so perhaps not. Hal Ashby came to directing with a broad hands-on experience of the film industry. Here, he shows his gift for blending edgy partners – the blackly comical and the nearly whimsical. Ruth Gordon, however, never lets Maude sink into whimsy: she's too spunky and matter-of-fact, and her one-liners are too funny.

WHAT'S UP, DOC?

Peter Bogdanovich, USA, 1972

CAST INCLUDES:
Barbra Streisand, Ryan
O'Neal, Madeline Kahn,
Kenneth Mars, Austin
Pendleton, Michael Murphy,
Philip (Phil) Roth
SCREENPLAY:
Buck Henry, David Newman,
Robert Benton
CINEMATOGRAPHY:
László Kovács
(Director of Photography)

In a hotel in San Francisco sit four identical tartan overnight bags. One contains rare rocks that are on their way to a conference of musicologists. One is full of valuable jewellery, one has top-secret government documents and one has a change of clothes. The scene is set for confusion, but all eventually resolves itself after a rip-roaring chase through the streets of San Francisco. *What's Up, Doc?* was number three at the box office for 1972, so audiences clearly delighted in Bogdanovich's happy homage to the screwball comedies of the thirties, particularly *Bringing Up Baby*.

The film showed, many murmured, how funny Streisand could be – before she lost her sense of humour.

EVERYTHING YOU ALWAYS WANTED TO KNOW ABOUT SEX* *BUT WERE AFRAID TO ASK

Woody Allen, USA, 1972

CAST INCLUDES:
Woody Allen, John Carradine,
Lou Jacobi, Louise Lasser,
Anthony Quayle,
Tony Randall
SCREENPLAY:
Woody Allen from the book
by David Reuben
CINEMATOGRAPHY:
David M. Walsh

Seven significant questions about sex are answered in the film's seven episodes. 1. Do Aphrodisiacs Work? 2. What is Sodomy? 3. Do Some Women Have Trouble Reaching Orgasm? 4. Are Transvestites Homosexuals? 5. What Are Sex Perverts? 6. Are the Findings of Doctors and Clinics Who Do Sexual Research and Experiments Accurate? 7. What Happens During Ejaculation?

It's clear that all director/scriptwriter Woody Allen needed from David Reuben's book was the title and the chapter headings. The rest of the genius is Allen's own. No one who has seen the film will forget the tears in the eyes of Gene Wilder as he gazes at Daisy, nor the neurotic nihilism of Woody Allen's Sperm #1 as it observes its dwindling chances of being able to make the leap.

BLAZING SADDLES

Mel Brooks, USA 1974

CAST INCLUDES:
Cleavon Little, Gene Wilder,
Slim Pickens, Harvey Korman,
Madeline Kahn, Mel Brooks,
Burton Gilliam, Dom DeLuise
SCREENPLAY:
Mel Brooks, Norman Steinberg,
Andrew Bergman, Richard
Pryor, Alan Uger, from a story
by Andrew Bergman
CINEMATOGRAPHY:
Joseph Biroc

Rescued from a railroad gang, Black Bart (Little) is appointed by a corrupt speculator and a crooked governor (both played by Brooks) to be the sheriff of Rock Ridge. Their hope is that the townsfolk will become so hostile and demoralized that it will be easy to overcome their resistance to selling up and leaving, so that a profitable railroad can be built through their land. Black Bart finds an unexpected ally in Waco Kid (Wilder), and the two come up with a plan to fool the would-be land-stealers and their henchmen by creating a replica cardboard town. Alongside the sexual revolution and flower power of the '60s and '70s strode the fast-growing power of the black civil rights movement. Hollywood rushed to create new black superhero roles, and 'Blaxploitation' movies were born in which the superstud black hero – Shaft, Superfly – always comes out on top, but is also suitably streetwise. For Blazing Saddles, Mel Brooks chose a breathtakingly incorrect formula: he would show up Hollywood's new black moral consciousness for what it was while simultaneously spoofing the western. Black Bart, therefore, quickly reveals that he is as incompetent as a sheriff as at everything else, while the thing that 'real' cowboys do best is fart.

MONTY PYTHON AND THE HOLY GRAIL

Terry Gilliam and Terry Jones, GB, 1975

A horseless King Arthur jogs across the countryside followed by a servant banging coconut shells together. The knight may be Sir Galahad the Pure, Sir Lancelot the Brave, Sir Bedevere the Quiet, Sir Robin the Not-Quite-So-Brave-as-Sir-Lancelot or Sir Not-Appearing-In-This-Film. The Monty Python team wanted their version of the King Arthur legend to be 'a film completely different from some of the other films which aren't quite the same as this one is'. They elected to achieve this by means of satire, whimsy and aggressive eccentricity, and by complementing their random gag-making with the visually imaginative creation of a mock medieval landscape, with every intention of deliberately courting controversy. Their success is summed up by all the critics, who said of the film: 'Makes *Ben-Hur* look like an epic.'

CAST INCLUDES:
Graham Chapman, John Cleese, Eric Idle, Terry Gilliam, Terry Jones, Michael Palin, Connie Booth, Carol Cleveland
SCREENPLAY:
Graham Chapman, John Cleese, Eric Idle, Terry Gilliam, Terry Jones, Michael Palin
CINEMATOGRAPHY:
Terry Bedford (uncredited)

ANIMAL HOUSE

John Landis, USA, 1978

CAST INCLUDES:
John Belushi, Tim Matheson, John Vernon, Verna Bloom, Tom Hulce, Cesare Danova
SCREENPLAY:
Harold Ramis, Douglas Kenney, Chris Miller
CINEMATOGRAPHY:
Charles Correll

Faber College, 1962. Some years ago, John 'Bluto' Blutarsky (Belushi) and Eric 'Otter' Statton (Matheson) were refused admittance to Omega, the Wasp fraternity, and consigned to Delta, the crap fraternity where the only thing the students do best is behave atrociously. Bluto and Otter are now at the forefront of Delta's toga parties, drunken binges, pot-smoking orgies and food fights. The college principal despises them and, following the fraternity's abysmal exam results, the whole of Delta is expelled. The Delta dorks decide that the best way to declare war on the college is to wreck the annual homecoming parade... 'Frantic', 'gross' and 'crude' are words frequently and lovingly applied to *Animal House*. The relentless pace of John Belushi's Bluto was the work of a consummate (and fondly remembered) professional. *Animal House* became one of the top earners in Universal's history and spawned many imitations, but it remained, for a considerable time, the most successful comedy movie ever produced.

AIRPLANE!

Jim Abrahams, David Zucker, Jerry Zucker, USA, 1980

CAST INCLUDES:
Robert Hays, Julie Hagerty,
Lloyd Bridges, Leslie Nielsen,
Robert Stack, Peter Graves,
Lorna Patterson
SCREENPLAY:
Jim Abrahams, David Zucker
and Jerry Zucker,
based on the teleplay *Flight
Into Danger* by Arthur
Hailey (uncredited) and the
screenplay *Zero Hour* by
Arthur Hailey, Hall Bartlett
and John C. Champion
(all uncredited)
CINEMATOGRAPHY:
Joseph Biroc

The experiences of Ted Striker (Hays) as a fighter pilot have left him with a deeply entrenched phobia of flying. However, when his air hostess girlfriend, Elaine (Hagerty), dumps him, he realizes he must follow her on her next flight if he is to win her back. Fortunately, he doesn't eat the poisonous fish that the airline serves for dinner but, as most of the crew (and the passengers) do, it falls to Ted to land the plane. With help from Elaine and an unflappable doctor (Nielsen), and in spite of help from a high-as-a-kite ground controller (Bridges) and an inflatable automatic pilot, Ted manages to land the plane safely.

Disaster movies had been one of the most successful Hollywood genres of the seventies, with such successes as *The Towering Inferno*, *Avalanche* and *Earthquake* – and the whole series of Airport movies. By the end of the decade, these catastrophe films were running thin on ideas, and the relentless parodying provided by *Airplane!* not only tolled their death knell but gave rise to a new style of knockabout spoof movie. *Airplane!*'s plot was based on Arthur Hailey's screenplay for the fifties B-movie *Zero Hour*. The AZZ team – Abrahams, Zucker and Zucker – held onto the B-movie tension (with the help of such B-movie stars as Bridges, Stack and Nielsen) – and added a laugh a second. 'Parody may be the lowest form of humour', observed *Variety* on *Airplane!*'s release, 'but few comedies in ages have rocked the laugh-metre this hard.'

TOOTSIE

Sydney Pollack, USA, 1982

Actor Michael Dorsey (Hoffman) is a deeply motivated young actor who has been branded 'unemployable': he says 'perfectionist', they say 'difficult'. Feeling that he knows exactly why girlfriend Sandy (Garr) didn't get chosen for a daytime hospital soap, he dresses as a woman, auditions as Dorothy Michaels and lands the role of Emily. Now he has to keep up his female guise – not easy, as he's fallen for his co-star, Julie (Lange), and Julie's father (Durning) has fallen for Dorothy. Eventually, he can stand it no more, and 'outs' himself during an episode of the soap.

Tootsie's film crew realized that, if they had bad news for Hoffman, they should keep it until he was playing Dorothy, because he was 'much nicer as a woman'. *Tootsie* is one of the top-grossing comedies of all time, and comes second on the American Film Institute's recent list of funniest-ever US movies – after that other great drag movie, *Some Like It Hot* (1959).

CAST INCLUDES:
Dustin Hoffman, Jessica Lange, Teri Garr, Dabney Coleman, Charles Durning, Bill Murray, Sydney Pollack, George Gaynes, Geena Davis
SCREENPLAY:
Larry Gelbart, Murray Schisgal, Barry Levinson (uncredited) Elaine May (uncredited) from a story by Don McGuire, Larry Gelbart
CINEMATOGRAPHY:
Owen Roizman

TRADING PLACES

John Landis, USA, 1983

A snobbish investor, Winthorpe III (Aykroyd), and a wily street con artist, Billy Ray Valentine (Murphy), find their positions reversed as part of a 'nurture versus nature' bet by two callous millionaires. Billy Ray realizes his new lifestyle will be over when the old guys settle their bet, so he and Louis get together to turn the tables. John Landis was riding high after *Animal House* (1978) and *The Blues Brothers* (1980). For *Trading Places*, he took a very archetypal theme – rich guy becomes poor guy, and poor guy becomes rich guy – and added a well-chosen cast, a fine script with excellent comic dialogue, and his own funny and delicate touches. There are also, underpinning it all, some important questions raised about money and the effect it has on people.

CAST INCLUDES:
Dan Aykroyd, Eddie Murphy, Ralph Bellamy, Don Ameche, Denholm Elliott, Jamie Lee Curtis, Kristin Holby
SCREENPLAY:
Timothy Harris, Herschel Weingrod
CINEMATOGRAPHY:
Robert Paynter

DID YOU KNOW?
Richard Pryor was originally considered for the role of Billy Ray.

ALL OF ME

Carl Reiner, USA, 1984

CAST INCLUDES:
Steve Martin, Lily Tomlin,
Victoria Tennant, Madolyn
Smith, Richard Libertini
SCREENPLAY:
Phil Alden Roninson from
the novel *Me Too* by Edwin
Davis III
CINEMATOGRAPHY:
Richard H. Kline

When the eccentric and wealthy Edwina Cutwater (Tomlin) learns that she is dying, she arranges for her soul to be transferred into the body of the young and lovely Terry (Tennant), for a sizeable sum. Roger Cobb (Martin) is the lawyer hired merely to sort out the final legalities but, on Edwina's death, her soul is somehow transferred to him and duly takes over the right side of his body – leaving him with what's left. When *The Jerk* – directed by Carl Reiner and starring Steve Martin in his first comedy – appeared in 1979, it was a hit. However, the reviews were so bad that Martin decided to follow it with the very 'unusual' musical drama, *Pennies From Heaven* (1981). This was a flop, and his next three movies fared little better. Then Carl Reiner phoned him with a script 'about a girl who gets into a guy's body'. Martin took some persuading to go with a story even odder than *Pennies*, but finally agreed. *All of Me* was released in 1984. The public loved it, and Steve Martin was duly elevated to the status of major comic star.

THIS IS SPINAL TAP

Rob Reiner, USA, 1984

The next project from film director Marty DiBergi (Reiner) is a documentary about Spinal Tap, a British heavy-metal band which has the enviable reputation of being 'one of England's loudest'. The band is on the US leg of their comeback tour which is scheduled to coincide with their new album, 'Sniff the Glove'. However, the tour is plagued with problems. The album hasn't arrived, there are hotel mix-ups, their Stonehenge stage set arrives in miniature form, some of the venues are appalling and the audiences are dwindling. Through it all, DiBergi observes, films and interviews to make a worthy filmed tribute to his favourite band. This is perhaps the spoof to end all spoofs. The inescapable factor that leads fans to a weak-kneed worship is that they could be real. Reiner's acute ear for the vernacular of 1980s' rock bands and the tedious, reverential films made about them is faultless. Only the truly terrible songs remind us that this is parody *par excellence*.

CAST INCLUDES: Rob Reiner, R.J. Parnell, David Kaff, Tony Hendra, Michael McKean, Christopher Guest, Harry Shearer,
SCREENPLAY: Christopher Guest, Michael McKean, H. Shearer, R.Reiner
CINEMATOGRAPHY: Peter Smokler

THE BREAKFAST CLUB

John Hughes, USA, 1985

Five high school students, who would not normally seek out each other's company, have to spend a Saturday together in detention. Brian the geek (Hall), Alison the basket case (Sheedy), Andy the jock (Estevez), John the jerk (Nelson) and Claire the prom queen (Ringwald). They start off at each other's throats but loosen up during a pot-smoking session and begin to see that they have far more in common than the stereotypes that separate them. Director Hughes recognized the plight of 1980s' teenagers and saw beyond the definitions inflicted on them by parents and teachers. His empathy with the wounds that hormones and changing family values could cause was a theme he returned to again and again. Hughes wrote the script for the film in only a few days, but then got the young cast to rehearse it several times as a play before shooting began, allowing the story to develop during that process. *The Breakfast Club* was the teenage-angst, Brat Pack movie that cast the mould for those that followed.

CAST INCLUDES:
Emilio Estevez, Anthony Michael Hall, Judd Nelson, Molly Ringwald, Paul Gleason, Ally Sheedy
SCREENPLAY:
John Hughes
CINEMATOGRAPHY:
Thomas Del Ruth

FERRIS BUELLER'S DAY OFF

John Hughes, USA, 1986

CAST INCLUDES:
Matthew Broderick, Alan Ruck, Mia Sara, Jeffrey Jones, Jennifer Grey, Cindy Pickett, Charlie Sheen
SCREENPLAY:
John Hughes
CINEMATOGRAPHY:
Tak Fujimoto

It's a beautiful day in Chicago, and Ferris Bueller (Broderick) plays hooky from school. He then persuades his best buddy Cameron (Ruck) to 'borrow' his father's irreplaceable 1961 red Ferrari, and they pick up Ferris's girlfriend, Sloane (Sara). The trio now set off on a joyride around Chicago, giving Ferris the chance to give his depressed friend Cameron some time and encouragement. One of the funniest and most delightful of John Hughes' 'Brat Pack' comedies, it is also the only one that doesn't feature Anthony Michael Hall and Molly Ringwald. The film does, however, have Brat-Packer Charlie Sheen in a side-splitting cameo role as a drugged-to-the-eyeballs boy. To get the necessary spaced-out effect, Sheen kept himself awake for 48 hours before the scene was shot.

A FISH CALLED WANDA

Charles Crichton, John Cleese (uncredited), GB/USA, 1988

ACADEMY AWARD

Best Actor in a
Supporting Role:
Kevin Kline

CAST INCLUDES:
John Cleese, Jamie Lee
Curtis, Kevin Kline,
Michael Palin,
Maria Aitken, Tom
Georgeson,
Patricia Hayes,
Geoffrey Palmer
SCREENPLAY:
John Cleese from the story
by John Cleese and
Charles Crichton
CINEMATOGRAPHY:
Alan Hume

Wanda (Curtis), a normal diamond-loving woman, Otto (Kline), her jewel-thief boyfriend (ex-CIA and a psychopath), the robbery's mastermind, George (Georgeson), and a verbally challenged animal-lover K-K-K-Ken (Palin) pull off a successful jewellery heist. Wanda then decides she wants all the diamonds for herself and tips the cops off about George – only to find she doesn't know where George has stashed the loot. She sets out to seduce George's tight-assed lawyer, Archie Leach, in whom George may have confided. A complex double-crossing caper ensues during which Archie falls in love, Otto becomes dangerously jealous, George stays safely out of the way and K-K-K-Ken's heart is broken when Otto eats his tropical fish – one of which is called Wanda. Incidentally, Cleese called his character Archie Leach because he and the real Archie Leach – i.e. Cary Grant – both came from the English town of Weston-super-Mare.

Embroiled in *A Fish Called Wanda* – 'A tale of murder, lust, greed, revenge and seafood' – are two Hollywood stars (Curtis and Kline), two members of the British Monty Python team (Cleese and Palin) and Charles Crichton, a director of such notably English Ealing comedies as *The Lavender Hill Mob* (1951). Somehow, this odd mix worked beautifully. Cleese requested Crichton to write the film as an old-fashioned romantic comedy, and that worked, too. The movie was the sleeper hit of the summer of 1988.

THE NAKED GUN:
FROM THE FILES OF POLICE SQUAD

David Zucker, USA, 1988

CAST INCLUDES:
Leslie Nielsen, Priscilla Presley, Ricardo Montalban, George Kennedy, O.J. Simpson, Susan Beaubian
SCREENPLAY:
Jim Abrahams, David Zucker, Pat Proft, Jerry Zucker
CINEMATOGRAPHY:
Robert (M.) Stevens

Fresh from tackling terrorism in Beirut, Lt Frank Drebin (Nielsen) is immediately detailed to investigate the near-fatal shooting of a fellow officer, Detective Nordberg (Simpson). Drebin starts the job where Nordberg left off, at a company owned by the much-respected Victor Ludwig (Montalban) whose assistant, Jane (Presley), Drebin falls for. Thanks to years of experience and granite-jawed determination (and Jane), Drebin uncovers a dastardly plot, by Ludwig, to assassinate Queen Elizabeth II when she attends a baseball game while on her state visit to the USA. It was acclaimed, when it first appeared, as the best movie ever made with the words 'Naked', 'Gun' and 'The' in the title; although a few sad people later challenged the word 'The'. From the creators of *Airplane!* (1980) and the brief but unforgettable (now that it's a cult) TV spoof series *Police Squad* came this spoof police movie. Jokes, visual gags and achingly funny moments are rained upon the viewer. The Zuckers, Abrahams and Proft have also taken the trouble to create endearing and well-rounded characters so that, despite the mayhem, the viewer still cares about what's happening to them. John Houseman, as an unflappable driving instructor, is irrepressibly funny in this, his last movie. *The Naked Gun 2 1/2: The Smell of Fear* (1991), and *Naked Gun 33 1/3: The Final Insult* (1994) followed.

CAST INCLUDES: Tom Hanks, Elizabeth Perkins, Robert Loggia
SCREENPLAY: Gary Ross, Anne Spielberg
CINEMATOGRAPHY: Barry Sonnenfeld

BIG

Penny Marshall, USA, 1988

Young Josh, at 12, is just reaching an awkward age. One minute it's Little League baseball, the next it's standing beside a blonde princess at a carnival fairground and being told you're too short to go on the ride. In that moment of mortification, young Josh encounters a fortune-telling machine and wishes that he'll become big. The next morning finds him with a 30-year-old body and a face he doesn't recognize. He runs away to New York with best mate Billy and gets a job in a toy factory. So in tune is he with the company's product that he is soon moving up the career ladder. Despite, however, the attentions of the attractive Susan (Perkins), Josh has begun to realize that all he wants to do is find the magic machine and get back to normal. Tom Hanks always played his 12-year-old Josh as a 12-year-old, and won a Best Actor Golden Globe and an Oscar nomination for his success. He was helped in this by director Penny Marshall, who had the actor playing young Josh, David Moscow, play each of big Josh's scenes first, so that Hanks could absorb the reactions and body language of a real 12-year-old.

HOME ALONE

Chris Columbus, USA, 1990

CAST INCLUDES:
Macaulay Culkin, Joe Pesci,
Daniel Stern, John Heard,
Catherine O'Hara
SCREENPLAY:
John Hughes
CINEMATOGRAPHY:
Julio Macat

The McCallister clan have gathered in Peter and Kate's Chicago home prior to flying off to spend Christmas in Paris. In the chaos of leaving, they overlook eight-year-old Kevin (Culkin). Once in the air, his absence is noticed but snowstorms prevent his distraught mother (O'Hara) from getting back to him. Kevin can't believe his luck. He watches forbidden videos, eats his favourite junk food and rifles through his brother's things. He does get scared, and when two burglars decide to break into the house he gets really scared. However, courage and resourcefulness come to the fore as he devises elaborate and painful booby traps to deter them. Macaulay Culkin had already appeared in a couple of films, but his extraordinarily self-possessed performance in *Home Alone* launched him to child superstardom. He earned $100,000 for the film; by the time he made *Home Alone 2* (1992), he was commanding $5 million. This massive Christmas hit did what it set out to with maximum hilarity, and Culkin was the cutest kid on the block for a long time.

GROUNDHOG DAY

Harold Ramis, USA, 1993

CAST INCLUDES:
Bill Murray, Andie MacDowell,
Chris Elliott, Stephen
Tobolowsky, Brian Doyle-
Murray, Maria Geraghty
SCREENPLAY:
Danny Rubin, Harold Ramis
from a story by Danny Rubin
CINEMATOGRAPHY:
John Baily

Phil Conners (Murray) is a nasty, cynical, people-hating TV weatherman. This year, as every year, he makes a much-resented trip to Punxsutawney, the 'Groundhog Capital', to broadcast the big news from Groundhog Day: if Punxsutawney Phil (the groundhog) appears, then spring has come; if he doesn't, it's six more weeks of winter. However, on awaking the next morning, it's Groundhog Day again. . . and on the next day, and the next. For a while, he enjoys taking advantage of his *déjà vu* knowledge – especially of how to impress his long-suffering producer, Rita (MacDowell). Next, frustration leads him to various forms of suicide, but he still wakes up the next day. Finally, however, though time and space remain stuck, he realizes that things within him are changing. He starts on the long job – for which he needs many Groundhog Days – of becoming a loveable human being. There haven't been many movies that play with concurrent time. *It's a Wonderful Life* (1946) examines how things might have been as a way of reevaluating how things are, but in *Groundhog Day*, the method is repetition until things are put right. The fact that such a potentially grim situation is hilarious owes it's weak-at-the-knees thanks to Rubin and Ramis's script and to the deep well of comedy talent that is Bill Murray.

GROSSE POINTE BLANK

George Armitage, USA, 1997

Martin Q. Blank (Cusack) is a hitherto successful hit man who has just hit burnout. After a bungled job, he gets the chance to redeem himself through a contract in Detroit. His old high school is in the Detroit suburb of Grosse Pointe and, coincidentally, it's holding his ten-year reunion. Once in Grosse Pointe, he searches out Debi (Driver), the girlfriend he stood up at the school prom. He discovers that various people are out to kill him, and his improving relationship with Debi goes sour when he has to kill a would-be assassin at the reunion dance. This is deadpan comedy of a high order. The perennially boyish-looking Cusack does a fine job of persuading us that he is a professional assassin. He placed Blank very much in the mould of 'Zen and the Art of Assassination'; all the nitty-gritty bits of the job are meticulously planned and carried out. Like many perfectionist professionals, he hasn't a clue how to conduct a relationship – but he discovers he wants to learn. Furthermore, his moral code has been to kill only bad people, but once his emotions have started to surface, it's much harder to make that distinction.

CAST INCLUDES:
John Cusack, Minnie Driver, Alan Arkin, Dan Aykroyd
SCREENPLAY:
Tom Jankiewicz, D.V. DeVincentis, Steve Pink, John Cusack
CINEMATOGRAPHY:
Jamie Anderson

AUSTIN POWERS: INTERNATIONAL MAN OF MYSTERY

Jay Roach, USA, 1997

CAST INCLUDES:
Mike Myers, Elizabeth Hurley, Michael York, Mimi Rogers, Robert Wagner, Seth Green, Fabiana Udenio
SCREENPLAY:
Mike Myers
CINEMATOGRAPHY:
Peter Deming

It's swinging 1967. Dr Evil (Myers) has failed to kill his archenemy, British secret agent Austin Powers (also Myers), and resolves to escape by means of his cryogenic freezing capsule and return later. Powers bravely offers to be frozen too, ready to destroy Dr Evil when he comes back. It's now 1997. Dr Evil thaws out, steals a nuclear weapon and holds the world to ransom. Austin Powers, however, is ready for him – debonair, defiant and defrosted – together with his new assistant, Vanessa Kensington (Hurley), whose job is to reacclimatize Powers to the no-fun nineties. Austin 'Shall we shag now, or shall we shag later?' Powers is an homage to 007 and a sixties' send-up, and is also full of lavatory humour. In addition, Myers' creation provides all the joys of appalling velvet fashion statements, matted hairy chests and Union-Jack-painted Minis. No joke has done its job until it's been thrashed into the ground and then stomped on – 'Shagadelic, baby!' The British love to send themselves up to the point of pain – and Myers loves to help.

THE BIG LEBOWSKI

Joel Coen, USA/GB, 1998

Jeff 'the Dude' Lebowski (Bridges) is an easy-going man. His life in LA is so laid-back as to be almost horizontal. His answer to most problems is 'Let's go bowling'. However, when his house is broken into by two gangsters who pee on his favourite rug, he finds himself becoming quite angry. Then, when he discovers that they think they are chasing Jeffrey Lebowski – 'the Big Lebowski' ('big' as in millionaire), whose wife owes them a lot of money – he's furious. The Dude sets off to demand compensation (or at least rug-cleaning) from the Big Lebowski, only to find himself enmeshed in a series of events that span a kidnapping scenario, the art world and the porn industry.

The Coen brothers' zany humour delights in weird characters – or characters so normal that they're weird. In this, their first (and possibly only) bowling movie, Dude's biggest bowling pal, Walter Sobchak (Goodman), is a Vietnam vet who attributes every cause and effect in life to the USA's involvement 'over there'. He does it when he's bowling, and he does it when he says he's not doing it. Donny (Buscemi), the other bowling pal, could be weird or 'normal', but we'll never know as the mere opening of his mouth provokes the order to 'Shut the … up'. Another Coen-inspired weirdo is Jesus (Turturro), a Latino bowler with a rare door-to-door mission.

Like the Dude, the Coens' movie doesn't really want to get anywhere, but it makes sure we are happy to bowl along with it.

CAST INCLUDES:
Jeff Bridges, John Goodman, Julianne Moore, Steve Buscemi, David Huddleston, Philip Seymour Hoffman, Tara Reid
SCREENPLAY:
Ethan Coen, Joel Coen
CINEMATOGRAPHY:
Roger Deakins

THERE'S SOMETHING ABOUT MARY

Bobby Farrelly, Peter Farrelly, USA, 1998

CAST INCLUDES:
Cameron Diaz, Matt Dillon,
Ben Stiller, Lee Evans,
Chris Elliott, Lin Shaye,
Jeffrey Tambor
SCREENPLAY:
Ed Decter, John J. Strauss,
Bobby Farrelly, Peter Farrelly
CINEMATOGRAPHY:
Mark Irwin

Ted Stroehmann (Stiller) is a high school geek with braces who is in love with Mary (Diaz), the loveliest girl in Rhode Island. After he helps her mentally handicapped brother (W. Earl Brown), she invites him to the prom. Ted turns that into an unforgettable night by getting his dick caught in his trouser zip. Thirteen years later Ted is still pining over Mary and, at the suggestion of friend Dom (Elliott), hires sleazy private detective Pat Healy (Dillon) to find her. Healy finds Mary living in Florida, but sends back a horrendous report of this beautiful and caring woman because he's fallen for her himself. In fact, he finds, every needy nerd in the state has discovered that there's something about Mary. When it comes to bad taste, Mel Brooks could learn a thing or three from the Farrellys. They have been practising for a couple of films now, and they don't seem to have missed much. There are jokes about whiteheads-on-the-eyeballs skin conditions, bodily fluids, the mentally handicapped, watering holes for gay men, the ugliness of the elderly (nude) and people in leg braces, and there are bucketfuls of semen. But somewhere behind (or underneath) all this are two very nice people called Ted and Mary who will be truly glad to know that they are part of what's making you laugh so hard.

AMÉLIE (LE FABULEUX DESTIN D'AMÉLIE POULAIN)

Jean-Pierre Jeunet, France/Germany, 2001

CAST INCLUDES:
Audrey Tautou,
Mathieu Kassovitz, Rufus,
Lorella Cravotta,
Serge Merlin
SCREENPLAY:
Guillaume Laurent (plus
dialogue) from the story
by Jean-Pierre Jeunet and
Guillaume Laurent
CINEMATOGRAPHY:
Bruno Delbonnel

Amélie (Tautou), an enchanting bubble of *joie de vivre* who lives in Paris, had a rather sad childhood: a mother who committed suicide and a father who couldn't cuddle. One day, a shocking piece of news causes her to drop something that dislodges a tile in the bathroom of her flat. Behind it she discovers a rusty tin box full of a boy's childhood treasures. She finds the man that the boy has become, and is uplifted by the happiness she brings to him with the box. She realizes that bringing people happiness is her life's work and sets about doing this in myriad ways. Eventually, she is able to bring about her own happiness. Joyful, romantic and charming, *Amélie* sprinkles colour everywhere yet it never strays into whimsy. It is a flawless gem of a film graced by flawless performances.

LOST IN TRANSLATION

Sofia Coppola, USA/Japan, 2003

Bob Harris (Murray) is a world-weary, past-his-prime actor who is in Tokyo to make whisky ads. He despises the job but is doing it for the money ($2 million) and to get away from a souring marriage. At the same hotel is Charlotte (Johansson), a 25-year-old philosophy graduate whose photographer husband, John (Ribisi), is making a video about an indie band – and doesn't really want her around. Bob and Charlotte, both feeling inwardly lost and outwardly strange in Tokyo, while away long hours together in strip clubs and karaoke bars, and spend charmed hours talking and listening. They know that these are short, magical moments – but where there's magic, there's hope. For this, her second movie, Sofia Coppola wrote the role of Bob for Bill Murray. When she finally tracked him down, all he would say was that he was 'inclined' to make the film – and then appeared on the day before shooting started in Tokyo. What followed was a new and wondrous Bill Murray. Both the acerbic grouch and unwilling romantic of *Groundhog Day* (1993) are there, but none of the Murray comic schtick. It's all available, however – that massive reservoir of comic talent lies just below this minimalist, romantic comedy of manners. Coppola creates a situation in which a sad Bob and a confused Charlotte can be safe with each other, where they can relax and find real laughter.

ACADEMY AWARD

Best Writing, Screenplay
Written Directly for the Screen:
Sofia Coppola

CAST INCLUDES:
Scarlett Johansson,
Bill Murray,
Akiko Takeshita,
Giovanni Ribisi
SCREENPLAY:
Sofia Coppola
CINEMATOGRAPHY:
Lance Acord

SHAUN OF THE DEAD

Edgar Wright, GB, 2004

Dumped by his girlfriend, ridiculed by his housemate and patronized by his mother, Shaun (Pegg) is the definitive loser. But when the world in which he has failed to succeed is suddenly turned on its head, he finally finds a purpose in life: saving people he cares about from the zombie holocaust. Conceived by Pegg and Wright (two of the creative forces behind British sitcom *Spaced*) as a kind of tribute to the George A. Romero 'trilogy of the dead' zombie movies, the first 'rom-zom-com' is a delightful mash-up of twisted Ealing comedy, '70s' zombie movie gore and postmodern romance. It's supposed to be as silly as it sounds and succeeds magnificently. Perhaps one of the main reasons lies in the way its lead characters behave and interact. There's an authenticity here that can only be achieved when the writers and director genuinely understand and are part of the same demographic to which their characters belong. Shaun and Ed are ordinary English 30-something overgrown kids and also people you'd like to go and have a pint with… assuming the zombie army loitering outside the pub will let you in.

CAST INCLUDES:
Simon Pegg, Kate Ashfield, Nick Frost, Lucy Davis, Dylan Moran, Peter Serafinowicz, Penelope Wilton, Bill Nighy
SCREENPLAY:
Simon Pegg, Edgar Wright
CINEMATOGRAPHY:
David M. Dunlap

ANCHORMAN

Adam McKay, USA, 2004

CAST INCLUDES:
Will Ferrell, Christina Applegate, Paul Rudd, Steve Carell, David Koechner, Fred Willard
SCREENPLAY:
Adam McKay, Will Ferrell
CINEMATOGRAPHY:
Thomas Ackerman

In 1970's San Diego, Ron Burgundy (Ferrell) is a big star thanks to his top-rated news show. But when a new addition to the testosterone-fuelled newsroom turns out to be a woman, Burgundy and his cronies are outraged. Ron Burgundy, the Scotch-swilling dog-lover whose apartment smells of rich mahogany, became an instant classic comedy creation when *Anchorman* was released in 2004. A mix of celebrity and saviour to the people of San Diego, Burgundy is given free reign to be a narcissistic misogynist with hilarious results. When Veronica Corningstone (Applegate) is parachuted in (ostensibly from another town, though she may as well come from modern times) to add a little balance, she becomes an excellent foil to Burgundy and the only sane person on screen. The chemistry between Ferrell and Applegate is marvellous and clearly sparked much of the endlessly quotable and largely improvised script. As Burgundy himself would say, 'Great story. Compelling, and rich.'

LITTLE MISS SUNSHINE

Jonathan Dayton, Valerie Faris, USA, 2006

CAST INCLUDES:
Abigail Breslin, Greg Kinnear,
Paul Dano, Alan Arkin,
Toni Collette, Steve Carell
SCREENPLAY:
Michael Arndt
CINEMATOGRAPHY:
Tim Suhrstedt

The disparate and highly strung Hoover family drive cross-country in order to take youngest progeny Olive (Breslin) to a kids' beauty pageant she has no hope of winning.

Lifting and improving upon ideas from virtually every family road movie (not to mention *The Simpsons*), *Little Miss Sunshine* cruised into cinemas in the summer of 2006 and set about becoming the sleeper hit of the year. Key to its success is a seriously clever script from debutante Michael Arndt (who also wrote the screenplay for *Toy Story 3*), who must have sweated blood to imbue his characters with such an impressive balance of absurdist satire and detailed realism. It's very much an actors' film, with the ensemble cast apparently encouraging each other to new heights of excellence. Although all are entirely credible, Olive's mother, Cheryl (Collette), appears the most 'normal'. Stretched too thin by a demanding and inconsiderate family, she's the glue that holds them all together. Father Richard (Kinnear) is a motivational speaker struggling to stay positive in the face of career meltdown, whilst Grandpa Edwin (Arkin on Oscar-winning form) is only along for the ride after being kicked out of his old people's home for taking drugs. Similarly, suicidal Proust scholar Uncle Frank (Carell, showing a very different side to his talents) has been kicked out of a psychiatric ward and has nowhere else to go, whilst brother Dwayne (Dano), a Nietzsche-loving teen strictly adhering to a vow of silence, is present in physical form only.

Clever, funny and touching, *Little Miss Sunshine* is an unexpected little gem.

BORAT: CULTURAL LEARNINGS OF AMERICA FOR MAKE BENEFIT GLORIOUS NATION OF KAZAKHSTAN

Larry Charles, USA, 2006

Kazakhstani TV presenter Borat Sagdiyev (Baron Cohen) and his producer Azamat (Davitian) are despatched to the US to learn more of its culture and people. There, he struggles to understand etiquette, is almost lynched at a rodeo and falls in love with Pamela Anderson. The documentary format is key when you consider the fundamental appeal of Baron Cohen's characters lies in watching them interact with real people. Borat is a witless, racist, anti-Semitic and sexist anachronism, but this reprehensible character is superb at exposing similar, genuine traits in others. He is able to engender a feeling of solidarity with 'fellow' anti-Semitics and sexists who, having unwisely let down their guard, speak in terms that can be shocking. Although the most extreme of the resulting interviews are fascinating and horrifying in equal measure, they're never less than hilarious. Director Larry Charles handles this challenging humour expertly and ensures the more abhorrent interviewees come across as the prostrate imbeciles they are.

CAST INCLUDES:
Sacha Baron Cohen,
Ken Davitian
SCREENPLAY:
Sacha Baron Cohen,
Anthony Hines, Peter
Baynham, Dan Mazer,
Todd Phillips
CINEMATOGRAPHY:
Anthony Hardwick,
Luke Geissbuhler

CAST INCLUDES: Ellen Page, Michael Cera, Jennifer Garner, Jason Bateman, Allison Janey, J.K. Simmons
SCREENPLAY: Diablo Cody
CINEMATOGRAPHY: Eric Steelberg

JUNO

Jason Reitman, USA, 2007

ACADEMY AWARD
Best Writing, Screenplay
Written Directly for the Screen:
Diablo Cody

Sixteen-year-old Minnesotan Juno MacGuff (Page) unexpectedly falls pregnant by her sort-of boyfriend Paulie Bleeker (Cera). Deciding to give the baby up for adoption proves the easy part but the pair must overcome numerous difficulties during the pregnancy. Written by an ex-stripper newcomer (Diablo Cody), directed by a man with just one little-seen feature on his CV (Jason Reitman) and starring a Canadian in her 20s playing a 16-year-old American schoolgirl, there was little reason to expect anything special from *Juno*. However, what starts out as a chaotic screwball comedy rapidly settles into a considered character study, the two styles brought together by a universal deftness of touch and perfect judgement. Cody's script crackles with smart one-liners and features an ingenious teenage patois that allows for some fantastic dialogue. Page and Cera excel as the likeable but confused teens. Page in particular garnered the critical plaudits (and an Oscar nomination) but Cera is just as impressive in a breakout role.

BRIDESMAIDS

Paul Feig, USA, 2011

CAST INCLUDES:
Kristen Wiig, Maya
Rudolph, Rose Byrne,
Melissa McCarthy,
Chris O'Dowd
SCREENPLAY:
Kristen Wiig, Annie
Mumolo
CINEMATOGRAPHY:
Robert D. Yeoman

Annie (Wiig), single and in her late 30s, is going nowhere. Her cake business has failed, she has no savings, she's sharing an apartment with a decidedly odd brother and sister and her no-strings-attached relationship with self-absorbed Ted is a source of constant misery and humiliation. The only bright spot is her best friend, Lillian (Rudolph), but when Lilian announces her engagement and asks Annie to be her maid of honour, things unravel even more.

Produced by Judd Apatow, the writer/director behind *Knocked Up* (2007) and *The 40-Year-Old Virgin* (2005), *Bridesmaids* was a huge commercial and critical success on its release. It was notable for breaking new ground by being a gross-out, female-driven comedy written by and starring women. Shrewdly honest about what's really going on in women's lives, it was deservedly nominated for Academy Awards for Best Supporting Actress for Melissa McCarthy and Best Original Screenplay.

FROZEN

Chris Buck, Jennifer Lee, USA, 2013

ACADEMY AWARD
Best Animated Feature
Best Original Song
('Let It Go')

Fearless optimist Anna (Bell) teams up with rugged mountain man Kristoff (Groff) and his loyal reindeer Sven in an epic journey, encountering Everest-like conditions, mystical trolls and a hilarious snowman named Olaf (Gad) in a race to find Anna's estranged sister Elsa (Menzel), whose icy powers have inadvertently trapped the kingdom of Arendelle in eternal winter.

Based loosely on the Hans Andersen tale *The Snow Queen*, *Frozen* is the gorgeously rendered computer-animated musical that has broken all records and pushed the boundary of what is possible in CGI. It has a winning score by husband-and-wife songwriting team Robert Lopez and Kristen Anderson-Lopez, including the film's big anthem, 'Let It Go', which won an Academy Award. A massive commercial and critical success, *Frozen* is the highest-grossing animated film of all time, accumulating $1.3 billion in worldwide box-office revenue and counting. Winning the Academy Award for Best Animated Feature was the icing on the cake, and its cultural impact and huge popularity show no signs of diminishing.

CAST INCLUDES:
(voices of) Kristen Bell,
Idina Menzel, Jonathan Groff,
Josh Gad
SCREENPLAY:
Jennifer Lee from
The Snow Queen by
Hans Christian Andersen
ART DIRECTION:
Michael Giaimo

THE GRAND BUDAPEST HOTEL

Wes Anderson, GB/Germany/USA, 2014

*T*he *Grand Budapest Hotel* recounts the adventures of Gustave H. (Fiennes), a legendary concierge at a famous European hotel between the wars, and Zero Moustafa, the lobby boy who becomes his most trusted friend. The story involves the theft and recovery of a priceless Renaissance painting and the battle for an enormous family fortune – all against the backdrop of a suddenly and dramatically changing continent.

Released to great critical acclaim, *The Grand Budapest Hotel* received nine Academy Award nominations and won four, including those for Best Production Design and Best Original Score for composer Alexandre Desplat. The film's visual style is a treat from start to finish, Anderson using ornate visual environments to explore emotional concepts, while Fiennes' performance is a tour de force.

CAST INCLUDES:
Ralph Fiennes,
F. Murray Abraham,
Mathieu Amalric,
Adrien Brody, Willem Dafoe,
Jeff Goldblum,
Harvey Keitel, Jude Law,
Bill Murray, Edward Norton
SCREENPLAY:
Wes Anderson
CINEMATOGRAPHY:
Robert D. Yeoman:

DRAMA

MR SMITH GOES TO WASHINGTON

Frank Capra, USA, 1939

ACADEMY AWARD
Best Writing, Original Story:
Lewis R. Foster

CAST INCLUDES:
Jean Arthur, James Stewart,
Claude Rains,
Edward Arnold, Guy Kibbee
SCREENPLAY:
Sidney Buchman
(screenplay),
Lewis R. Foster (story)
CINEMATOGRAPHY:
Joseph Walker

When a congressional seat becomes available, the politicians are looking for someone who will play ball with the established regime, maintaining the status quo and keeping his personal views in check. While those in power think they have found the perfect man in Jefferson Smith (Stewart), it soon becomes clear that he is both a shrewd man and incorruptible. Frank Capra's stirring insight into government and powers manages to fulfil its aims, whilst injecting a certain amount of humour into the proceedings. Master at bringing the trials of humanity to the big screen (*It's a Wonderful Life*, 1946), Capra uses his unique talent for dealing with big ideas in simple ways to portray a man fighting for his ideals against the odds. Jefferson begins full of optimism for his new role of patriotic duty but soon discovers that, even at the top, the greed for power and wealth can corrupt moral ideals of service and duty to your country. When it transpires that tycoon James Taylor (Arnold) is bolstering his real-estate business with money that he's procured from public funds, it becomes Mr Smith's duty to expose this blatant corruption. The moral path is no easy walk, however, and cynical insiders try to ruin his career. This film was a definite turning point for James Stewart, who won acclaim, from both the Academy and the audiences, for his heartfelt performance. Though it criticized the system, this movie also proved that democracy held within it the means of its own redemption.

THE GRAPES OF WRATH

John Ford, USA, 1940

Following one family's struggle to survive during the Great Depression, *The Grapes of Wrath* struck a real chord with audiences of the time. Documenting real events, it is part historical document, part social observation, but above all a film that charts the strength and resilience of the farming families that suffered virtual devastation, as their livelihoods were lost and they faced starvation and homelessness. Tom Joad (Fonda) returns to his Oklahoma farm from a stint in prison to find his family packing up and preparing to make the long journey to California in search of work. They are representative of the many thousands of people who made the same difficult trek, having been forced from their smallholdings by the moneymen. Based on the John Steinbeck novel of the same name, Ford's film doesn't attempt to dilute the message of the book or play to a Hollywood formula. Tom is still the same flawed hero, guilty of murder and far from perfect, but it's his everyman qualities that see him applauded as the voice of the common people, refusing to just roll over and die while those in power profit from his plight. The only real major deviation from the book is the ending, when Steinbeck's shocking and heart-rending climax is transformed into something a little more palatable for a cinema audience.

CAST INCLUDES:
Henry Fonda, Jane Darwell,
John Carradine,
Charley Grapewin,
Dorris Bowdon,
Russell Simpson
SCREENPLAY:
Nunnally Johnson
(screenplay),
John Steinbeck (novel)
CINEMATOGRAPHY:
Gregg Toland

ACADEMY AWARDS
Best Actress in a Supporting
Role: Jane Darwell
Best Director: John Ford

CITIZEN KANE

Orson Welles, USA, 1941

CAST INCLUDES:
Orson Welles, Joseph Cotton,
Dorothy Comingore,
Agnes Moorehead,
Ruth Warrick, Ray Collins
SCREENPLAY:
Herman J Mankiewicz and
Orson Welles
CINEMATOGRAPHY:
Gregg Toland

ACADEMY AWARD
Best Original Screenplay:
Herman J. Mankiewicz,
Orson Welles

Charles Foster Kane (Welles) utters the word 'Rosebud' with his dying breath and the film deals with the attempt by friends, acquaintances and colleagues to give meaning to these apparently innocuous and random syllables by means of flashbacks of his life. Still regarded by many as the best film ever made, its reputation hasn't lessened with the passing of time, and the accolades still pour in when any definitive list of movie greats is put together. The praise is deserved for many reasons, not least the fact that Orson Welles was only 25 years old when he co-wrote, starred in and directed *Citizen Kane*. This accomplishment was all the greater because, for its time, the film was highly innovative in many respects, particularly in revolutionizing cinematography. As we dwell on the dying words of a lonely man, we are literally thrown into the middle of his life when he was a highly successful newspaper publisher, who built his up his empire from humble beginnings to become one of America's most powerful businessmen. However, success and happiness don't always go hand in hand, and this soon becomes apparent as Kane begins to lose the power he has become accustomed to and his empire starts crumbling around him. The film is said to have been based on real-life newspaper magnate William Randolph Hearst, although this is difficult to prove as Welles created an amalgamation of various well-known paper men of the time. And what of Rosebud? The secret behind the word is revealed right at the end, but after so much searching and surmising, the truth is something of a surprise.

THE LOST WEEKEND

Billy Wilder, USA, 1945

Charting one man's desperate battle with alcoholism, *The Lost Weekend* is probably the most honest and pragmatic study of this often misinterpreted and misunderstood disease ever produced. There is no romanticism or masculine bravado employed to excuse or try and play down Don Birnnam's (Milland) frenzied nose dive for the bottle at every possible opportunity during this fateful 48 hours. Displaying the telltale signs of many alcoholics, such as hiding booze around the house, lying, and sneaking into bars, we meet Don one particular weekend when he and his brother, Wick (Terry), are supposed to be going down to stay with their parents. Having managed to stay dry for a while, it's more than Don can bear to be in the same room as a half-bottle of bourbon. The thought of it tortures him and tears him apart and, once he has given in, there's no going back; it's a downward spiral into the depths of human pain and despair. Milland manages to keep the film within the realms of reality with his truly agonizing performance, for which he won an Oscar. It's a subject that was crying out to be tackled but it was a brave choice and one that didn't sit easily with the original audience.

CAST INCLUDES:
Ray Milland, Jane Wyman, Phillip Terry, Howard Da Silva, Doris Dowling
SCREENPLAY:
Charles Brackett and Billy Wilder from the novel by Charles R. Jackson
CINEMATOGRAPHY:
John F. Seitz

THE BEST YEARS OF OUR LIVES

William Wyler, USA, 1946

This film is as timeless as the subject it tackles; men returning from war. Just how do people cope with their reintegration into everyday life back home when they have seen and suffered so much? Wyler's three protagonists each has their own inner demons to deal with and they must somehow try to reconcile their Second World War experiences with family life and the mundane normality of Boone City. This film is a poignant reminder of the hidden costs of war and the confusion of the men who fight for their country, only to find that they and the land for which they suffered have been altered irrevocably by the experience. It won seven Academy Awards, including Best Director for William Wyler, Best Actor for Fredric March and Best Supporting Actor for Harold Russell.

CAST INCLUDES:
Myrna Loy, Fredric March, Dana Andrews, Teresa Wright, Virginia Mayo, Harold Russell
SCREENPLAY:
Robert E. Sherwood and MacKinlay Kantor from the novel *Glory For Me*
CINEMATOGRAPHY:
Gregg Toland

GREAT EXPECTATIONS

David Lean, GB, 1946

CAST INCLUDES:
John Mills, Anthony Wager,
Valerie Hobson, Jean
Simmons, Bernard Miles,
Martita Hunt
SCREENPLAY:
Anthony Havelock-Allan, David
Lean, Cecil McGivern, Ronald
Neame and Kay Walsh from
the novel by Charles Dickens
CINEMATOGRAPHY:
Guy Green

Despite a number of later film and television interpretations of the famous work, Lean's is the one that is still remembered and referred to as the classic version. Pip, the protagonist, is invited to the house of the bitter Miss Havisham (Hunt), who was abandoned by her fiancé on their wedding day many years ago and is yet to recover from the blow. She lives with her adopted daughter, Estella (Simmons), for whom Pip is to be the playmate. An anonymous benefactor soon sees Pip move to London and, although he believes he is being made respectable enough to marry the beautiful Estella, it isn't, in fact, Miss Havisham who is paying. She has been rearing her young charge in the art of breaking hearts, as revenge for her own heartbreak. An evocative and epic production, the opening scenes will haunt you forever.

IT'S A WONDERFUL LIFE

Frank Capra, USA, 1946

In this now much-lauded movie, Frank Capra explores the value and virtue of an 'ordinary' life of decency and integrity to the wider society of which it is a part. George Bailey (Stewart) dreamt of being a famous explorer when he was a boy, but the death of his father meant forsaking his dreams of travel and remaining in the town of Bedford Falls to run the family business. When misfortune strikes, George despairs and contemplates suicide. His guardian angel (Travers) appears to help him take stock, to see the value of his life. He asks him what the world would have been like if George hadn't been born and subsequently takes him on a tour of his life as if he had never existed, revealing the many ways in which George has contributed to the lives of those around him. Capra created a timeless piece of cinema that related so directly to the human psyche that it could not fail but to touch the hearts of audiences. However, it wasn't until long after the film was first released that it really gained in popularity, and it still attracts new fans today.

CAST INCLUDES:
James Stewart, Donna Reed,
Lionel Barrymore, Thomas
Mitchell, Henry Travers
SCREENPLAY:
Frances Goodrich, Albert
Hackett, Frank Capra, Jo
Swerling (additional scenes),
Philip Van Doren Stern from
the story *The Greatest Gift*
CINEMATOGRAPHY:
Joseph F. Biroc, Joseph Walker

THE BICYCLE THIEF
LADRI DI BICICLETTE

Vittorio De Sica, Italy, 1948

CAST INCLUDES:
Lamberto Maggiorani,
Enzo Staiola, Lianella Carell,
Gino Saltamerenda,
Vittorio Antonucci
SCREENPLAY:
Oreste Biancoli, Vittorio De
Sica, Gerardo Guerrieri,
Suso Cecchi d'Amico, Adolfo
Franci, Cesare Zavattini,
Cesare Zavattini (story) from
the novel by Luigi Bartolini
CINEMATOGRAPHY:
Carlo Montuori

A slice of life in poverty-stricken, post-war Rome, *The Bicycle Thief* is a simple tale that offers far more than its linear structure and uncomplicated characterizations suggest. Ricci (Maggiorani) queues at the same spot each morning with other men, hoping to gain work. When a job is offered one day, he jumps at the chance, only to discover that a bicycle is required. Ricci has pawned his in order to buy food for his family, but Ricci's wife, Maria (Carell), eagerly strips their bed of its sheets so that the bicycle can be retrieved from the pawnbrokers and Ricci can take the job. Providing a rare insight into post-war Italy at the time, there's a clever irony in play that sees Ricci putting up film posters as part of his job; the glamour of the silver screen staring down, larger than life, as the people below try to scrape a living. Needless to say, Ricci's bicycle is stolen from him and he scours the streets of Rome to no avail, looking for the thief. It's a cycle of poverty and desperation that he very nearly continues when he is tempted to steal another bicycle from someone else to replace his, in order to keep his job. Often cited as one of the greatest films ever made, the simplicity of such a human tale hasn't been lost.

CAST INCLUDES:
Bette Davis, Anne Baxter,
George Sanders, Celeste
Holm, Gary Merrill
SCREENPLAY:
Joseph L. Mankiewicz
CINEMATOGRAPHY:
Milton R. Krasner

ALL ABOUT EVE

Joseph L. Mankiewicz, USA, 1950

A rollercoaster ride through the glitzy world of 1950s' American theatre, this classic film with its six Oscar wins and star line-up was always destined to remain a favourite. Its showbiz connotations still resonate today and its upfront behind-the-scenes analysis of the cynical yet all-encompassing theatrical milieu is a joy to watch. The divine Bette Davis is engrossing in her portrayal of Margo Channing, an actress at the end of the line but unsure how to go about doing anything else. When aspiring artiste Eve Harrington (Baxter) appears, Margo becomes her mentor. It's actually Margo, however, who really benefits from her generosity, having lost sight of who she really is after years of accolades and acting parts. By taking Eve under her wing, she can be proactive rather than having her every move mapped out for her. As the film develops, however, Eve's ulterior motives begin to surface and we sense that she may be trying to pursue her own career. Mankiewicz succeeded in re-creating a world within a world, inhabited by snappy and memorable characters that transport us right to the stage.

SUNSET BOULEVARD

Billy Wilder, USA, 1950

CAST INCLUDES:
William Holden, Gloria Swanson, Erich von Stroheim, Nancy Olson, Fred Clark, Lloyd Gough
SCREENPLAY:
Charles Brackett, Billy Wilder, D.M. Marshman Jr.
CINEMATOGRAPHY:
John F. Seitz

ACADEMY AWARDS

Best Art Direction-Set Decoration, Black-and-White:Hans Dreier, John Meehan, Sam Comer, Ray Moyer
Best Music, Scoring of a Dramatic or Comedy Picture: Franz Waxman
Best Writing, Story and Screenplay: Charles Brackett, Billy Wilder, D.M. Marshman Jr.

Still regarded as the greatest film ever made on the subject of Hollywood, *Sunset Boulevard* charts the ill-fated meeting of faded star Norma Desmond (Swanson) and screenwriter on the make, Joe Gillis (Holden). Living in virtual isolation in a mansion, Norma spends her lonely days dreaming of how she could become a big name once again. Joe comes across the decrepit mansion and the lonely has-been by chance. Gillis is struggling to make it big, and the dichotomy between the woman who's been at the top and the man who's scrabbling at the bottom provides an interesting take on the asinine world of stardom and the film industry. Norma not only employs Gillis to work on her comeback script, but she falls in love with him in the process, showering him with expensive gifts. Unbeknown to her, Gillis is also working with young studio writer Betty (Olson) on a collaboration and, rather than returning any amorous feelings towards Norma, Gillis falls for Betty and things get complicated. In an industry where youth and beauty are pretty much a prerequisite for continued employment, Norma struggles to come to terms with her fall from grace. For Gillis to go behind her back is an unqualified affront, after all the kindness she feels she has shown him. Norma believes she owns the young writer, as she has owned many people in the past, and this only serves to highlight the materialistic nature and egocentric view that presides over Norma's Hollywood. A warped outlook perhaps, but one that ends in murder and Norma Desmond's last great close-up. Erich von Stroheim gives an astounding performance as her former director/lover and now butler.

ACE IN THE HOLE

Billy Wilder, USA, 1951

CAST INCLUDES:
Kirk Douglas, Jan Sterling,
Porter Hall, Robert Arthur,
Frank Cady, Richard Benedict
SCREENPLAY:
Billy Wilder, Walter Newman,
Lesser Samuels
CINEMATOGRAPHY:
Charles Lang

Sacked from his job at a big newspaper, reporter Chuck Tatum (Douglas) resorts to taking a job on a small New Mexican paper. Whilst travelling to cover a local event, he literally stumbles across the story that could relaunch his career. The subject is the unfortunate Leo Minosa (Benedict), who has become trapped after a cave collapsed. In a film that seems even more pertinent today than it did in the 1950s, the whole media institution is taken apart, examined and condemned, along with those who come along for the ride. When a good story is pursued to the detriment of its subject, the rules governing common decency are flouted and the news is no longer simply the news; it is a form of entertainment. This is the case in *Ace in the Hole*; the story has all the human interest elements that will guarantee it extended headlines but, in order to prolong the public interest and ensure his return to the big time, Chuck needs Leo to remain trapped in the cave for as long as possible. The relatively quick recovery option is therefore eschewed in favour of a much lengthier rescue plan, jeopardizing the man's health but keeping the assembled public and press more than happy. Based on a true story in which the man actually died before being rescued, Wilder's film is a brave and blatant attack on the media, which, not surprisingly, won him little praise or acclaim at the time of its release.

ON THE WATERFRONT

Elia Kazan, USA, 1954

CAST INCLUDES:
Marlon Brando, Karl Malden,
Lee J. Cobb, Rod Steiger,
Pat Henning, Eva Marie Saint
SCREENPLAY:
Budd Schulberg,
Malcolm Johnson
(suggested by articles)
CINEMATOGRAPHY:
Boris Kaufman

Loosely based on the real-life experiences of director Elia Kazan, *On the Waterfront* was essentially a justification for his actions during attempts in the 1950s to 'cleanse' America of its Communist elements. Kazan named contemporaries whom he believed to be involved with the Communist Party. In the film Brando plays the part of Terry Malloy, errand boy for a notoriously corrupt docker's union, where workers are kept quiet and life is sweet for the men at the top. When he's unwittingly involved in a murder, he decides it's time to re-evaluate his principles and make some tough decisions. Marlon Brando was at the height of his career when he starred in this eight-Oscar-winning film, but it was talent and not fame that really drove home the message and still has people today talking about the film in terms of a classic.

REBEL WITHOUT A CAUSE

Nicholas Ray, USA, 1956

Our first encounter with Jim Stark (Dean) is as he lies in the gutter, drunk. A fitting image for a film that predominantly deals with alienation and disquiet amongst the youth of 1950s' America. Jim is by no means a wayward loser, however; he is a symbol of the shifting dynamic of a country adapting to monumental social and political change. *Rebel Without a Cause* follows Jim *et al* as they purposefully misspend their youth, looking for answers to unanswerable questions. Parental indifference is offered up as one justification for the meaningless violence, as if a lack of love can be counteracted with acts of hate; attention-seeking behaviour that will fill the void left by absent intimacy. The 1950s was certainly a time when the generation gap was growing, as the Victorian values of a pre-war America began to be replaced by a more forward-thinking outlook and the youth found their voice but weren't yet sure how to use it. In the film, the bonds of friendship replace those of family, and Jim, Judy and Plato come to represent a surrogate family unit, providing each other with a reassuring emotional-support network. Jim is out to prove himself though, despite the security that his friendships provide, and the famous 'chicken run' scene really sums up the film. Stolen cars are revved up to race over the edge of a cliff, the drivers jumping out at the very last minute, thus demonstrating the universal and timeless display of male bravado and pride. James Dean was the personification of this period in America's history. His moody screen dominance made him an overnight sensation and his untimely death made him a legend.

CAST INCLUDES:
James Dean, Natalie Wood,
Sal Mineo, Jim Backus,
Ann Doran
SCREENPLAY:
Stewart Stern, Irving
Shulman from the story by
Nicholas Ray
CINEMATOGRAPHY:
Ernest Haller

12 ANGRY MEN

Sydney Lumet, USA, 1957

DID YOU KNOW?
Reginald Rose's TV play script was left virtually intact in its move to film.

CAST INCLUDES:
Martin Balsam, John Fiedler,
Lee J. Cobb, E.G. Marshall,
Jack Klugman, Ed Binns,
Jack Warden, Henry Fonda,
Joseph Sweeney, Ed Begley,
George Voskovec,
Robert Webber
SCREENPLAY:
Reginald Rose
CINEMATOGRAPHY:
Boris Kaufman

Twelve jury members are sent out to deliberate over the verdict of a murder trial. If the defendant is found guilty, he will be sentenced to death, so the life of a fellow human being hangs in the balance and these men must decide on his fate. Almost the entire film is set in the jury room where the 12 white, male jurors ponder over the case that has been played out in court over the preceding six days. What initially appears to be a relatively clear-cut case of premeditated murder slowly becomes more complicated, and the discussion turns into a heated deliberation over the absolute certainty that the defendant is guilty. Lumet is undoubtedly attacking the American legal system in this film and, despite the quite uniform gender, race and class make-up of the jury, a surprising number of prejudices and issues emerge within the confines of the room and the matter at hand. The defendant is non-white, and racism is a key factor in many of the men's justifications of returning with a plea of 'guilty beyond reasonable doubt'. However, when juror number eight (Fonda) starts planting the seeds of doubt in their minds, there's a shift in the dynamic of the film. By keeping the action contained in just one location, the audience is treated to a more genuine experience, becoming fully engrossed in the actual process involved in this monumental responsibility.

THE SEVENTH SEAL (DET SJUNDE INSEGLET)

Ingmar Bergman, Sweden, 1957

CAST INCLUDES:
Gunnar Björnstrand,
Bengt Ekerot, Nils Poppe,
Max von Sydow,
Bibi Andersson
SCREENPLAY:
Ingmar Bergman from his
play *Trämålning*
CINEMATOGRAPHY:
Gunnar Fischer

Set against the backdrop of 14th-century Sweden, in the midst of the plague and the holy crusades, a knight (von Sydow) and his squire, Jöns (Bjönstrand), return home. Having escaped death during his perilous travels, the knight enters a church and comes face to face with it, in the form of a hooded man. It transpires that the shadowy figure has been following the knight on his homeward journey. Although dealing with a subject so dark and bleak, the film is thought-provoking and directed with such skill that the viewer is drawn in and forgets the depressing issues that are being played out on screen. Bergman was a master of this broody genre of filmmaking, always exploring the complexities of human existence and religious beliefs. Death is necessarily omnipresent in this country racked with plague and suffering, but to feature it in such a tangible way is both shocking and obvious. The knight plays chess with Death, a significant imagery that Bergman employs to describe his own personal hypotheses about God and religion.

SWEET SMELL OF SUCCESS

Alexander Mackendrick, USA, 1957

J.J. Hunsecker (Lancaster) is a man who's used to being fawned over and treated like royalty. A famous newspaper columnist whose words send reverberations around Manhattan, he lives the playboy lifestyle, enjoying the good life as if it's his birthright. A small-fry publicity agent by the name of Falco (Curtis) is one of Hunsecker's sources, sifting through the proverbial dustbins of New York's small talk to provide fodder for the famous column inches. Director Mackendrick makes no real attempt to highlight any redeeming features that might be hidden in these two men. The film is about media sensationalism, entertainment procured at other people's expense and, as such, niceties would be superfluous. We are shown a world of greed and envy, two of the deadly sins that these men carry around with them like weights about their necks, imprisoning them in their shallow world with blinkered vision.

CAST INCLUDES: Burt Lancaster, Tony Curtis, Susan Harrison, Martin Milner, Sam Levene
SCREENPLAY: Clifford Odets, Ernest Lehman from the novelette by Ernest Lehman
CINEMATOGRAPHY: James Wong Howe

VERTIGO

Alfred Hitchcock, USA, 1958

CAST INCLUDES:
James Stewart, Kim Novak, Barbara Bel Geddes, Tom Helmore, Henry Jones
SCREENPLAY:
Alec Coppel, Samuel A. Taylor, Pierre Boileau and Thomas Narcejac from the novel *d'Entre les Morts*
CINEMATOGRAPHY:
Robert Burks

When his fear of heights starts to impinge on his effectiveness as a police officer, John Ferguson (Stewart) is compelled to leave the force. At a loose end, a friend asks a favour; he wants Ferguson to follow his wife, as she's been acting strangely. Ferguson obliges but it doesn't take long for him to become infatuated with the beautiful Madeleine (Novak). When eventually they meet, it's obvious that the feeling is mutual, however Ferguson's demons come back to haunt him once more, as he is unable to save Madeleine from a fatal fall from a bell tower. *Vertigo* is a summation of all that Hitchcock did best; the suspense, the tension, the coercion of the camera to suit the mood, and the almost remote female lead. In a plot that twists and retraces until we're not sure who is who any more, a tall tale of deception and intrigue is built up. When Ferguson meets a woman bearing a remarkable resemblance to Madeleine, soon after her death, the intrigue really starts to escalate, and Hitchcock builds the notion of one man's obsession with obtaining perfection as he tries to mould the lookalike into an exact replica of the love he lost prematurely. Dealing with human neuroses in such a groundbreaking manner was part of the genius that earned Hitchcock his awesome reputation.

À BOUT DE SOUFFLE

Jean-Luc Godard, France, 1960

CAST INCLUDES:
Jean-Paul Belmondo, Jean Seberg, Daniel Boulanger, Jean-Pierre Melville, Henri-Jacques Huet, Van Doude, Claude Mansard, Jean-Luc Godard
SCREENPLAY:
Jean-Luc Godard from a story by François Truffaut
CINEMATOGRAPHY:
Raoul Coutard

Michel (Belmondo) thinks of himself as a young Humphrey Bogart, but he's really just a small-time hood. While stealing a car, out in the country, he shoots a policeman who is following him. He goes back to Paris to hide out in the room of his American girlfriend, Patricia (Seberg), who's a student and wants to be a journalist. She tells him she may be pregnant. They spend time fooling around, making love and talking – and making 'getaway' money by stealing and selling more cars. Michel wants to leave the country, but Patricia is uncertain. She'd rather be an American intellectual in Paris. Michel's name and picture are now on the front pages of newspapers. The police are everywhere and they are closing in. 'Modern movies begin here,' say the critics. Godard's film was the start of the French New Wave – a reaction against the existing structure and narrative of French film.

TO KILL A MOCKINGBIRD

Robert Mulligan, USA, 1962

CAST INCLUDES:
Gregory Peck, Mary Badham, Phillip Alford, Robert Duvall, John Megna, Frank Overton, Brock Peters, James Anderson
SCREENPLAY:
Horton Foote (screenplay), Harper Lee (novel)
CINEMATOGRAPHY:
Russell Harlan

ACADEMY AWARDS

Best Actor in a Leading Role: Gregory Peck
Best Art Direction-Set Decoration, Black-and-White: Alexander Golitzen, Henry Bumstead, Oliver Emert
Best Writing, Screenplay Based on Material from Another Medium: Horton Foote

Set in the American deep south in the 1930s, when racial intolerance was still the norm, *To Kill a Mockingbird* is the adaptation of Harper Lee's outstanding novel of the same name. In order to do justice to the book it was imperative that Mulligan had the right cast, and his choice of Peck for the part of lawyer Atticus Finch was clearly a stroke of genius. Finch takes on the case of Tom Robinson (Peters), a black man accused of rape. The law of being innocent until proven guilty seems lost on a prejudiced populace, and this is a clear-cut tale of racism and injustice as seen through the eyes of Finch's daughter, Scout (Badham). Following lengthy court proceedings, Robinson is found guilty, a charge which we know to be incorrect – the flagrant racist undertones leave a nasty taste in one's mouth. Robinson's most vocal accuser is the venom-filled Bob Ewell (Anderson), the father of the alleged victim, but he merely verbalizes what the majority of the white townsfolk are thinking. Despite the tragic conclusion to the trial, the story offers some hope, not least in the portrait of Finch as a single parent, instilling principles of decency and morality into his children, who can clearly see the inexcusable injustice for what it is. We are left with the facts, and the world is left with a film that reflects on a tainted period in history, but one which still has repercussions today.

8½

Federico Fellini, Italy/France, 1963

Ostensibly a film about a director at a creative impasse in his career, it has often been remarked that *8½* was at least semi-autobiographical, reflecting many of the difficulties Fellini was experiencing in his own work and life. Film director Guido (Mastroianni) is being hassled to begin production on his next film, but inspiration eludes him and personal crises fill his thoughts and, to a greater extent, his dreams. Indeed, it is during the dream sequences that we really learn about the true themes of the film – sexual desire, frustration and a feeling of isolation as a human being among them. Guido has a wife and a mistress, both of whom want their fair share of him. But, once he has divided himself amongst the hungry hopefuls waiting to pounce on the yet-to-be-confirmed film, there's not a whole lot left. It seems only in sleep is he free to explore the dark imaginings and desires of his mind, and where Fellini has a creative free rein to really push forward Guido's character. Fellini's work was often misunderstood as being too highbrow for the average audience, but it was generally a lack of linear structure in his films that forced people to interpret the stories for themselves. He doesn't make it easy for his audience but it's ultimately a more fulfilling experience.

CAST INCLUDES:
Marcello Mastroianni,
Claudia Cardinale,
Anouk Aimée, Rossella Falk,
Sandra Milo
SCREENPLAY:
Ennio Flaiano, Tullio Pinelli,
Federico Fellini, Brunello
Rondi. Story by Federico
Fellini and Ennio Flaiano
CINEMATOGRAPHY:
Gianni Di Venanzo

BELLE DE JOUR

Luis Buñuel, France/Italy, 1967

CAST INCLUDES:
Catherine Deneuve,
Jean Sorel, Michel Piccoli,
Geneviève Page,
Pierre Clémenti
SCREENPLAY:
Luis Buñuel, Jean-Claude
Carrière from the novel by
Joseph Kessel
CINEMATOGRAPHY:
Sacha Vierny

Séverine (Deneuve) is a breathtakingly beautiful young woman who has been married to her doctor husband (Sorel) for a year. In that time they haven't slept together, Séverine preferring to stay in the guest room, and herein lies the backbone of Buñuel's stunning exposition of sexual desires and frustrations. However, despite its gritty subject matter, Buñuel never allows it to stray into smutty territory. Séverine's curiosity eventually leads her to the brothel of Madame Anaïs (Page). We are aware that it's just a matter of time before she's on the payroll, and despite potentially humiliating treatment at the hands of some of her clients, Séverine is finally able to succumb to the urges that fill her sexually explicit dreams. As she is only able to see customers in the afternoons while her husband works, Séverine is given the name Belle de Jour. A truly perceptive look at some of the darker aspects of human desire, Buñuel's film emancipates its frustrated female lead in a way few films at the time dared.

THE GRADUATE

Mike Nichols, USA, 1967

CAST INCLUDES:
Anne Bancroft, Dustin Hoffman, Katharine Ross, William Daniels, Murray Hamilton
SCREENPLAY:
Calder Willingham, Buck Henry from the novel by Charles Webb
CINEMATOGRAPHY:
Robert Surtees

ACADEMY AWARD
Best Director: Mike Nichols

This iconic movie has any number of famous images and oft-repeated lines of dialogue associated with it. Recent college graduate Ben has reached an indecisive crossroads in his life and is ripe for the plucking by the sexually aware but unsatisfied Mrs Robinson, the wife of his father's business partner. The Graduate was a real film of the moment, speaking volumes about the America it represented, a populace uncertain and full of trepidation, rather like Ben, who makes a flustered refusal to Mrs Robinson's blatant offer of sex. It isn't long, however, before her advances are more successful and Ben quickly loses his inhibitions, embarking on a crazy affair. The adventure abruptly ends when Ben is introduced to the Robinsons' daughter, Elaine (Ross), and decides that she's the girl for him.

GUESS WHO'S COMING TO DINNER

Stanley Kramer, USA, 1967

CAST INCLUDES:
Spencer Tracy, Sidney Poitier, Katharine Hepburn, Cecil Kellaway, Beah Richards, Katharine Houghton
SCREENPLAY:
William Rose
CINEMATOGRAPHY:
Sam Leavitt

When the premise of a film is a girl bringing her fiancé home to meet her parents, it doesn't sound like much of a story. Make the girl white, the fiancé black and remember that it's 1960s' America, and things start to look a little more interesting. Joanna Drayton (Houghton) has been brought up in a liberal household but her impending marriage to an African-American is set to test her parents' (Hepburn and Tracy) views to the limits. John Wade Prentice (Poitier) is a distinguished doctor so it seems likely that any reluctance to give their blessing to the impending union must be based solely upon the colour of his skin. This particular aspect of the script was originally criticized by many people, as there didn't appear to be any real dilemma. However, by basing any prejudices solely on colour, the potential for excuses over poor job prospects or differing social backgrounds was removed, leaving the real issue to be discussed. In a topic that still has relevance today, people are asked to put their values on the line; it's all very easy to be a vocally progressive liberal but when the issues come walking through your front door, can you still stand by your beliefs with such heartfelt enthusiasm? Joanna's parents cite concerns for the couple's acceptance by society at large as their major issue, but is this a thin veil covering their own deep-rooted anxieties?

EASY RIDER

Dennis Hopper, USA, 1969

CAST INCLUDES:
Peter Fonda, Dennis Hopper,
Antonio Mendoza,
Phil Spector,
Mac Mashourian,
Jack Nicholson
SCREENPLAY:
Peter Fonda, Dennis Hopper,
Terry Southern
CINEMATOGRAPHY:
László Kovács

The ultimate road movie that launched a thousand more, *Easy Rider* follows the journey of Wyatt (Fonda) and Billy (Hopper) as they rev up their motorbikes and leave LA for the narcotics-fuelled adventure they've risked everything to take. With drug references aplenty, hippy protagonists and a great score, this film was destined to be a hit with the misunderstood generation, all clamouring to be a part of the free and easy lifestyle it portrayed, living beyond the constraints of a law-abiding society. It's not one big, carefree orgy of cannabis and casual sex, however, and tragedy strikes more than once as the boys land themselves in trouble. They begin to realize that not everyone they meet appreciates their values and it's not such an easy ride after all; enter George Hanson (Nicholson), the lawyer who helps them out

when they're arrested in redneck Middle America. George is intrigued and goes on to join them on their freedom crusade. He soon becomes infatuated with the lure of the open road, the antithesis of his own, sedentary life. Chemical highs help him gain awareness of the wider world beyond his limited experience, and he is one step closer to realizing his somewhat uninspired dream of visiting a famous brothel in New Orleans. The cinematography is crafted to back up the whole essence of the film and it works wonderfully as a means of reiterating the central themes of freedom and escapism. However, when death is the ultimate price for a sense of freedom, the viewer is asked to question the ethics of opting out of the mainstream and going solo.

THE LAST PICTURE SHOW

Peter Bogdanovich, USA, 1971

CAST INCLUDES:
Timothy Bottoms, Jeff Bridges,
Cybill Shepherd, Ben
Johnson, Cloris Leachman,
Ellen Burstyn
SCREENPLAY:
Larry McMurtry,
Peter Bogdanovich from the
novel by Larry McMurtry
CINEMATOGRAPHY:
Robert Surtees

Nothing much happens in the Texan town of Anarene, but that's the beauty of this film; it's the quintessential uniformity and conformity that makes space for the growth of the quirky characters. Sam (Johnson) owns the town's only picture house, the Royal Theater, and this is the hub of much activity, not least the attempted seduction of Jacy Farrow (Shepherd) by the local adolescent boys. What the boys don't realize is that she is well aware of her sexuality and how to use it to best further her plans. As time slips by and life plods along in Anarene, the event of note is that the picture house is closed, rendered superfluous by the television set. In a town noticeably void of action or incident, this in itself represents a changing era as people become even more insulated and housebound. The film won two Oscars.

NASHVILLE

Robert Altman, USA, 1975

ACADEMY AWARD
Best Music, Original Song:
Keith Carradine, for the song
'I'm Easy'

With songs galore throughout the entire film, we are thrown headfirst into America's country music capital whilst witnessing the machinations of the presidential candidate elections. Comebacks, showdowns, backstabbing and heartbreak are all par for the course in this all-singing, all-dancing epic. Robert Altman is the archetypal large-cast director and *Nashville* is no exception. He seems to relish the task of introducing as many characters as the plot can physically handle, then giving them all the space to develop. The film is an anomalous mix of music and politics; potentially strange bedfellows but ones that produce an exceptional film at the hands of this master craftsman. In a virtually unprecedented move amongst directors, Altman made no

CAST INCLUDES:
David Arkin, Barbara Baxley,
Ned Beatty, Karen Black,
Ronee Blakley, Timothy Brown
SCREENPLAY:
Joan Tewkesbury
CINEMATOGRAPHY:
Paul Lohmann

changes to Joan Tewkesbury's script, which obviously paid off, showing a great deal of cinematic altruism and a perceptive eye. The storylines interweave naturally but the separate strands and relationships between them are too intricate to begin to analyze. Needless to say, it all comes together to form a toe-tapping story of great magnitude, where the characters are larger than life and dish up a real slice of America.

ONE FLEW OVER THE CUCKOO'S NEST

Milos Forman, USA, 1975

CAST INCLUDES:
Jack Nicholson,
Louise Fletcher, William
Redfield, Michael Berryman,
Peter Brocco
SCREENPLAY:
Bo Goldman and Lawrence
Hauben from the novel by
Ken Kesey
CINEMATOGRAPHY:
Haskell Wexler

When petty criminal R.P. McMurphy (Nicholson) opts for a stint in a pyschiatric hospital over a prison sentence, he believes he's getting off lightly. A natural free spirit and no passive accepter of authority, it isn't long before he is trying to rebel against the dominating and degrading atmosphere. In a film that clearly wears its heart on its sleeve when dealing with the difficult subject of mental health and its treatment, this is really only a subplot to the central theme; the subjugation of the individual and enforced conformity to the rules of society. Nicholson plays the part of the subversive anarchist with suburb intuition, proving beyond reasonable doubt that if people have their identities removed they lose the very human traits that make them individuals. McMurphy provides an alternative path for some of the patients, showing them snippets of the life they deserve; a brief glimpse of the freedoms most will never enjoy. In the end, McMurphy's undermining of the hospital rules leads to his own downfall as he is kept on as a patient and prescribed treatments that will inevitably take away his individuality and worse. *One Flew over the Cuckoo's Nest* was the first film in 41 years to win all five of the top Academy Awards, which is a considerable feat considering that it very nearly didn't get made.

CAST INCLUDES:
Sylvester Stallone, Talia Shire,
Burt Young, Carl Weathers,
Burgess Meredith
SCREENPLAY:
Sylvester Stallone
CINEMATOGRAPHY:
James Crabe

ACADEMY AWARDS

Best Director: John G. Avildsen
Best Film Editing: Richard
Halsey, Scott Conrad
Best Picture: Irwin Winkler,
Robert Chartoff

ROCKY

John G. Avildsen, USA, 1979

When local boxer Rocky gets a once in a lifetime stab at the heavyweight championship, it's almost a given that he'll lose. Male pride and a misguided sense of possibility propel Rocky into one of the most famous workouts the big screen has ever known, with the underdog giving it his all for this one chance at the big time. It's a clichéd and much-used storyline that nevertheless manages to suspend our disbelief for the likeable guy who just might be able to prove them all wrong. *Rocky* is one of those feel-good films where, from the opening credits, you're cheering for the protagonist. Stallone wrote and starred in the film that secured his status as a household name, and he did such a great job of creating a character that he moulded into so perfectly that it's difficult to separate the two.

ALL THE PRESIDENT'S MEN

Alan J. Pakula, USA, 1976

CAST INCLUDES:
Dustin Hoffman,
Robert Redford, Jack Warden,
Martin Balsam, Hal Holbrook
SCREENPLAY:
William Goldman from the
book by Carl Bernstein and
Bob Woodward
CINEMATOGRAPHY:
Gordon Willis

ACADEMY AWARDS
Best Actor in a Supporting
Role: Jason Robards
Best Art Direction-Set
Decoration: George Jenkins,
George Gaines
Best Sound: Arthur Piantadosi,
Les Fresholtz, Rick Alexander
as Dick Alexander,
James E. Webb
Best Writing, Screenplay
Based on Material from
Another Medium:
William Goldman

When junior reporters Carl Bernstein (Hoffman) and Bob Woodward (Redford) are sent to cover the trial of the burglary at National Democratic Headquarters, they end up exposing the biggest scandal in the history of American politics and one that eventually leads to the resignation of President Nixon. Penned by seasoned screenwriter William Goldman (*Butch Cassidy and the Sundance Kid*), *All the President's Men* is essentially a film that charts the perseverance and doggedness of the reporters, to try and discover the truth, despite the many obstacles placed in their path. As such, it sings the praises of investigative journalism as an essential and necessary public function, bringing to light corruption and high-level political scandal. Their progress is almost thwarted on a number of occasions, not least by the pedantic editor of the *Washington Post*, who is loathe to publish any accusations without full 'on the record' back-up. Salvation comes in the form of the dubiously named 'Deep Throat' (Holbrook), whose true identity is kept a closely guarded secret, but who points them in the right direction and provides them with enough information to be able to eventually expose the Watergate scandal in the newspaper. Hoffman and Redford are both at the peak of their talents here, working off one another to produce an exciting, highly charged race against time, as they try not only to ensure they collect enough evidence to break the story, but also that another newspaper doesn't get there before them.

RAGING BULL

Martin Scorsese, USA, 1980

Martin Scorsese's finest hour came about thanks to the real-life story of boxer Jake LaMotta (De Niro). Ostensibly a film charting the highs and lows of the boxer's tumultuous career, it is actually so much more. The harrowing but visually stunning fight scenes were both inspired and gruelling, taking much longer to film than anticipated. However, both Scorsese and De Niro's pedantic attention to detail paid off, and they were rewarded with the greatest fight sequences to ever grace a cinema screen. As LaMotta punches his way to supremacy in the ring, his acute jealousy over his wife means she ends up on the receiving end of his knockout blows. With no grounds for his suspicions, he is left with nothing but his own neuroses as a justification for his deplorable actions against the one constant in his life. LaMotta's downfall is swift and unforgiving. He takes his beatings in a subservient way, accepting his punishment and his flawed character with a poignancy that is deserving of pity. Like many of the difficult roles De Niro has taken on in his career, he put everything he had into the preparation for *Raging Bull*, psyching himself up to play this mentally and physically draining part. He certainly did it justice, and won an Oscar for his efforts.

CAST INCLUDES:
Robert De Niro, Cathy Moriarty, Joe Pesci, Frank Vincent, Nicholas Colasanto, Theresa Saldana
SCREENPLAY:
Paul Schrader, Mardik Martin from the book by Jake LaMotta, Joseph Carter and Peter Savage
CINEMATOGRAPHY:
Michael Chapman

THE KING OF COMEDY

Martin Scorsese, USA, 1983

CAST INCLUDES:
Robert De Niro, Jerry Lewis, Diahnne Abbott, Sandra Bernhard, Shelley Hack
SCREENPLAY:
Paul D. Zimmerman
CINEMATOGRAPHY:
Fred Schuler

Some people will do just about anything to get their 15 minutes of fame and Rupert Pupkin (De Niro) is one of them. Absolutely convinced of his prowess as a stand-up comedian, Rupert is just looking for his one shot at the big time. He has chosen Jerry Langford's show as his route to fame and fortune and just needs to persuade the host (Lewis) to give him a slot. Rupert decides the only solution is to kidnap Jerry. In a rare departure from their usual genre, Scorsese and De Niro create an ingenious comedy that manages to entertain whilst looking at a genuine phenomenon. De Niro is wonderful as the desperate, starstruck Rupert, excusing his actions on the grounds of necessity. Rupert does get his 15 minutes and a whole lot more to boot, Scorsese telling us what we already know about the crazy world of celebrity worship. Everyone's cheering for the insane kidnapping comic, exactly as we're supposed to.

DANGEROUS LIAISONS

Stephen Frears, USA/GB, 1988

CAST INCLUDES:
Glenn Close, John Malkovich, Michelle Pfeiffer, Swoosie Kurtz, Keanu Reeves, Mildred Natwick, Uma Thurman
SCREENPLAY:
Christopher Hampton from his play and the novel by Choderlos de Laclos
CINEMATOGRAPHY:
Philippe Rousselot

If you want to see the best example of an actor who is absolutely convincing and practically born to play a certain role, watch John Malkovich in *Dangerous Liaisons*. His potent mix of sensual provocateur and evil manipulator is truly mesmerizing, and the crackling rapport between Malkovich and Close is exquisite. Set in 18th-century France, the lavishly decadent backdrop provides a rich source of visual endorsement for the blatant innuendo and mischievous undertones of a script sharpened to a knife edge. Our bored leads get sadistic pleasure out of the corruption of relationships and, having once been in one together, they are now famously free from the constraints of love and bitter enough to destroy the happiness of others by whatever means they can.

RAIN MAN

Barry Levinson, USA, 1988

CAST INCLUDES:
Dustin Hoffman, Tom Cruise, Valeria Golino, Gerald R. Molen, Jack Murdock
SCREENPLAY:
Ronald Bass, Barry Morrow from his story
CINEMATOGRAPHY:
John Seale

When Charlie Babbit's (Cruise) father dies, he is left with more than he bargained for. In lieu of money or property, Charlie discovers instead that he has an older brother, Raymond (Hoffman), who he knew nothing about and who has been left the lion's share of the inheritance. Charlie initially decides to avail himself of his entitled share of his father's estate, but matters are complicated by the discovery that his brother is autistic and he must first learn how to communicate with him, gain his trust and try to understand him before he can wheedle the fortune away from him. The brilliance of the film is borne out more in its simplicity than any daring attempts at boundary breaking. For the most part, the audience and Charlie are simultaneously learning about Raymond's condition, becoming by turn shocked, amazed and distressed by the intricacies of this hitherto little-understood affliction. The irony occurs when it becomes apparent that Raymond has no appreciation of money and, from Charlie's perspective, this means he has no use for his inheritance. However, as they travel across the country together, a mutual understanding develops, and a brotherly bond begins to emerge, putting a slight damper on Charlie's plans. Hoffman takes character acting to a new level in this film (he won an Oscar) and the rapport between the two leads is the ultimate secret of its success.

DO THE RIGHT THING

Spike Lee, USA, 1989

Sal's Pizzeria has been trading for 20 years and now represents one of just a couple of white businesses in a black area. Tensions begin to surface in the most innocuous way, when local activist Buggin' Out (Esposito) berates the fact that owner Sal (Aiello) exclusively has photos of white people on his board of fame in the restaurant; where are the African-American heroes? History has proved time and again that the smallest incident can lead to the biggest confrontations and this is a great match to use to ignite the flame of racial violence. This was one of the most open, honest and realistic discussions of race in America at its time of release. Spike Lee, known for courting controversy, didn't let the critics down with this film, in which violence erupts in a normally quiet Brooklyn neighbourhood. Without prophesying, condoning or condemning, Lee merely tells it like it is, leaving the viewer to put their own spin on the whys and wherefores of racial tension and integration in American inner cities. The story occurs against the backdrop of the hottest day of summer and there are definite symbolic overtones with regard to temperatures and tempers racing towards boiling point, both in this isolated incident and as a reflection of America in general.

CAST INCLUDES:
Danny Aiello, Ossie Davis,
Ruby Dee, Richard Edson,
Giancarlo Esposito,
Spike Lee
SCREENPLAY:
Spike Lee
CINEMATOGRAPHY:
Ernest R. Dickerson

It's a clever metaphor that allows Lee to push people over the edge in a way that seems justified. *Do the Right Thing* is a film that makes you sit up and pay attention, reflecting on its message long after the credits roll. And if that's not the mark of a great film, then nothing is.

DID YOU KNOW?
The title comes from a Malcolm X quote: 'You've got to do the right thing.'

RAISE THE RED LANTERN
DA HONG DENG LONG GAO GAO GUA

Yimou Zhang, China/Hong Kong/Taiwan, 1991

CAST INCLUDES:
Li Gong, Caifei He, Jingwu Ma, Cuifen Cao, Qi Zhao
SCREENPLAY:
Ni Zhen from the novel by Su Tong
CINEMATOGRAPHY:
Zhao Fei, Lun Yang

When Songlian (Gong) arrives at her new home, it is not with a sense of happy anticipation but one of resigned acceptance. The fourth wife of a wealthy Chinese man, Songlian had different ideas about where her future might take her, but her mother offered her as a concubine and she was unable to refuse. *Raise the Red Lantern* is dramatic in its scope, using cinematography and limited locations to convey the sense of a comfortable prison. This is how the four women live, each trying to curry favour with the master of the house, replicating that which occurs in everyday life within the confines of their quarters. The film teaches us about the life of the concubine but it also illustrates human emotion and adaptability; these women have accepted their future and they learn to fight for their survival, much as they would in the outside world, of which, incidentally, they know nothing. If they are antagonistic or ambivalent towards the newest addition to the household, it's because they fear for their own position in the miniature hierarchy that has been created amongst them.

GLENGARRY, GLEN ROSS

James Foley, USA, 1992

ACADEMY AWARD
Best Actor in a Supporting Role: Al Pacino

CAST INCLUDES:
Jack Lemmon, Al Pacino, Ed Harris, Alan Arkin, Kevin Spacey, Alec Baldwin
SCREENPLAY:
David Mamet from his play
CINEMATOGRAPHY:
Juan Ruiz Anchía

Estate agents are often at the receiving end of ranting tirades about time wasting, money-grabbing and superficiality. Here we get to see behind the scenes of one particular agency and discover that the smiles are fake, the confidence erroneously bolstered and the big bucks elusive, to say the least. Based on a play by David Mamet, who based his play on his own experiences, *Glengarry, Glen Ross* is a sad tale of desperate men trying to sell real estate to people who don't want to buy it. The rules of supply and demand are disproportionately unbalanced against these pitiable individuals as they sell their very souls for the possibility of a commission. The leads are out of date, but it's all they have to go on, so they plod on with the cold-calling, hoping for a miracle. When Blake (Baldwin) arrives in the office to announce a new contest, they only sink lower into their mire of despondency as, this time, their jobs are on the line; win and you get a Cadillac, lose and you're out. With its all-star cast, this film couldn't fail to procure a certain positive following; however this doesn't necessarily result in timeless appreciation. What Foley and his cast have achieved is that perfect combination of talent and altruistic acting, which allows each man's ability to really shine and bring the piece together, without ever focusing too specifically on the stars behind the characters.

THE PLAYER

Robert Altman, USA, 1992

CAST INCLUDES:
Tim Robbins, Greta Scacchi,
Fred Ward, Whoopi Goldberg,
Peter Gallagher
SCREENPLAY:
Michael Tolkin
CINEMATOGRAPHY:
Jean Lépine

Studio Executive Griffin Mill (Robbins) is the man-who-can when it comes to getting films made. However, hot on his heels is Larry Levy (Gallagher), whose alliterated name and shameful ambition prove him to be a dangerous contender for Mill's pole position. Larry's takeover bid is strengthened somewhat by Mill's distress at being hounded by a writer bearing a grudge, which leaves him shaken and not quite on top form. When he receives one malicious postcard too many, he personally goes after the scribe he believes to be the culprit, but ends up killing him and becoming the subject of a manhunt. Often discussed and used as a learning tool, Robert Altman's scathing satirical exposé of the Hollywood machine deserves its cult-like status. With potentially the most star-studded cast ever to appear together in a film (many doing so for a paltry sum), he creates a vapid world of superficial characters and wannabes, all clamouring to step onto whichever rung of the ladder they can lift their waxed, tanned and toned legs. As the film progresses, we see Mill falling for his victim's girlfriend (Scacchi), whilst being chased by a police force that includes Whoopi Goldberg and Lyle Lovett. Hollywood is sent up big time, from the lowly screenwriter to the top dog, in all its glitzy, glamorous, back-stabbing glory. One has to wonder whether any other director could have got away with it.

FORREST GUMP

Robert Zemeckis, USA, 1994

CAST INCLUDES:
Tom Hanks, Robin Wright
Penn, Gary Sinise, Mykelti
Williamson, Sally Field
SCREENPLAY:
Eric Roth from the novel by
Winston Groom
CINEMATOGRAPHY:
Don Burgess

Forrest Gump (Hanks) is a bit slow, the conventional anti-hero going nowhere and destined to melt into life's background. However, he has a talent; he can run like the wind, and so he embarks on a rather accidental tour of the highs and lows of 1960s' and 1970s' America. He meets US presidents and becomes a college football star and a Vietnam War hero in the process. The film is a bit of a potted history of mid-20th-century America, with a definite positive vibe being attributed to the country's history. However, the amazing special effects elevate the film to something much greater than a simple retelling of events, as archive footage is used to fantastic effect to place Forrest right in the thick of the action. Underlying the whole story are Forrest's feelings for Jenny (Robin Wright), the girl who he's loved since childhood. Winning six Oscars, including one for Hanks, *Forrest Gump* captured the hearts and imaginations of millions of cinemagoers, as the message made clear that everyone can be a hero, and everyone can live their dreams.

THE SHAWSHANK REDEMPTION

Frank Darabont, USA, 1994

When Andy Dufresne's wife and her lover are found murdered, having been shot in bed, her husband (Robbins) is the prime suspect. This supposition swiftly becomes assumption, as it emerges that Andy had discovered the affair and the couple had a heated, alcohol-fuelled argument shortly before the murders took place. When circumstantial evidence is added to the obvious motive, the only possible outcome is a conviction. And so, as Andy begins his life sentence in Shawshank Jail, the film begins in earnest.

The Shawshank Redemption examines issues such as hope, despair and friendships in times of adversity and the harsh realities of a life sentence. However, it is human resilience that is lingered on throughout the film and, for this to be fully explored, Andy is paired up with the reflective 'Red' (Freeman), who provides the voice-over to Andy's silent initiation and eventual apparent resignation to his situation. Andy is the archetypal example of just how much physical and mental torment human beings can endure and, like everyone else in prison, Andy learns to get by. His business background and education elevate him to a certain status, as he takes on the role of accountant to the prison's staff. Despite this surface display of equality, it isn't long before Andy is reminded, in no uncertain terms, that he will always be a con, inferior to all but fellow cons, regardless of his brain. However, it is Andy who has the last laugh. *The Shawshank Redemption* arrived quietly then escalated as word spread and people fell in love with this simple tale of human traits.

CAST INCLUDES:
Tim Robbins, Morgan Freeman, Bob Gunton, William Sadler, Clancy Brown
SCREENPLAY:
Frank Darabont, based on the short story *Rita Hayworth and Shawshank Redemption* by Stephen King
CINEMATOGRAPHY:
Roger Deakins

DID YOU KNOW?
Frank Darabont wrote the script in eight weeks.

SHAKESPEARE IN LOVE

John Madden, USA/GB, 1998

It seems fitting that a film about Shakespeare should be in the form of a comedy. After all, in his day, Shakespeare was a playwright for the masses, something that seems to have been forgotten with passing time. This is certainly a film for the masses, as its light-hearted look at 15th-century writer's block humanizes Shakespeare as never before. It offers an interpretation of his life that certainly demystifies the often staid impressions we've conjured up of the great bard. Will Shakespeare (Fiennes) is a dashing young playwright, struggling to complete his latest work, *Romeo and Ethel, the Pirate's Daughter*. Viola de Lesseps (Paltrow) arrives on the scene to provide some much-needed inspiration but she is betrothed to the Earl of Wessex (Firth), who is planning to whisk her off to America. It's to its credit that a film set in 1500s' England can strike a chord today, and this is certainly down to the well-structured and taut screenplay, co-penned by the hugely talented playwright Tom Stoppard. There are numerous echoes of modern wit and we are shown that people don't change all that much. They laugh, they love, they work, they play and politics are omnipresent.

CAST INCLUDES:
Joseph Fiennes, Gwyneth Paltrow, Geoffrey Rush, Tom Wilkinson, Judi Dench, Colin Firth
SCREENPLAY:
Marc Norman and Tom Stoppard
CINEMATOGRAPHY:
Richard Greatrex

ALL ABOUT MY MOTHER
TODO SOBRE MI MADRE

Pedro Almodóvar, Spain/France, 1999

Esteban (Azorin) has always wanted to learn the truth about the father he has never seen, but on the day his mother, Manuela (Roth), finally decides to reveal the information, Esteban dies. A devastated Manuela embarks on a journey from Madrid to Barcelona in search of the missing man, befriending loners and misfits en route. Almodóvar is the king of characterization and *All About My Mother* is no exception. The characters are quirky but realistically so. Who else could put a transvestite prostitute, a pregnant nun and a lesbian acting couple together in the same film and get away with it? It is the examination of the trials and tribulations of this disparate group and, more essentially, their experiences as women that form the crux of the story. As all the main characters necessarily have such different takes on the theme of womanhood, the film is never stilted or stereotypical. It is insightful, humorous and genuinely engaging.

CAST INCLUDES:
Cecilia Roth, Marisa Paredes, Candela Peña, Antonia San Juan, Penélope Cruz, Eloy Azorin
SCREENPLAY:
Pedro Almodóvar
CINEMATOGRAPHY:
Affonso Beato

AMERICAN BEAUTY

Sam Mendes, USA, 1999

When a film begins with the voice-over of a middle-aged man telling us that in a year from now he'll be dead, we know we are in for something different. Lester Burnham (Spacey) is the quintessential middle-class white American, trapped in a life that has leached him of all passion and zeal. On the outside he has much to envy: great house, great lifestyle, attractive wife (Bening) and daughter, but, as we delve beneath the surface, we begin to realize that all is not roses in the Burnham household. His marriage has deteriorated into a campaign of snide comments and sarcasm, and his daughter is ambivalent towards him – an insult far greater than hate or rebellion. So when he catches the eye of her beautiful friend Angela (Suvari), it's enough to give his sad existence a new sense of excitement and purpose.

Mendes' directorial debut was the archetypal '90s' film that expressed the repressions of American suburbia, peering through the curtains and delving into the characters' lives. Lester's midlife sexual obsession is more wake-up call than realistic chase, giving him a whiff of the excitement he once experienced when life was more meaningful. Meanwhile, his unsatisfied wife embarks on an affair with a sleazy estate agent and his daughter becomes involved with the strange boy living across the road who videos her from his bedroom. Gradually the apparently quiet neighbourhood is revealed in all its quirky, ugly nakedness.

ACADEMY AWARDS
Best Actor in a Leading Role:
Kevin Spacey
Best Cinematography:
Conrad L. Hall
Best Director: Sam Mendes
Best Picture:
Bruce Cohen, Dan Jinks
Best Original Screenplay:
Alan Ball

CAST INCLUDES:
Kevin Spacey, Annette Bening, Thora Birch, Wes Bentley, Mena Suvari
SCREENPLAY:
Alan Ball
CINEMATOGRAPHY:
Conrad L. Hall

TRAFFIC

Steven Soderbergh, USA, 2000

CAST INCLUDES:
Benicio Del Toro, Michael
Douglas, Jacob Vargas,
Catherine Zeta-Jones,
Erika Christensen
SCREENPLAY:
Stephen Gaghan based on
the original television series,
Traffik by Simon Moore
CINEMATOGRAPHY:
Steven Soderbergh
(as Peter Andrews)

Two narcotics cops intercept a huge drug delivery on the borders of Mexico, only to have the haul and glory taken from them by a General Salazar. Meanwhile, in America, Robert Wakefield (Douglas) is given the impossible task of clamping down on the drug problem. Throw into the mix a group of privileged kids getting high on cocaine and wealthy housewife Helena La Jolla (Zeta-Jones) unknowingly lunching on the proceeds of her husband's drug deals, and you have a film that really delves into all sides of the seedy world of drugs. Originally a television series, *Traffik* was developed into a feature film at a time when Western governments were unsuccessfully fighting real-life drug wars. Here, Soderbergh relates some of the real stories behind the headlines, albeit through fictionalized characters and scenarios. Class, background or status does not limit drug dealing and usage and that essentially is the problem. The dichotomy between tackling the issue hands-on at street level and overseeing it from the comfort of a plush office are all too obvious. The institutionalized drugs phenomenon is too huge for anyone to even make a dent in the supply trade, or to curb demand. However, like all great battles, the wounded keep fighting until the bitter end.

CAST INCLUDES:
Imelda Staunton, Phil Davis,
Peter Wight,
Adrian Scarborough,
Heather Craney,
Eddie Marsan, Daniel Mays
SCREENPLAY:
Mike Leigh
CINEMATOGRAPHY:
Dick Pope

VERA DRAKE

Mike Leigh, GB, 2004

In 1950s' London, Vera Drake (Staunton), a housewife and cleaner with a devoted family, secretly carries out illegal abortions in the belief she is helping desperate women with nowhere else to turn. Mike Leigh continues his mission to elucidate the lives of working class Britons through cinema, this time applying one of his beautifully constructed narratives to a period setting. By placing the film in a time of different laws and social attitudes to our own, he allows us to identify and sympathize with his lead character. Whilst there may still be those who object, a modern audience is unlikely to find her actions to be anything other than the purest altruism. But the viewer is still tested by an unflinching focus on both the procedural detail and emotional stress involved. There is a rich tapestry of characters living refreshingly authentic lives and everybody in Vera's world is somehow affected when her secret vocation is exposed. It's in the reactions of her family and neighbours that all the joy, pain and love of life are paraded for our benefit.

THE LIVES OF OTHERS (DAS LEBEN DER ANDEREN)

Florian Henckel von Donnersmarck, Germany, 2006

CAST INCLUDES:
Ulrich Mühe, Sebastian Koch, Martina Gedeck, Ulrich Tukur, Thomas Thieme, Hans-Uwe Bauer
SCREENPLAY:
Florian Henckel von Donnersmarck
CINEMATOGRAPHY:
Hagen Bogdanski

In the early 1980s the GDR, East Germany's brutal communist government, oversees a police state rife with secret cameras, bugs, informants and misery. After a playwright attracts the suspicions of a senior party official, agents are assigned to run a surveillance operation. As is often the case when examining the darker aspects of a nation's history, it has taken a generation of filmmakers who matured in their aftermath to deliver films this balanced and analytical. Director von Donnersmarck was just 11 at the time the film is set and, as such, his grasp of the social realities have the authenticity of personal experience whilst maintaining an objective perspective. The narrative delicately interweaves the lives of several characters, each trapped and repressed by the state in slightly different ways. Fascinating in its insights into a shadowy chapter of European history and devastating in its emotional impact, *The Lives of Others* is a hugely accomplished film, repaying the investment demanded of the viewer tenfold.

VOLVER

Pedro Almodóvar, Spain, 2006

CAST INCLUDES:
Penélope Cruz, Carmen Maura, Lola Dueñas, Blanca Portillo, Yohana Cobo
SCREENPLAY:
Pedro Almodóvar
CINEMATOGRAPHY:
José Luis Alcaine

Raimunda (Cruz) travels from Madrid to the peculiar village of Alcanfor in order to tend the grave of her mother, Irene, and visit Paula (Cobo), the beloved aunt who raised her. After a strange meeting with Paula, Raimunda returns home to find her husband, Paco, dead, killed by their young daughter as she fended off his physical assault. Whilst trying to dispose of the body she receives a phone call informing her of Paula's death, the catalyst for a series of increasingly surreal challenges. Over the last couple of decades Spanish filmmaker Pedro Almodóvar has been quietly building up a repertoire of stylish modern classics like *Talk to Her* and *All About My Mother*. With *Volver* he has expertly built on an accumulated strength and produced his most focused and impressive film so far. Every ounce of emotion is wrung from an alternately heartbreaking and heartwarming story about a group of working-class Spanish women trying to turn a crisis into an opportunity. Although proceedings focus on Raimunda and her daughter, Almodóvar still indulges his fondness for a female ensemble cast and Raimunda's sister Sole (Dueñas) and friend Agustina (Portillo) are important pieces of the puzzle. But it's all about Penélope Cruz who is devastating as the put-upon but determined Raimunda.

THE DIVING BELL AND THE BUTTERFLY (LE SCAPHANDRE ET LE PAPILLON)

Julian Schnabel, France, 2007

CAST INCLUDES:
Mathieu Amalric, Emmanuelle Seigner, Marie-Josée Croze, Anne Consigny, Patrick Chesnais, Niels Arestrup
SCREENPLAY:
Ronald Harwood
CINEMATOGRAPHY:
Janusz Kaminski

The true story of French magazine editor Jean-Dominique Bauby (Amalric). After suffering a stroke he is diagnosed with 'locked-in syndrome', a condition which leaves him almost totally paralysed. From his bed he determines to dictate a memoir to book editor Claude Mendibil (Consigny) by blinking his left eye, the only means of communication available to him. It's rare for films about disability and personal tragedy to offer anything genuinely inspiring. Too often they amount to little more than exploitative tear-jerkers, the affliction used merely as a shortcut to emotional payoff. With *The Diving Bell and the Butterfly* (the former refers to Bauby's broken body, the latter his great imagination), director Julian Schnabel has crafted a completely original and genuinely moving film. He places us in Bauby's position by allowing access to the thoughts running through his mind (via a voice-over) and shooting much of the film from Bauby's bedridden perspective. As a result, we're drawn right in and offered an unsettling glimpse of a frustrating world. Amalric is sensational in the central role, and in addition to his bedridden period, we see Bauby through flashbacks to happier times. Sadly Bauby died immediately after his book was published but this remains an original film with an exceptional power to inspire.

ATONEMENT

Joe Wright, GB, 2007

CAST INCLUDES:
Keira Knightley, James McAvoy, Saoirse Ronan, Brenda Blethyn, Romola Garai
SCREENPLAY:
Christopher Hampton, Ian McEwan (novel)
CINEMATOGRAPHY:
Seamus McGarvey

ACADEMY AWARD
Best Achievement in Music Written for Motion Pictures, Original Score: Dario Marianelli

Robbie (McAvoy), a servant's son, begins a relationship with Cecilia (Knightley). Due to a series of misinterpreted coincidences, Cecilia's 13-year-old sister Briony (Ronan) is given reason to believe Robbie is a deviant. After a cousin is raped by an unknown assailant, Briony falsely claims it to have been Robbie. Director Joe Wright took on a book which is blessed and cursed in equal measure: a beautifully detailed text and a hugely passionate following. Detail that might add rich texture if handled well can just as easily weigh a film down, and although existing fans will flock to see it, they can also be the most unforgiving critics. This film is a rare achievement. A costume drama about class, love and loss which eschews the more predictable and staid aspects of the genre in favour of a vibrantly original approach.

THE KING'S SPEECH

Tom Hooper, GB, 2010

CAST INCLUDES:
Colin Firth, Geoffrey Rush,
Helena Bonham Carter
SCREENPLAY:
David Seidler
CINEMATOGRAPHY:
Danny Cohen

ACADEMY AWARDS

Best Motion Picture of the
Year: Iain Canning, Emile
Sherman, Gareth Unwin
Best Performance by an Actor
in a Leading Role: Colin Firth
Best Achievement in
Directing: Tom Hooper
Best Writing, Original
Screenplay: David Seidler

In 1930s' Britain, Prince Albert (Firth), second son of King George V (Michael Gambon), suffers with a severe stammer. Although sceptical there could be any cure, he is finally convinced by his wife, Elizabeth (Bonham Carter), to work with Australian speech therapist Lionel Logue (Rush). Initially their clashing personalities ensure little progress is made. But when the abdication of his older brother thrusts Albert onto the world stage, he once again seeks help from Logue. In many ways this small story about a minor footnote in the history of the British monarchy had no right becoming one of the most successful films of the decade. The fact that it did so well is surely down to the incredibly high standard of work produced right across the board. The screenplay is a beautifully constructed narrative flush with the sort of dialogue actors fantasize about getting their teeth into. In the pivotal roles, Firth and Rush give arguably the best performances of either of their careers under the exquisitely subtle direction of Tom Hooper. Together they explore a subject that at first seems limited, a simple speech impediment that may or may not be curable. But once we start to understand the affliction as psychological rather than physical, the film opens up. Through Logue's gentle probing of the new king, it's able to touch on powerful themes such as familial responsibility and the way we deal with pressure, failure and personal flaws.

THE ARTIST

Michael Hazanavicius, France, 2011

CAST INCLUDES:
Jean Dujardin, Bérénice Bejo, John Goodman, James Cromwell, Uggie
SCREENPLAY:
Michael Hazanavicius
CINEMATOGRAPHY:
Guillaume Schiffman

At the peak of his powers as a headline performer in silent cinema, George Valentin (Dujardin) takes aspiring young actress Peppy Miller (Bejo) under his wing and sets her on course for stardom. As silent cinema dies, Valentin fails to make the crossover to 'talkies' and loses touch with Miller, by now a huge success. Bankrupt, heartbroken and badly injured in a fire, Valentin hits rock bottom before eventually being reunited with Miller. In a reversal of their previous relationship she helps her old mentor find a place in the new Hollywood. Few in the industry expected much from a black-and-white, foreign and essentially silent film by an almost unknown director. Somehow he managed to tap into a mainstream blockbuster crowd with this idiosyncratic little gem. *The Artist* is one of the most charming and stylistically original films in years and as a result an often jaded and lazy audience were treated to something beautiful. A film of such passionate delight that it's heartwarming just to think of modern cinemagoers being exposed to something so wonderful.

DID YOU KNOW?
The Artist won five Oscars at the 2012 Academy Awards.

THE HELP

Tate Taylor, USA/India/UAE, 2011

CAST INCLUDES:
Emma Stone, Viola Davis, Octavia Spencer, Bryce Dallas Howard, Jessica Chastain, Ahna O'Reilly, Allison Janney
SCREENPLAY:
Tate Taylor (screenplay), Kathryn Stockett (novel)
CINEMATOGRAPHY:
Stephen Goldblatt

Set in Mississippi during the 1960s, Skeeter (Stone) is a Southern society girl who returns from college determined to become a writer, but turns her friends' lives – and a Mississippi town – upside down when she decides to interview the black women who have spent their lives taking care of prominent Southern families. Aibileen (Davis), Skeeter's best friend's housekeeper, is the first to open up – to the dismay of her friends in the tight-knit black community. Though arguably guilty of glossing over its racial themes, *The Help* rises on the strength of its cast – particularly Viola Davis, whose performance is powerful enough to carry the film on its own, and Octavia Spencer who won an Oscar for Best Supporting Actress.

ZERO DARK THIRTY

Kathryn Bigelow, USA, 2012

After the terrorist attacks of 11 September 2001, CIA rookie agent Maya (Chastain) is assigned to Pakistan to learn (reluctantly) how to use extreme duress on suspects in order to discover the whereabouts of Osama bin Laden. She becomes obsessed in her pursuit of him, and finally, in 2011, it appears her work will pay off. A US Navy SEAL team is sent to kill or capture bin Laden. But only Maya is confident that bin Laden is where she says he is. A chronicle of the decade-long hunt for the al-Qaeda terrorist leader, *Zero Dark Thirty* is gripping, suspenseful and brilliantly crafted, dramatizing the hunt for bin Laden with intelligence and an eye for detail. The film reunites the Oscar-winning team of director-producer Kathryn Bigelow and writer-producer Mark Boal (*The Hurt Locker*).

ACADEMY AWARD
Best Achievement in
Sound Editing:
Paul N.J. Ottosson

CAST INCLUDES:
Jessica Chastain, Jason
Clarke, Reda Kateb,
Kyle Chandler, Jennifer Ehle,
Harold Perrineau,
Jeremy Strong, J.J. Kandel
SCREENPLAY:
Mark Boal
CINEMATOGRAPHY:
Greig Fraser

DALLAS BUYERS CLUB

Jean-Marc Vallée, USA, 2013

CAST INCLUDES:
Matthew McConaughey,
Jennifer Garner,
Jared Leto, Denis O'Hare,
Steve Zahn, Michael O'Neill,
Dallas Roberts
SCREENPLAY:
Craig Borten, Melisa Wallack
CINEMATOGRAPHY:
Yves Bélanger

Dallas, 1985. Electrician and sometime rodeo rider Ron Woodroof (McConaughey) works hard and plays hard. While in hospital for a work-related injury, he discovers that he is HIV-positive, and will probably die within 30 days. Racist and homophobic, Ron is initially in angry denial, believing HIV to be a homosexual disease. He begins to research treatments and how to get hold of them by any means possible. Refused help via legal channels, he takes matters into his own hands – tracking down alternative treatments from all over the world and selling them to fellow patients, many of whom he would once have shunned. Their shared struggle for dignity and acceptance is at the heart of this film, although the success of *Dallas Buyers Club* rests squarely on Matthew McConaughey's scrawny shoulders. He carries the burden gracefully with what might be a career-best performance.

ACADEMY AWARDS

Best Performance by an
Actor in a Leading Role:
Matthew McConaughey
Best Performance by an
Actor in a Supporting Role:
Jared Leto
Best Achievement in
Makeup and Hairstyling:
Adruitha Lee, Robin Mathews

12 YEARS A SLAVE

Steve McQueen, USA/GB, 2013

In the pre–Civil War United States, Solomon Northup (Ejiofor), a free black man from upstate New York, is abducted and sold into slavery. Facing cruelty (personified by a malevolent slave owner, portrayed by Michael Fassbender), as well as unexpected kindnesses, Solomon struggles not only to stay alive, but also to retain his dignity. In the 12th year of his unforgettable odyssey, Solomon's chance meeting with a Canadian abolitionist (Brad Pitt) will forever alter his life. Based on an incredible true story of one man's fight for survival and freedom, *12 Years a Slave* is far from comfortable viewing. However, its unflinchingly brutal look at American slavery is also brilliant – and quite possibly essential – cinema. It deservedly won three Oscars at the 2014 Academy Awards, including Best Picture.

CAST INCLUDES:
Chiwetel Ejiofor, Lupita Nyong'o, Michael Fassbender, Michael Kenneth Williams, Benedict Cumberbatch

SCREENPLAY:
John Ridley, based on the book by Solomon Northup

CINEMATOGRAPHY:
Sean Bobbitt

DID YOU KNOW?
On-location shooting in Louisiana took only 35 days with one camera.

ACADEMY AWARDS
Best Motion Picture of the Year:
Brad Pitt, Dede Gardner, Jeremy Kleiner, Steve McQueen, Anthony Katagas
Best Performance by an Actress in a Supporting Role:
Lupita Nyong'o
Best Writing, Adapted Screenplay:
John Ridley

BOYHOOD

Richard Linklater, USA, 2014

CAST INCLUDES:
Ellar Coltrane, Patricia Arquette, Ethan Hawke, Lorelei Linklater
SCREENPLAY:
Richard Linklater
CINEMATOGRAPHY:
Lee Daniel, Shane F. Kelly

DID YOU KNOW?
Hawke would have taken over as director if Linklater was to die during the production.

Filmed over 12 years with the same cast, Richard Linklater's *Boyhood* is a ground-breaking story of growing up as seen through the eyes of a child named Mason (a breakthrough performance by Ellar Coltrane), who literally grows up on screen before our eyes. Starring Ethan Hawke and Patricia Arquette as Mason's parents and newcomer Lorelei Linklater as his sister, Samantha, *Boyhood* charts the rocky terrain of childhood like no other film has before. Snapshots of adolescence from road trips and family dinners to birthdays and graduations and all the moments in between become transcendent, set to a soundtrack spanning the years.

Both a nostalgic time capsule of the recent past and an ode to growing up and parenting, *Boyhood* is a revelation: epic in technical scale but intimate in narrative scope. It is a sprawling investigation of the human condition and a 12-year cinematic odyssey that stunned audiences and is widely regarded as a masterpiece.

THE REVENANT

Alejandro G. Iñárritu, USA, 2015

Based on the true story of 19th century bear trapper Hugh Glass, *The Revenant* is the film that finally earned DiCaprio that long-awaited Academy Award for Best Actor. While exploring the uncharted American wilderness in 1823, Glass sustains injuries from a brutal bear attack. When his hunting team leaves him for dead, Glass must utilize his survival skills to find a way back home while avoiding natives on their own hunt. Grief-stricken and fueled by vengeance, Glass treks through the wintry terrain to track down John Fitzgerald, the former confidant who betrayed and abandoned him. *The Revenant* deservedly won three Academy Awards and five BAFTAS, and managed to gross a worldwide total of over $500 million against a budget of $135 million. It received rave reviews, although some criticized its historical accuracy as regards the romantic relationship that develops between Glass and a Pawnee woman, for which there is no real evidence. The film saw its crew deal with harsh conditions, which included DiCaprio allegedly eating a wild bison's liver to get into character (the actor is a vegetarian, meaning he promptly threw up afterwards). It's blood, sweat and a lot of snow – not one for the faint-hearted.

CAST INCLUDES:
Leonardo DiCaprio,
Tom Hardy, Domhnall
Gleeson, Will Poulter
SCREENPLAY:
Alejandro G. Iñárritu,
Mark L. Smith

ACADEMY AWARDS

Best Actor:
Leonardo DiCaprio
Best Director:
Alejandro G. Iñárritu
Best Cinematogrpahy:
Emmanuel Lubezki

DID YOU KNOW?
DiCaprio started axe-throwing competitively during the shoot.

HORROR

NOSFERATU

F.W. Murnau, Germany, 1922

Realtor Hutter (von Wangenheim) is driven mad by the vampire Count Orloc (Schreck), who then goes to Bremen to find Hutter's wife, Ellen (Schröder), with whom he has become infatuated. For Count Orloc, read 'Count Dracula', as this is actually one of the earliest incarnations of Bram Stoker's famous creation in all but legal paperwork (which Murnau was unable to secure). This version of Dracula presents the Count as more repulsive and wretched than the book's almost debonair figure, and it's certainly more politically charged. There is a potent theory that Orloc is actually a representation of Lenin, and the film a German propaganda piece warning of the Communist threat from Russia. The vampire's arrival at Bremen, in a black coffin and followed by hundreds of 'plague'-carrying rats, isn't the most subtle of allegories, but there's much more to this film than fear of the Bolsheviks. Murnau and his collaborators created possibly the most accomplished and beautiful film to that date, in any genre. Allegedly a student of the 'method' school of naturalistic acting, Schrek's performance was so believable that many of the crew were apparently too scared to approach him.

CAST INCLUDES:
Max Schreck, Gustav von Wangenheim, Greta Schröder, Alexander Granach, Georg H. Schnell
SCREENPLAY:
Henrik Galeen
CINEMATOGRAPHY:
Günther Krampf, Fritz Arno Wagner

THE PHANTOM OF THE OPERA

Rupert Julian, USA, 1925

CAST INCLUDES:
Lon Chaney, Mary Philbin, Norman Kerry, Arthur Edmund Carewe, Gibson Gowland
SCREENPLAY:
Walter Anthony from the novel by Gaston Leroux
CINEMATOGRAPHY:
Milton Bridenbecker, Virgil Miller, Charles Van Enger (all uncredited)

A famous opera singer is forced to relinquish her role in a new production by a threatening Phantom (Chaney). She is replaced by the unknown Christine Daae (Philbin), a woman we soon discover the Phantom is in love with. But how will she respond to him? There have been over a dozen screen versions of this tale, but this is generally considered the definitive one. The sets are extraordinary, but the first and best reason to see this film is Lon Chaney's performance. He brings such a carefully considered and well-balanced sensitivity to the ambiguous Phantom that it's impossible to imagine anyone else in the role. And any viewers who tend not to be scared by films of this age will have to think again, as the unmasking is guaranteed to leave even the most hardened of modern audiences aghast.

FREAKS

Tod Browning, USA, 1932

CAST INCLUDES:
Henry Victor, Harry Earles,
Daisy Earles, Olga Baclanova
SCREENPLAY:
Clarence Aaron, 'Tod'
Robbins
CINEMATOGRAPHY:
Merritt B. Gerstad

Cleopatra (Baclanova), a trapeze artist in a carnival, schemes with her lover, Hercules (Victor), to cheat midget Hans (Harry Earles) out of a large inheritance. Although his girlfriend, Frieda (Daisy Earles), is on to the scam, Hans is hopelessly in love with Cleopatra.

Tod Browning was already a renowned horror director after his *Dracula* (1931) starring Bela Lugosi created the Western template for scary movies, but nobody was expecting *Freaks*. In *Freaks*, Browning created a vision made all the more real by his use of mainly non-professionals in his cast. All Browning has to do to create his desired effect is show us the members of the carnival's freak show, a method he employs so comprehensively the film sometimes appears more like a documentary (in fact in some countries it was marketed as one to evade local censorship). Banned in numerous countries, it said much about these societies' attitude to people with physical disfigurements. Medical advances in the First World War allowed previously fatal injuries to be treated, and as a result, physical disfigurement became a more common sight, and one that was fascinating to American audiences in particular. Hollywood would not miss this opportunity and indirectly exploited it in many of its pioneering horror films (*The Phantom of the Opera* and *The Hunchback of Notre Dame* in particular), but *Freaks* is the most honest. It is uncompromising, challenging and absolutely unique.

KING KONG

Merian C. Cooper, Ernest B. Schoedsack, USA, 1933

CAST INCLUDES:
Fay Wray, Robert Armstrong,
Bruce Cabot, Frank Reicher,
Sam Hardy
SCREENPLAY:
Merian C. Cooper, Edgar
Wallace, James Ashmore
Creelman and Ruth Rose
CINEMATOGRAPHY:
Edward Linden, J.O. Taylor,
Vernon L. Walker

A group of Americans, including beautiful actress Ann Darrow (Wray), discover a giant ape whilst exploring the remote Skull Island. After the monster is taken to New York for exhibition, it escapes and runs amok in search of Darrow.

Over 70 years old, King Kong remains one of the most popular mythical monsters of cinema. Unlike his contemporaries Frankenstein and Dracula, Kong hasn't yet been the subject of a worthy remake or sequel, leaving this vision the undisputed definitive, which is no bad thing.

Produced (like many other monster classics) in the early 1930s, Hollywood had just got to grips with sound and was ready to innovate in other areas of cinema, particularly visual effects. Although there was a large team working on the job, Kong's impressive blending of live action and the innovative technique of stop-motion are attributed mainly to Willis H. O'Brien (who took the sole credit of chief technician on the film). By today's standards the ape may lack realism, but the personality expressed in his face cannot (yet) be mimicked so endearingly in CGI. At the time, it looked real enough to cause entire audiences to panic through sheer confusion, something else CGI is yet to do. But Kong is only one of the legends to appear in the film: credit must also go to the lungs of Fay Wray, who will always be remembered as having the best scream in the movies. 'The Most Awesome Thriller of All Time' declared the promotional posters. Perhaps it isn't quite true anymore, but it's certainly still impressive.

BRIDE OF FRANKENSTEIN

James Whale, USA, 1935

CAST INCLUDES: Boris Karloff, Colin Clive, Valerie Hobson, Elsa Lanchester, Ernest Thesiger
SCREENPLAY: William Hurlbut, John L. Balderston, Mary Shelley *(book)*
CINEMATOGRAPHY: John J. Mescall

Following on directly from the 1931 version, we soon discover Doctor Henry Frankenstein (Clive) and his creation were not killed. With the monster on the loose again, and the mad Doctor Pretorius (Thesiger) attempting to create a bride for the monster, the townsfolk have never been in more danger. Based on Mary Shelley's classic novel and directed by James Whale, the seminal 1931 masterpiece *Frankenstein* wouldn't seem to support a sequel (with the monster appearing to die at the end). But the *Bride of Frankenstein*'s inspired opening (an impossibly theatrical dramatisation of Mary Shelley revealing to Lord Byron and Percy Shelley that, 'the story doesn't end there') ensures its plausibility. Considered by many to be better than its predecessor, *Bride of Frankenstein* is more personal. The monster becomes a much more sympathetic character, and Frankenstein himself is less the selfish egomaniac and more a solemn, regretful figure. This leaves a gap in the screenplay for a cackling, psychotic villain and the abhorrent Doctor Pretorius fills it with a ravenous zeal. His presence is just one of many elements that make *Bride of Frankenstein* probably the most important film of the era.

DEAD OF NIGHT

Alberto Cavalcanti, Charles Crichton, Basil Dearden, Robert Hamer, GB, 1945

Walter Craig (Johns), an architect meeting a group of people for the first time, realizes he has dreamt the whole experience before. As each person recounts a tale of personal brushes with the supernatural, he begins to recall more, eventually remembering how the dream turns into a nightmare. A successful compendium of spooky stories, this dry comic-horror is a joy to watch, and the credits read like a who's who of the 'up-and-comers' who would later shape British cinema. Each character brings something different to the film, making it a diverse but coherent exercise in storytelling. Five strangers each recount a spooky tale, and the red herring of the bunch, penned by H.G. Wells, is particularly good. The transition between tales is subtle and seamless, and the amiable group of storytellers are all a pleasure to watch, so much so it's possible to forget the film's a horror… until the grimly surreal conclusion.

CAST INCLUDES:
Mervyn Johns, Roland Culver, Mary Merrall, Barbara Leake
SCREENPLAY:
John Baines, E.F. Benson, T.E.B. Clarke, Angus MacPhail, H.G. Wells
CINEMATOGRAPHY:
Jack Parker, Stanley Pavey, Douglas Slocombe

LES DIABOLIQUES

Henri-Georges Clouzot, France, 1955

CAST INCLUDES:
Simone Signoret, Véra Clouzot, Paul Meurisse
SCREENPLAY:
Pierre Boileau from the novel *Celle qui n'était*, Henri-Georges Clouzot, Jérôme Géronimi
CINEMATOGRAPHY:
Armand Thirard

The wife and mistress of a tyrannical schoolmaster conspire to murder their tormentor. When the body inexplicably disappears they find it increasingly difficult to keep up their façade. Shot and edited with a simplicity that makes it a pleasure to watch, this French classic of suspense was hugely influential. Its restrained style, rare but effective shocks and inventive ending clearly influenced Hitchcock when making *Psycho*, and subsequently created a template for the suspense thriller. Paul Meurisse is suitably dastardly as the openly abusive 'victim,' Michel Delasalle. He intimidates everyone at the boarding school he runs (but is owned by his wife), including the other teachers, limiting their wine to two glasses per meal and berating their stupidity in front of the children. But it's the sympathetic killers who are centre stage for most of the film, and under Henri-Georges Clouzot's delicate direction, they are both superb. The more interesting character is the long-suffering and sickly wife, Christina (Véra Clouzot), trapped in the marriage by her religious convictions and aware Michel longs for her death so he can inherit her family fortune. The most impressive aspect of the film, though, is the taut and inventive screenplay. Clouzot and Jérôme Géronimi's adaptation of Pierre Boileau's novel may be the perfect example of how to write a suspense thriller.

CAST INCLUDES: Peter Cushing, Christopher Lee, Michael Gough, Melissa Stribling, Carol Marsh, John Van Eyssen
SCREENPLAY: Jimmy Sangster, from the novel by Bram Stoker
CINEMATOGRAPHY: Jack Asher

DRACULA

Terence Fisher, GB, 1958

Jonathan Harker arrives at a remote castle somewhere in Germany to catalogue the library of Count Dracula (Lee). We soon learn the profession of librarian is a cover for Harker's real identity – a student of vampirism, and that he is there to kill the count. After his failure, Dracula leaves the castle in search of Harker's family and friends, none of whom are aware of the oncoming threat, with the exception of the eminent Dr Van Helsing (Cushing). This is the first stab at the vampire count by legendary British studio, Hammer. Although the film takes considerable liberties with the novel (mainly to tighten the pacing and focus on the salient points), it remains the most popular filmed version, largely due to the excellent performances from the two leads. Christopher Lee is a commanding Dracula, the role for which he will always be remembered. His entrance (in shadow at the top of a staircase) is alarming even by modern standards, and the hospitable charm with which he conducts himself is in stark contrast to the wretched, reclusive incarnations of some other features. As effective as it is, this isn't the scariest horror movie ever made, nor is it the most technically impressive, but it might just be the most charming and enjoyable.

PSYCHO

Alfred Hitchcock, USA, 1960

Secretary Marion Crane (Leigh) steals the $40,000 she has been instructed to bank. Immediately skipping town, she heads for her lover's California home. Stopping to spend the night at a quiet motel on the way, she finds a shy young man having problems with his mother.

Hitchcock's masterpiece of terror hasn't dated a bit in the years since its release. The ominous opening chords of Bernard Herrmann's now famous theme (set against the stylish credit design of Saul Bass) makes our hearts beat faster, as well as making it immediately clear that whatever lies ahead, it's not going to be agreeable to any of the characters.

But Hitchcock intended to mislead us from the start. For the first half-hour the film is a straight crime thriller, featuring an established star on the run for embezzlement – classic Hitchcock material that comfortably fits the assumptions one might have had upon entering the cinema. *Psycho* was his first foray into horror, and even then it didn't happen until a third of the way through the film.

Shot in black-and-white (mainly to evade the censor's scissors), the film is stunning. Every shot is framed with subtle beauty, and every cut carefully considered to achieve precisely the intended effect. But none of this is news. The film appears in almost every 'all-time top ten' list devised, and for good reason. The interesting thing is just how unusual all this is for a horror film. Hitchcock lavished *Psycho* with at least as much care and attention as he did any of his films, and he did it at a time when the genre wasn't taken seriously. Horror (like sci-fi) was for drive-ins, existing only as exploitation B-movies since the demise of Universal's classic *Frankenstein*, *Dracula* and *Wolfman* pictures, while the British Hammer films had yet to make any impact in the States. What *Psycho* did was change the way cinemagoers thought about an entire genre. It made horror respectable again.

CAST INCLUDES:
Anthony Perkins, Janet Leigh,
Vera Miles, John Gavin,
Martin Balsam
SCREENPLAY:
Joseph Stefano from the novel
by Robert Bloch
CINEMATOGRAPHY:
John L. Russell

PEEPING TOM

Michael Powell, GB, 1960

CAST INCLUDES:
Karlheinz Böhm (as Carl Boehm), Moira Shearer, Anna Massey, Maxine Audley, Brenda Bruce
SCREENPLAY:
Leo Marks
CINEMATOGRAPHY:
Otto Heller

Mark (Karlheinz Böhm, credited here as Carl Boehm), a reclusive, voyeuristic focus puller and photography enthusiast, forms an awkward friendship with a female neighbour that threatens to expose his secret obsession – murdering women in order to capture a record of their expression at the moment of death. Michael Powell's sleazy horror-drama has aged remarkably well since it first baited the national newspapers with its provocative and upsetting presentation of a disturbed man's brutal hobby. Upon release it was effectively sunk by the critics, who were upset by the subject matter and the ruthless incrimination of the viewer with inventive camerawork. The film eventually resurfaced thanks to a new generation of directors (including Martin Scorsese), who cited it as an influence. Böhm excels in the lead. Emotionally crippled, he is an uncomfortable presence on screen, making the viewer squirm whenever he comes into contact with a woman. The explanation for his dysfunctional behaviour lies in his childhood. As we soon learn, his father forced him to grow up on camera as the subject of bizarre experiments, often engineering cruel and torturous circumstances in order to elicit a response. As a result, Mark is unable to relate to reality or people in the flesh, only through the camera lens he spends much of the film hiding behind.

VILLAGE OF THE DAMNED

Wolf Rilla, GB, 1960

CAST INCLUDES:
George Sanders, Barbara Shelley, Michael Gwynn, Laurence Naismith, John Phillips
SCREENPLAY:
Stirling Silliphant, Wolf Rilla, Ronald Kinnoch (as George Barclay) from the novel by John Wyndham
CINEMATOGRAPHY:
Geoffrey Faithfull

All the residents of the English village of Midwitch briefly pass out at the same time and for the same duration. Some time later it's discovered all the women capable of bearing children are pregnant. Stranger still, when the children are born, they all possess an eerie physical resemblance and age unusually quickly. One of the best and last entries to the 1950s'-era paranoid horror/sci-fi series, *Village of the Damned* is a wonderfully crisp and subtle example of British cinema. The use of children is a chillingly effective device, while Sanders as the kindly schoolteacher is superb. The photography is beautiful throughout, and director Wolf Rilla keeps everything moving along at a brisk pace (the film is only 77 minutes long). The result is a modest, highly watchable little classic.

THE BIRDS

Alfred Hitchcock, USA, 1963

ACADEMY AWARD
Best Effects,
Special Visual Effects:
Ub Iwerks

CAST INCLUDES:
Tippi Hedren, Rod Taylor,
Jessica Tandy, Suzanne
Pleshette, Veronica
Cartwright
SCREENPLAY:
Evan Hunter from the
novella by Daphne Du
Maurier
CINEMATOGRAPHY:
Robert Burks

After a chance meeting in a pet shop, rich socialite Melanie Daniels (Hedren) decides to give Mitch Brenner (Taylor) a surprise visit at his family home in the quiet coastal town of Bodega Bay, but this is a Hitchcock movie, and the local birds seem to know it.

Although long associated with the genre, Hitchcock only actually made two horror movies (*Psycho* being the other) and, as is the way with Hitchcock movies, things are hardly done by the book. Hitchcock must have loved spending the first half-hour pretending this was going to be a romantic comedy, but when he starts to drop in an increasing number of clues to the violence ahead, it really begins to get interesting. Prophetic moments such as the seagull scratching Melanie's head and the bird crashing into the window of the Brenner's home become more frequent, brilliantly building the viewers' sense of unease and culminating in a chilling climax. One of the great achievements here is to make plausible most of the characters' relaxed and unsuspicious manner, while the audience is fed all the ominous events and touches required for the tension to mount and mount.

THE HAUNTING

Robert Wise, GB, 1963

CAST INCLUDES:
Julie Harris, Claire Bloom,
Richard Johnson, Russ
Tamblyn, Fay Compton
SCREENPLAY:
Nelson Gidding from the
novel by Shirley Jackson
CINEMATOGRAPHY:
Davis Boulton

A huge, rambling mansion that has seen several mysterious deaths in its 90-year history is leased to an eccentric British professor who is convinced that ghosts exist. Together with the skeptical Luke (Tamblyn), who stands to inherit the house, psychic Theodora (Bloom) and insecure Eleanor (Harris), Dr John Markway (Johnson) moves in to the building to test his theories. On face value *The Haunting* could seem like any other haunted house movie to have graced the screen over the years, but that isn't so. Firstly, the characters are all hugely successful, something generally not achieved in this usually cheap and cheerless sub-genre. Enthusiastic Dr Markway (who inevitably finds a supernatural explanation for the most mundane event) is an infectious presence who has even the sceptical Luke doubting himself. Claire Bloom is excellent as the sophisticated Theodora, but the real achievement is Julie Harris's Eleanor, who must carry the film as the central character and provide a voice-over that runs throughout. The film is also helped along by the production values. The house is supposed to be immense and some beautiful lighting and camerawork show it off as such. The most likely explanation for the film's universal success is the presence of legendary director Robert Wise, who fitted it in between *West Side Story* and *The Sound of Music*.

ROSEMARY'S BABY

Roman Polanski, USA, 1968

ACADEMY AWARD
Best Actress in a
Supporting Role:
Ruth Gordon

CAST INCLUDES:
Mia Farrow, John
Cassavetes, Ruth Gordon,
Sidney Blackmer
SCREENPLAY:
Roman Polanski from the
novel by Ira Levin
CINEMATOGRAPHY:
William A. Fraker

Young newlyweds Guy and Rosemary (Cassavetes and Farrow) move into a New York apartment block and befriend the neighbours. When the elderly couple next door become a little too friendly for Rosemary, the warnings of a woman who recently committed suicide in the building come to mind. Roman Polanski's haunting gothic tale of devil worship is a well-crafted and surprisingly understated psychological horror. Using little more than the power of suggestion, Polanski builds a horribly uncomfortable environment. Farrow (married to Polanski at the time) is notable in the lead, a brittle but devoted wife who is pushed to one side when her husband's career takes off. But it's the ambiguous neighbour, Minnie Castevet (Gordon), who steals the show (and an Oscar).

NIGHT OF THE LIVING DEAD

George A. Romero, USA, 1968

CAST INCLUDES: Duane Jones, Judith O'Dea, Karl Hardman, Marilyn Eastman, Keith Wayne
SCREENPLAY: John A. Russo, George A. Romero
CINEMATOGRAPHY: George A. Romero

A small group of people are trapped in a house when the dead rise up and walk again, hungry for human flesh. Shot in grainy black-and-white on a miniscule budget, *Night of the Living Dead* surprised even its investors when it became the most successful independent film of its time, uniting audiences and (most) critics, leading one to famously dub it, 'the best film ever made in Pittsburgh'. The first instalment in director George A. Romero's 'Trilogy of the Dead' (*Dawn of the Dead* came next in 1978, followed by *Day of the Dead* in 1985), *Night of the Living Dead* is his most successful social commentary, challenging some of the anachronistic beliefs still prevalent even in the late 1960s. One of the more obvious examples of this is the casting of African-American newcomer Duane Jones in the lead, particularly effective after a blonde actor is seemingly set up for the role and then killed early on. Jones is excellent; the dominant presence in every scene, he inevitably takes on the role of leader within the metaphorical society that develops inside the house. But it's not all politics – Romero is equally comfortable with straight horror. Notable highlights include the half-eaten corpse that Barbara (O'Dea) stumbles upon when entering the house, its eye hanging out and face torn away. And the now famous scene of a sickly young girl suddenly recovering enough to lunge at her mother is one of horror cinema's great moments. *Night of the Living Dead* marked the debut for almost everyone involved, including Romero, but notwithstanding it's still one of the genre's best examples.

CAST INCLUDES:
Ellen Burstyn, Max von Sydow, Jason Miller, Lee J. Cobb, Linda Blair
SCREENPLAY:
William Peter Blatty
CINEMATOGRAPHY:
Owen Roizman

THE EXORCIST

William Friedkin, USA, 1979

In leafy Georgetown, Washington, successful actress Chris Macneil (Burstyn) begins to worry about her daughter, Regan (Blair), whose strange behaviour eventually becomes a matter for the church. William Peter Blatty's novel had a difficult filming. Rumours still abound today of a curse on the production that caused at least two tragic deaths and a fire that burnt down much of the studio and production offices. Controversy and trouble even followed the film into release, with some church leaders declaring it a blasphemy and cinemagoers sent into a moral outrage by the language and imagery employed. However, this didn't affect the film's success. In spite of the structure (the slow build is very drawn-out compared to its contemporaries) and the harrowing finale (in which Blair achieves one of the most impressive performances by a child actor in the history of cinema), it was a massive success at the box office, proving that intelligent and demanding horror films had an audience. Although two sequels followed, neither came close to this formidable and essential classic.

DON'T LOOK NOW

Nicholas Roeg, GB, 1973

CAST INCLUDES:
Julie Christie, Donald
Sutherland, Hilary Mason
SCREENPLAY:
Allan Scott, Chris Bryant from
a story by Du Maurier
CINEMATOGRAPHY:
Anthony Richmond,
Nicolas Roeg

After the tragic drowning of their young daughter, John and Laura Baxter (Sutherland and Christie) move to Venice, where Laura meets two mysterious sisters, one of whom claims to be a psychic in contact with their daughter. It is pedigree alone that makes this benchmark classic essential viewing. Directed by Nicholas Roeg, adapted from a short story by Daphne Du Maurier and starring Donald Sutherland and Julie Christie, the film lives up to expectations. The work of lesser-known contributors, like cinematographer Anthony Richmond, is also not to be overlooked. There are so many beautiful touches to this film. The striking vision of a child running in a red coat is an unforgettable image, and the way in which Richmond's camera weaves through the dark Venetian alleyways beautifully mirrors the manner in which Roeg leads us through the psychological screenplay, never revealing what's around the next corner until it's upon us. What strikes hardest, however, is the sheer emotional clout this collective of talents have at their disposal.

THE WICKER MAN

Robin Hardy, GB, 1973

CAST INCLUDES:
Edward Woodward,
Christopher Lee, Diane
Cilento, Britt Ekland,
Ingrid Pitt
SCREENPLAY:
Anthony Shaffer
CINEMATOGRAPHY:
Harry Waxman

A letter detailing the abduction of a young girl brings police officer Sergeant Howie (Woodward) to a remote Scottish island. He is met with a complete lack of cooperation from the strange locals, who all claim the girl never existed. Firmly established as one of Britain's greatest horror films, *The Wicker Man* sees career-best performances from Edward Woodward (better known as TV's *The Equalizer*) as the deeply religious Howie, and also Christopher Lee as the island's pagan Lord Summerisle. The two men spark fantastically off each other, Summerisle being a source of spiritual consternation for Howie. Director Robin Hardy crafts the film beautifully. From the first frames, he instils the island with an air of authenticity that extends to the smallest detail, making the place and its inhabitants totally believable in spite of the peculiarities. When Howie arrives at the inn, he finds the locals singing what first appears to be a song of adoration for the landlord's beautiful (and flattered) daughter, Willow (Ekland). We soon realize that the song proclaims her a slut, yet she is still grateful. These small moments develop the island's quietly surreal personality very well, and provide numerous opportunities to outrage Howie, whose difficulty equating the island's Godless beliefs to his own deep Christian faith lies at the heart of the film.

THE TEXAS CHAIN SAW MASSACRE

Tobe Hooper, USA, 1974

CAST INCLUDES:
Marilyn Burns, Allen Danziger, Paul A. Partain, Edwin Neal, Gunnar Hansen
SCREENPLAY:
Kim Henkel, Tobe Hooper
CINEMATOGRAPHY:
Daniel Pearl

A teenage girl, her wheelchair-bound brother and a few friends intend to spend a brief holiday in the family's rundown old summer house. In need of petrol, a nearby home seems an obvious source, but the neighbours aren't too friendly. Based (very loosely) on the serial killer Ed Gein's brutal crimes, the story couldn't be simpler. One by one the kids wander into a neighbour's house and suffer a grizzly demise at the hands of Leatherface (Hansen). But he's not the only psychopath in the film. Unusual (though not exclusive) is the use of an entire family as murderers. It might seem excessive, but it's perfectly in tune with the rest of director Tobe Hooper's extreme and uncompromising vision, creating a numerical balance between the hunter and hunted (briefly anyway). But much more importantly, it announces, with authority, that there are places in America where inbred, deviant crackpots like this can carry out full lives in a structured social order. Escaped lunatics or serial killers must either remove themselves from society or conceal their true nature. Here Hooper creates a functional, open group, but so far removed from our idea of society as to have no awareness of its basic rules; therefore they have none of the weaknesses inherent in other killers such as the need to remain unidentified or to kill someone specific. That aside, it's still the most harrowing and terrifying film ever made.

CAST INCLUDES: Roy Scheider, Robert Shaw, Richard Dreyfuss
SCREENPLAY: Peter Benchley, Carl Gottlieb
CINEMATOGRAPHY: Bill Butler

JAWS

Steven Spielberg, USA, 1975

ACADEMY AWARDS
1976
Best Film Editing: Verna Fields
Best Music, Original Score: John Williams
Best Sound: Robert L. Hoyt, Roger Heman Jr., Earl Madery, John R. Carter

When a great white shark chooses the waters off peaceful holiday destination Amity Island for its feeding ground, Police Chief Brody (Scheider) must call on experts for help. Directed by Steven Spielberg, this film is exemplary. John Williams' indelible score, the sublime editing, gorgeous cinematography and perfect casting and acting all contribute to putting it streets ahead of contemporary mainstream cinema, let alone contemporary horror cinema. The bold decision to tease the viewer with tantalizing glimpses of the shark until the very end (Spielberg modestly jokes because it never worked) is hugely successful, making the phantom-like monster all the more of a threat. With the cheer-inducing finale providing the ultimate in satisfaction, it's fair to say a better horror-thriller will probably never be made.

THE OMEN

Richard Donner, USA, 1976

When the child of the wealthy American ambassador to the UK, Robert Thorn (Peck), dies at birth, he substitutes another baby and avoids revealing the tragedy to his wife, Katherine (Remick). Some years later the child has developed a fear of churches and is surrounded by a subtle web of quiet observers. But when some of these mysterious people begin to die under bizarre circumstances, Thorn begins to suspect his son may not be what he seems.

Richard Donner's epic is a deeply disturbing addition to the horror genre, exploring the traditional concept of good versus evil. It raises questions about faith and, depending on the viewers' own beliefs and opinions, will be interpreted in many different ways. The subject and material are treated with respect throughout, and Donner was obviously aware that casting would be vital if he was to achieve the carefully considered performances he required. Peck's awesome stature provides substantial authority to both the film and character of Thorn, a somewhat sombre figure devoted to his wife and 'son'. Lee Remick is also impressive, and the ever dependable David Warner is superb as the ambiguous photographer Keith Jennings.

A film with such a dark tone also requires a carefully conceived visual style if it is to remain even, and acclaimed cinematographer Gilbert Taylor (who had previously worked with Polanski, Kubrick and Hitchcock and would later shoot *Star Wars*) created a harsh and uncompromising style that never permits the viewer to relax. Along with its similarly themed contemporary, *The Exorcist*, *The Omen* has stood the test of time well, retaining its curious ability to use fear in order to make us consider our own views on faith.

ACADEMY AWARD
Best Music, Original Score:
Jerry Goldsmith

CAST INCLUDES: Gregory Peck, Lee Remick, David Warner, Billie Whitelaw, Harvey Stephens
SCREENPLAY: David Seltzer
CINEMATOGRAPHY: Gilbert Taylor

CARRIE

Brian De Palma, USA, 1976

CAST INCLUDES:
Sissy Spacek, Piper Laurie,
Amy Irving, William Katt,
Betty Buckley, Nancy Allen
SCREENPLAY:
Lawrence D. Cohen from the
novel by Stephen King
CINEMATOGRAPHY:
Mario Tosi

A frail teenage girl with psychic powers is bullied relentlessly by the girls at her high school, and browbeaten into a constant state of guilt by her fanatically religious mother. Future A-list director Brian De Palma (*The Untouchables*, *Mission Impossible*) had spent 15 years directing shorts and minor movies before adapting this Stephen King favourite. Dealing directly with issues such as puberty and physical change (frequently alluded to via metaphor in horror) is an uncompromising but successful technique, and one that ensures *Carrie*'s place amongst the most emotionally powerful examples of the genre. Due to her ignorance, Carrie's (Spacek) first period is a distressing and public experience, seized upon by her tormentors, and also signifies the onset of her psychic capabilities; clearly the two events are linked. Carrie's mother, Margaret (Laurie), does little to support her daughter. More than a little mad, she is too busy harassing the neighbours with prophecies of eternal damnation. She is an oppressive presence, refusing Carrie privacy and preventing her from taking part in the normal activities of a teenage girl. She has inadvertently raised a disaffected, nervous daughter, who is no more able to understand relationships than she is her strange powers. Piper Laurie is excellent, but Spacek's astonishing turn in the lead is a frank and unselfconscious career-best performance.

DID YOU KNOW?
Stanley Kubrick made the cast of *The Shining* watch this film to get in the mood for filming a horror picture.

ERASERHEAD

David Lynch, USA, 1977

CAST INCLUDES:
Jack Nance (as John
Nance), Charlotte Stewart,
Allen Joseph, Jeanne Bates
SCREENPLAY:
David Lynch
CINEMATOGRAPHY:
Herbert Cardwell,
Frederick Elmes

Mary X (Stewart), the girlfriend of Henry Spencer (Nance), falls pregnant and delivers a very peculiar baby into a dark and troubled world. The plot of *Eraserhead* – the epitome of David Lynch's challenging style – cannot be summed up in words. The above does technically happen, but we are deep into the realm of experimental surrealism here, and anything definable and explainable has no place. Whether Henry's whole life is a dream or whether Lynch believes this bizarre and desolate world should be perceived as reality is not made clear, but neither is it important. What is important is the extent to which this surreal nightmare affects the audience. This film is an uncontrolled stream of Lynch's consciousness; bizarre, repulsive and upsetting – just as a horror should be.

HALLOWEEN

John Carpenter, USA, 1978

CAST INCLUDES:
Donald Pleasence, Jamie Lee Curtis, Nancy Kyes, P.J. Soles, Tony Moran
SCREENPLAY:
John Carpenter, Debra Hill
CINEMATOGRAPHY:
Dean Cundey

Over a decade after the six-year-old Michael Myers (Moran) murdered his sister on Halloween night, he escapes from an asylum and returns to his hometown. John Carpenter's wildly creative *Halloween* is now well established as one of the genre's greatest treasures as well as the film that created the slasher movie. The story is simple: bad guy wants to kill teenagers (ideally promiscuous ones). But the plot is not what makes *Halloween* so scary. Myers comes across as so remorselessly evil and detached that his backstory is effectively superseded by the hugely successful realization of the character. His blank face (actually a William Shatner mask painted white) gives away nothing, and it's all the more effective for being presented in leafy, sunny suburbia. But Myers wouldn't exist without Carpenter (or co-writer Debra Hill). The five-minute, one-take opening sequence, all seen through Myers' eyes, is bravura filmmaking that places us uncompromisingly in the shoes of a murderer. *Halloween* is simply the most important horror film of the last 40 years, and absolutely essential viewing

DAWN OF THE DEAD

George A. Romero, USA, 1978

The sequel to *Night of the Living Dead* starts where its predecessor left off, with zombies now outnumbering the living and the remnants of society in chaos. Two SWAT officers and a young couple set out in search of safety in a helicopter, eventually finding a shopping mall, that, once cleared and barricaded, they decide will act as an ideal temporary safe haven. But it soon becomes apparent that help may not be coming any time soon. George A. Romero, the godfather of zombie movies, had a lot to live up to when returning to the material of his hugely successful debut. Perhaps unexpectedly, Romero decides to take a swipe at consumerism. Unsubtle though it may be, it has stood the test of time magnificently. One of the underlying themes of greed rapidly leading to death is another effective message in a film that demands to be taken seriously as social commentary as well as a kick-ass zombie flick.

CAST INCLUDES: David Emge, Ken Foree, Scott H. Reiniger, Gaylen Ross
SCREENPLAY: George A. Romero
CINEMATOGRAPHY: Michael Gornick

THE SHINING

Stanley Kubrick, USA, 1980

CAST INCLUDES:
Jack Nicholson, Shelley
Duvall, Danny Lloyd,
Scatman Crothers
SCREENPLAY:
Stanley Kubrick, Diane
Johnson from the novel by
Stephen King
CINEMATOGRAPHY:
John Alcott

Former teacher Jack Torrance (Nicholson) takes a job as the winter caretaker of a huge, isolated mountain hotel. He and his wife, Wendy (Duvall), and son, Danny (Lloyd), are left alone in the place we soon learn to be haunted.

In 1980 Stanley Kubrick released his critically panned *The Shining* upon a very confused audience, most of whom found it too long, too slow and too hard to understand. Today the film is rightly considered one of the masterpieces of cinema, and the dialogue and imagery have become ingrained in popular culture. Jack Nicholson's showboating performance as the insane Torrance, at the time considered too over the top, is now his best known and beloved role. He chews his way through the countless scenes of twitching hysteria with such a demonic dedication it's impossible to take your eyes off him.

The remote and overbearing Overlook Hotel (casually established as being built on an Indian burial mound) takes on the second-most potent personality of the film. The endless corridors weaving like arteries around the upper floors feel as if they could conceal any number of horrors (and do), while the gigantic halls have an eerie look to them, as if they remember the past horrors and anticipate their repetition. Without question one of the scariest films ever made, there are few sudden shocks, very little direct violence and no deaths until the last ten minutes. But the audience must withstand a huge amount of creeping psychological pressure brought on by a combination of qualities, any of which on its own would make the film a must-see – the performances, the smoothly hypnotic camerawork, and particularly the disorienting dips into Jack's broken mind as he chats with a former caretaker or wanders through a huge ballroom filled with dancers.

Perhaps the most powerful quality is the film's totally unique nature. There is no reference in cinema, nothing even similar exists, so there's no way to predict what might happen next.

FRIDAY THE 13TH

Sean S. Cunningham, USA, 1980

CAST INCLUDES:
Betsy Palmer, Adrienne
King, Harry Crosby, Laurie
Bartram, Jeannine Taylor,
Kevin Bacon
SCREENPLAY:
Victor Miller
CINEMATOGRAPHY:
Barry Abrams

In the late 1950s, Camp Crystal Lake suffered a terrible tragedy when a boy was drowned and two revenge killings were carried out. For 20 years the summer camp remains deserted until a young couple arrive with a group of teenagers, planning to reopen for business. But they don't heed the warnings of the locals and the kids start dropping like flies. When John Carpenter blew the horror genre wide open with *Halloween* in 1978, writer Victor Miller and director Sean S. Cunningham took their opportunity to jump on the bandwagon. At little expense they produced what looked like being a quirky rip-off, and whilst there is an element of truth in this, *Friday the 13th* is a quality imitation. The graphic violence makes the audience feel like victims, but we are also incriminated with the killer by the clever use of first person perspective camera shots. We are forced to see through his eyes as the teenagers are observed from the shadows. The twist at the end is one of the greatest in horror history, and the final scare is both unexpected and inspired.

THE FOG

John Carpenter, USA, 1980

CAST INCLUDES: Adrienne Barbeau, Jamie Lee Curtis, Janet Leigh
SCREENPLAY: John Carpenter, Debra Hill
CINEMATOGRAPHY: Dean Cundey

One hundred years after six townsfolk killed a group of wealthy lepers planning to settle just up the coast, the spirits of the murdered sailors return in a bank of glowing fog to kill the descendants of the six men and reclaim their gold. Much has been written about how director John Carpenter changed the direction of horror with *Halloween* in 1978, but his next feature was to be an old-fashioned ghost story. The quote that opens the film – 'Is all that we see or seem but a dream within a dream?' – implies the director's intent to make the film's reality ambiguous. The scene that follows – a group of children around a late-night campfire listening to a story of sailors seeking vengeance – only reinforces this. Although there are fairy-tale implications, the movie is not short on proper scares. The sailors are terrifying, and the fact that they are glimpsed only as shadows or through fog makes their presence all the more alarming. However, the film's great success lies primarily with the excellently conceived and realized characters. Such high levels of tension cannot be generated without caring for the imperilled townsfolk. One particularly effective device is the single mother and local DJ acting as the eyes and guiding voice for the town in her lighthouse-based radio station. From the lighthouse she can see the fog, but is agonizingly isolated and vulnerable. Like a good captain, we worry she might go down with the ship. *The Fog* is a true classic of horror cinema and one of Carpenter's career highlights.

AN AMERICAN WEREWOLF IN LONDON

John Landis, GB, 1981

CAST INCLUDES:
David Naughton,
Jenny Agutter, Griffin Dunne,
John Woodvine
SCREENPLAY:
John Landis
CINEMATOGRAPHY:
Robert Paynter

ACADEMY AWARD
1982
Best Makeup: Rick Baker

Two American students on a hitchhiking holiday around England fail to heed the words of the locals in a Yorkshire pub and find themselves lost at night on the moors. After being attacked by a strange beast, the lone survivor recuperates in London, but it's not long before he starts to realize his condition isn't improving in the way he had expected.

From the opening shot of the two naïve boys (Naughton and Dunne) arriving in a cattle truck, surrounded by sheep on the way to the slaughterhouse, it's clear this is going to be an inventive and humorous affair. Indeed, director Landis is better known for his funny bone than bloody bones, with credits such as *Animal House*, *The Blues Brothers* and *Trading Places* making him a highly revered and influential comedy director. But whilst his tongue remains firmly in his cheek throughout (after feeding one night, the werewolf wakes naked in human form and must queue for the bus home), you underestimate at your peril the utterly terrifying events that take place in between the smirks. One dream sequence in particular is guaranteed to leave you chilled, and the werewolf's attacks themselves are built with tension and finished with violence that seems strong even by today's standards.

Another aspect of the film that still deserves credit is the special make-up effects. Rick Baker did a stunning job, both in the werewolf transformation scene and with the dozens of lacerated and decomposing characters, all of which had to be created with prosthetics and mechanics. There isn't a frame that doesn't stand up in the digital era.

An American Werewolf in London is a unique movie, as scary as any horror and as satirical as any comedy.

THE THING

John Carpenter, USA, 1982

CAST INCLUDES:
Kurt Russell, Wilford Brimley,
T.K. Carter, David Clennon,
Keith David
SCREENPLAY:
Bill Lancaster from the story
by John W. Campbell Jr.
CINEMATOGRAPHY:
Dean Cundey

In the Antarctic, an American scientific research base is invaded by an ancient alien capable of taking on the form of any human it comes into contact with. This excellent adaptation of John W. Campbell's short story, *Who Goes There?*, provides (like so many great horrors) a very simple situation and group dynamic on which the filmmakers can build tension. When we're introduced to the isolated men at the start, a tense atmosphere already exists. Later, when it must develop with the influence of The Thing itself, it becomes infinitely more threatening. Alongside *Halloween*, *The Thing* features Carpenter's best achievements in this area. But unlike *Halloween*, *The Thing* didn't kickstart a sub-genre (though it did help dramatically in the advancement of special make-up effects technology); instead it almost deliberately bucks the slasher trend only four years after Carpenter started it. Part homage to 1950s' sci-fi B-movies, part original creation, the film contains one of Carpenter's best characters, the surly helicopter pilot R.J. MacReady, a role Kurt Russell fits into magnificently. Although not a huge success on release (possibly a less demanding alien movie in the shape of *E.T.* was part of the reason), *The Thing* has since achieved a huge fan base and has become one of the best-loved horror staples of late-night TV.

POLTERGEIST

Tobe Hooper, USA, 1982

CAST INCLUDES:
Jo Beth Williams, Craig T.
Nelson, Beatrice Straight,
Heather O'Rourke,
Zelda Rubinstein
SCREENPLAY:
Steven Spielberg, Michael
Grais, Mark Victor
CINEMATOGRAPHY:
Matthew F. Leonetti

A young girl discovers she can communicate with a supernatural spirit through the TV. Strange things soon start to happen in the Freeling home, and the docile presence becomes more of a threat. Although directed by Tobe Hooper (*The Texas Chain Saw Massacre*), the presence of producer Steven Spielberg has clearly tempered Hooper's violent and distressing style. Spielberg has always had a skill for presenting upsetting details and events in a manner not overtly threatening (*Jurassic Park*, for example). Apparently Tobe Hooper didn't realize any of this when he took the job and has always wanted to release his own, hardcore, version. However, Hooper realizes the haunted house premise very successfully, and (another Spielberg influence) a lot of time is spent establishing the characters and relationships that remain at the heart of the film. In particular, Carol Anne (O'Rourke), the youngest daughter and link to the spirits, provides a performance so rich and intelligent it's impossible to believe she was only six.

A NIGHTMARE ON ELM STREET

Wes Craven, USA, 1984

CAST INCLUDES:
John Saxon, Ronee Blakley,
Heather Langenkamp,
Amanda Wyss, Jsu Garcia,
Robert Englund
SCREENPLAY:
Wes Craven
CINEMATOGRAPHY:
Jacques Haitkin

Teenager Nancy (Langenkamp) is having vivid nightmares in which a sinister figure is attempting to kill her. When people start turning up dead and she discovers her friends are having the same dream, the local parents are forced to reveal a horrible secret from their past. This is probably the best known of the 1980s' slasher-movie wave. As David Lynch would do later in *Blue Velvet* and *Twin Peaks*, Wes Craven delights in creating an impossibly perfect vision of small-town America, a transparent bubble of safety filled with fresh-faced teenagers (including a young Johnny Depp) who, once they start becoming victims of the town's nasty secret, are left helplessly vulnerable. The character of Freddy Krueger (Englund) is a masterstroke, instantly becoming one of the most identifiable figures in film horror.

THE FLY

David Cronenberg, USA, 1986

ACADEMY AWARD
Best Make-up:
Chris Walas, Stephan Dupuis

Seth Brundle (Goldblum), an eccentric scientist experimenting in the field of matter transportation, is amalgamated with a housefly at the genetic level. At first unaware, he gradually mutates into a deranged beast. Differing dramatically from the 1958 original, Cronenberg's version is a gruesome meditation on disease and deformity, both subjects he visited in earlier films such as *Rabid*, *Shivers* and *Scanners*. But *The Fly* is more accessible than his previous work, which may go some way to explaining its crossover success, becoming a box-office hit and ubiquitous presence in the video collections of '80s' teenagers. Goldblum is perfectly cast as the brilliant but doomed young scientist. Already an expert in idiosyncratic mannerisms and intonation, here he displays a surprisingly touching chemistry with Davis. The repugnant

CAST INCLUDES:
Jeff Goldblum, Geena Davis,
John Getz, Joy Boushel
SCREENPLAY:
David Cronenberg, Charles
Edward Pogue (based on
George Langelaan's story)
CINEMATOGRAPHY:
Mark Irwin

development of the fly itself is the most memorable aspect of the film. Cronenberg clearly relishes the excuse (and budget) to be as repugnant as possible, turning in one of his best films, and one of the best horror/sci-fi crossovers to date.

EVIL DEAD 2

Sam Raimi, USA, 1987

CAST INCLUDES:
Bruce Campbell, Sarah Berry, Dan Hicks, Kassie DePaiva, Ted Raimi, Denise Bixler
SCREENPLAY:
Sam Raimi, Scott Spiegel
CINEMATOGRAPHY:
Peter Deming

In a remote woodland shack, young couple Ash and Linda (Campbell and Bixler) discover a tape recording left by a mysterious scientist claiming there is an evil, supernatural presence in the surrounding woods. In the first *Evil Dead* movie, Raimi created a tense zombie classic as a tribute to hero George A. Romero. Although this superior sequel is essentially a remake, Romero has lost some ground to the three stooges as Raimi's chief muse. *Evil Dead 2* has a truly unique tone, stemming from Raimi's appreciation of star Bruce Campbell's considerable gift for physical comedy. The scene in which Ash must defend himself from his own (possessed) right hand is a definitive moment. You know this is no ordinary zombie movie when the hand throws him into a wall and flips him head over heels before Ash gets the better of it and – ever resourceful – removes it with a chainsaw. After trapping the squirming hand under a bucket, a copy of *Farewell to Arms* is placed on top as a weight. The movie was a success on release but with the passing of time, it has become increasingly popular, and its star a certified legend of the genre. A third movie followed (*Army of Darkness*) and successfully re-created the spirit in a higher budget form, but it is this second instalment that remains the best example of comedy-horror ever to be produced in the cinema.

ANGEL HEART

Alan Parker, USA, 1987

CAST INCLUDES:
Mickey Rourke, Robert De Niro, Lisa Bonet, Charlotte Rampling, Stocker Fontelieu
SCREENPLAY:
Alan Parker from the novel by William Hjortsberg
CINEMATOGRAPHY:
Michael Seresin

Harry Angel (Rourke) is a cynical private detective working small-time cases in 1950s' New York. Wealthy client Louis Cyphre (De Niro) comes to him with a seemingly straightforward missing person case. Angel takes it, believing Cyphre is simply owed money by a man who disappeared 12 years previously. But then those involved begin turning up dead. Comparisons with cynical private dicks like Philip Marlowe and Sam Spade are inevitable, but Angel's cynicism doesn't stem from a loss of faith in society; he never had any faith to begin with. And unlike the films Marlowe and Spade appeared in, *Angel Heart* is not a straight detective story, though it uses one as the framework for something original and terrifying. Just what the missing person owes Louis Cyphre is one of several alarming revelations that drag the viewer into the realm of psychological horror. Shot in a grainy and dirty style by cinematographer Michael Seresin, *Angel Heart* is unforgettable, engrossing and intelligent.

MISERY

Rob Reiner, USA, 1990

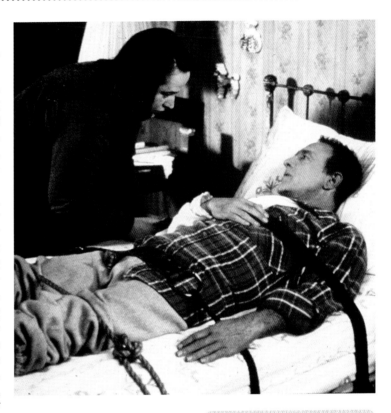

Novelist Paul Sheldon (Caan) crashes his car on a remote New England road and is rescued by friendly nurse Annie Wilkes (Bates). Coincidentally she is a big fan of his books and in particular, the heroine Misery Chastaine. Recuperating in her house, Sheldon soon realizes Annie is more than a little unhinged and effectively he becomes a prisoner. Stephen King's literary adaptations are notoriously hit or miss. The success of *Misery* stems from the experience and talent involved. Director Rob Reiner had an exceptional run-up to *Misery*. Successive hits including *Stand By Me*, *The Princess Bride* and *When Harry Met Sally* made him one of the hottest directors in Hollywood and gave him the power to pick his collaborators. Employing the talents of veterans like actor James Caan, cinematographer Barry Sonnenfeld and screenwriter William Goldman, Reiner carefully composed a tense thriller, into which he injected Kathy Bates, the adrenalin shot to the film. She is magnificent as Sheldon's deranged superfan and her impressive performance rightly earned her an Academy Award. As with many of the genre's best examples, *Misery* doesn't assault the viewer prematurely. Instead, it carefully establishes the situation and then starts to build tension, making any act of violence seem all the more extreme and effective. The best example of this is the drastic measure Annie takes to prevent Sheldon's escape. In King's book she removes his feet, but the alternative here is even more upsetting to witness.

CAST INCLUDES:
James Caan, Kathy Bates,
Richard Farnsworth
SCREENPLAY:
William Goldman from
the novel by Stephen King
CINEMATOGRAPHY:
Barry Sonnenfeld

TREMORS

Ron Underwood, USA, 1990

CAST INCLUDES:
Kevin Bacon, Fred Ward,
Finn Carter, Michael Gross
SCREENPLAY:
S.S. Wilson, Brent Maddock
from a story by S.S. Wilson,
Brent Maddock, Ron
Underwood
CINEMATOGRAPHY:
Alexander Gruszynski

A female seismologist working outside the small desert town of Perfection discovers inexplicable tremors. Before long she finds herself trapped with two idiot roughnecks and a scattering of locals when strange, subterranean monsters lay siege. Ron Underwood's first theatrical outing as director is an inventive hotchpotch of 1950s' sci-fi hokum. Brimming with genre references, it proudly wears its B-movie badge all the way to the drive-in. The gleefully stereotypical characters are a delight, particularly brainless cowboys Valentine (Bacon) and Earl (Ward), who possess a huge array of one-liners and a great chemistry. The local survivalist, Burt (Gross), whose house is stocked with explosives, weapons and enough water to last five years, also deserves a special mention for comedy relief. The monsters, or 'Graboids', are not exactly the scariest cinematic creation (they even have a sense of humour), and the fun most of the cast seem to be having trying to kill them doesn't exactly instil terror, but that's not the idea. There's no intention to scare – classic genre stereotypes are gently mocked for the viewers' amusement, without the film ever trying to be too clever. Charming and unpretentious fun.

THE SILENCE OF THE LAMBS

Jonathan Demme, USA, 1991

CAST INCLUDES:
Jodie Foster, Anthony
Hopkins, Scott Glenn,
Anthony Heald, Ted Levine
SCREENPLAY:
Ted Tally from the novel by
Thomas Harris
CINEMATOGRAPHY:
Tak Fujimoto

When the FBI cannot catch a brutal serial killer, Clarice Starling (Foster), a trainee agent, is sent to interview a convicted cannibal psychopath, Hannibal Lecter (Hopkins). Starling must attempt to gain profiling information from Lecter without revealing too much of herself. The film won the five most coveted Academy Awards (Picture, Director, Actor, Actress, Adapted Screenplay) at the 1992 ceremony, and it's easy to see why. Hopkins is totally convincing in a role that makes the skin crawl, and Demme pulls off the trick of disguising a violent and upsetting horror as a thriller, smuggling it into the theatres before anyone noticed, and all without having to compromise a single, brutal frame. Slick, intelligent, stunningly photographed and suspenseful to the end, this is a horror film that earned its huge success.

SCREAM

Wes Craven, USA, 1996

CAST INCLUDES:
David Arquette, Neve Campbell, Courteney Cox, Skeet Ulrich, Rose McGowan, Matthew Lillard
SCREENPLAY:
Kevin Williamson
CINEMATOGRAPHY:
Mark Irwin

One year after the murder of teenager Sidney Prescott's (Campbell) mother, a serial killer starts carving his way through her friends in a sleepy American town. Wes Craven's hugely inventive and amusing 'postmodern' slasher was so successful it both reinvigorated and changed the genre. Or rather, reverted it. John Carpenter wrote the rule book with *Halloween* in 1978, and nothing much changed until a wave of (arguably) more intelligent and serious horror films became popular in the late 1980s (*Angel Heart*, *Silence of the Lambs*, *Misery*, etc.). For *Scream*, Craven decided to dig out the old rule book, dust it down, add a few notes on self-referential mockery and throw all his skill and experience into a glossy and slightly watered-down slasher movie for a new generation. The result is a fantastically enjoyable film that works as both a sly comedy and an excellent addition to the genre.

RINGU

Hideo Nakata, USA, 1998

CAST INCLUDES: Nanako Matsushima, Miki Nakatani, Hiroyuki Sanada
SCREENPLAY: Hiroshi Takahashi from the novel by Kôji Suzuki
CINEMATOGRAPHY: Junichirô Hayashi

Rumours of a mysterious videotape that causes the death of anybody who views it attracts the attention of a reporter. When her son accidentally sees it, she must race against the clock to discover its secret before his inevitable death. Director Hideo Nakata found huge success in the West as well as in his native Japan with this slick and highly original chiller. He uses everything at his disposal to build a sense of fear. The dark and moody visuals are particularly effective, with rain used to block out light, while the incredible intensity of the video itself threatens to reduce the audience to a collective of cowering wrecks every time extracts are shown. The opening sequence is a minor masterpiece in itself. Here, two schoolgirls discuss the rumour of a videotape that kills when one reveals that she has not only seen it but also received a phone call claiming that she would die in seven days (something common to all the victims). As if that isn't enough, exactly seven days have passed since the call. Strange things start to happen in the house, culminating in the girl's unexplained death. Her face stiff and disfigured by some unimaginable fear is as disturbing as any image from the horror cinema portfolio. Nakata's demanding and imaginative film is a harrowing watch, but it's also rewarding, paying you back everything you've invested – as long as you can bear to watch to the end. Don't bother with the American remake – the Japanese original runs rings around it.

THE SIXTH SENSE

M. Night Shyamalan, USA, 1999

CAST INCLUDES:
Bruce Willis, Haley Joel Osment, Toni Collette, Olivia Williams, Trevor Morgan
SCREENPLAY:
M. Night Shyamalan
CINEMATOGRAPHY:
Tak Fujimoto

Malcolm Crowe (Willis), a child psychologist disillusioned by his tragic failure in an earlier case and suffering a crumbling marriage, offers to help Cole Sear (Osment), a small boy with the troubling ability to see dead people.

Night Shyamalan's subtle and controlled ghost story is a triumph of more than just filmmaking. Shyamalan was a Hollywood nobody, having written and directed two largely unseen features. It was unlikely a major star would risk teaming up with him, even for an action movie or romantic comedy – traditionally safe genres. However, Shyamalan was peddling the most terrifying of screenplays for any established action star in need of a hit – a highly original, intelligent horror story. Fortunately Willis went for it, and Shyamalan's inspired casting paid off. Audiences were comforted by a familiar face and flocked to see a demanding, slow-paced horror film.

Although another large reason for the film's success is the famous twist ending, it's more than a collection of gimmicks. Shyamalan's hypnotic and methodical style envelops us, the perfectly paced screenplay reveals plot points in carefully measured doses and a few good, solid scares are sprinkled over the top when necessary (Shyamalan has clearly learned a lot from Stanley Kubrick's *The Shining*). Willis's subtle and thoughtful performance is certainly a career highlight, but the revelation here is Haley Joel Osment's eerie and vulnerable Cole Sear, a role that won him an Academy Award nomination at the age of just 12.

THE BLAIR WITCH PROJECT

Daniel Myrick and Eduardo Sánchez, USA, 1999

CAST INCLUDES:
Heather Donahue, Joshua
Leonard, Mike Williams
SCREENPLAY:
Daniel Myrick and
Eduardo Sánchez
CINEMATOGRAPHY:
Neal Fredericks

In 1994 the legend of the Blair Witch attracted three young documentary makers to the small Maryland town of Burkittesville. After setting off into the woods, they were never seen again. Five years on, *The Blair Witch Project* has been pieced together from the film found scattered, but does it explain what happened to them? In the early 1990s, glossy horror-thrillers such as *Misery* and *Silence of the Lambs* took horror out of the hands of 1970s'- and 1980s'-genre firebrands like Wes Craven and John Carpenter, making it mainstream. Although Craven soon applied a twist to the slasher formula with *Scream* in 1996, it was Daniel Myrick and Eduardo Sánchez who made the greatest innovation with the bizarre marketing campaign for this film. The story of the missing filmmakers was presented as true, and huge publicity was generated. In the face of this gimmick, it's easy to forget just how scary the film is. The shaky, handheld 16mm film and video creates a (deliberately) stomach-churning effect and helps build the tension, which is the cornerstone of the film's effectiveness.

AUDITION

Takashi Miike, Japan, 2000

CAST INCLUDES:
Ryo Ishibashi, Eihi Shiina,
Tetsu Sawaki, Jun Kunimura
SCREENPLAY:
Daisuke Tengan from the
novel by Ryu Murakami
CINEMATOGRAPHY:
Hideo Yamamoto

Widowed for seven years, TV producer Shigeharu Aoyama (Ishibashi) lives with his teenage son, Shigehiko (Sawaki). Deciding it's time to remarry and realizing he has little idea how to go about finding a wife, he asks a friend for advice. At first he's not keen to take up his suggestion of sitting in on casting auditions for young actresses, but he soon succumbs to the pressure of loneliness and whilst leafing through candidates' resumés sets his heart on a girl even before the audition. A tentative courtship follows, but is the girl hiding something? Prolific and challenging Japanese director Takashi Miike finally broke through in the West with this alternately touching and gruelling 'romantic horror'. An emotionally wrenching opening gives way to a gentle, touching romance as two psychologically scarred people appear to find love. Eihi Shiina is superb as Asami Yamazaki, the *femme fatale* whose façade doesn't start to crumble until Aoyama has fallen hopelessly in love with her, in spite of the warnings of those close to him. Her recollections of a tortured childhood alert the viewer to the kind of excruciating violence that lies ahead when Miike destroys the film's narrative in a blaze of harrowing abhorrence that he seems to relish. If David Lynch decided to make a cross between *Boxing Helena* and *Solaris*, it might look something like this.

THE OTHERS

Alejandro Amenábar, USA, 2001

CAST INCLUDES:
Nicole Kidman, Fionnula Flanagan, Christopher Eccleston, Alakina Mann, James Bentley, Eric Sykes
SCREENPLAY:
Alejandro Amenábar
CINEMATOGRAPHY:
Javier Aguirresarobe

1940s' Jersey. A neurotic mother of two children, both allergic to daylight, battles to maintain a large house with the assistance of three increasingly suspicious servants, her husband seemingly having been killed in the war. Essentially a modern reworking of assorted haunted house themes, writer/director Alejandro Amenábar adds some interesting ideas to the formula whilst abiding by strict genre rules. The house in which almost the entire film takes place is suitably gothic and spooky. Isolated from a village we never see and permanently enveloped in fog, it's shot with an elegant, lingering style that helps it do what every haunted house must – take on a personality. This is aided by the children's allergy to light, an ingenious plot device that creates both a genuine threat to their lives and a good excuse for the terminal darkness that becomes part of the building's overbearing interior identity. Moving the children from room to room requires huge feats of planning: interference or impediment could prove fatal as every inner door must be kept locked and curtains drawn wherever they go. Conversely, light becomes a refuge for Grace (Kidman), the heart of the film. Her struggle with loneliness and motherhood and her neurotic fall into madness are portrayed perfectly by the excellent Kidman, who infuses the character with the same gothic elegance possessed by the house.

CAST INCLUDES:
Cillian Murphy, Naomie Harris, Noah Huntley, Brendan Gleeson, Christopher Eccleston
SCREENPLAY:
Alex Garland
CINEMATOGRAPHY:
Anthony Dod Mantle

28 DAYS LATER...

Danny Boyle, USA, 2001

Twenty-eight days after animal rights' activists release a virus that transforms people into wild zombie-like lunatics, an uninfected man (Murphy) wakes up in hospital. Together with a small group of survivors, he starts on a long trek to find safety and the possibility of a new life. But in a crumbling society, it's not just the infected who pose a threat. Danny Boyle (*Trainspotting*) turns his hand to zombie movies and succeeds in injecting new blood. Where Romero's classic zombies shuffle and stumble, Boyle's incarnations run like rabid dogs. This twist isn't entirely new – David Cronenberg has used many of the essential elements here before (and successfully), but these are the first cinema zombies that seem to launch themselves at you from the screen. What sets *28 Days Later…* aside is its daring in all quarters – shooting on digital cameras, sticking to a UK setting, casting unknowns in lead roles while potentially deterring core fans with radical innovations. Fortunately, the gamble paid off – the film was a huge success and its place in the cult horror hall of fame is assured.

CAST INCLUDES: Leigh Whannel, Cary Elwes, Danny Glover,
Ken Leung, Dina Meyer, Tobin Bell
CINEMATOGRAPHY: David A. Armstrong
SCREENPLAY: Leigh Whannell, James Wan (story),
Leigh Whannell (story)

SAW

James Wan, USA, 2004

Two men wake up chained to pipes in a filthy bathroom with no memory of each other or how they got there. A tape recording tells them one must kill the other in order to save his family, but the hacksaws they've been left won't cut the chains. So begins the latest venture for serial killer Jigsaw (Bell), a psychotic intent on teaching the value of life to those he has deemed unworthy. The *Saw* franchise has become so devalued in the face of second-rate sequels that it's easy to forget just how good the original is. Made on a shoestring budget and powered by the creativity of co-writer/director James Wan, *Saw* had a monumental impact on the horror genre and defined the now thriving 'torture-porn' movement. It's appeal lies less in sustained tension than in marvelling at (and, inevitably, recoiling from) the ingenious instruments with which Jigsaw administers his own peculiar justice. This sort of thing clearly isn't for everybody. If you aren't ready to revel in the pain, humiliation and, ultimately, death of 'wrongdoers', you may have some ethical qualms with the film. But if you can stomach the torture, *Saw* is one of the most original and unpredictable horror films for years.

THE DESCENT

Neil Marshall, GB, 2005

CAST INCLUDES:
Shauna Macdonald, Natalie
Jackson Mendoza, Alex Reid,
Saskia Mulder, MyAnna
Buring, Nora-Jane Noone,
Oliver Milburn
SCREENPLAY:
Neil Marshall
CINEMATOGRAPHY:
Sam McCurdy

One year after Sarah's (Macdonald) husband and daughter are killed in a car crash, she meets up with a group of girlfriends and sets out on a caving expedition. After a rockslide traps them all in a mountain, they realize they're being picked off by strange creatures who live in the darkness. British filmmaker Neil Marshall made a splash with his 2002 horror debut *Dog Soldiers*. Sticking to what he knows best, the follow-up is even scarier and infinitely more accomplished. Part of the success lies in a concept that sees six young women confined in caves and pursued by mysterious creatures. It's a setup that allows for a 'proper' horror atmosphere thick with dread and tension: if you're scared of the dark, this will leave you in pieces. Ditto if you're claustrophobic, and if you're not entirely sure about horrifying monsters stalking petrified, vulnerable women… perhaps it's best to leave this one altogether. Even if you nail the scares, a poor character dynamic will still sink a film like this. With *Dog Soldiers* Marshall demonstrated his aptitude for casting and handling actors, and does so again in *The Descent*. All the women come across as real people, clearly defined and properly fleshed out, which becomes increasingly important as they gradually realize they should be more afraid of each other than the 'crawlers' pursuing them.

THE ORPHANAGE (EL ORFANATO)

Juan Antonio Bayona, Mexico, 2007

Married couple Laura (Rueda) and Carlos (Cayo) move into a beautiful new home that was once the orphanage in which Laura grew up. Although an ostensibly happy couple, they face several challenges, not least of which being their young adopted son Simón's (Príncep) HIV, for which he must receive regular treatment. After deciding to reopen the orphanage for handicapped children Simón vanishes without a trace. As the months pass, Laura increasingly hears and feels the presence of other children and calls in a parapsychologist to investigate.

With successes like *Hellboy* and *Pan's Labyrinth* under his belt, Mexican filmmaker Guillermo del Toro has found himself in a position to shepherd new talent into the lion's den that is the modern international film industry. First to benefit from his production experience are Spaniards Sergio G. Sánchez (who wrote the screenplay) and debutante director Juan Antonio Bayona. Between the three of them they've created a truly nerve-shredding experience and one of the most terrifying films of recent times. Set almost entirely in and around the eerie building of the title, tension seeps into everything as we constantly expect the creaking floor or shadowy corner to provide the next unsettling surprise. The suspense never drops and towards the end, as we approach the shocking climax, becomes almost unbearable as Laura must play a strange children's game... apparently all on her own.

CAST INCLUDES: Belén Rueda, Fernando Cayo, Roger Príncep, Geraldine Chaplin, Montserrat Carulla, Mabel Rivera
SCREENPLAY: Sergio G. Sánchez
CINEMATOGRAPHY: Oscar Faura

LET THE RIGHT ONE IN (LÅT DEN RÄTTE KOMMA IN)

Tomas Alfredson, Sweden, 2008

CAST INCLUDES:
Kåre Hedebrant, Lina
Leandersson, Per Ragnar,
Henrik Dahl, Karin Bergquist
SCREENPLAY:
John Ajvide Lindqvist
CINEMATOGRAPHY:
Hoyte Van Hoytema

Oskar (Hedebrant), a 12-year-old boy bullied at school, meets Eli (Leandersson), a girl who appears to be about the same age. As a serial killer terrorizes the district, the children develop a close friendship, which is complicated when Oskar realizes his new companion is a vampire. At first glance, *Let the Right One In* appears to be part of the trend for romanticizing vampires. At the heart of the story is a forbidden love between youngsters from two incompatible societies: human and vampire. Comparisons with Stephanie Meyer's *Twilight* series are inevitable but largely superficial. *Let the Right One In* is a much darker tale with staggering performances from such young actors. It is a genuine study in character and relationship, and far from being 'merely' a horror movie.

DRAG ME TO HELL

Sam Raimi, USA, 2009

CAST INCLUDES:
Alison Lohman, Justin Long,
David Paymer, Lorna Raver,
Dileep Rao, Adriana Barraza
SCREENPLAY:
Sam Raimi, Ivan Raimi
CINEMATOGRAPHY:
Peter Deming

Christine (Lohman), an eager young loan officer, is chasing promotion at her bank. When a mysterious old woman is denied an extension on her loan repayments, she places a curse on Christine, who then spends three days being terrorized by a demon. In the '80s and '90s, filmmaker Sam Raimi defined the modern horror-comedy with his *Evil Dead* triptych. After going on to conquer mainstream Hollywood with the hugely successful *Spider-Man* films, he has returned to the gnarled roots of his movie career with a terrifying and hilarious triumph. It's tempting to think Raimi is here to show the new boys how it should be done. The film pointedly avoids the thematic ground trampled by the likes of *Saw* and *Hostel* whilst also refusing to offer us a traditional rent-a-psycho to terrorize a bevy of beautiful bimbos (seemingly a legal requirement in modern American horror). Instead, Raimi reverts to a more timeless approach, with a mysterious curse the motivation for a plot populated by realistic characters. In Christine, Raimi and Lohman have fashioned the most believable horror heroine for years, imbued with all the contradictory personality traits fostered by real people. We identify with her and are subsequently drawn into her nightmare. There's an endearing honesty and simplicity to this film that should appeal to those for whom modern horror cinema has become needlessly gratuitous.

MUSICAL

42ND STREET

Lloyd Bacon, USA, 1933

CAST INCLUDES:
Warner Baxter, Bebe Daniels,
George Brent, Ruby Keeler,
Guy Kibbee, Una Merkel,
Ginger Rogers, Ned Sparks,
Dick Powell, Allen Jenkins
SCREENPLAY:
Rian James, James Seymour
and Whitney Bolton
(uncredited) from the novel
by Bradford Ropes
CINEMATOGRAPHY:
Sol Polito

DID YOU KNOW?
The movie was adapted
as a Broadway musical
and opened in 1980.

The word goes up and down the street: producers Jones and Day are doing a new show – *Pretty Lady*. Rich business magnate Abner Dillon (Kibbee) is backing the musical to please leading lady Dorothy Brock (Daniels). Veteran director Julian Marsh (Baxter), though a sick man, signs up because he needs the money. He picks 50 girls by looking at their legs, including stage-worn showgirls Lorraine (Merkel) and Annie (Rogers) and wide-eyed newcomer Peggy (Keeler). Marsh drives the girls through tough rehearsals, off-stage relationships are in an uproar and, on the eve of first night, Dorothy hurts her ankle. Peggy is sent on instead – and comes back a star.

42nd Street changed the direction of the backstage musical. It was a tale, not of glamour, but of the grim reality of theatre life, with its heartbreaks and grinding work schedules. It was also the film that saved Warner Brothers from bankruptcy and set it on course to become a major studio. Furthermore, in *42nd Street*, the Broadway choreographer Busby Berkeley came into his own on film. He contrasts real-life on 42nd Street with his superb chorus-girl revue pieces and the extraordinary camera angles used to film them, creating kaleidoscopes, waves and chandeliers of exquisitely dressed girls. Warner Brothers promptly signed Berkeley to a seven-year contract. Ruby Murray was an exciting new kid on the block, too.

GOLD DIGGERS OF 1933

Mervyn LeRoy, USA, 1933

CAST INCLUDES:
Warren William,
Joan Blondell,
Aline MacMahon,
Ruby Keeler, Dick Powell,
Guy Kibbee, Ned Sparks,
Ginger Rogers
SCREENPLAY:
Erwin S. Gelsey, James
Seymour, David Boehm,
Ben Markson from the play
by Avery Hopwood
CINEMATOGRAPHY:
Sol Polito

Three out-of-work chorus girls, Carol (Blondell), Trixie (MacMahon) and Polly (Keeler), learn that producer-friend Barney Hopkins (Sparks) hopes to be putting on a new show. Barney hears Brad Roberts (Powell) at the piano and discovers that he is also a fine singer-songwriter – and has money to back the show. Brad's wealthy family disapprove of his showbusiness tendencies and, when they hear he is engaged to Polly, brother Lawrence (William) arrives with a lawyer, Peabody (Kibbee), to put a stop to it. Carol and Trixie turn their 'gold-digger' charms on the men and everyone gets married or engaged – and the show goes on. *Gold Diggers of 1933* was Busby Berkeley's second job as dance director for Warner Brothers, and it is even more elaborate than *42nd Street*. The show blasts open with 54 girls dressed in silver-coin costumes singing 'We're in the Money' with 'front girl' Ginger Rogers singing a chorus in pig Latin. 'The Shadow Waltz' has 74 girls – some on a spiralling staircase, others forming the petals of a flower as seen from one of Berkeley's overhead crane shots.

THE GAY DIVORCEE

Mark Sandrich , USA , 1934

The famous dancer Guy Holden (Astaire) is travelling with his attorney-friend Egbert (Horton) in England when he meets and falls for Mimi (Rogers). Egbert is a friend of Mimi's Aunt Hortense (Brady), and the pair are trying to get Mimi divorced from her geologist husband, Cyril (Austin). They arrange for a hired correspondent to give Cyril reason to divorce Mimi. However, Mimi mistakes Guy for the correspondent and invites him to her room at midnight. When all is later explained, Mimi asks Cyril for a divorce so she can marry Guy, but Cyril says he forgives her. However, the waiter recognizes Cyril as a man who already has another wife. When Egbert and Hortense announce that they've married, Guy and Mimi respond by dancing. Following their show-stopping 'Carioca' in *Flying Down to Rio* (1933) – the result of almost accidental pairing – RKO gave Astaire and Rogers star billing in *The Gay Divorcee*. Here they developed the elegant, sophisticated dance style most associated with them, and danced to two Cole Porter numbers, including 'The Continental', a sensational song and dance routine that lasts for over 20 minutes. It also won the first Oscar for a song.

CAST INCLUDES:
Fred Astaire, Ginger Rogers, Alice Brady, Edward Everett Horton, Erik Rhodes, Eric Blore, Lillian Miles, Charles Coleman, William Austin, Betty Grable
SCREENPLAY:
George Marion Jr., Dorothy Yost, Edward Kaufman, Robert Benchley from the unproduced play by J. Hartley Manners
CINEMATOGRAPHY:
David Abel

TOP HAT

Mark Sandrich, USA, 1935

CAST INCLUDES: Fred Astaire, Ginger Rogers, Edward Everett Horton, Erik Rhodes, Eric Blore, Helen Broderick
SCREENPLAY: Allan Scott, Dwight Taylor, Károly Nóti based on the play *The Girl Who Dared* by Alexander Faragó and Aladar Laszlo
CINEMATOGRAPHY: David Abel

Two strangers, Jerry Travers (Astaire) and Dale Tremont (Rogers), meet by accident. Their budding romance is soon confused by a whole roster of mistaken identities. However, Jerry manages to win over the, by now, sceptical Dale with some romantic dances in delightful settings – 'Isn't This a Lovely Day' in a bandstand during a rainstorm in London and 'Cheek to Cheek' beside the canals of Venice. *Top Hat*, RKO's biggest box-office hit of the 1930s, is an exquisite production: the elegant costumes, art-deco sets, toe-tapping music and delightful lyrics (both by Irving Berlin) are all divine. This was the fourth film with Astaire and Rogers and it is possibly the best known and best loved. The dance sequences are the stuff of legend – who can forget Astaire practising his tap routine in his hotel late at night or when he puts on his 'Top Hat, White Tie, and Tails'? 'Cheek to Cheek' is without a doubt one of the duo's most romantic song and dance routines – Astaire nicknamed Rogers 'Feathers' because her beautiful satin and ostrich feather gown moulted as she danced.

SHOW BOAT

James Whale, USA, 1936

CAST INCLUDES:
Irene Dunne, Allan Jones,
Charles Winninger,
Paul Robeson, Helen Morgan,
Helen Westley, Queenie
Smith, Sammy White,
Donald Cook, Hattie
McDaniel, Francis X.
Mahoney, Marilyn Knowlden,
Sunnie O'Dea
SCREENPLAY:
Oscar Hammerstein from
the novel by Edna Ferber
CINEMATOGRAPHY:
John J. Mescall

Julie LaVerne (Morgan) is the leading lady on the Mississippi showboat under the helm of Cap'n Andy Hawks (Winninger). When a local sheriff accuses Julie of being a mulatto, she and husband Steve (Cook) have to leave the boat. Hawks' daughter, Magnolia 'Nola' (Dunne), replaces her and falls in love with the new leading man, Gaylord Ravenal (Jones). They marry, have a daughter, Kim (Knowlden), and then go to Chicago, where Gaylord's gambling ruins them. He leaves in shame, and Nola goes back to the stage. When she retires, Kim (O'Dea) goes on to sing on Broadway – where they meet Gaylord again. Most of the cast had been in one or other of the stage productions of Edna Ferber's story. The unexpected choice was to use classic horror filmmaker James Whale as the director. However, it certainly works: people speak of the 1936 *Show Boat* as the one with soul.

ALEXANDER'S RAGTIME BAND

Henry King, USA, 1938

It's Prohibition-era New York. Young Roger Grant (Power) has abandoned his classical music training to form his own 'Alexander's Ragtime Band'. He hires Stella Kirby (Faye) as his singer and soon finds he is in love with her – but so is pianist Charlie Dwyer (Ameche). Roger and Charlie battle over the love of Stella for some 25 years. In the meantime, Roger meets Jerry (Merman), another vocalist, and Stella opts for Broadway and marries Charlie. After many more mix-ups and adventures – including the First World War – everyone meets up again and settles down with the right partner. This lavish musical is a sumptuous all-star showcase for 28 of Irving Berlin's songs. The movie took its title from Berlin's hit of 1911 – a song which, ironically, was not in ragtime. 'Easter Parade', 'Heat Wave', 'A Pretty Girl Is Like a Melody' – they're all here. As Jerome Kern said, 'Irving Berlin has no place in American music. He is American music'.

ACADEMY AWARD
Best Music, Scoring:
Alfred Newman

CAST INCLUDES: Tyrone Power, Alice Faye, Don Ameche, Ethel Merman, Jack Haley, Jean Hersholt, Helen Westley, John Carradine
SCREENPLAY: Kathryn Scola, Richard Sherman, Lamar Trotti
CINEMATOGRAPHY: J. Peverell Marley

THE WIZARD OF OZ

Victor Fleming, King Vidor, USA, 1939

Kansas farm-girl Dorothy (Garland) is feeling sad because a nasty neighbour wants to have her dog Toto put to sleep. She is planning to run away when a tornado blows away the farmhouse. When it comes to ground, Dorothy finds she's in the Land of Oz. She sets off to find the Wizard, who will help her to get home. On the way she meets a Scarecrow who needs a brain, a Tin Man who wants a heart, a Cowardly Lion who desperately needs courage and the Good Fairy of the North (who, she hopes, will save her from the Wicked Witch of the West). Her adventures show her that there's no place like home. Once you see *The Wizard of Oz*, ideas such as the Yellow Brick Road and 'Somewhere Over the Rainbow' will be with you forever. The songs fitted perfectly into the plot, advancing the surprise-a-minute storyline. The role of the Wizard was written with W.C. Fields in mind but, when MGM didn't offer enough money, he apparently told them he was too busy writing the script for *You Can't Cheat an Honest Man*!

CAST INCLUDES:
Judy Garland, Frank Morgan, Ray Bolger, Bert Lahr, Jack Haley, Billie Burke, Margaret Hamilton, Charley Grapewin, Pat Walshe, Clara Blandick
SCREENPLAY:
Noel Langley, Florence Ryerson, Edgar Allan Woolf
CINEMATOGRAPHY:
Harold Rosson

ACADEMY AWARDS
Best Music, Original Score: Herbert Stothart
Best Music, Original Song: Harold Arlen, E.Y. Harburg for 'Over the Rainbow'

YANKEE DOODLE DANDY

Michael Curitz, USA, 1942

CAST INCLUDES:
James Cagney, Joan Leslie, Walter Huston, Richard Whorf, Irene Manning, George Tobias, Rosemary DeCamp, Jeanne Cagney
SCREENPLAY:
Robert Bruckner and Edmund Joseph from a story by Robert Bruckner
CINEMATOGRAPHY:
James Wong Howe

The composer, singer and dancer George M. Cohan (Cagney) has been invited to meet President Franklin D. Roosevelt, whom he has recently 'spoofed' in a musical comedy called 'I'd Rather Be Right'. He tells the president his rags-to-riches life story and is given a congressional medal, after which he goes out to join in a Second World War parade where young soldiers are singing his song 'Over There'. George Cohan's life and career were firmly tidied up and sanitized for this musical; however both his amazing output of music – especially such heartfelt patriotic numbers as 'Grand Old Flag' and 'Over There' – and Cagney's incredible input into the movie role (earning him a well-deserved Oscar) did give the USA a much-needed tonic at that miserable point in the Second World War.

THE GANG'S ALL HERE

Busby Berkeley, USA, 1943

Rich, young Andy Mason (Ellison) is on leave from the army when he meets and falls for beautiful showgirl Edie (Faye). By the time morning comes, he's won her heart and her hand – although he hasn't given her his real name. He then has to leave to report for active duty in the Pacific. In due course Andy completes his term of duty and comes home with a medal. To celebrate his return, his parents have arranged to put on a benefit show in which Edie's troupe will be performing. Their meeting will be unavoidable, as will her discovery of his true identity – and of Vivian, who is another lady for whom he seems to be coming home.

CAST INCLUDES:
Alice Faye, Carmen Miranda, Phil Baker, Benny Goodman, Eugene Pallette, Charlotte Greenwood, Edward Everett Horton, Tony De Marco, James Ellison, Dave Willock
SCREENPLAY:
Walter Bullock from a story by Nancy Wintner, George Root Jr. and Tom Bridges
CINEMATOGRAPHY:
Edward Cronjager

The plot of a Busby Berkeley movie is never much to marvel at but, for *The Gang's All Here*, it sinks to the level of a conversation stopper. Its only purpose is to give Alice Faye the opportunity to sing some lovely songs, to let Benny Goodman swing, to enable Pallette, Greenwood and Horton to be, as always, deliriously funny, to give Busby Berkeley the opportunity to create some wondrously outrageous chorus-line numbers – and to allow spike-heeled Carmen Miranda to wear her nine-foot-high Tutti Frutti Hat. The number involving the hat, the strawberries and the banana girls is a crowning moment of Technicolor, movie-musical kitsch.

MEET ME IN ST. LOUIS

Vincente Minnelli, USA, 1944

The Smith family lives at 5135 Kensington, St Louis: Anna (Astor) and Alonzo (Ames), their son, Lon (Daniels), and their four daughters – Rose (Bremer), Esther (Garland), Agnes (Carroll) and Tootie (O'Brien). In the spring, Esther falls in love with the new boy next door, John Truett (Drake). Then their father announces that he has received a position in New York and they will be moving after Christmas.

At the winter dance, Esther tells John about having to leave St Louis and he asks her to marry him. Tootie waits at the window for Santa to arrive; she is worried that he won't be able to find her next year. Esther comforts her little sister and sings 'Have Yourself a Merry Little Christmas', but Tootie runs out into the snow and smashes her snowmen. The doctor is called to help calm her, and Alonzo decides that his family needs to stay in St Louis. The last scene shows the Smith family and John at the World's Fair which has come to town.

This was only Minnelli's third film, yet his ability to work with the songs, which slip seamlessly into the story, is masterly. Indeed, the film didn't follow a putting-on-a-show formula; instead, Minnelli took a suburban-life story and, without letting it get sentimental, told of simple, family things in superb colour. The songs include 'The Boy Next Door', 'The Trolley Song' and 'You Are For Loving'. The producer Arthur Freed dubbed the singing voice of Leon Ames.

CAST INCLUDES:
Judy Garland, Margaret O'Brien, Mary Astor, Lucille Bremer, Leon Ames, Tom Drake, Marjorie Main
SCREENPLAY:
Fred F. Finklehoffe, Irving Brecher
CINEMATOGRAPHY:
George (J.) Folsey

THE RED SHOES

Michael Powell, Emeric Pressburger, GB, 1948

CAST INCLUDES:
Anton Walbrook, Marius
Goring, Moira Shearer,
Robert Helpmann, Léonide
Massine, Albert Bassermann,
Ludmilla Tchérina,
Esmond Knight
SCREENPLAY:
Michael Powell,
Emeric Pressburger from
the fairy tale by
Hans Christian Andersen
CINEMATOGRAPHY:
Jack Cardiff

Ballerina Vicky Page (Shearer) and composer Julian Craster (Goring) join the famous Lermontov (Walbrook) ballet company. Vicky falls in love with Julian and is groomed for the lead in his ballet *The Red Shoes*, which is a great success. But Lermontov demands that she choose between her career and her lover. For Vicky, the strain is too great... One of Powell and Pressburger's best-loved films; for many, seeing it is an eye-opening and inspirational cinematic moment. It is also ranked, by British Film Institute members, as the ninth-best British film ever made. Not so for studio boss J. Arthur Rank (the dominant force in British filmmaking), who walked out during the gala performance. The special effects used to heighten the drama of the ballet sequence are still sensational, and the Technicolor photography, production design and score are all perfect.

ON THE TOWN

Stanley Donen, Gene Kelly, USA, 1949

CAST INCLUDES:
Gene Kelly, Frank Sinatra,
Betty Garrett, Jules Munshin,
Vera-Ellen, Florence Bates,
Alice Pearce, George
Meader, Judy Holliday
SCREENPLAY:
Adolph Green, Betty
Comden from a play by
Adolph Green and
Betty Comden
CINEMATOGRAPHY:
Harold Rosson

Three sailors, Gabey (Kelly), Chip (Sinatra) and Ozzie (Munshin) – who are on 24-hour shore leave – want to find some 'good-looking broads' with whom to taste the Big Apple. Gabey falls for the current 'Miss Turnstiles' – the monthly calendar girl featured on the subway who, this month, is Ivy Smith (Vera-Ellen). Chip is pounced on by Hildy (Garrett), a 'let's get physical' taxi driver, and Ozzie is snapped up by museum researcher Claire (Miller), who sees him as her missing link to Neanderthal Man. Once Gabey finds Ivy, the three couples set out to have a good time – which they do, judging by the number of New York City cops who end up chasing after them. A ballet by Jerome Kern led to a 1944 Broadway hit by Betty Comden and Adolph Green (who also played Claire and Ozzie in it), who went on to write the screenplay after MGM bought the play. Much of the movie was filmed on location (unheard of at that time) in New York, including the scenes in the old Brooklyn Navy Yard and those on top of the Empire State Building – tough on Munshin, who was afraid of heights. Great numbers from Leonard Bernstein's score include 'New York, New York', 'On the Town', 'Prehistoric Man' and 'Main Street'.

AN AMERICAN IN PARIS

Vincente Minnelli, USA, 1951

CAST INCLUDES: Gene Kelly, Leslie Caron, Oscar Levant, Georges Guétary, Nina Foch
SCREENPLAY: Alan Jay Lerner (and story)
CINEMATOGRAPHY: John Alto, Alfred Gilks

Before being called up for the First World War, Jerry Mulligan (Kelly) was an artist. Now that the war is over, he's decided to continue painting in Paris. Life in Paris is good: painting, meeting his pianist-friend Adam (Levant) in sidewalk cafés and attempting to sell his paintings on sunny street corners. Furthermore, he has attracted the attentions of an elegant older woman, Milo Roberts (Foch), who purports to be an art patron. But now Jerry has seen the girl of his dreams, Lisa (Caron). In spite of Milo's obvious jealousy and Lisa's existing boyfriend, Jerry knows he must follow his heart. The elements of *An American in Paris* that people still speak of with rapture are the little French nymph that is Leslie Caron, the glorious dancer that is Gene Kelly, and the closing 13-minute ballet sequence, the like of which many viewers have never seen before. Vincente Minnelli was a groundbreaking director of musicals and the perfect partner for Kelly on this project. It's often said that it is the ballet that won the film its six Oscars.

ACADEMY AWARDS

Best Art Direction: Cedric Gibbons, E. Preston Ames, Edwin B. Willis
Best Cinematography, Color: Alfred Gilks, John Alton
Best Costume Design, Color: Orry-Kelly, Walter Plunkett
Best Music: Johnny Green, Sally Chaplin
Best Picture: Arthur Freed
Best Writing, Story and Screenplay: Alan Jay Lerner

CAST INCLUDES: Gene Kelly, Donald O'Connor, Debbie Reynolds, Jean Hagen, Millard Mitchell, Cyd Charisse, Douglas Fowley, Rita Moreno
SCREENPLAY: Betty Comden, Adolph Green
CINEMATOGRAPHY: Harold Rosson

SINGIN' IN THE RAIN

Stanley Donen, Gene Kelly, USA, 1952

It's 1927 and *The Jazz Singer* has been seen — and heard. However, silent stars are still worshipped, none more so than Don Lockwood (Kelly) and his beautiful on-screen partner Lina Lamont (Hagen). Their fans believe them to be a 'hot' off-screen item, too. Unfortunately Lina's voice is so dreadful that, once they have heard her in a sound movie, no fan will ever swoon again. However, Don has met a lovely studio hopeful called Kathy Seldon (Reynolds), who has a charming voice. The plan is to hide Kathy on set and have her speak for Lina — but Lina is not amused. Before becoming a big-time musical producer, Arthur Freed wrote song lyrics with composer Nacio Herb Brown. He thought there was mileage in those songs, and commissioned scriptwriters Comden and Green to write a movie around them. However, when *Singin' in the Rain* first appeared, it was mostly greeted with indifference. The compilation film *That's Entertainment* (1974) is often credited with showing people what they were missing.

THE BAND WAGON

Vincente Minnelli, USA, 1953

Has-been Hollywood-musical star Tony Hunter (Astaire) is in New York to try and revive his dying career. His old friends, Lester and Lily Marton (Levant and Fabray), have an idea for a light-hearted pop musical and have asked Tony to star in it. They ask Jeffrey Cordova (Buchanan) to direct it because his Broadway successes will attract backers. However, Jeffrey decides to turn the show into 'meaningful' theatre and hires top ballerina Gaby Gerard (Charisse) as Tony's co-star. This is a disastrous move: she thinks he's too old, he thinks she's too tall, their styles don't blend and, at the off-Broadway try-out, the backers withdraw. However, washed-up Tony takes the helm, and things start to come right.

For serious musical lovers, if *An American in Paris* (1951) or *Singin' in the Rain* (1952) is not top of their list, then *The Band Wagon* almost certainly is. It has the Minnelli magic, a great score, an Astaire who's probably never been better and a Charisse who's at the peak of her perfection. On top of all that, there is the elegant Jack Buchanan, revelling in a part that enables him to scene-steal more than once. Minnelli, once again, revealed his genius in the closing dance sequence. Here the 'Girl Hunt Ballet' is a Mickey Spillane–type takeoff with Astaire in cream suit and black shirt and Charisse in red dress and black mesh tights – and seduction oozing from every step.

CAST INCLUDES:
Fred Astaire, Cyd Charisse,
Oscar Levant, Nanette Fabray,
Jack Buchanan, James Mitchell,
Robert Gist
SCREENPLAY:
Betty Comden, Adolph Green
CINEMATOGRAPHY:
Harry Jackson

GENTLEMEN PREFER BLONDES

Howard Hawks, USA, 1953

CAST INCLUDES:
Jane Russell, Marilyn Monroe,
Charles Coburn, Elliott Reid,
Tommy Noonan, George
Winslow, Marcel Dalio, Taylor
Holmes, Norma Varden,
Howard Wendell
SCREENPLAY:
Charles Lederer from the
novel by Anita Loos and the
play by Joseph Fields and
Anita Loos
CINEMATOGRAPHY:
Harry J. Wild

'Two Little Girls From Little Rock', lounge singers Lorelei (Monroe) and Dorothy (Russell), are setting off on a transatlantic cruise to (as Lorelei reminds us) 'Europe France'. Dorothy wants to meet a nice, manly man, though she's not averse to luxury. Lorelei wants to meet rich men – though she already has, at home, one rich beau whom she's encouraging, by her absence, to marry her. Lorelei settles for the elderly Sir Francis 'Piggy' Beekman, who owns diamond mines, but Lady Beekman rocks the boat when she discovers her diamond tiara has been given to Lorelei. Dorothy is smitten with Ernie Malone (Reid), but discovers he's been hired by Lorelei's beau's father to spy on her. Then it's time to disembark for Paris, and the game gets more challenging as the stakes get higher…

Marilyn Monroe's musical comedies are exquisitely funny because she is the perfect straight person. Marilyn is sometimes sexy-funny in her on-stage role within the musical, but other than that, she's as straight as a die. She's also an excellent female buddy; her relationships with other women (or 'women', in *Some Like It Hot*, 1959), are both honest and realistic. Then, there is the joy of the musical numbers – even if only five songs do barely a musical make. The fact that she is an entertainer on a cruise ship means that all the stops can be pulled out: the 'Diamonds Are a Girl's Best Friend' dress is stunningly pink, and 'When Love Goes Wrong' is full-blown after-dinner decadence. And Jane is very good, too.

SEVEN BRIDES FOR SEVEN BROTHERS

Stanley Donen, USA, 1954

CAST INCLUDES:
Jane Powell, Howard Keel,
Jeff Richards, Russ Tamblyn,
Tommy Rall, Marc Platt, Matt
Mattox, Jacques d'Amboise,
Julie Newmar (Newmeyer),
Nancy Kilgas, Betty Carr,
Virginia Gibson, Ruta Lee
(Kilmonis), Norma Doggett
SCREENPLAY:
Albert Hackett, Frances
Goodrich, Dorothy Kingsley
CINEMATOGRAPHY:
George (J.) Folsey

ACADEMY AWARD
Best Music, Scoring of a
Musical Picture:
Adolph Deutsch, Saul Chaplin

Oregon farmer Adam Pontipee (Keel) goes off to town to find himself a wife. He espies the lovely Milly (Powell), marries her and takes her home – where she finds six more Pontipee boys. Milly gives them all a bath and a proper dinner and starts teaching them how to be courteous to ladies. One night, between tending the farm and dancing up a storm, the boys listen to Adam's story of the 'Sobbin' (Sabine) Women. Inspired by this, they head into town to carry off their own women. Milly is furious and bars the men from the house, but spring comes, and things start to blossom. . .

Seven Brides for Seven Brothers was a mystifyingly (to the studio) massive success when it opened, and has remained enormously popular ever since. The choreography, say the critics, or the superb score. Nonsense. *Seven Brides* is pure Mills and Boon: women being carried off against their will by handsome, virile men who then are given a rough time before the women give in. It's romantic bliss. It's probably also the first time, in a musical, that boys really danced like boys. The putting-up-a-house competition between the girls' former town beaux and their new farmyard suitors is one of the most vigorous and energetic boots-and-braces dance routines on film. Gloriously politically incorrect.

A STAR IS BORN

George Cukor, USA, 1954

CAST INCLUDES:
Judy Garland, James Mason, Jack Carson, Charles Bickford, Tommy Noonan, Lucy Marlow, Amanda Blake, Irving Bacon, Hazel Shermet, Lotus Robb
SCREENPLAY:
Moss Hart from 1937 screenplay by Dorothy Parker, Alan Campbell, William A. Wellman and 1937 story by William A. Wellman and Robert Carson
CINEMATOGRAPHY:
Sam Leavitt

Norman Maine (Mason), once a huge star but now washed up by a steady stream of alcohol, helps the career of singer and dancer Esther Blodgett (Garland). As Esther – now Vicki Lester and Mrs Norman Maine – goes from strength to strength, Norman's downhill path escalates. He sees that he is damaging her career and her life, and realizes that this can't go on. Judy Garland sang superbly in *A Star Is Born*, and Cukor's direction enabled her to show her full range of acting talents. By this time Judy was 32 and, given the stresses in her life, her nerves, the pills and the booze, the fact that she managed to play a very young woman who lovingly cherishes her wreck of a star (an excellent Mason) – a path she found herself on more and more frequently – was an amazing achievement.

OKLAHOMA!

Fred Zinnemann, USA, 1955

Cowboy Curly McLain (MacRae) is courtin' Laurey (Jones), a sweet farm girl, and has invited her to a 'social'. She wants to go, but thinks he'll get bigheaded if he realizes how much she likes him. To make Curly jealous, she agrees to go with the hired hand, Jud (Steiger), but he's so moody she wishes she hadn't. However, Jud has been in love with Laurey for a good while – and would kill to stop anyone else getting her. This delightful Rogers and Hammerstein operetta was, not surprisingly, a big hit on Broadway before director Fred Zinnemann turned it into an exuberant film. MacRae and Jones have beautiful voices that blend effortlessly and phrase lyrics superbly.

ACADEMY AWARDS
Best Music, Scoring of a Musical Picture:
Robert Russell Bennett, Jay Blackton, Adolph Deutsch
Best Sound, Recording:
Fred Hynes
(Todd-AO Sound Dept.)

CAST INCLUDES: Gordon MacRae, Gloria Grahame, Gene Nelson, Charlotte Greenwood, Shirley Jones, Eddie Albert, James Whitmore, Rod Steiger
SCREENPLAY: Sonya Levien, William Ludwig from the play *Green Grow the Lilacs* by Lynn Riggs and Oscar Hammerstein
CINEMATOGRAPHY: Floyd Crosby, Robert Surtees

HIGH SOCIETY

Charles Walters, USA, 1956

There are three men in the life of Tracy Lord (Kelly). The first is C.K. Dexter-Haven (Crosby), or 'Dex', who was her childhood sweetheart and from whom she is now divorced. Dex, a successful jazz musician, now lives nearby and wants Tracy back. The second is George Kittredge, a safe, sound (but dull) businessman whom she is about to marry. The third is Mike Connor (Sinatra), a reporter for *Spy* magazine, which is threatening to run an exposé on Tracy's playboy father (Blackmer) unless given an 'exclusive' on her wedding. Mike, however, has also fallen in love with Tracy. Is Tracy caught in a terrible dilemma, or is she just spoilt for choice? *High Society* is a reworking of Philip Barry's play *The Philadelphia Story*, already filmed in 1940. John Patrick's instructions were to rework it just enough to make room for nine Cole Porter songs. As a result, *High Society* offers Crosby singing 'Now You Has Jazz' with Louis Armstrong and Sinatra and Crosby's 'Well, Did You Evah!', a song which had previously been sung in *DuBarry Was a Lady*, in 1939 on Broadway, by Betty Grable and Charles Walters – *High Society*'s director. This was Kelly's last film before becoming Princess of Monaco, and her engagement ring in the film is her own.

CAST INCLUDES:
Bing Crosby, Grace Kelly, Frank Sinatra, Celeste Holm, John Lund, Louis Calhern, Sidney Blackmer, Louis Armstrong
SCREENPLAY:
John Patrick from the play *The Philadelphia Story* by Philip Barry
CINEMATOGRAPHY:
Paul Vogel

THE KING AND I

Walter Lang, USA, 1956

After the death of her husband, an Englishwoman, Anna (Kerr), travels with her son to become English teacher to the many children of King Mongkut of Siam. She has some initial clashes of wills with him before realizing that, although proud, he has a curious mind and wishes to learn. She finds the notion of polygamy unacceptable but king and governess view each other with affection and respect. *The King and I* is a feast of costumes, settings, drama, forbidden romance and wonderful songs. There is also a very fine performance by Kerr as a brave, firm but warm-hearted woman. However, the film belongs to Yul Brynner. No one has ever made a role so much their own. He began with it on stage, took it into film and then onto television. In the course of 34 years, he played it over 4,600 times.

CAST INCLUDES:
Deborah Kerr, Yul Brynner, Rita Moreno, Martin Benson, Terry Saunders, Rex Thompson, Carlos Rivas, Patrick Adiarte, Alan Mowbray, Geoffrey Toone
SCREENPLAY:
Ernest Lehman from the play by Oscar Hammerstein II and the book *Anna and the King of Siam* by Margaret Landon
CINEMATOGRAPHY:
Leon Shamroy

FUNNY FACE

Stanley Donen, USA, 1957

CAST INCLUDES:
Audrey Hepburn,
Fred Astaire, Kay Thompson,
Michel Auclair,
Robert Flemyng, Dovima,
Suzy Parker, Sunny Hartnett,
Jean Del Val, Virginia Gibson,
Sue England, Ruta Lee,
Alex Gerry,
Iphigenie Castiglioni
SCREENPLAY:
Leonard Gershe
CINEMATOGRAPHY:
Ray June

One day, Jo Stockton (Hepburn), a young intellectual who works in a Greenwich Village bookstore, is descended on by one of *Quality* magazine's photoshoots. She appears in some of the pictures taken by fashion photographer Dick Avery (Astaire), and the editor, Maggie Prescott (Thompson), realizes they've found their new '*Quality* girl'. Jo agrees to go to Paris for a big fashion shoot, but only so that she can meet her guru, 'emphatheticalism' founder Professor Flostre (Auclair). Once in Paris, Dick and Jo find their budding attraction for each other has 'bumpy ride' written all over it. Audrey Hepburn goes, in a flash, from being a mousey frump in a shapeless sack to a vision of extraordinary elegance and loveliness in Givenchy. In addition, she does her own singing and graceful dancing (ballet trained), and she and Astaire did manage to put a sizzle into their dances and romantic moments together – despite his being twice her age and Paris having its wettest-ever summer. Beautiful Gershwin songs and exquisite settings, costumes and photography make *Funny Face* a feast for the senses.

PAL JOEY

George Sidney, USA, 1957

CAST INCLUDES:
Rita Hayworth, Frank Sinatra, Kim Novak, Barbara Nichols, Bobby Sherwood, Hank Henry, Elizabeth Patterson
SCREENPLAY:
Dorothy Kingsley from the play by John O'Hara
CINEMATOGRAPHY:
Harold Lipstein

Renowned ladies' man Joey Evans (Sinatra) arrives in San Francisco looking for nightclub entertainment work and lands a job at The Barbary Coast Club. Almost at once, he meets Linda English (Novak), a chorus girl who is as genuine as she is lovely, and Vera Simpson (Hayworth), a burlesque queen who retired after marrying well and who is now widowed but still very rich. Joey starts romancing both of them, one for his heart and one for his bank balance (he wants to open his own nightclub), but will he get away with it?

After the tremendous success of *Cover Girl* in 1944, starring Rita Hayworth and Gene Kelly, Harry Cohn of Columbia bought the rights to the Broadway musical *Pal Joey* (in which Kelly had also starred), intending to unite the pair on screen again. However, Louis B. Mayer owned Kelly's contract, and his price for the loan-out was too high. It was 17 years before Cohn did manage to film *Pal Joey*. By that time, Hayworth was ready to play woman-of-the-world Vera, rather than Linda, the ingénue – and Sinatra's Joey had become much less of a heel. Hayworth sings 'Bewitched, Bothered and Bewildered' beautifully, and 'The Lady Is a Tramp' became one of Sinatra's signature tunes.

SOUTH PACIFIC

Joshua Logan, USA, 1958

CAST INCLUDES:
Rossano Brazzi, Mitzi Gaynor,
John Kerr, Ray Walston,
Juanita Hall, France Nuyen,
Russ Brown, Jack Mullaney,
Ken Clark, Floyd Simmons
SCREENPLAY:
Paul Osborn
CINEMATOGRAPHY:
Leon Shamroy

ACADEMY AWARD
Best Sound: Fred Hynes
(Todd-AO SSD)

It is 1943 in the South Pacific Solomon Islands. The US armed forces want to set up a naval base, for which they need the help of French plantation owner Emile de Becque (Brazzi). Nurse Nellie Forbush (Gaynor) and Becque have become very close, but she refuses to marry him because he has children by a Polynesian woman (now dead). Lt Joseph Cable (Kerr) is also on the islands on a dangerous mission. He has met and fallen for a Polynesian girl, Liat (Nuyen), but he has difficulty proposing because of her ethnic background. Lots of difficult decisions must be made in this war-torn time. Joshua Logan cast a wide net when looking for Nellie: Elizabeth Taylor, Audrey Hepburn and Doris Day were all considered – but Mitzi Gaynor did the best screen test.

WEST SIDE STORY

Jerome Robbins, Robert Wise, USA, 1961

DID YOU KNOW?
West Side Story won ten Oscars at the 1962 Academy Awards.

The streets of New York's West Side are home to two warring gangs: the Puerto Rican Sharks, whose leader is Bernardo (Chakiris), and the 'Anglo' Jets, led by Riff (Tamblyn). However, Bernardo's sister, Maria (Wood), and Tony (Beymer), an ex-member of the Jets, have fallen in love. The streets of New York begin to rumble with the anger of both gangs, and soon death is stalking those streets. *West Side Story* is still one of the best-ever film adaptations of a stage musical. Jerome Robbins, director and choreographer of the hit Broadway version, shared directing credits with Robert Wise. This appears to have been a troubled relationship, with Robbins insisting on levels of perfection that the budget and schedule couldn't absorb. Although stylized, the dance routines fit the energy and language of Leonard Bernstein's groundbreaking score so well that they still have street cred today.

CAST INCLUDES: Natalie Wood, Richard Beymer, Russ Tamblyn, Rita Moreno, George Chakiris, Simon Oakland, Ned Glass
SCREENPLAY: Ernest Lehman, from the play by Arthur Laurents, based on the play *Romeo and Juliet* by William Shakespeare
CINEMATOGRAPHY: Daniel L. Fapp

VIVA LAS VEGAS

George Sidney, USA, 1964

CAST INCLUDES:
Elvis Presley, Ann-Margret, Cesare Danova, William Demarest, Nicky Blair
SCREENPLAY:
Sally Benson
CINEMATOGRAPHY:
Joseph Biroc

Racing-car driver Lucky Jackson (Presley) has come to Las Vegas for the Grand Prix, but currently lacks an engine. While being a waiter at a casino to earn the engine money, he meets Rusty (Ann-Margret), a swimming instructor at his hotel. While they are having a really good time together, he loses the money he has saved. Lucky has also been having problems with rival driver Elmo (Danova). In the end, how lucky will he be?

It was unusual for Elvis to share the limelight with anyone, but here Ann-Margret gets equal billing and on-screen time. This certainly worked well on screen because this was Elvis's most successful film on release to the theatres, and he and Ann-Margret were, apparently, as hot an item off-screen as they were on. Las Vegas (not yet ruined by commercialism) was a lovely venue, the songs were good, and Rusty and Lucky danced their little socks off (a talent contest was introduced to give them maximum opportunity). Elvis seemed more involved, acting-wise, than he had been for some time. A sage critic has described him, in movies, as being 'The Jedi master of emoting without bothering with facial expressions'.

CAST INCLUDES:
Julie Andrews, Dick Van Dyke, David Tomlinson, Glynis Johns, Karen Dotrice, Matthew Garber
SCREENPLAY:
Bill Walsh, Don DaGradi from the books by P.L. Travers
CINEMATOGRAPHY:
Edward Colman

MARY POPPINS

Robert Stevenson, USA, 1964

London, 1910. When Mary Poppins (Andrews) floats down into the lives of the boisterous but rather unappreciated Banks children, Jane (Dotrice) and Michael (Garber), things take a magical turn for the better. Their many amazing outings include a visit to her friend Bert (Van Dyke), a chimney sweep, street artist and one-man band. Walt Disney had wanted to make this film since his young daughters told him about P.L. Travers' books, but it took 20 years for him to overcome her objections. Even then, after seeing the finished film, she produced a list of changes she wanted the studio to make. Disney cast Andrews as Mary Poppins (her film debut) but had to delay shooting till baby Emma arrived. Fortunately, Andrews got the author's seal of approval after Ms Travers heard her voice on the phone.

DID YOU KNOW?

Mary Poppins won five Oscars at the 1965 Academy Awards.

A HARD DAY'S NIGHT

Richard Lester, GB, 1964

CAST INCLUDES:
John Lennon, Paul McCartney,
George Harrison,
Ringo Starr, Wilfrid Brambell,
John McCartney
(Paul's grandfather),
Norman Rossington,
John Junkin, Victor Spinetti,
Anna Quayle
SCREENPLAY:
Alun Owen
CINEMATOGRAPHY:
Gilbert Taylor

The Beatles (John, Paul, George and Ringo) have just finished a gig and are racing for a train, pursued by screaming girls, bewildered policemen and reporters asking the customary inane questions. Waiting on the train for them is Paul's grandfather (Brambles), who causes all kinds of trouble by giving them very bad advice. The gang then travels on, with their road crew, to a television studio to prepare for a TV special. The boys don't like rehearsals and run-throughs and take every chance to split or goof around. However, the show itself is a great success.

A Hard Day's Night is the Beatles' own look at the phenomenon of Beatlemania and how, by clowning, joshing, acting crazy and working very hard, they combined being Beatles with staying sane. The four chose Richard Lester to direct because they thought his *The Running Jumping & Standing Still Film* from 1959 (about British radio comedians, The Goons) was brilliant. Liverpool playwright Alun Owen worked with them on the script. Lester takes the movie at a tremendous pace, which echoes the boys' wackiness and their *joie de vivre*. The humour was their own – 'What do you call that hairstyle you're wearing?' 'Arthur.'

MY FAIR LADY

George Cukor, USA, 1964

Phonetics Professor Henry Higgins (Harrison) accepts a bet from fellow academic Colonel Pickering (Hyde-White). The bet is that Higgins, in six months, cannot turn Cockney flower-seller Eliza Doolittle (Hepburn) into a lady. He succeeds, but omits to give Eliza any of the credit for their success. She storms off, threatening to accept the proposal from one of her new young beaux. Warner Brothers' beautifully staged musical was their most expensive film to date, but it recouped its expenses by being one of the year's five most successful films. The songs are unforgettable: 'I Could Have Danced All Night', 'I'm Getting Married in the Morning', 'Wouldn't It Be Loverly'. Hepburn was disappointed that, after singing in *Funny Face* (1957), the studio insisted on Marnie Dixon dubbing her songs. Julie Andrews, too, had been very disappointed not to play Eliza (her role on Broadway), but, at the Oscars ceremony, she thanked Jack Warner for leaving her free to win Best Actress for *Mary Poppins*.

CAST INCLUDES:
Audrey Hepburn,
Rex Harrison, Stanley
Holloway, Wilfrid Hyde-White,
Gladys Cooper, Jeremy Brett,
Theodore Bikel
SCREENPLAY:
Alan Jay Lerner
CINEMATOGRAPHY:
Harry Stradling Sr.

DID YOU KNOW?
My Fair Lady won eight Oscars at the 1965 Academy Awards.

LES PARAPLUIES DE CHERBOURG (THE UMBRELLAS OF CHERBOURG)

Jacques Demy, France, 1964

CAST INCLUDES:
Catherine Deneuve,
Nino Castelnuovo,
Anne Vernon, Marc Michel,
Ellen Farner, Mireille Perrey,
Jean Champion, Pierre
Caden, Jean-Pierre Dorat
SCREENPLAY:
Jacques Demy
CINEMATOGRAPHY:
Jean Rabier

Guy Foucher (Castelnuovo) and Geneviève Emery (Deneuve) are in love. He is a mechanic and gas station attendant; she lives with her mother (Vernon) and works in her mother's umbrella shop. Guy is shipped out to do his national service in Algeria, and Geneviève discovers she is pregnant. The umbrella shop gets into financial difficulties but is saved by Roland Cassard (Michel), a suave and handsome man of means. He proposes to Geneviève, knowing her situation, and she has to decide between love and security. For many, Jacques Demy's musical is magical. Its simple, bittersweet love story is treated as an operetta: every word is sung. The theme tune sweeps across the heartstrings, and every scene is tuned with chords of colour: a sweater here is echoed by a van there; the luminous tint of a flower will be reflected in an umbrella. This wonderful panoply of colours had begun to fade in the original film, but it was lovingly restored in 1994.

THE SOUND OF MUSIC

Robert Wise, USA, 1965

CAST INCLUDES:
Julie Andrews, Christopher Plummer, Eleanor Parker, Richard Haydn, Peggy Wood, Charmian Carr, Heather Menzies, Nicholas Hammond, Duane Chase

SCREENPLAY:
Ernest Lehman from Maria Augusta Trapp's novel

CINEMATOGRAPHY:
Ted (D.) McCord

DID YOU KNOW?

The Sound of Music won five Oscars at the 1966 Academy Awards.

Maria (Andrews), who is a postulant in an abbey in Austria, is told by Mother Superior (Wood) that she doesn't have the decorum to become a full-time nun. She's sent to do the work of God with the Von Trapp family near Salzburg. Baron Von Trapp (Plummer), an ex-naval officer, is still grieving for his wife, and the house is not a happy place. However, everything changes when Maria encourages the children to sing. Von Trapp and Maria fall in love and get married, and the whole family enters a singing contest. Just at that moment, however, Germany occupies Austria, and Von Trapp is called on to serve in the German Navy...

The Sound of Music could have been very different. The director was nearly William Wyler, who spent some time working on the script and looking at locations. Von Trapp could have been Yul Brynner, Sean Connery or Richard Burton; Doris Day and Audrey Hepburn both turned down the role of Maria. The opening shot nearly didn't happen: every time the helicopter carrying the camera flew over her, the downdraft knocked Julie Andrews off her feet. Would-be Von Trapp children included Kurt Russell, Richard Dreyfuss and the four eldest Osmond Brothers (Alan, Jay, Merrill and Wayne).

FUNNY GIRL

William Wyler, USA, 1968

Would-be show girl Fanny Brice (Streisand), born in 1891 and raised in the Jewish slums of New York City, meets and subsequently marries handsome gambler Nick Arnstein (Sharif), who brings her to the attention of musical impresario Florenz Ziegfeld (Pidgeon). Ziegfeld hires her for his new Ziegfeld Follies show. Her comic flair has great appeal and soon she is one of the Follies' biggest stars. Yet, while the star of her ambition is rising, her marriage is moving into rocky waters.

Streisand had already starred in the Broadway production but, as so often happens, the producers were anxious that a Broadway star wouldn't have the box-office appeal to turn a costly project into a massive profit. Streisand, in conjunction with the venerable William Wyler's direction, gave Columbia its highest-grossing production of the '60s – and she won the Best Actress Oscar.

CAST INCLUDES:
Barbra Streisand, Omar Sharif, Kay Medford, Anne Francis, Walter Pidgeon, Lee Allen, Mae Questel, Gerald Mohr
SCREENPLAY:
Isobel Lennart based on the play by Isobel Lennart
CINEMATOGRAPHY:
Harry Stradling Sr.

ACADEMY AWARD
Best Actress in a Leading Role: Barbra Streisand; tied with Katharine Hepburn for *The Lion in Winter*

WOODSTOCK

Michael Wadleigh, USA, 1970

It's the summer of 1969 and the Vietnam War is being fought. In the USA, a three-day rock festival is being held at Woodstock, a 600-acre farm near Bethel, New York. The 12 cameras filming the event record the mud, the skinny-dipping, the drugs and the chaos. The movie nearly didn't happen. At the last moment, Michael Wadleigh threw together a production team – just in case Woodstock turned out to be more than just another rock concert. They shot 120 miles of film that was edited down to roughly three hours by Thelma Schoonmaker and Martin Scorsese. A surprising number of bands asked not to be included because they didn't feel their performances were good enough. *Woodstock* is still the definitive rock-festival movie, and possibly unparalleled as a summary of a generation.

CAST INCLUDES:
Richie Havens, Joan Baez, Joe Cocker, Arlo Guthrie, Lawrence Ferlinghetti
SCREENPLAY:
None - documentary
CINEMATOGRAPHY:
Don Lenzer, David Myers, Richard Pearce, Michael Wadleigh, Al Wertheimer

ACADEMY AWARD
Best Documentary, Features: Bob Maurice

CABARET

Bob Fosse, USA, 1972

CAST INCLUDES:
Liza Minnelli, Michael York, Helmut Griem, Joel Grey
SCREENPLAY:
Jay Presson Allen from the book *Berlin Stories* by Christopher Isherwood, the play *I Am a Camera* by John Van Druten and *Cabaret* by Joe Masteroff
CINEMATOGRAPHY:
Geoffrey Unsworth

DID YOU KNOW?
Cabaret won eight Oscars at the 1973 Academy Awards.

Berlin, 1930, and the Nazis are on the rise. Brian Roberts (York) comes to Berlin. He meets Sally Bowles (Minnelli), the daughter of a US diplomat, who earns her living at the Kit-Kat Club. Sally wants to be an actress, and 'anything goes' to achieve that aim. Bob Fosse's masterpiece of a musical will forever be as effective, despite all the 1930s' events and accessories. The characters are fashionable and timeless. The hopelessness and gloom lurking around every corner is historically immediate and archetypal. The brilliant routines in the Kit-Kat Club are both a shaft of much-needed fun and a clear warning of the approach of something dreadful. Minnelli's performance is perfect; what a tragedy that no one was truly able to catch that brilliance again. Few musicals bear watching as often as this one.

THE ROCKY HORROR PICTURE SHOW

Jim Sharman, USA, 1975

CAST INCLUDES:
Tim Curry, Susan Sarandon, Barry Bostwick, Richard O'Brien, Nell Campbell, Jonathan Adams, Peter Hinwood, Meat Loaf
SCREENPLAY:
Jim Sharman, Richard O'Brien from his play *The Rocky Horror Show*
CINEMATOGRAPHY:
Peter Suschitzky

Denton, Ohio. Janet (Sarandon) and Brad (Bostwick) have just got engaged and are driving off to share the good news when their car breaks down in a thunderstorm. Looking for help, they stumble across the castle of Dr Frank-N-Furter (Curry), a transvestite who is entertaining alien transsexual guests from the galaxy of Transylvania. He invites the young couple to witness the unveiling of blonde, bemuscled Rocky Horror (Hinwood), his artificially created love-toy for the relieving of sexual tension. Frank-N-Furter makes Brad and Janet his 'guests' for the night, after which Denton will never seem the same again. Richard O'Brien's play of the same name had done very well on the London stage, but the filmed version bombed both with the critics and at the box office. Then, word got around that the film was in the wrong slot, that it was a midnight movie, and slowly the tide turned. Now, some 30 years later, *The Rocky Horror Picture Show* has been on continuous release in various cinemas all over the world. Nor is it just a word-of-mouth success and a cult movie: it's a full-blown event, a ritual. People come dressed for the occasion and there are dances, actions, props and sing-alongs.

SATURDAY NIGHT FEVER

John Badham, USA, 1977

CAST INCLUDES:
John Travolta, Karen Lynn Gorney, Barry Miller, Joseph Cali, Paul Pape, Donna Pescow, Bruce Ornstein, Julie Bovasso, Martin Shakar
SCREENPLAY:
Norman Wexler from article by Nik Cohn
CINEMATOGRAPHY:
Ralf D. Bode

Tony Manero (Travolta) has a dreary job during the day, but on Saturday nights he's king of the dance floor. The disco is where he's popular and admired, unlike home where he's mocked by his father and compared with his brother. Then he meets Stephanie (Gorney) at the club. They both want more out of life, and the first step is to see if they can win the upcoming dance contest. *Saturday Night Fever* has a magic and an energy that exceed the sum of its parts. The no-hoper Brooklyn kids escaping the grind at the disco are not easy to like: they're sexist, racist, selfish and charmless. Tony is really no better, except that Travolta's Tony at least has charm. In addition, Travolta dancing – or even just swaggering along – to the Bee Gees' soundtrack (the all-time biggest seller until Jackson's 'Thriller') is irresistible.

NEW YORK, NEW YORK

Martin Scorsese, USA, 1977

Jimmy Doyle (De Niro), a saxophone player, and Francine Evans (Minnelli), a lounge singer, meet in Times Square on V-J Day and decide they're meant for each other. Slightly further down the line, Jimmy's controlling, selfish nature is well to the fore, and Francine has turned into a doormat. Then, when she's accompanying him to an audition, her sensational voice is discovered. Her career begins to eclipse his – but at a cost to their relationship. Martin Scorsese has meticulously re-created the musical scene in post-war New York – the late-night atmosphere (those smoky browns), a whole new interweaving of poverty and wealth, and the big-band numbers themselves. He also deals with the tough realism, for musicians, of life on the move: the tedium of the travelling and the one-night stands, with happier moments to be found in companionship, a card game or a comfortable room for the night.

CAST INCLUDES:
Liza Minnelli, Robert De Niro, Lionel Stander, Barry Primus, Mary Kay Place, Georgie Auld, George Memmoli, Dick Miller
SCREENPLAY:
Earl Mac Rauch, Mardik Martin from a story by Earl Mac Rauch
CINEMATOGRAPHY:
László Kovács

He also deals with the reality that, not even in musicals, is there always a happy ending. De Niro gets neatly under Jimmy's skin, and, other than *Cabaret* (1972), this is the closest anyone's got to finding Minnelli.

GREASE

Randal Kleiser, USA, 1978

CAST INCLUDES:
John Travolta, Olivia Newton-John, Stockard Channing, Jeff Conaway, Barry Pearl, Michael Tucci, Kelly Ward, Didi Conn, Jamie Donnelly, Dinah Manoff, Eve Arden
SCREENPLAY:
Bronte Woodard
CINEMATOGRAPHY:
Bill Butler

Southern California, 1950s. It's school vacation and, while away on holiday, Danny Zuko (Travolta) meets, and has a short, sweet summertime romance with, lovely Australian Sandy Olsson (Newton-John). School starts up again – and there's Sandy, who's on a student-exchange programme. Romance is trickier this time round. Danny is the leader of the leather-jacketed, slick-haired, tough T-Birds. Sandy is so cute, pretty, clean and wholesome that not even the Pink Ladies gang wants her. Danny has his image to think about – and Rizzo (Channing) wants Danny back. Both Danny and Sandy have to find a way to win the other back. The producers claimed to want new faces for *Grease* the movie, but most of the cast had been in productions of the stage musical – including Travolta as Doody. Travolta, here, is as sizzling as in *Saturday Night Fever* (1972), plus showing he can sing as well as dance. Newton-John plays both goody-goody and hot-stuff girl with equal charm, and her slinky, high-heeled, black-clad power-babe is the *Grease* clip most often shown. Knock-out success though it was, *Grease* did virtually nothing for the careers of anyone involved.

ALL THAT JAZZ

Bob Fosse, USA, 1979

CAST INCLUDES:
Roy Scheider, Jessica Lange, Leland Palmer, Ann Reinking, Cliff Gorman, Ben Vereen, Erzsebet Foldi
SCREENPLAY:
Robert Alan Aurthur, Bob Fosse
CINEMATOGRAPHY:
Giuseppe Rotunno

Joe Gideon (Scheider) is feeling the strain. He's auditioning the dancers and working on the choreography for his new show, while also editing a film – which doesn't leave much time for ex-wife, Audrey (Palmer), girlfriend, Kate (Reinking), or daughter, Michelle (Foldi). Joe is also ignoring symptoms of heart disease and having regular sessions with his Angel of Death (Lange), during which they travel through many painful memories. Heart-surgery time comes along – but is he ready to die? It's not a completely autobiographical piece, but Bob Fosse has based quite a bit of *All That Jazz* on his own life. Although not a dancer, Roy Scheider was chosen as Joe/Fosse because of his great dancer's body. Ann Reinking is both a perfect and a bizarre choice: she was Fosse's mistress for years, and won a Tony for her choreography of the 1990 version of Fosse's Broadway musical *Chicago* – from whence comes 'All That Jazz'. Fosse has left nothing out of this movie – except restraint. Nevertheless, this love song to theatre and show business is far more brilliant than over the top.

THE BLUES BROTHERS

John Landis, USA, 1980

CAST INCLUDES:
John Belushi, Dan Aykroyd,
James Brown, Cab Calloway,
Ray Charles, Aretha Franklin,
Steve Cropper, Carrie Fisher,
John Candy, Henry Gibson
SCREENPLAY:
Dan Aykroyd, John Landis
CINEMATOGRAPHY:
Stephen M. Katz

On being released from prison, Joliet 'Jake' Blues is met by brother Elwood and, together, they visit the home where they were raised by nuns. The home is in debt and $5,000 is urgently needed to keep it open. What to do? Reform their band and stage a lucrative concert, of course. Facts about *The Blues Brothers* abound: Elwood and Jake are two cities southwest of Chicago; five film directors appear in the film (John Landis, Dan Aykroyd, Frank Oz, John Candy and Stephen Spielberg); the film breaks the world record for the number of cars crashed. John Landis has achieved a rare thing with *The Blues Brothers*: he's taken a slot from *Saturday Night Live* and made it work as a movie. Not that it appeared to work to start with: it was trashed by critics and ignored by audiences. Gradually, however, the video sales rose and rose, and they keep on rising.

FAME

Alan Parker, USA, 1980

CAST INCLUDES:
Irene Cara, Lee Curreri,
Laura Dean, Antonia
Franceschi, Boyd Gaines,
Albert Hague, Tresa Hughes,
Steve Inwood, Paul McCrane,
Anne Meara, Joanna Merlin
SCREENPLAY:
Christopher Gore
CINEMATOGRAPHY:
Michael Seresin

A new school year has started at the New York City High School for the Performing Arts, and a new batch of hopefuls is ready and waiting, each with a burning desire to succeed. Eight of them begin to get to know one another and to share in each other's triumphs and failures, happiness and heartbreaks – knowing that not all of them are going to make it.

Alan Parker likes the combination of music, film and kids, or so his films would seem to suggest: there's *Bugsy Malone* (1976), *Fame*, *Pink Floyd: The Wall* (1982), *The Commitments* (1991), plus, of course, the less-youthful *Evita* (1996). As a teen movie, *Fame* is much more focused than the bulk of the Brat Pack genre that would be projected onto kids in the 1980s, and the energy, enthusiasm and creativity of *Fame*'s whole young cast is awesome. A quarter of a century later, the big show-numbers still work.

ACADEMY AWARDS
Best Music, Original Score:
Michael Gore
Best Music, Original Song:
Michael Gore, Dean Pitchford
for the song 'Fame'

LITTLE SHOP OF HORRORS

Frank Oz, USA, 1986

Poor orphaned, nerdy Seymour (Moranis) works in a flower shop – as does Audrey (Greene), with whom Seymour is in love. Audrey, however, has a boyfriend, Orin Scrivello (Martin), an obnoxious and sadistic motorbike-riding dentist. One day, just after an eclipse of the moon, Seymour finds a strange plant. He names it Audrey II. The plant starts to grow, and soon it is enormous. Seymour becomes famous and popular but is beginning to think he must give up his new-found fame as the plant feeds on blood, and now it's big enough to eat whole corpses. . . Rick Moranis has, here, leapt from being a rather easy-to-ignore actor to being the heart and soul of *Little Shop of Horrors*. He makes us believe in Audrey II (he's the one it talks to) and we feel for him in his blossoming love affair with Audrey I. Furthermore – he can sing! In addition, Frank Oz's laid-back directing style is warm and easy, and there are the hilarious and scene-stealing guest turns – including Bill Murray as a masochistic patient.

CAST INCLUDES:
Rick Moranis, Ellen Greene, Vincent Gardenia, Steve Martin, Tichina Arnold, Michelle Weeks, Tisha Campbell, Levi Stubbs (voice of Audrey II), James Belushi, John Candy, Christopher Guest, Bill Murray, Stan Jones (narrator/voice)
SCREENPLAY:
Howard Ashman, Charles B. Griffith (1960 screenplay)
CINEMATOGRAPHY:
Robert Paynter

MOULIN ROUGE!

Baz Luhrmann, USA, 2001

CAST INCLUDES:
Nicole Kidman, Ewan McGregor, John Leguizamo, Jim Broadbent, Richard Roxburgh, Garry McDonald
SCREENPLAY:
Baz Luhrmann, Craig Pearce
CINEMATOGRAPHY:
Donald (M.) McAlpine

DID YOU KNOW?
Moulin Rouge! won two Oscars at the 2002 Academy Awards.

Montmartre, Paris, 1889. A penniless young writer (McGregor) falls for a beautiful courtesan (Kidman), the star dancer at the Moulin Rouge (a bordello, burlesque show and dance hall), whom a jealous duke covets. Baz Luhrmann pulls out all the stops for *Moulin Rouge!* – indeed, he has a whole battery of new stops. This Australian director, with a background in opera, has the cast sing their own songs – songs that were not around in 1889. Everything from Elton John's 'Your Song' via 'All You Need Is Love' and 'Like a Virgin' to 'Roxanne' is in there, but it all fits beautifully around the velvet curtains and the elegant boudoir. Sound, music, colour, texture, voluptuousness, movement, dance, flavours, tragedy, love – it's all here in this 21st-century musical.

CHICAGO

Rob Marshall, USA, 2002

CAST INCLUDES: Taye Diggs, Clive Saunders, Catherine Zeta-Jones, Renée Zellweger, Richard Gere, Lucy Liu, Christine Baranski, Dominic West, Sean McCann, John C. Reilly, Chita Rivera, Queen Latifah
SCREENPLAY: Bill Condon from the play by Maurine Dallas Watkins and the musical by Bob Fosse and Fred Ebb
CINEMATOGRAPHY: Dion Beebe, James Chressanthis

Murderesses Velma Kelly and Roxie Hart find themselves on death row together and fight for the fame that will keep them from the gallows in 1920s' Chicago. *Moulin Rouge!* (2001) announced the return of the screen musical, and *Chicago* moved in to carry on the flame. *Chicago* had done well on Broadway, first in 1975 and again in 1997 – there is always a production of it going on somewhere. Bob Fosse, the main man behind the original *Chicago*, had grown up in that city in the 1920s and 1930s and knew the mobsters, the murderers, the cops on the make and the heated headlines. Fortunately, all that energy, drama, gloss and sleaze is still there on the screen.

DID YOU KNOW?
Chicago won six Oscars at the 2003 Academy Awards.

A PRAIRIE HOME COMPANION

Robert Altman, USA, 2006

A *Prairie Home Companion* is an old-fashioned radio variety show featuring folk and country music, wholesome skits and storytelling. In this fictionalized account of its final recording (the show is very real and still going strong), numerous performers come and go whilst head of security Guy Noir (Kline) tries to identify a mysterious stranger. Robert Altman's last film as director is an affectionate and amusing portrait of an American institution. A staple of rural middle-American life for over 30 years, this at first seems like an odd subject for Altman to tackle, but his formless style and penchant for an ensemble cast make it a perfect match. Amongst that cast is another great creative force in host and writer Garrison Keillor. It's his script that lends authenticity and provides the heart of the film, whilst his 'character' exudes the absent-minded amiability that defines the homely tone. But beyond the melodious affability, this is a film about change, and specifically death. This is the last show of its kind and a blank-faced hatchet man (Jones) is en route to close it down. Elsewhere death could, quite literally, be stalking the halls.

CAST INCLUDES:
Garrison Keillor, Meryl Streep, Lily Tomlin, Virginia Madsen, Lindsay Lohan, Kevin Kline, Tommy Lee Jones, Woody Harrelson, Maya Rudolph, John C Reilly
SCREENPLAY:
Garrison Keillor
CINEMATOGRAPHY:
Ed Lachman

SWEENEY TODD:
THE DEMON BARBER OF FLEET STREET

Tim Burton, USA, 2007

CAST INCLUDES:
Johnny Depp, Helena
Bonham Carter, Alan
Rickman, Timothy Spall,
Sacha Baron Cohen
SCREENPLAY:
John Logan,
Stephen Sondheim,
Hugh Wheeler (musical)
CINEMATOGRAPHY:
Dariusz Wolski

ACADEMY AWARD
Best Achievement in
Art Direction:
Dante Ferretti (art director),
Francesca Lo Schiavo
(set decorator)

In Victorian London, the innocent Benjamin Barker (Depp) is exiled by the villainous Judge Turpin (Rickman). Fifteen years later, Barker returns as Sweeney Todd and opens a barber shop above the pie shop of widow Mrs Lovett. Together they hit upon an ingenious way for Todd to exact revenge on those who wronged him, whilst at the same time supplying Mrs Lovett with much-needed meat for her pies.

Adapted from Stephen Sondheim's 1979 Broadway musical (which itself was influenced by Christopher Bond's 1973 play), this tale has long been a temptation for filmmakers in search of a challenge. At various times actors from Russell Crowe to Richard Dreyfuss have been attached to star, and directors such as Sam Mendes were rumoured to take the reins. Such talent would doubtless produce a great film, but thank goodness it was left to Tim Burton and Johnny Depp to bring the murderer to screen life. The macabre themes and gruesome content could have been tailor-made for the pair responsible for films like *Edward Scissorhands* and *Sleepy Hollow*. Every frame is brimming with the sort of ominous beauty that is Burton's calling card and, although not a trained singer, Depp is perfect as the once-upstanding citizen rendered a cadaverous ghoul by injustice. Bonham Carter makes an equally impressive Mrs Lovett, just as tragic and twisted as her bloodthirsty tenant. Watch out, too, for a hilarious turn from Sacha Baron Cohen as a potential rival to Todd.

MAMMA MIA!

Phyllida Lloyd, USA, 2008

On an idyllic Greek island, Sophie (Seyfried), beloved daughter of single mum Donna (Streep), is preparing for her marriage to Sky (Cooper). After discovering that her father is one of three men from her mother's past, Sophie decides to secretly invite them all to her big day, convinced she'll be able to tell which one is her father.

It had to happen. The stage production has played for over a decade in nearly 200 countries, so a film adaptation was inevitable. What wasn't so obvious was whether the camp absurdity of the Abba-themed musical would transfer successfully to the screen. But fear not, the songs of Benny Andersson and Bjorn Ulvaeus seem to work their peculiar magic just as effectively. Even if the film

hadn't sparked near riots amongst delirious zealots around the world, the plain numbers show it reached well beyond its core audience of Abba aficionados, with international takings making it one of the 50 most successful films in history. Clearly it's the wonderful music that's the basis of the film's success, but it's important to recognize the cast, too. By populating the film with (let's be honest here) enthusiastic amateurs, director Phyllida Lloyd has cleverly avoided intimidating the audience with the sort of flawless vocal performances we're all used to in this sort of film. As a result, the more relaxed and less self-conscious audience had no qualms about getting involved, and spontaneous sing-alongs were a hallmark of the film's theatrical run.

CAST INCLUDES:
Meryl Streep, Amanda Seyfried, Julie Walters, Christine Baranski
SCREENPLAY:
Catherine Johnson, Judy Craymer
CINEMATOGRAPHY:
Haris Zambarloukos

ROMANCE

SUNRISE

F.W. Murnau, USA, 1927

CAST INCLUDES:
George O'Brien, Janet
Gaynor, Margaret Livingston,
Bodil Rosing, J. Farrell
McDonald, Ralph Sipperly,
Jane Winton, Arthur
Housman, Eddie Boland
SCREENPLAY:
Carl Mayer from the novella
Die Reise nach Tilsit by
Hermann Sudermann. Titles
by Katherine Hilliker and
H.H. Caldwell
CINEMATOGRAPHY:
Charles Rosher, Karl Struss

ACADEMY AWARDS
Best Actress in a
Leading Role:
Janet Gaynor
Also for *Seventh Heaven*
(1927) and *Street Angel*
(1928).
Best Cinematography:
Charles Rosher, Karl Struss
Best Picture, Unique and
Artistic Production

A city woman (Livingston), on holiday in the country, has an affair with a young married farmer. She wants him to murder his wife (Gaynor) and go with her. The husband plans a boating 'accident' but can't go through with it. In a state of anguish, he and his wife take a tramcar to the city, and reaffirm their vows in a church where a wedding is taking place. On the way home in the boat, a tremendous storm blows up. He is washed ashore, but it appears she is lost. The city woman reappears, thinking he has followed her plan and he all but strangles her in his despair as he waits for news of his wife.

Murnau is one of the great silent directors, indeed, one of the great men of cinema. Cinema buffs and cameramen still can't figure out how he accomplished half the things he did, but are unanimous in affirming the brilliance of his camerawork, lighting, framing, back-screen projection – the lot. It is a tragedy that he made only three more films before being killed in a car crash at the age of 42. In the first year of Academy Award presentations, Janet Gaynor won the very first Best Actress Oscar for *Sunrise* (and two previous films); *Sunrise* won the first Oscar for Unique and Artistic Picture.

IT HAPPENED ONE NIGHT

Frank Capra, USA, 1934

When spoilt young Ellie Andrews (Colbert) weds a mercenary playboy, her rich banker father (Connolly) whisks her away on the family yacht until he can have the marriage annulled. Ellie dives overboard and sets off to join her husband. On the way she meets hungover, just-been-fired reporter Peter Warne (Gable). He recognizes her and, in exchange for his not telling papa, she agrees to give him her story. To avoid discovery, they take to hitchhiking and fall in love, but more complications lie in store. Nobody wanted to make this film, the first of many wonderful 1930s' screwball comedies – no one except Frank Capra and his scriptwriter Robert Riskin. No one wanted to star in it either, but eventually they got Gable on loan from MGM, because Louis B. Mayer was annoyed with him and thought this would be fitting punishment, and Claudette Colbert, provided they paid her twice her usual fee and didn't expect her to work for more than four weeks. This was the first film to win the Oscars' grand slam: Best Picture, Director, Actor, Actress and Screenplay.

CAST INCLUDES:
Clark Gable, Claudette Colbert, Walter Connolly, Roscoe Karns, Jameson Thomas, Alan Hale, Arthur Hoyt, Blanche Frederici, Charles C. Wilson
SCREENPLAY:
Robert Riskin from the story *Night Bus* by Samuel Hopkins Adams
CINEMATOGRAPHY:
Joseph Walker

CAMILLE

George Cukor, USA, 1936

CAST INCLUDES:
Greta Garbo, Robert Taylor, Lionel Barrymore, Elizabeth Allan, Jessie Ralph, Henry Daniell, Lenore Ulric, Laura Hope Crews, Rex O'Malley
SCREENPLAY:
Zoe Akins, Frances Marion, James Hilton from the novel and the play *La Dame aux camélias* by Alexandre Dumas fils
CINEMATOGRAPHY:
William (H.) Daniels, Karl Freund

Paris, 1847. Beautiful Marguerite 'Camille' Gautier, currently the mistress of the Baron de Varville (Daniell), is one of the most sought-after women in Paris. She is content with her life of parties and soirées until she meets the charming and honest Armand Duval (Taylor) and falls in love with him. Unfortunately, he can't afford to support her, so she must continue to depend on the baron while meeting Armand in secret. Alexandre Dumas fils created, in his original novel and play, the symbol of the camellia to represent illicit sexual love. It was the badge of the mistress, and it is very fitting that Garbo, the brightest star in the Hollywood firmament, should take on the role of the definitive movie mistress. Between them, Garbo and Cukor (the 'women's director'), plus a sensitive contribution from Robert Taylor, turn what could easily have been a tear-jerker into a classic.

WUTHERING HEIGHTS

William Wyler, USA, 1939

CAST INCLUDES:
Merle Oberon, Laurence Olivier, David Niven, Flora Robson, Donald Crisp, Geraldine Fitzgerald
SCREENPLAY:
Charles MacArthur, Ben Hecht, John Huston (uncredited), from the novel by Emily Brontë
CINEMATOGRAPHY:
Gregg Toland

Mr Earnshaw (Kellaway) lives with his children, Cathy and Hindley, at Wuthering Heights on the Yorkshire moors. He takes in a starving gypsy child named Heathcliff. As they grow up, Heathcliff (Olivier) is accepted by all except Hindley (Williams) who, when his father dies, condemns Heathcliff to a life of servitude in the stables. Heathcliff only stays because of Cathy (Oberon). Although she loves him, too, Cathy marries the more prosperous Edgar Linton (Niven). Heathcliff leaves for the Americas, but things get stormy when he returns. For many, this is the ultimate tale of doomed love, unrequited passions and revenge. It also garnered much critical acclaim. In 1939 – described more than once as the 'greatest year in motion-picture history' – it earned eight Academy Award nominations and won one, for Best Cinematography.

THE SHOP AROUND THE CORNER

Ernst Lubitsch, USA, 1940

CAST INCLUDES:
James Stewart, Margaret Sullavan, Frank Morgan, Joseph Schildkraut, Sara Haden, Felix Bressart
SCREENPLAY:
Samson Raphaelson, Ben Hecht (uncredited), from the play *Parfumerie* by Miklós László
CINEMATOGRAPHY:
William H. Daniels

Budapest, Hungary, in the 1930s. Alfred Kralik (Stewart) works at Matuschek & Co, the gift shop around the corner. Alfred has been telling his fellow shop assistants about the dream girl with whom he is currently having a pen-pal correspondence, when in walks Miss Klara Novak (Sullavan), a young woman who is looking for a job. Alfred and Klara hit it off badly almost immediately. Six months later, things are worse – although the pen-pal relationship grows ever more loving. Then, one day, Alfred and Klara both arrange to meet their correspondents after work. Which Alfred will meet which Klara? Margaret Sullavan had many down patches in her short life, and there was a general lament that this glorious actress made so few films. Sullavan had a great fondness for Stewart, encouraging him and helping him get parts, and the chemistry between them, here, in Lubitsch's subtle, polished, timeless romantic comedy, is delightful. Miklós László's tale was used again for pen pals Judy Garland and Van Johnson in *In the Good Old Summer Time* (1949) and by e-mail pals Meg Ryan and Tom Hanks in *You've Got Mail* (1998).

WATERLOO BRIDGE

Mervyn LeRoy, GB, 1940

CAST INCLUDES:
Vivien Leigh, Robert Taylor,
Lucile Watson, Virginia Field,
Maria Ouspenskaya,
C. Aubrey Smith
SCREENPLAY:
S.N. Behrman, Hans Rameau,
George Froeschel, from the
play by Robert E. Sherwood
CINEMATOGRAPHY:
Joseph Ruttenberg

An ageing Colenol Roy Cronin (Taylor), on the eve of the Second World War, stands on London's Waterloo Bridge remembering the beautiful girl he met there during the First World War – Myra Lester (Leigh), a ballet dancer – and how they fell wildly in love. They can't find a way to get married before he leaves for the front, so she misses a performance in order to say goodbye to him and is fired from the ballet company. Poverty, and the news that he is believed dead, drive her to prostitution. Then, while working one night, she sees him. Their passionate reunion is marred for her by what she has become, and she realizes – for his sake – their love must end. *Waterloo Bridge* had poignant war connections of its own. It went into production in 1939 as Hitler was invading Poland and it premièred in New York on the day (14 May 1940) that Nazi bombs flattened Rotterdam. It is certainly a weepie, but in the hands of Mervyn LeRoy and its two stars, it was a lyrical weep rather than a soggy one. Both Leigh and Taylor said that *Waterloo Bridge* was their favourite film and, for Taylor, it marked the first appearance of what was to become his trademark moustache.

THE PHILADELPHIA STORY

George Cukor, USA, 1940

CAST INCLUDES:
Cary Grant, Katharine Hepburn, James Stewart, Ruth Hussey, John Howard, Roland Young, John Halliday, Mary Nash, Virginia Weidler
SCREENPLAY:
Donald Ogden Stewart, Waldo Salt (uncredited) from the play by Philip Barry
CINEMATOGRAPHY:
Joseph Ruttenberg

On the eve of the wedding of Philadelphia heiress Tracy Samantha Lord (Hepburn) to wealthy and worthy George Kitteridge (Howard), her first husband appears – the wealthy and deliciously unworthy C.K. Dexter Haven (Grant). Another uninvited 'guest' that morning is a scandal concerning her errant father, Seth Lord (Halliday) – who also hasn't been invited but turns up anyway. Two reporters also turn up, but will hold back on the Seth scandal in exchange for the wedding exclusive. This was the fourth (and final) outing for Grant and Hepburn as a comedy pair. Their ease with each other brought a fine resonance to Tracy and Dex's divorced status, and George Cukor directs a fine script with great style. The result is a classic romantic screwball, remade as the Kelly/Crosby/Sinatra musical *High Society* in 1956.

THE LADY EVE

Preston Sturges, USA, 1941

CAST INCLUDES:
Barbara Stanwyck, Henry Fonda, Charles Coburn, Eugene Pallette, William Demarest, Eric Blore, Melville Cooper, Martha O'Driscoll, Janet Beecher, Robert Greig, Dora Clement, Luis Alberni
SCREENPLAY:
Preston Sturges from the story by Monckton Hoffe
CINEMATOGRAPHY:
Victor Milner

Jean Harrington (Stanwyck), aboard an ocean liner, introduces herself to millionaire Charles Pike (Fonda) by ensuring that he trips over her foot. Jean and her father, 'Colonel' Harrington (Coburn), are, in fact, cardsharps on board to 'work' the ship. She finds herself falling in love with Charles, but promises her father not to announce her feelings until the end of the voyage. Meantime, someone else warns Charles and he then cuts her dead. Jean swears revenge. Preston Sturges' directorial debut, *The Great McGinty* (1940), so impressed the critics that the studio encouraged him to make another film (*Christmas in July,* 1940) straight away. By the time he got to *The Lady Eve*, his third, he was being offered front-line stars. Both critics and audiences greatly approved of Stanwyck and Fonda's comic talents, and further comedy vehicles were lined up for them. Sturges usually based his scripts on his own stories, although this one is attributed to (Oscar-nominated) Monckton Hoffe. However, he does tell the story of once opening the door to his first wife and talking to her for quite a while without recognizing her.

CASABLANCA

Michael Curtiz, USA, 1942

CAST INCLUDES:
Humphrey Bogart, Ingrid
Bergman, Paul Henreid,
Claude Rains, Conrad Veidt,
Sydney Greenstreet,
S.Z. Sakall, Madeleine LeBeau
SCREENPLAY:
Julius J. Epstein, Philip G.
Epstein, Howard Koch,
Casey Robinson (uncredited),
from the play *Everybody
Comes to Rick's* by Murray
Burnett and Joan Alison
CINEMATOGRAPHY:
Arthur Edeson

Casablanca, December 1941. Wartime refugees heading for freedom come to Casablanca, desperately seeking the necessary documents. Most of them find their way to Rick's Café Américain, run by Richard 'Rick' Blaine, a cynical expatriate and former soldier of fortune. Rick deals in such papers. He acquires two invaluable letters just before underground leader Victor Laszlo (Henreid) and his wife Ilsa (Bergman) arrive. Rick and Ilsa had been lovers, and he still bears the scars of her leaving. Now, he has the chance to turn Victor over to the SS and flee Casablanca with Ilsa. What will he choose to do? Surely the best-loved of all the Hollywood classics and certainly one of the favourites of all time, *Casablanca* had everything going for it. Bogart is at his enigmatic best playing the antihero for all he's worth, Bergman is beautiful and there are some great performances from the likes of Claude Rains and Sydney Greenstreet in the supporting cast. Even now, you only have to hear the opening bars of 'As Time Goes By', by Herme Hupfeld, and you are immediately transported to exotic Casablanca – which was in fact the back lot of the Warner Brothers' studio. As to *Casablanca*'s famous lines, a sure sign of a picture's cult status, the usually misquoted closing line is 'Louie, I think this is the beginning of a beautiful friendship' (a last-minute dub-in), while 'Play it again, Sam' comes from the Marx Brothers' *A Night in Casablanca* (1946).

NOW, VOYAGER

Irving Rapper, USA, 1942

Charlotte Vale (Davis) is a depressed and frumpish young woman, completely dominated by her heartlessly selfish mother (Cooper). A well-wisher introduces her to Dr Jaquith (Rains), who persuades her to come to his sanatorium for analysis and treatment. When she leaves, she's an elegant and confident woman. She goes on a cruise and falls in love with kind and attentive Jerry Durrance (Henreid), but he's already married. When she returns home, her refusal to comply so frustrates her mother that she dies of a heart attack. Charlotte's guilt drives her back to the sanatorium but she isn't there for long.

Now, Voyager is one of the women's pictures – one with a five-hankie rating. Davis was very brave to agree to looking so deeply unattractive during the opening scenes. Barbara Stanwyck had started the movement of female stars not always looking like stars with *Stella Dallas* (written by *Now, Voyager*'s author), but Davis went the whole way – shapeless dress; hair scraped back in a bun; thick, coarse eyebrows; unbecoming glasses and no make-up. Fortunately, by the end of the film, she gets to leave audiences with a very different impression. She also has one of the best-ever last lines – 'Oh Jerry, don't let's ask for the moon. We have the stars.'

CAST INCLUDES:
Bette Davis, Paul Henreid, Claude Rains, Gladys Cooper, Bonita Granvill, John Loder, Ilka Chase, Lee Patrick, Franklin Pangborn, Katharine Alexander, James Rennie, Mary Wickes, Janis Wilson
SCREENPLAY:
Casey Robinson from the novel by Olive Higgins Prouty
CINEMATOGRAPHY:
Sol Polito

BRIEF ENCOUNTER

David Lean, GB, 1945

CAST INCLUDES:
Celia Johnson, Trevor Howard,
Stanley Holloway, Joyce Carey,
Cyril Raymond, Everley
Gregg, Marjorie Mars,
Margaret Barton
SCREENPLAY:
Anthony Havelock-Allan,
David Lean, Ronald Neame
(all uncredited) from the play
Still Life by Noel Coward
(also uncredited)
CINEMATOGRAPHY:
Robert Krasker

Mrs Laura Jesson (Johnson) and Dr Alec Harvey (Howard) meet at Milford Junction railway station when he gently removes some grit from her eye. They meet again by accident, go to the cinema, and arrange to meet the following week. When they go to a restaurant, Laura is deeply embarrassed when they run into old friends. Alec takes her to a friend's flat but, when the friend comes back unexpectedly, she runs away. Alec finds her at the station and tells her he loves her and that he has accepted a job abroad. Can she really be about to say goodbye to him, for the last time, at their station?

A superb five-hankie movie, thanks in no small part to Rachmaninov's 'Second Piano Concerto', *Brief Encounter* was a courageous undertaking for Lean – as shown by its rather mediocre on-release box-office returns. In choosing Noel Coward's very middle-class story with a somewhat middle-aged cast (even Trevor Howard, in his first starring role, was 29), with non-star names and without a happy ending, he wasn't embarking on a profitable route. However, the honesty and sensitivity with which he depicted those events has stood the test of time well. *Brief Encounter* is a classic.

BEAUTY AND THE BEAST (LA BELLE ET LA BÊTE)

Jean Cocteau, René Clément (uncredited), France, 1946

CAST INCLUDES:
Jean Marais, Josette Day,
Marcel André, Mila Parély,
Nane Germon
SCREENPLAY:
Jean Cocteau (also story and
dialogue), Jeanne-Marie
Leprince de Beaumont
CINEMATOGRAPHY:
Henri Alekan

A merchant (André), for whom business is not going well, lives with his daughters – Belle (Day) and her two sisters – and a son whose friend wishes to marry Belle. She, however, feels she must look after her father. One day on his way home, the merchant stumbles into the extraordinary castle of a mysterious Beast (Marais). The Beast tells him he must die – or send one of his three daughters in his place. The loyal Belle sets off immediately, and is slowly won over by the Beast. Cocteau's film of this famous fairy tale is a ripe choice for psychosexual interpretations. This was his first feature film embodying all of his gifts as an artist: as a poet, writer and painter, and his many years of studying the art of film. He was persuaded to make this movie by his long-term lover Jean Marais, who played the triple role of Beast, the Prince and Avenant (Belle's suitor). 'Genius' was the word used to describe Cocteau the filmmaker from the outset. No one, before, had used a film to express so many artistic media.

THE GHOST AND MRS MUIR

Joseph L. Mankiewicz, USA, 1947

London/Cornwall, at the turn of the 20th century. Recently widowed, Lucy Muir (Tierney) is struggling with a bossy but well-meaning family. She decides to move with daughter Anna (Wood) to a house in Cornwall. She meets the house ghost, the crotchety Captain Daniel Gregg (Harrison). As their friendship grows, and her money dwindles, he persuades her to write a book about his seafaring life and it becomes a bestseller. Then, she meets the charming Miles Fairly (Sanders), and the Captain sadly says goodbye to her before wiping the memory of him from her mind. However, Mr Fairly isn't really charming, and Gregg hasn't really left her forever. A wonderful score by Bernard Hermann perfectly complements this deeply romantic movie, and in Tierney's hands, the lovely Lucy's assertiveness grows until she is a woman of feisty resolve.

CAST INCLUDES: Gene Tierney, Rex Harrison, George Sanders, Edna Best, Vanessa Brown, Anna Lee, Robert Coote, Natalie Wood, Isobel Elsom, Victoria Horne
SCREENPLAY: Philip Dunne from the novel by R.A. Dick
CINEMATOGRAPHY: Charles Lang Jr.

ADAM'S RIB

George Cukor, USA, 1949

CAST INCLUDES:
Spencer Tracy, Katharine Hepburn, Judy Holliday, Tom Ewell, David Wayne, Jean Hagen, Hope Emerson, Eve March, Clarence Kolb
SCREENPLAY:
Ruth Gordon, Garson Kanin
CINEMATOGRAPHY:
George J. Folsey

Mr and Mrs Bonner, Adam and Amanda (Tracy and Hepburn), are legal professionals. Each of them lands a new job, which happens to be prosecuting (him) and defending (her) the accused woman in an attempted-murder trial. Doris Attinger (Holliday) tried (but failed) to shoot her husband on catching him with a floozie (Hagen). Hepburn makes the trial an equality-of-the-sexes battle, claiming that the husband, Warren Attinger (Ewell), wouldn't be found guilty of the same crime. She turns the courtroom into a circus. Husband Adam, already needled by Amanda's encouragement of an ingratiating suitor (Wayne), finds himself increasingly angry. The Bonner marriage is looking a little strained. Adam's Rib was the sixth of nine Tracy–Hepburn pairings, and many consider it to be their best. Their good friends, Garson Kanin and Ruth Gordon, had written Adam's Rib especially for them. Furthermore, all four were so impressed with Judy Holliday's film debut that they made sure she got the starring role in Born Yesterday (1950). In spite of the intensity of the battle played out here, the Kanins' point was that there is very little difference between the sexes – and as Tracy states at the end, 'Viva la difference – hurrah for that little difference.' And the romance? Well, if the Bonners hadn't been such a loving couple, there would have been no point in having a fight.

THE QUIET MAN

John Ford, USA, 1952

CAST INCLUDES:
John Wayne, Maureen O'Hara, Barry Fitzgerald, Ward Bond, Victor McLaglen
SCREENPLAY:
Frank S. Nugent from the story Green Rushes by Maurice Walsh
CINEMATOGRAPHY:
Winton C. Hoch

ACADEMY AWARDS
Best Cinematography, Color: Winton C. Hoch, Archie Stout
Best Director: John Ford

In America, Sean Thornton (Wayne) was a boxer, but he retires after accidentally killing a man in the ring. Now, he has returned to his Irish hometown of Innisfree, a place, he hopes, where he can finally be at peace. Sean's first move is to buy the cottage in which he was born. This alienates the town bully, Danabar, who wanted that land for his own use. Sean then meets and falls for Danabar's sister, Marie Kate (O'Hara), a red-haired colleen with a passionate heart. The director John Ford, while working away on westerns, was trying to drum up the backing for The Quiet Man, a homage to the Emerald Isle of his roots. The big studios refused, but eventually Republic, the westerns and B-movies studio, agreed as long as Ford made them a western first. Ford made them Rio Grande, and they funded The Quiet Man.

ROMAN HOLIDAY

William Wyler, USA, 1953

Ann (Hepburn), a very young princess visiting Rome on a goodwill tour, with all its ceremonies, speeches and interviews, suddenly reaches the end of her tether and bolts – just as the sedative her doctor gave her takes effect. She wakes up on the sofa of Joe Bradley (Peck), an American journalist who recognizes her. She wants someone to show her some fun, and he wants an exclusive story, so off they go. She gets a haircut, they go on a wild scooter ride through the streets of Rome and they dance on a barge on the Tiber while his paparazzi friend, Irving (Albert), tries to take pictures. Too soon, she has to decide whether duty to her country comes before freedom and newly kindled love, and he has to discover whether he can put his heart and his honour before his scoop. Most of the people who saw Hepburn in *Roman Holiday* were seeing her for the first time. She'd had some very minor roles in mostly minor films, but this was the moment when this slender, innocent, impish Gigi of a girl walked elegantly into the centre of the screen. With Peck as her stalwart, manly and honourable escort, the romance of unrequited love reaches its peak in their deliciously bittersweet final moment on screen together.

CAST INCLUDES:
Gregory Peck, Audrey Hepburn, Eddie Albert, Hartley Power, Harcourt Williams, Margaret Rawlings, Tullio Carminati, Paolo Carlini, Claudio Ermel

SCREENPLAY:
Ian McLellan Hunter, John Dighton, story by Dalton Trumbo (credited to Ian McKellan Hunter)

CINEMATOGRAPHY:
Henri Alekan, Franz (F.) Planer

ACADEMY AWARDS
Best Actress in a Leading Role: Audrey Hepburn
Best Costume Design, Black-and-White: Edith Head
Best Writing, Motion Picture Story: Ian McLellan Hunter, Dalton Trumbo

TO CATCH A THIEF

Alfred Hitchcock, USA, 1955

CAST INCLUDES:
Cary Grant, Grace Kelly,
Jessie Royce Landis
SCREENPLAY:
John Michael Hayes based
on the novel by David Dodge
CINEMATOGRAPHY:
Robert Burks

John Robie (Grant) was a cat burglar – specializing in expensive gems, and known by the respectful title of 'The Cat' – until he took up comfortable retirement on the Riviera. Now there's a 'copy Cat' about and, as Robie is under suspicion, he feels that, to prove his innocence, he must catch the jewel thief himself. In this detective work he is assisted by the beautiful and wealthy playgirl Frances Stevens (Kelly). Initially, she believes he's guilty but thinks no less of him for that. Thrilled by the idea that he may be a master thief, her main interest is in catching him – for herself. Alfred Hitchcock was a stickler for order and control in his films so, when he found congenial and trustworthy collaborators, he liked to hang on to them. Kelly and Grant were two of his favourite actors. On this occasion he coaxed Grant out of his threatened retirement by offering him the chance of playing opposite Grace Kelly, the new movie sensation, as a suave and sexy hero in a sophisticated and romantic comedy drama – with Riviera locations thrown in. Moreover, the role would be especially attractive to Grant because the film was a genuine whodunnit – and Grant could keep everyone guessing until the end.

ACADEMY AWARD
Best Cinematography,
Colour: Robert Burks

AN AFFAIR TO REMEMBER

Leo McCarey, USA, 1957

CAST INCLUDES:
Cary Grant, Deborah Kerr,
Richard Denning
SCREENPLAY:
Leo McCarey, Delmer Daves,
Donald Ogden Stewart
(originally uncredited) from
the story by Leo McCarey
and Mildred Cram
CINEMATOGRAPHY:
Milton (R.) Krasner

Charming, handsome Nicky Ferrante (Grant) and glamorous nightclub singer Terry McKay (Kerr) are on the same cruise from Europe to New York where they will both be meeting up with their intended. However, it's love at first sight for Nicky and Terry. The story was good enough to have been made more than once – as *Love Story* in 1939, starring Irene Dunne and Charles Boyer. In 1994, Glenn Gordon Caron directed it with Warren Beatty, Annette Bening and Katharine Hepburn. Bollywood lovers can see it as *Mann* (1999), directed by Indra Kumar, starring Aamir Jhan and Manisha Koirala and with Sharmilla Tagore as Grandma. The scriptwriters of *Sleepless in Seattle* (1993) have clearly seen it, and the ultimate accolade – a spoof – comes courtesy of *The Muppets Take Manhattan* (1984).

THE LONG, HOT SUMMER

Martin Ritt, USA, 1958

CAST INCLUDES:
Paul Newman, Joanne Woodward, Anthony Franciosa, Orson Welles, Lee Remick, Angela Lansbury, Richard Anderson

SCREENPLAY:
Irving Ravetch and Harriet Frank Jr. from the stories *Barn Burning* and *The Spotted Horses*, and the novel *The Hamlet* by William Faulkner

CINEMATOGRAPHY:
Joseph LaShelle

Ben Quick (Newman) has a reputation for barn burning that keeps him on the move. This summer finds him in the southern town of Frenchman's Bend, being given a lift in their automobile by two young ladies, Clara Varner (Woodward) and Eula Varner (Remick). Clara is the daughter of Will Varner (Welles), who owns most of the town, and Eula is the wife of his son Jody (Franciosa). When Will Varner gets back to town, he's not amused to learn that there's a barn burner about but, on meeting Ben, Varner decides he likes him enough to give him Jody's job in the store and to encourage him to marry Clara – at 23, already a spinster. Clara is cool with Ben until he nettles her enough to get her temperature rising – and then how the sparks do fly. Among Martin Ritt's students at the Actors' Studio in New York (where he taught for many years) were Paul Newman, Joanne Woodward, Anthony Franciosa and Lee Remick – all of whom were offered parts in *The Long, Hot Summer*. A rich vein of sexual tension was added to their on-screen pairing by Newman and Woodward's off-screen love affair. They had known one another for a while, but couldn't get married until Newman's wife agreed to a divorce. Within a week of that divorce being finalized, they were married.

PILLOW TALK

Michael Gordon, USA, 1959

Jan Morrow (Day) is a successful interior designer whose business and personal life are interrupted by songwriter Brad Allen (Hudson), with whom she shares a phone line. All day long he sings his songs down the phone to his various girlfriends. One day Brad sees Jan and recognizes her voice from hearing it so often on the phone, and decides to have some fun. The romantic comedies of the '50s are wittily romantic, but with a heart of candyfloss. However, for this kind of film, Hudson and Day are a perfect pairing. She was America's sweetheart: bubbly and cutely rebellious but as wholesome as apple pie. Hudson's extraordinary good looks took him into brooding roles in tormented melodramas. *Pillow Talk* gave them both the chance of something new. Hudson got to deliver snappy, stinging lines, and Day got the chance to remind people that she was a great comedienne and a sexy lady. The film was a box-office smash.

CAST INCLUDES:
Rock Hudson, Doris Day, Tony Randall, Thelma Ritter, Nick Adams, Julia Meade, Allen Jenkins, Marcel Dalio
SCREENPLAY:
Maurice Richlin, Stanley Shapiro, Russell Rouse, Clarence Greene
CINEMATOGRAPHY:
Arthur E. Arling

ACADEMY AWARD
Best Writing, Story and Screenplay - Written Directly for the Screen: Russell Rouse, Clarence Greene, Stanley Shapiro, Maurice Richlin

THE APARTMENT

Billy Wilder, USA, 1960

CAST INCLUDES:
Jack Lemmon, Shirley MacLaine, Fred MacMurray, Ray Walston, Jack Kruschen, David Lewis, Hope Holiday, Joan Shawlee
SCREENPLAY:
Billy Wilder and I.A.L. Diamond
CINEMATOGRAPHY:
Joseph LaShelle

The life of Manhattan insurance clerk C.C. Baxter (Lemmon) is a nightmare. It shouldn't be – he has all his superiors writing glowing reports about him – but the price is the key to his apartment for their extramarital affairs. Baxter himself is in love with elevator girl Fran Kubelik (MacLaine). However, he's distressed to discover that Fran has been visiting his apartment with the company boss. Fran is similarly distressed to learn that the boss is having other extramarital affairs. Billy Wilder very skilfully sets up the funny side of *The Apartment*'s scenario before peeling the humour away, layer by layer, till we see the bleakness beneath. An optimistic streak, however, is maintained by the honestly cheerful Miss Kubelik, until her own world becomes too grim. Jack Lemmon seems to have been liberated by his portrayal as Daphne in *Some Like It Hot* (1959). He finds new depths here that allow him to forge the perfect balance between the film's comic top layer and its darker implications.

BREAKFAST AT TIFFANY'S

Blake Edwards, USA, 1961

CAST INCLUDES:
Audrey Hepburn, George
Peppard, Patricia Neal,
Buddy Ebsen, Martin Balsam,
José Luis de Villalonga, John
McGiver, Alan Reed
SCREENPLAY:
George Axelrod from the
novel by Truman Capote
CINEMATOGRAPHY:
Franz (F.) Planer

Holly Golightly (Hepburn) won't thank you for referring to her origins in Texas – not since she came to New York and found ways to allow grateful men to fund her glamorous existence. Any time Holly is feeling blue, she takes a trip to Tiffany's – the only jewellery store worth browsing in. Her new neighbour, Paul (Peppard), doesn't judge her: he has his own rich lady friend. Little by little, Holly and Paul are getting closer, but any kind of 'real' relationship terrifies Holly. Audrey Hepburn is everyone's instant call-up image of *Breakfast at Tiffany's*. However, she nearly wasn't. The novel's author, Truman Capote, had always seen Marilyn Monroe in that role, but her drama coach vetoed the idea as Monroe was in the process of changing her image. Nevertheless, Hepburn always said that she felt she was miscast.

UN HOMME ET UNE FEMME

Claude Lelouch, France, 1966

Anne Gauthier (Aimée) is a widowed production assistant in the movie business. Her young daughter, Françoise (Amidou), attends a boarding school in Deauville. There, Anne meets racing-car driver Jean-Louis Duroc (Trintignant), a widower with a son at the school. When she misses her train, Jean-Louis offers her a lift back to Paris. As the two become increasingly attracted to one another, they slowly begin to reveal their feelings and the painful and tragic elements in their pasts that locked them into themselves. Indeed, they are performing the age-old ritual of falling in love. When Lelouch's *A Man and a Woman* appeared, it was as if a small cyclone tore through all the awards ceremonies and film festivals the world over, winning everything as it went. It also, having been so cheaply made (Lelouch did nearly everything on the movie), made a good-sized fortune. For all it's stylistic innovations, it is the sensual romance of two powerfully attractive stars that made it such a hit.

CAST INCLUDES: Anouk Aimée, Jean-Louis Trintignant, Pierre Barouh, Valérie Lagrange, Antoine Sire, Souad Amidou, Henri Chemin, Yane Barry
SCREENPLAY: Claude Lelouch, Pierre Uytterhoeven
CINEMATOGRAPHY: Claude Lelouch

BAREFOOT IN THE PARK

Gene Saks, USA, 1967

Newly married Paul (Redford) and Corie (Fonda) start wedded life in their bijou but problem-riddled fifth-floor (no elevator) flat. Paul is a sensible and dedicated young lawyer, while Corie is a bubbly free spirit who wants him to stay home and play. To her, he seems completely unspontaneous; for his part, Corie is beginning to give him a headache. Meantime, Corie's mother (Natwick) is lonely, and regularly staggers up the five flights – and on up to the sixth, after meeting the charming Mr Velasco (Boyer). Paul, feeling totally worn down by work, Corie and a terrible cold, consoles himself with a lot of whisky, and soon he and Corie are in the middle of a full-scale newlywed crisis.

Adapted by Neil Simon from his own hilarious Broadway hit, *Barefoot in the Park* transferred to the screen with Redford and Natwick reprising their original roles. The stars of the film, however, are probably the stairs. Anyone entering the flat (little more than one room – and the setting for 75 per cent of the film) is out of breath – including all the reluctant workmen who are trying to tame the flat's eccentricities. Redford and Fonda are a charismatic couple, and Mildred Natwick, as Ethel, Corie's mother, brilliantly delivers her very funny lines and well deserves her Oscar nomination.

CAST INCLUDES: Robert Redford, Jane Fonda, Charles Boyer, Mildred Natwick, Herb Edelman, Mabel Albertson, Fritz Feld, James Stone, Ted Hartley, Paul E. Burns
SCREENPLAY: Neil Simon from his own play
CINEMATOGRAPHY: Joseph LaShelle

LOVE STORY

Arthur Hiller, USA, 1970

CAST INCLUDES:
Ali MacGraw, Ryan O'Neal, John Marley, Ray Milland, Russell Nype, Katharine Balfour, Sydney Walker, Robert Modica, Walker Daniels, Tommy Lee Jones
SCREENPLAY:
Erich Segal
CINEMATOGRAPHY:
Richard (Dick) C. Kratina

Oliver Barrett IV (O'Neal) is studying law at Harvard, while Jenny Cavalleri (MacGraw) is majoring in music at Radcliffe. They meet and quarrel a lot until, in a long kiss, they find undying love. Jenny is going to Paris to further her music studies, but shelves this plan when Oliver proposes marriage. Enter the fathers-in-law, and a few other complications. Paramount was very grateful for *Love Story*. They were lamenting a seriously disappointing year for hit films when this modestly budgeted little movie blew the roofs of box offices everywhere. *Love Story* was one of the first movies to gross $100 million on first release – and a good deal more after that. It was also one of the first times that an author wrote a best-selling book from a screenplay. Francis Lai's Oscar-winning theme music has become a classic, and the two veteran Hollywood actors, Milland and Marley, are superb. Five hankies, minimum.

A NEW LEAF

Elaine May, USA, 1971

CAST INCLUDES:
Walter Matthau, Elaine May, Jack Weston, George Rose, James Coco, Doris Roberts, Renée Taylor, William Redfield, Graham Jarvis
SCREENPLAY:
Elaine May from the story *The Green Heart* by Jack Ritchie
CINEMATOGRAPHY:
Gayne Rescher

Ageing, snobbish, bachelor playboy Henry Graham (Matthau) has run out of money. He reluctantly takes his butler's advice to get himself a rich wife and stumbles upon millionairess Henrietta Lowell (May) – myopic, clumsy, awkward, a frump and a botanist. Henry intends to marry and then murder her because he doesn't want to be married or to share her wealth with anyone. He agrees to go with her on a field trip, and the perfect murder moment arrives when their canoe overturns in rapids (she can't swim) – but what does he see on the bank? *A New Leaf* is an exquisitely funny film. It's scripted by Elaine May and is her debut as a director. It was the subject of a court battle with Paramount: May's version was nearly three hours long with a dark subplot and she wanted her name removed. She didn't succeed, and what is left of the film is certainly as much as one could want. Matthau has probably never been better than as this arrogant, heartless, selfish, insensitive, greedy and homicidal man. May is incomparable as a disaster zone who still manages to be sweet and naïvely sexy. Henry's redemption – which he fights to the last – is the more funny and delightful because it's engineered by a woman who has no idea that anything's changed.

THE WAY WE WERE

Sydney Pollack, USA, 1973

It's the late 1930s, and Katie Morosky and Hubbell Gardner meet at university. They are from very different backgrounds: she's Jewish, outspoken and a political activist; he's from a Wasp family and wants to be a writer. There's a mutual underlying attraction that neither of them follows up. However, some years later, when they meet up again, they embark on a wonderful romance despite their ideological differences. They get married and, by the time they move out to California, it's the early 1950s and people are being blacklisted as Communist sympathizers. Katy (now pregnant) is still as vocal as ever and she and Hubbell decide they must part. Years later, they bump into each other again, and the magic is still there. The critics mauled *The Way We Were*, but the public loved it. Perhaps it was the theme song – which went on to be a monumental hit and won an Oscar; perhaps it was the unexpectedly strong on-screen chemistry between Redford and Streisand; perhaps it was the strength of the plot that was heartwrenching without being sentimental; perhaps it was the five-hankie ending – whatever it was, it worked.

CAST INCLUDES:
Barbra Streisand, Robert Redford, Bradford Dillman, Lois Chiles, Patrick O'Neal, Viveca Lindfors, Allyn Ann McLerie, Murray Hamilton, Herb Edelman, Diana Ewing, Sally Kirkland
SCREENPLAY:
Arthur Laurents, David Rayfiel (uncredited)
CINEMATOGRAPHY:
Harry Stradling Jr.

DID YOU KNOW?
The film won four Academy Awards, including Best Director for Woody Allen.

ANNIE HALL

Woody Allen, USA, 1977

CAST INCLUDES:
Woody Allen, Diane Keaton, Tony Roberts, Carol Kane, Paul Simon, Shelley Duvall, Janet Margolin
SCREENPLAY:
Woody Allen and Marshall Brickman
CINEMATOGRAPHY:
Gordon Willis

Successful New York comedian Alvy Singer (Allen) begins an affair with would-be singer Annie Hall (Keaton). Alvy becomes jealous and they split up for a while. They are reconciled in time to fly to Hollywood and pursue career possibilities for Alvy, and although they split up once and for all, their affair still has more to offer Alvy. *Annie Hall* was advertised as a 'nervous romance' and finds Allen expanding his range of cinematic comedy ingenuity. He also gives strong indications as to where his work is now: when, for instance, Alvy's in bed with Annie, he says that 'this is the most fun I've ever had without laughing', showing his readiness to move beyond all-out comedies into the world of direct feeling. And Ralph Lauren's clothes for Annie caused a fashion revolution.

10

Blake Edwards, USA, 1979

CAST INCLUDES: Dudley Moore, Julie Andrews, Bo Derek, Robert Webber, Dee Wallace (Stone), Sam J. Jones, Brian Dennehy, Max Showalter
SCREENPLAY: Blake Edwards
CINEMATOGRAPHY: Frank Stanley

George Webber (Moore) is a writer of hit songs who's going through a midlife crisis. He has a lovely home, a fulfilling career, a nice car and Samantha (Andrews), his beautiful and intelligent girlfriend. But he's feeling the onset of age, and his lust for life seems to be diminishing. Then, on the beach, he sees an angel in white. It's Jenny (Derek), a blonde, perfectly proportioned goddess of a girl – who happens to be about to get married. She's not just a perfect '10' (the top of George's beauty scale), she's an '11'. She represents his youth, and he pursues her, uphill and down. Will he catch her? Will she be the answer to his dreams? Blake Edwards uses *10* to remind us that 40 is a dangerous age. At 40, men are much more at home with fantasy than reality, and George is not really at all comfortable with the actual free spirit of sexual revolution that Jenny represents. The male menopause is upon him; old age itself seems like a dreaded disease and the only way to put it off is with a last fling. Dudley Moore was able to remind the world, in *10*, how very funny he is, Julie Andrews got to play a role – very effectively – that was elegant and sexy, and Bo Derek was responsible for a new hairstyle.

THE FRENCH LIEUTENANT'S WOMAN

Karel Reisz, GB, 1981

CAST INCLUDES:
Meryl Streep, Jeremy Irons, Hilton McRae, Emily Morgan, Charlotte Mitchell, Lynsey Baxter, Jean Faulds, Peter Vaughan, Colin Jeavons, Liz Smith, Patience Collier John Barrett, Leo McKern
SCREENPLAY:
Harold Pinter from the novel by John Fowles
CINEMATOGRAPHY:
Freddie Francis

Anna (Streep) and Mike (Irons) are starring in the film of a story set in Lyme Regis in 19th-century England. It tells of the infatuation of Charles Smithson (Irons) with the strangely fascinating Sarah Woodruff (Streep), even though he is engaged to Ernestina (Baxter). Sarah, on the other hand, is supposedly a 'wronged' and, therefore, tainted woman. So involved does Charles become that he feels obliged to break his engagement to Ernestina. He then finds that Sarah has vanished, and resolves to try to find her. Meanwhile, Anna and Mike are carrying on an illicit affair that bears extraordinary similarities to the parts they are playing. John Fowles' magnificent novel was not an easy undertaking for Harold Pinter to adapt for the screen. It has, for example, a narrator, and it also has alternative endings. Pinter chose to put the original story within a film so that the detachment of the filmmaking process would echo the function of the narrator. Contemporary insight on the plight of the Victorian characters would also be provided by the observations of the film-within-a-film actors playing the parts. Interestingly, Charles and Sarah's affair is a lot more passionate than Anna and Mike's.

AN OFFICER AND A GENTLEMAN

Taylor Hackford, USA, 1982

CAST INCLUDES:
Richard Gere, Debra Winger,
David Keith, Robert Loggia,
Lisa Blount, Lisa Eilbacher,
Louis Gossett Jr., Tony Plana,
Harold Sylvester,
David Caruso
SCREENPLAY:
Douglas Day Stewart
CINEMATOGRAPHY:
Donald (E.) Thorin

Loner Zack Mayo (Gere) decides he's getting too like the alcoholic father he was stuck with when his mother died. He decides to shake off escalating delinquency by signing up for Naval Officer's Candidate School with the aim of becoming a navy pilot – a longheld dream. Once there, he falls foul of his tough drill instructor (Gossett Jr.), who puts Mayo to the test. He also warns the recruits about the local girls who are desperate to catch a pilot husband; however, when Paula (Winger) catches him, he thinks he might want to stay caught. With a compelling central romance, Mayo's development, though predictably inspirational, is worth watching because this is Gere at his very best. Deborah Winger, too, is excellent, making more than the most of a very underwritten part, and Louis Gossett Jr. was Oscar-winning.

OUT OF AFRICA

Sydney Pollack, USA, 1985

Dane Karen Blixen (Streep), despairing of being a spinster forever, goes to Kenya to enter a marriage of convenience with Baron Bror Blixen-Finecke (Brandauer). Together, they start a coffee plantation. When the First World War breaks out, Bror joins a provisional army and Karen runs the plantation by herself. When Bror returns, and she feels his philandering ways have gone too far, she throws him out. She herself has met big-game hunter Denys Hatton (Redford). They are soon having a passionate affair, but their relationship becomes ever more turbulent. The Kenyan scenery is staggering and the chemistry between Streep and Redford is tangible; all in all, a beautifully observed and skilfully directed picture.

DID YOU KNOW?
Out of Africa won seven
Oscars at the 1986
Academy Awards.

CAST INCLUDES: Meryl Streep, Robert Redford, Klaus Maria Brandauer,
Michael Kitchen, Malick Bowens, Joseph Thiaka, Stephen Kinyanjui
SCREENPLAY: Kurt Luedtke from the memoirs of Isak Dinesen and
the book *Silence Will Speak* by Errol Trebinski
CINEMATOGRAPHY: David Watki

NINE ½ WEEKS

Adrian Lyne, USA, 1986

CAST INCLUDES:
Mickey Rourke, Kim Basinger, Margaret Whitton, David Margulies, Christine Baranski
SCREENPLAY:
Sarah Kernochan, Zalman King, Patricia Louisianna Knop from the novel by Elizabeth McNeill
CINEMATOGRAPHY:
Peter Biziou

John (Rourke) buys and sells money on Wall Street. Elizabeth (Basinger) works at a SoHo art gallery. Their eyes lock in a Chinese grocery store in Manhattan and then meet again in a flea market. He takes her to his houseboat on the Hudson and offers her an erotic affair. They play every kind of sex game, usually with him in control. He seduces her with endearments and expensive gifts, while insisting on an ever more debasing sexual itinerary. Soon, Elizabeth has to decide whether the hedonistic pleasure is worth the total annihilation of her self, or whether she can find a way to cut free from her sensual imprisonment. When Adrian Lyne's *Nine 1/2 Weeks* opened, there hadn't been a mainstream movie quite as open about lust and sex since *Last Tango in Paris* (1972). Lyne creates an enormous amount of sexual tension by making it a foreplay movie. The orgasms are in the build-up, the ideas, John's commands, and are further heightened, for the viewer, by the scenes of (mainly her) everyday life. On one level, he and she are deeply aroused while, on another, they are frozen, as much objects as are their clothes and sex toys. This is Rourke 'while he was still hot'. The beautiful Basinger had, apparently, body doubles for all the intimate scenes.

THE PRINCESS BRIDE

Rob Reiner, USA, 1987

CAST INCLUDES:
Cary Elwes, Mandy Patinkin, Chris Sarandon, Christopher Guest, Wallace Shawn, André the Giant, Fred Savage, Robin Wright (Penn), Peter Falk, Peter Cook, Mel Smith, Carol Kane, Billy Crystal
SCREENPLAY:
William Goldman from his own book
CINEMATOGRAPHY:
Adrian Biddle

A grandfather (Falk) settles down to read a bedtime story to his sick grandson (Savage). The story tells of Westley, a farm hand who works for – and loves – the beautiful Buttercup (Robin Wright). When she realizes she loves him too, he sets out to earn his fortune so they can be married. After a time, she learns that he has been killed by pirates. Brokenhearted, Buttercup offers no resistance when Prince Humperdinck decides he wishes to marry her. In fact, he really wishes to murder her, thus causing a war from which he can profit. However, just in time, a dark stranger appears, bent on rescuing her. For the children, director Rob Reiner preserves the magic of a fairy tale; for the grown-ups, he reminds them of the magic and leaves them helpless with laughter. Oh, and they all lived happily ever after.

DIRTY DANCING

Emile Ardolino, USA, 1987

CAST INCLUDES:
Jennifer Grey, Patrick Swayze, Jerry Orbach, Cynthia Rhodes, Jack Weston, Jane Brucker, Kelly Bishop, Lonny Price, Max Cantor
SCREENPLAY:
Eleanor Bergstein
CINEMATOGRAPHY:
Jeff Jur

It's the summer of 1963. Frances 'Baby' Houseman (Grey) is on holiday with her family in a Catskills resort. The activities on offer seem very tame until she hears pulsating music coming from the staff lodge. Inside there's some steamy dancing going on, and the steamiest dancer is Johnny Castle (Swayze), the resort dance instructor. When Johnny's partner has to rest up – after an unwanted pregnancy (not Johnny's fault) and a botched abortion – Baby offers to help him out, dance-wise, and the two get close – and steamy. Baby's father then gets Johnny fired, but will he find a way to return before the big dance contest? *Dirty Dancing*'s soundtrack really took off, with the Oscar-winning '(I've Had) The Time of My Life' a particularly huge hit. Swayze and Grey certainly have chemistry – and she manages to convince the world she, as Baby, is only 17 (not 27). Beloved by romantics everywhere, it's also memorable for its iconic lines, most notably 'Nobody puts Baby in a corner' and 'I carried a watermelon' – although perhaps you had to be there.

WHEN HARRY MET SALLY

Rob Reiner, USA, 1989

Harry (Crystal) and Sally (Ryan) meet when sharing a car trip from graduation at Chicago University to post-college life in New York City. This quickly turns into 18 hours of bickering and they conclude they have nothing in common. One important discussion point was 'Can men and women be friends without sex getting in the way?' 'No,' says Harry; 'Yes,' says Sally. Five years pass before their paths cross again and the arguing resumes. Sally now has a businessman boyfriend and Harry is engaged to be married. Another five years pass; Sally's boyfriend has gone, and Harry's wife has left him for another man. This time they sleep together. Can two friends sleep together and still love each other in the

CAST INCLUDES:
Billy Crystal, Meg Ryan, Carrie Fisher, Bruno Kirby, Steven Ford, Lisa Jane Persky, Michelle Nicastro
SCREENPLAY:
Nora Ephron
CINEMATOGRAPHY:
Barry Sonnenfeld

morning? *When Harry Met Sally* is a family affair. Rob Reiner and Nora Ephron cheerfully admit that there's a lot of Rob in Harry and a good deal of Nora in Sally. Reiner inter-slots the various stages of Harry and Sally with short interviews in which elderly couples talk about how, long ago, they met (real stories, although performed by actors), thus lending much more gravitas to the issues of coupledom. The film looks at a relationship that takes a long while to grow, with all the perils and pleasure of first being friends.

PRETTY WOMAN

Garry Marshall, USA, 1990

CAST INCLUDES:
Richard Gere, Julia Roberts,
Ralph Bellamy,
Jason Alexander,
Laura San Giacomo,
Alex Hyde-White,
Amy Yasbeck,
Elinor Donahue,
Hector Elizondo
SCREENPLAY:
J.F. Lawton
CINEMATOGRAPHY:
Charles Minsky

Out-of-towner Edward Lewis (Gere) is a ruthless, high-powered young businessman. While driving down Sunset Boulevard, he decides to pick up a prostitute – Vivian (Roberts). After a night with Viv, he asks her to stay on at his hotel: he enjoys her company and he needs a partner for social events. He gives her money to get some 'decent' clothes, but the fashion stores ignore her. However, Barney (Elizondo), the hotel manager, comes to her aid and soon she's looking properly classy. After a delightful week of events and togetherness which is full of surprises for both, commitment-phobe Edward pays Viv off – and then finds he misses her badly. Even his ruthlessness has softened since knowing her. But can he find her, and will she have him?

Pretty Woman tells of a callous man played by a mega–sex symbol who hires a hooker – for a week! – and then dumps her, and yet it's no more licentious or vicious than a warm Cinderella fairy tale (without the wicked step-family). Yet, at the same time, in Garry Marshall's hands, there's a completely straightforward element to their business dealings that merely makes them all the more accessible and friendly. Romance seldom comes in as good a package.

GHOST

Jerry Zucker, USA, 1990

CAST INCLUDES:
Patrick Swayze, Demi Moore,
Whoopi Goldberg,
Tony Goldwyn
SCREENPLAY:
Bruce Joel Rubin
CINEMATOGRAPHY:
Adam Greenberg

ACADEMY AWARDS
Best Actress in a Supporting
Role: Whoopi Goldberg
Best Writing, Screenplay
Written Directly for the
Screen: Bruce Joel Rubin

Sam (Swayze) and Molly (Moore) are very much in love. On their way home one night, a mugger shoots Sam. On regaining consciousness, he discovers that there are a lot of strange people about, and some of them walk through walls. Gradually, the 'people' he meets show him that he's a) dead, b) a ghost and c) still there because he's got a job to do. By skulking around he learns that he was intentionally murdered because he was about to uncover a crime committed by his friend Carl (Goldwyn), and now Molly is in danger. He finds pseudo-psychic Oda Mae (Goldberg), and has to convince her that she can understand him – and help Molly. Swayze and Moore are very affecting as the leads, and the film allows Whoopi Goldberg to be hilariously and Oscar-winningly splendid.

AGE OF INNOCENCE

Martin Scorsese, USA, 1993

ACADEMY AWARD
Best Costume Design:
Gabriella Pescucci

CAST INCLUDES:
Daniel Day-Lewis, Michelle
Pfeiffer, Winona Ryder,
Alexis Smith, Geraldine
Chaplin, Mary Beth Hurt, Alec
McCowen, Richard E. Grant,
Miriam Margolyes, Robert
Sean Leonard, Siân Phillips
SCREENPLAY:
Jay Cocks, Martin Scorsese
from the novel by
Edith Wharton
CINEMATOGRAPHY:
Michael Ballhaus

New York in the late 19th century, and Newland Archer (Day-Lewis) is engaged to the pretty Miss May Welland (Ryder) when Countess Ellen Olenska (Pfeiffer), May's cousin, appears on the scene. She left America to marry a dashing Polish count but, having found him unfaithful and abusive, has returned in order to divorce him. Ellen is a disturber of the status quo and, therefore, a social outcast. When this upper layer of New York society realizes that Newland has fallen in love with Ellen (in fact, with her intelligence and courageous independence as much as her beauty), they silently close ranks, determined to save Newland from himself. Nothing could be a less-obvious entry in Scorsese's filmography than this, but his main interest is the Mafia-like structure of this society. Its restrictive rules and codes are set in stone and its retributions forged in steel. Yet, heartless and claustrophobic though it appears, Newland realizes how much care went into his 'preservation', and how many sacrifices others also made.

SLEEPLESS IN SEATTLE

Nora Ephron, USA, 1993

Sam (Hanks), a recent young widower, and his son, Jonah (Malinger), are still grieving for their wife and mother when they move to Seattle for a fresh start. After a while, Jonah decides Sam is no better and what they need is a new wife and mom. Jonah phones Dr Marcia's national radio talk show, and Sam finds himself on the air baring his soul. Millions of women listen in and think they are the answer to Sam's problems – including Annie (Ryan), an engaged journalist in Baltimore. Jonah likes Annie's letter; he feels she's the one and sets up the ultimate make-or-break meeting. Often slated as a woman's movie, the comedic performances of Hanks and Ryan, not to mention the cute Jonah, save this feel-good picture from pure schmaltz. The romance flies off in all the wrong directions, as do the protagonists. However, this is a full-scale, no-holds-barred romantic screwball (which acknowledges *An Affair to Remember*, 1957) with a novel twist at the end. If you like Meg Ryan, you'll cry your eyes out in the closing scene; if you don't, then you may cry your eyes out for poor little Jonah and Sam.

CAST INCLUDES:
Tom Hanks, Meg Ryan, Bill Pullman, Ross Malinger, Rosie, O'Donnell, Gaby Hoffmann, Victor Garber, Rob Reiner
SCREENPLAY:
Nora Ephron, David S. Ward, Jeff Arch from the story by Jeff Arch
CINEMATOGRAPHY:
Sven Nykvist

THE ENGLISH PATIENT

Anthony Minghella, USA, 1996

CAST INCLUDES:
Ralph Fiennes, Juliette Binoche, Willem Dafoe, Kristin Scott Thomas, Naveen Andrews, Colin Firth, Julian Wadham, Jürgen Prochnow
SCREENPLAY:
Anthony Minghella from the novel by Michael Ondaatje
CINEMATOGRAPHY:
John Seale

Italy, in the last days of the Second World War. A badly burned man, 'the English patient', can travel no further with a hospital convoy, so nurse Hanna (Binoche) sets up a makeshift camp in which to stay and tend to him. Gradually, his memory returns. He is not English but the Hungarian Count Laszlo de Almasy (Fiennes). Based in Cairo, he met Katharine Clifton (Scott Thomas), a young woman disappointed by her husband, and soon Laszlo and Katharine are in the throes of a passionate affair. Love and tragedy, passion and violence come together in Anthony Minghella's masterful reworking of Ondaatje's 1992 Booker Prize–winning novel. Although this is a romantic epic, his characters are not allowed to get too overblown; they remain believable in this exquisitely produced and nine-Oscar-winning film.

ROMEO + JULIET

Baz Luhrmann, USA, 1996

A television anchorwoman (Moore), on the news, is announcing the tragic death of two star-crossed lovers and the incidents that led up to it. The gang war between the Montagues and the Capulets has been bad recently, resulting in a huge shoot-out at a gas station. Around that time, the parents of Juliet Capulet arrange a party at which they hope Juliet (Danes) will become engaged to the very eligible Dave Paris (Rudd). However, Romeo Montague (DiCaprio) arrives, after which he and Juliet can't take their eyes off each other. They are secretly married by Father Laurence (Postlethwaite), and hope this will bring about a truce between the families. Alas, this is not to be.

For some, Baz Luhrmann's take on *Romeo and Juliet* will be lost in a muddle of furniture and objects, a mass of jangling sounds and a whirlwind of visuals. For others, it will be visually stunning and highly entertaining. We first meet the lovers in a scene, as erotic as it is unusual, when their eyes meet through a crowded fish tank before Juliet is swept away to dance with her intended. They make love with their eyes, with their body language, with their smiles and through the fire-field of passion between them. Even impending tragedy can't dilute this moment. The youth and undoubted talents of DiCaprio and Danes made this movie a huge success with a younger audience, making Shakespeare highly accessible in the process. The timeless story of teenage love ruined by family strife had not been told for a new generation since Zeffirelli's masterpiece in 1968.

CAST INCLUDES:
Leonardo DiCaprio, Claire Danes, Diane Venora, Miriam Margolyes, John Leguizamo, Harold Perrineau, Carlos Martín Manzo Otálora, Paul Sorvino, Brian Dennehy, Pete Postlethwaite, Paul Rudd
SCREENPLAY:
Craig Pearce, Baz Luhrmann from the play by William Shakespeare
CINEMATOGRAPHY:
Donald (M.) McAlpine

TITANIC

James Cameron, USA, 1997

CAST INCLUEDS:
Leonardo DiCaprio, Kate Winslet, Billy Zane, Kathy Bates, Bill Paxton, Gloria Stuart, Frances Fisher, Bernard Hill Jonathan Hyde, David Warner, Victor Garber
SCREENPLAY:
James Cameron
CINEMATOGRAPHY:
Russell Carpenter

ACADEMY AWARDS

Best Art Direction-Set Decoration
Best Cinematography
Best Costume Design
Best Director
Best Effects, Sound Effects Editing
Best Effects, Visual Effects
Best Film Editing
Best Music, Original Dramatic Score
Best Music, Original Song: for 'My Heart Will Go On'
Best Picture
Best Sound

A treasure hunter (Paxton), looking for a diamond in the wreck of the *Titanic*, discovers in a safe the nude picture of a young woman. After it is shown on television, Rose Dawson (Stuart), aged 101, comes forward. She, Rose (Winslet), was that young girl on the ship. She was travelling with her mother (Fisher) and a wealthy man (Zane), whom she desperately didn't want to marry. She was about to throw herself over the rails when she was stopped by Jack (DiCaprio), a young man who had won his steerage ticket in a poker game. They fell in love and spent every moment together until the iceberg broke the ship apart. Even then, they determined to stay together.

James Cameron spent a huge budget and five extra months on perfecting his *Titanic*. Most people know the story and many of the statistics. His aim, therefore, was to show the human heart of this disaster and the sheer scale of the *Titanic* itself. He takes us there: into the state rooms, the dining rooms, the cabins and the engine rooms – first kitted out and decorated as they should be, and then with everything undone by water. Having got the outer scale of this tragedy in place, he tells the inner story through the heartbreak of a third-class boy and a first-class girl.

AS GOOD AS IT GETS

James L. Brooks, USA, 1997

CAST INCLUDES:
Jack Nicholson, Helen Hunt,
Greg Kinnear, Cuba Gooding
Jr., Skeet Ulrich,
Shirley Knight,
Yeardley Smith
SCREENPLAY:
Mark Andrus,
James L. Brooks from the
story by Mark Andrus
CINEMATOGRAPHY:
John Bailey

Melvin Udall (Nicholson) is a famous writer of romantic fiction, although the 'real' Melvin is a rude, selfish, obsessive-compulsive misanthrope. However, at the only restaurant where he will eat (using his own plastic cutlery), waitress Carol (Hunt) tolerates him fondly. When gay neighbour Simon (Kinnear) is beaten up one night, Melvin is prevailed upon to look after Melvin's dog, Verdell, and his icy, previously dogophobic heart begins to thaw a little. Then, when Carol leaves the restaurant to look after her asthmatic son, he's shocked to discover how upset he is – and not just about the change to his routine. Nicholson is at his best when he's at his nastiest, and Melvin is a perfect (and Oscar-winning) Nicholson part. Hunt also won an Oscar for her role as the long-suffering Carol.

HUA YANG NIAN HUA (IN THE MOOD FOR LOVE)

Kar Wai Wong, Hong Kong/France, 2000

CAST INCLUDES:
Maggie Cheung, Tony Leung,
Siu Pinglam, Tung Cho 'Joe'
Cheung (as Cheun Tung Joe),
Rebecca Pan, Lui Chun
SCREENPLAY:
Kar Wai Wong
CINEMATOGRAPHY:
Christopher Doyle,
Mark Lee (Li Pingbin)

Hong Kong, 1962. Two couples have just rented rooms next-door to each other in a cramped apartment building. First, there is newspaper editor Chow Mo-Wan (Leung) and his wife. The second couple are Su Li-zhen (Cheung), a beautiful secretary who is now Mrs Chan, and her executive husband. With their spouses often away, Chow and Li-zhen spend most of their time together as friends. They have everything in common from noodle shops to martial arts. Then, they are shocked to discover that their spouses are having an affair. Hurt and angry, they find comfort in their growing friendship even as they resolve to remain true to their marriage vows, even if their spouses are not. Wong Kar Wai is noted for shooting without a script and for visuals that are dripping with colour and moods of all kinds. Maggie Cheung and Tony Leung are two of the biggest stars in Asia. The combination results in a stunning movie. Drawn to each other first out of lust and then from escalating desire, this honourable pair faces, every day, the double pain of rejection by their spouses and the new, unrequited-love scenario into which they've put themselves. Together, director and actors eroticize this sexual tension to a point where it seems impossible that their resolve can hold.

PUNCH-DRUNK LOVE

Paul Thomas Anderson, USA, 2002

CAST INCLUDES:
Adam Sandler, Jason
Andrews, Don McManus,
Emily Watson
SCREENPLAY:
Paul Thomas Anderson
CINEMATOGRAPHY:
Robert Elswit

Barry Egan (Sandler), a small businessman with anger issues and a devotion to collecting air miles, falls in love with the unusual Lena (Watson). Obstacles ranging from Barry's unpredictable rage to his seven crazed sisters conspire to hamper their relationship. From the obligatory stint on TV's *Saturday Night Live* through early film hits like *The Wedding Singer*, by the late '90s Adam Sandler had become one of the most successful mainstream American comics of his generation. But while contemporaries like Jim Carrey and Ben Stiller had found success with more challenging material, Sandler was typecast as the guy who just got angry and smashed stuff up. It must have seemed rather unlikely that an art-house film would come along that required such a character, but director Paul Thomas Anderson is a fairly unlikely filmmaker. Keen to do something completely different and wanting a broad commercial hit, Anderson and Sandler moulded the air-miles-obsessed Egan into what is essentially a more rounded and developed version of Sandler's established screen persona, which will be quite a shock for anyone familiar with it. As with Jim Carrey and *The Truman Show*, *Punch-Drunk Love* gave Sandler an instant credibility that he's still tapping today.

BEFORE SUNSET

Richard Linklater, USA, 2004

CAST INCLUDES:
Ethan Hawke, Julie Delpy,
Vernon Dobtcheff
SCREENPLAY:
Richard Linklater, Julie Delpy,
Ethan Hawke
CINEMATOGRAPHY:
Lee Daniel

Nine years after a brief liaison, Jesse (Hawke), an American writer, and Celine (Delpy), a French environmentalist, meet again when Jesse visits Paris as part of a book tour. With only a few hours before Jesse must leave, they wander the streets of Paris. After first introducing us to Jesse and Celine in *Before Sunrise* in 1995, director Richard Linklater has chosen to revisit the formerly young romantics to show how the intervening decade has changed them. In the first film, wide-eyed students Jesse and Celine meet, fall in love and then must part. *Before Sunset* examines a much more interesting scenario with the two meeting again, but this time with responsibilities. As they stroll around Paris, the way in which awkward niceties soon give way to deeper discussions of love, life and regret suggests the pair still share a common chemistry and strong feelings for each other. As before, Hawke and Delpy are incredible, their sparing and realistic acting styles so perfectly in tune they don't seem to be acting at all, whilst the film itself displays a rare honesty and charm that surpasses even that of its predecessor.

ETERNAL SUNSHINE OF THE SPOTLESS MIND

Michel Gondry, USA, 2004

CAST INCLUDES:
Jim Carrey, Kate Winslet,
Gerry Robert Byrne,
Elijah Wood
SCREENPLAY:
Charlie Kaufman
CINEMATOGRAPHY:
Ellen Kuras

When Joel (Carrey) discovers ex-girlfriend Clementine (Winslet) has undergone a procedure to remove all memory of their relationship, he decides to do the same. As memories of their time together flood through his mind on their way to the recycle bin, Joel begins to wonder if they did the right thing in splitting up. After a shaky start to his filmmaking career with 2001's *Human Nature*, director Michel Gondry struck gold with this unconventional romance. Scripted by the only screenwriter bold enough to try and show the entire arc of a relationship from start to finish (wunderkind Charlie Kaufman), *Eternal Sunshine* is a touching, intelligent and surreal fairy tale about the importance of realizing what you have before it's gone. Carrey plays down the crazed loon aspect of his persona in favour of the sort of superbly played vulnerability we see too little of from him. Carrey's is actually the less dynamic screen presence, with Winslet's pixyish Clementine bursting with a vivacious exuberance that will charm even the most cynical of viewers. Mystifying, melancholy and moving in equal measure.

SLUMDOG MILLIONAIRE

Danny Boyle, GB, 2008

Jamal Malik (Patel), an 18-year-old orphan from the streets of Mumbai, finds himself competing on TV game show *Who Wants to Be a Millionaire*. His unexpected success leads police to become suspicious and he is arrested for cheating. During his police interview, Malik recounts the story of his life, explaining how he came to know the answer to each question in the quiz. When director Danny Boyle started filming Vikas Swarup's novel *Q&A*, he can't have had any idea it would lead to him being named Best Director at the 2009 Academy Awards, and the film itself achieving Best Picture. It won eight Oscars in total. Like many of the best 'uplifting' films it can be dark. Boyle knows the final emotional payoff is entirely dependent on what has come before, and as a result doesn't flinch from showing us the appalling circumstances under which his characters live. The mantra of 'the more you invest, the bigger your reward' has never been better demonstrated on film.

CAST INCLUDES: Dev Patel, Freida Pinto, Rubina Ali, Ayush Mahesh Khedekar, Madhur Mittal, Anil Kapoor
SCREENPLAY: Simon Beaufoy, Vikas Swarup (novel)
CINEMATOGRAPHY: Anthony Dod Mantle

SCIENCE FICTION & FANTASY

METROPOLIS

Fritz Lang, Germany, 1927

CAST INCLUDES:
Alfred Abel, Gustav Fröhlich,
Brigitte Helm, Rudolf Klein-
Rogge, Fritz Rasp
SCREENPLAY:
Fritz Lang from the novel by
Thea von Harbou
CINEMATOGRAPHY:
Karl Freund, Günther Rittau

Some time in the future, society has split into two distinct groups. The thinkers, who live in luxurious penthouses, and the workers, who toil in mines. The leader's son, Freder Frederson (Fröhlich), visits the mines to witness firsthand the roots of his society, but discovers a people on the verge of revolution. Georges Méliès may have travelled to the moon in 1914, but *Metropolis* marks the birth of the true science-fiction film, laying down a framework of themes and stylistic concepts that have changed very little in nearly 80 years. Virtually all of the genre's worthwhile additions have been influenced in some way by Fritz Lang's inspired and ambitious film. As with many classics from the silent era, numerous cuts have appeared on home video and DVD over the years, varying hugely in picture quality, but even the murkiest transfer can't obscure the film's rich, gothic, production design and incredible visual style. Beautiful skyscrapers reach above the clouds while claustrophobic mine shafts burrow into the ground. The potent visuals stay in the mind long after the film has ended. The army of workers shuffling to and fro, the Tower of Babel and the giant clock all leave indelible images, and there are countless other impressive achievements to discover upon watching this truly spectacular film.

LOST HORIZON

Frank Capra, USA, 1937

CAST INCLUDES:
Ronald Colman, Jane Wyatt,
John Howard, Margo,
Thomas Mitchell
SCREENPLAY:
Robert Riskin from the novel
by James Hilton
CINEMATOGRAPHY:
Joseph Walker

ACADEMY AWARDS
Best Art Direction:
Stephen Goosson
Best Film Editing:
Gene Havlick, Gene Milford

Famous British diplomat Bob Conway (Colman) is kidnapped and taken to the surreal Tibetan settlement of Shangri-La. At first, he and his four companions are intent on escape, but its strange, supernatural appeal begins to win them over. One of the most impressive and spectacular films of the era, it was made and released between world wars. Conway is a man dedicated to ending war; early on in the film he hypothesizes that when made foreign secretary, he will lay down Britain's arms and others will follow his lead. In Shangri-La, he and his companions find a place where just such a thing has happened. Beautiful and enchanting, virtual immortality is assured, as is the complete absence of disputes, needs and problems of any kind — something that appeals immediately to Conway.

THE DAY THE EARTH STOOD STILL

Robert Wise, USA, 1951

A flying saucer lands in Washington, sending the world into a state of paranoia. Its two occupants are Klaatu (Rennie), a humanoid, and Gort (Martin), his robot. Their warnings to mankind of the dangers of atomic power prove difficult to accept. Robert Wise's impeccably produced classic differs substantially from standard 1950s sci-fi hokum. Based on a short story by Harry Bates, the film largely avoids the exploitation of America's Cold War paranoia, opting instead to issue a warning of mankind's potential for atomic self-destruction. The alien visitor charged with relaying this message of peace hardly receives a warm welcome. Justifying his race's concerns about us, Klaatu is met with violence and distrust upon his arrival. After being shot

and arrested by the jittery military authorities, our society receives some redemption at the hands of an imaginative young boy, Bobby (Gray), and his liberal mother, Helen (Neal). It's the open-minded who are presented as our potential saviours, whilst the petty ignorance and reactionary approach of the media and government prove to be our greatest liability. *The Day the Earth Stood Still* is probably the best and most rewarding of the 1950s' political sci-fi movie cycle. Featuring an excellent score from Hitchcock collaborator Bernard Herrmann, impressive effects and great performances, the film is as enjoyable and relevant today as it must have been on its release.

CAST INCLUDES:
Michael Rennie, Patricia Neal,
Billy Gray, Lock Martin
SCREENPLAY:
Edmund H. North from
Harry Bates story *Farewell
to the Master*
CINEMATOGRAPHY:
Leo Tover

WAR OF THE WORLDS

Byron Haskin, USA, 1953

Aliens from Mars seek to colonize Earth by means of invasion and the total annihilation of the human race. When the military prove to be inadequate, a group of scientists battle against the odds to find a solution. Given the subject and the timing, one might expect *War of the Worlds* to be a flagship of 1950s' Cold War paranoia movies, but at times it seems keen to convince us otherwise. There are many references to nations uniting against a common foe, with information and ideas constantly exchanged between countries. Although no Communist nations are evident in the alliance that forms, the extent of our awareness of other nations within the story is unusual for the time, as are the numerous shots of international landmarks being destroyed. America's military are presented as woefully inadequate, and its greedy, selfish citizens destroy the best hope for survival – hardly propaganda filmmaking. As a result of this more even-handed approach, it's easier to enjoy the film in its own right.

ACADEMY AWARD
Best Effects, Special Effects:
Gordon Jennings

CAST INCLUDES:
Gene Barry, Ann Robinson,
Les Tremayne, Robert
Cornthwaite
SCREENPLAY:
Barré Lyndon from the
novel by H.G. Wells
CINEMATOGRAPHY:
George Barnes

FORBIDDEN PLANET

Fred M. Wilcox, USA, 1956

CAST INCLUDES:
Walter Pidgeon, Anne
Francis, Leslie Nielsen,
Robby the Robot
SCREENPLAY:
Irving Block, Allen Adler,
Cyril Hume, based on
William Shakespeare's play
The Tempest
CINEMATOGRAPHY:
George J. Folsey

After contact with the colonists of distant planet Altair 4 is lost, a spaceship is dispatched to investigate. The crew find only two survivors – the others have apparently been killed by a strange creature – but the planet holds more surprises. A sci-fi movie with a substantial budget was an unusual thing in the 1950s; even more unusual was the decision to shoot in colour. Basing the story on William Shakespeare's *The Tempest* completes the film's trilogy of baffling facts. But it all makes sense when you consider MGM made *Forbidden Planet* to take advantage of the massive popularity of sci-fi B-movies, reasoning that a lavishly produced colour epic, partly written by the definitive star writer, would be even more successful than the cheap exploitation movies so popular at drive-ins. As a result, the film avoids the era's genre clichés. Instead the intention seems to be to make a glossy but intelligent family adventure movie within the liberating framework of science fiction.

INVASION OF THE BODY SNATCHERS

Don Siegel, USA, 1956

CAST INCLUDES:
Kevin McCarthy, Dana Wynter, Larry Gates, King Donovan
SCREENPLAY:
Richard Collins, Jack Finney, Daniel Mainwaring
CINEMATOGRAPHY:
Ellsworth Fredericks

Local doctor Miles Bennell (McCarthy) returns to his hometown of Santa Mira to find numerous patients claiming their relatives have been replaced by imposters. His suspicions aroused, it's not long before he discovers the horrible truth. Shot in 19 days for just $300,000, Don Siegel's potent Cold War classic is one of the era's defining movies. Irrelevant to the way in which the ambiguous allegories are interpreted (anti-McCarthyist, anti-Communist, anti-conformity, etc.), it remains a highly effective exercise in paranoia. The film's great success lies primarily in its observations of everyday life. An invader mimicking normal human activity in order to go unnoticed, but with an indefinable uniformity to its mannerisms, is just enough to chill the spine, making for more uneasy viewing than any number of monsters in flying saucers attacking American landmarks. *Invasion of the Body Snatchers* is a good old-fashioned B-movie with an unusually potent concoction of classic genre allegory and social commentary. After watching it, close study of friends and family is unavoidable.

JASON AND THE ARGONAUTS

Don Chaffey, USA, 1963

The son of a fallen king, Jason gathers the best athletes and warriors in Greece. Supposedly aided by the gods, he sets sail for the end of the world, where he hopes to find the magical golden fleece that will bring him to power. The name of a special effects artist isn't something one expects to see above a film's title, but to genre fans, Ray Harryhausen's name has been a byword for fantasy and imaginative stop-motion for 50 years. Although he would make more films (*Clash of the Titans, One Million Years BC*), Harryhausen considers *Jason* to be the culmination of his technique and career. The film uses Greek mythology as a backdrop, allowing for a succession of impressive monster-themed set pieces and

CAST INCLUDES:
Todd Armstrong, Nancy Kovack, Gary Raymond, Laurence Naismith, Niall MacGinnis
SCREENPLAY:
Beverley Cross, Jan Read
CINEMATOGRAPHY:
Wilkie Cooper

the presence of the gods themselves, pulling the strings of mankind from Mount Olympus. The highlight of the film, and Harryhausen's definitive creation, are the skeleton warriors Jason must defeat in the film's finale. A triumph of creativity over available technology, they launch into hand-to-hand combat with the real actors. It was nearly 30 years before CGI could render such imaginative animation in a more technically convincing manner, and even now there is no way to replicate the charm.

DR STRANGELOVE OR: HOW I LEARNED TO STOP WORRYING AND LOVE THE BOMB

Stanley Kubrick, GB, 1964

CAST INCLUDES:
Peter Sellers, George C. Scott, Sterling Hayden, Slim Pickens, Peter Bull
SCREENPLAY:
Stanley Kubrick, Terry Southern and Peter George from his novel *Red Alert*, aka *Two Hours to Doom*
CINEMATOGRAPHY:
Gilbert Taylor

Insane Air Force Brigadier General Jack D. Ripper (Hayden) issues the 'go' code to his bomber wing through fear of an eventual Communist invasion. While the planes armed with nuclear bombs head for their Russian targets, US President Merkin Muffley tries to find a way to minimize the inevitable international carnage.

Whilst trying to adapt Peter George's *Red Alert*, a serious novel about a holocaust caused by inflexible military and political policy, Kubrick realized it was impossible to make a straight movie of the ridiculous scenario. A switch to satire proved much more successful, and allowed for a second collaboration between Kubrick and Peter Sellers (the first being their auspicious partnership on *Lolita* two years earlier).

Sellers is awesome, playing three of the film's five main roles. Strangelove (a former Nazi scientist now researching weapon systems for the Americans) is a fantastic comic creation, a man completely unable to control a bizarre affliction which causes him to refer to the president as '*mein Führer*' and randomly perform Nazi salutes. The film treads a dangerously fine line between horrific bad taste and powerful satire. Fortunately the judgement is consistently spot on.

PLANET OF THE APES

Franklin J. Schaffner, USA, 1968

CAST INCLUDES:
Charlton Heston, Roddy
McDowall, Kim Hunter,
Maurice Evans, Linda Harrison
SCREENPLAY:
Michael Wilson, Rod Serling
from the novel by Pierre Boulle
CINEMATOGRAPHY:
Leon Shamroy

Astronaut George Taylor (Heston) crash-lands on an unknown planet. He is soon captured by its dominant inhabitants, an advanced society of apes capable of speech and with a rudimentary grasp of technology. *Planet of the Apes* quickly became a sensation when it was released in 1968. It was the first film to generate widespread merchandising, in addition to spawning four direct sequels and spin-off television and cartoon shows. But before the formula was impoverished, the film had some very salient points to make about 1960s' concerns. Effectively holding a mirror up to mankind, the ape society is a slightly exaggerated reflection of our own. Segregated into strict classes, the apes treat the indigenous, speechless humans like animals. Faced with the unknown, the apes respond in a typically human manner, reacting with fear.

2001: A SPACE ODYSSEY

Stanley Kubrick , USA, 1968

A monolith, previously seen to stimulate the evolution of primitive apes, is discovered buried on the moon. Once uncovered, it sends a radio signal towards Jupiter. In an attempt to learn more about it, the spaceship *Discovery* is dispatched to the signal's destination. Starting with the origin of man and ending with the next stage of our evolution, Kubrick could hardly have anticipated how ambitious the project would become when he first met author Arthur C. Clarke and suggested they collaborate on 'the proverbial good science-fiction picture'. After ransacking Clarke's oeuvre, they settled on a short story, *The Sentinel*, that would form the basis of the film. The completed screenplay presented numerous challenges. Aside from the technical difficulties, the story called for a total absence of dialogue in the first and last half-hour, while the bulk of the film features just three characters, one of which is a computer. This minimalist narrative style only serves to emphasize the enormous themes Clarke and Kubrick set out to tackle.

ACADEMY AWARD
Best Effects, Special Visual
Effects: Stanley Kubrick

CAST INCLUDES:
Keir Dullea, Gary Lockwood,
William Sylvester,
Douglas Rain
SCREENPLAY:
Stanley Kubrick, Arthur C.
Clarke (from his short story)
CINEMATOGRAPHY:
Geoffrey Unsworth

A CLOCKWORK ORANGE

Stanley Kubrick, GB, 1971

In a violent future, society is on the verge of crumbling. A revolutionary new process, designed to reform criminals in the minimum time possible, is tested on convicted murderer Alex (McDowell) with mixed results.

Stanley Kubrick never made a film that didn't court controversy, but *A Clockwork Orange* caused more than all his previous work combined. Blamed for almost every crime of the day, the film was eventually withdrawn from release in the UK at the request of the director, but only after his family received death threats (technically it was never banned as urban legend claims). Accusations that the film endorses violence are laughable; although the attire and dialogue of the protagonist may have been adopted by self-conscious sociopaths of the time, the film's 136 minutes of gruelling violence (much of it suffered by Alex) is hard to accept as incitement. However, such indictments haven't affected the film's true purpose and power. Novelist Anthony Burgess's warning of a dystopian future in which criminal gangs and violent yobs maraud freely, with little concern for prosecution, has proved more prophetic than he could have imagined (similarly, the violence depicted in the film doesn't seem extreme by modern cinema standards). This ensures the film's primary themes of social commentary resonate just as well today. Stylish, terrifying, influential, brutal; there are few adjectives one cannot apply to *A Clockwork Orange*.

CAST INCLUDES:
Malcolm McDowell, Patrick Magee, Michael Bates, Warren Clarke, John Clive
SCREENPLAY:
Stanley Kubrick from the novel by Anthony Burgess
CINEMATOGRAPHY:
John Alcott

SILENT RUNNING
Douglas Trumbull, USA, 1972

CAST INCLUDES:
Bruce Dern, Cliff Potts,
Ron Rifkin, Jesse Vint
SCREENPLAY:
Deric Washburn, Michael
Cimino, Steven Bochco
CINEMATOGRAPHY:
Charles F. Wheeler

In the future, all plant life on Earth has died out and the only remaining specimens orbit in giant glass globes attached to spaceships. Lowell Freeman (Dern) is a botanist responsible for maintaining one of the vessels. A devoted naturalist, he is devastated when instructions come through ordering the destruction of the globes. In 1972, Douglas Trumbull, a renowned special-effects artist, was ready to step behind the camera. With environmental concerns more prominent in the post-1960s' era, he chose to marry ecological themes with his own innovative special-effects techniques, simultaneously making a potent statement and creating the aesthetic juxtapositions that define the film's visual style. The sight of his (totally convincing) spaceships, each with visible forests and gardens safely contained within enormous glass bubbles, is one of the most inspiring visions of the genre. The powerful central performance, contrasting style (heightened by folk-queen Joan Baez's soundtrack) and compelling message make it one of the most unusual and valuable films of the time.

SOLARIS (SOLYARIS)
Andrei Tarkovsky, USSR, 1972

CAST INCLUDES:
Natalya Bondarchuk,
Donatas Banionis, Jüri
Järvet, Nikolai Grinko,
Vladislav Dvorzhetsky
SCREENPLAY:
Stanislaw Lem (novel),
Fridrikh Gorenshtein,
Andrei Tarkovsky
CINEMATOGRAPHY:
Vadim Yusov

Psychologist Kris Kelvin (Banionis) is sent to Solaris, a space station monitoring a planet of the same name. The ocean world has many strange, unexplained properties, and as Kelvin soon discovers, it seems to be affecting the crew on board the station. Tarkovsky's meditation on guilt, desire, religion and the nature of the human conscience is a powerful and ambitious vision. Intellectually gruelling and hugely demanding, it is often compared to Stanley Kubrick's *2001: A Space Odyssey*, sharing a hypnotic pace, incredible atmosphere, and determination to tackle the most ambitious subjects. The planet can be seen as a representation of God, something the scientists are unable to understand by the mere application of established theories. Kelvin's eventual acceptance of its influence requires him to relinquish his scientific beliefs and embrace something that he can never understand. The planet's emotionally tortuous influence on the crew is to impose a deceased loved one upon them. In Kelvin's case, his guilt and regret over the death of former wife, Hari (Bondarchuk), is interpreted, and the woman materializes on the station. We witness Kelvin's changing reaction to her, along with the change in his own personality, portrayed with a detailed, well-judged and ambiguous performance from Banionis.

SLEEPER

Woody Allen, USA, 1973

CAST INCLUDES:
Woody Allen, Diane Keaton,
John Beck, Mary Gregory
SCREENPLAY:
Woody Allen,
Marshall Brickman
CINEMATOGRAPHY:
David M. Walsh

In 2173, Miles Monroe, a clarinet player and owner of a New York health food store, is brought out of cryogenic suspension by radical scientists in order to carry out a mission that will hopefully lead to the toppling of the oppressive government state. Unfortunately, he becomes separated from the militants and wanders around lost in a bizarre future.

Woody Allen's only real excursion into sci-fi (despite *Zelig* and numerous other flirtations with the genre) is also one of his most popular films. Deciding the visual freedom afforded by an imaginary, futuristic reality would suit a more physical performance, Allen employs many tricks used in the silent era by the likes of Harold Lloyd and Keystone Kops, adding to the plethora of comedy styles he experiments with throughout the film. Whilst relying on the sci-fi comedy cornerstone – the premise that nothing works in the future – he also pokes fun at the ignorance of our future selves. The fascist government of *Sleeper* bears some similarity to those of *Brazil*, *Fahrenheit 451* and *Metropolis*, but Allen's approach is very different here. Instead of cleverly exposing the flaws of an overbearing state, Allen just mocks it, presenting the authorities as a bunch of buffoons not worthy of a more intelligent or satirical assault. *Sleeper* is one of the most accessible films of Allen's early career. Concise and consistently funny, it's a benchmark of sci-fi comedy.

CAST INCLUDES:
Yul Brynner, Richard
Benjamin, James Brolin
SCREENPLAY:
Michael Crichton
CINEMATOGRAPHY:
Gene Polito

WESTWORLD

Michael Crichton, USA, 1973

An enormous theme park re-creates three historic environments, complete with robotic characters and extraordinary attention to detail. Two wealthy visitors (Benjamin and Brolin) inadvertently offend the meanest robot gunslinger in town (Brynner), who embarks on a vendetta when the machines go haywire. Dealing with almost exactly the same subject as his later film adaptation, *Jurassic Park*, Michael Crichton makes his point in a more subtle and simple manner here. As in his subsequent dino-thriller, Crichton meditates on the ramifications of mankind's ability to play God, but there are some interesting changes. Where *Jurassic Park* was a romantic optimist's dream, *Westworld* is a commercially motivated corporate resort. This crucial difference allows the film to play with more intellectually satisfying (though perhaps less exhilarating and astounding) themes like consumerism and capitalism. Its greatest success lies in the Gunslinger's protracted, relentless pursuit of Benjamin's character. Crichton draws every last bit of tension imaginable from the basic premise, his successful treatment clearly inspiring James Cameron's *Terminator*.

DARK STAR

John Carpenter, USA, 1974

CAST INCLUDES:
Brian Narelle, Cal Kuniholm,
Dre Pahich, Dan O'Bannon
SCREENPLAY:
John Carpenter, Dan
O'Bannon
CINEMATOGRAPHY:
Douglas Knapp

Four very bored men have been travelling through deep space for 20 years. Their job is to destroy unstable planets, making the area safe for settlement. Starting life as a student film, Carpenter later found funding to expand his 'hippie sci-fi' short into a feature-length comedy. Spoofing *2001: A Space Odyssey* (a tagline was cheeky enough to proclaim it 'A Spaced-Out Odyssey'), one of the film's cleverest aspects is the spoofing of *2001*'s themes as well as the format. Where Kubrick and others use man's reliance on fundamentally flawed technology to draw attention to our dehumanization, Carpenter uses it as a comedic device. The eponymous spaceship has been clattering about the universe for 20 years and is riddled with malfunctions. It's a shame Carpenter has seldom returned to comedy – based on this evidence, his gift is immense. In *Dark Star,* he and collaborator Dan O'Bannon have made the most intelligent and influential sci-fi comedy of them all.

CLOSE ENCOUNTERS OF THE THIRD KIND

Steven Spielberg, USA, 1977

CAST INCLUDES:
Richard Dreyfuss, François
Truffaut, Teri Garr, Melinda
Dillon, Bob Balaban
SCREENPLAY:
Steven Spielberg
CINEMATOGRAPHY:
William A. Fraker, Douglas
Slocombe, Vilmos Zsigmond

An Indiana everyman is one of a small group of people to witness a group of UFOs. The encounter leaves him obsessively attempting to mould a shape implanted in his mind, as he becomes increasingly disengaged from his family. 'We are not alone', ran the tagline for *Close Encounters*, the film in which Steven Spielberg laid down his manifesto for popular cinema domination. He had already had a huge hit with *Jaws* two years earlier, but here we see all his trademark beats together for the first time. A difficult father-son relationship (as well as an absent father/lost child scenario), shadowy authorities, and a plucky mother coping with it all – Spielberg has never been afraid to tell personal stories. Yet, as with many of his films, it's also quite dark. Roy Neary's (Dreyfuss) descent into madness is every bit as real and disturbing as one might expect, eventually costing him his family. *Close Encounters* may not be perfect, but one would need ice for blood not to be touched by its innocent charm and infectious sense of wonder.

ACADEMY AWARDS
Best Cinematography:
Vilmos Zsigmond
Special Achievement Award:
Frank Warner for sound
effects editing

STAR WARS: EPISODE IV – A NEW HOPE

George Lucas, USA, 1977

CAST INCLUDES:
Mark Hamill, Harrison Ford,
Carrie Fisher, Alec Guinness,
David Prowse
SCREENPLAY:
George Lucas
CINEMATOGRAPHY:
Gilbert Taylor

ACADEMY AWARDS

Best Art Direction-
Set Decoration:
John Barry,
Norman Reynolds,
Leslie Dilley, Roger Christian
Best Costume Design:
John Mollo
Best Effects, Visual Effects:
John Stears, John Dykstra,
Richard Edlund, Grant
McCune, Robert Blalack
Best Film Editing:
Paul Hirsch, Marcia Lucas,
Richard Chew
Best Music, Original Score:
John Williams
Best Sound:
Don MacDougall, Ray West,
Bob Minkler, Derek Ball

A naïve young farm boy (Hamill), a mystical old sage (Guinness) and a smuggler (Ford) get caught up in an intergalactic rebellion. After directing *THX1138* and the hugely successful *American Graffiti*, George Lucas found himself in great demand in 1974. *Apocalypse Now* looked to be next on his slate, having been prepped by collaborator Francis Ford Coppola, and suitably in keeping with the young director's previous mature and intelligent work. Instead, he surprised everyone by heading off to England to make a Flash Gordon movie with tin robots, space wizards and a seven-foot dog.

The film's success at the box office (and in exploiting its promotional and merchandizing potential) is now legendary. If you adjust for inflation, the worldwide gross stands at nearly $2 billion, and that doesn't include revenue from sequels, video games and merchandise. Nor does it reflect the large proportion of the populace who consider the film an abomination. Quite why it remains so divisive is hard to understand. There are certainly flaws, particularly in the dialogue and performances, but these are generally no more relevant to the film's critics than to its fans, detractors preferring to cite vague concerns over the film's influence on Hollywood's increasing commercialism. But that is to miss the point entirely. It is inevitable that success will bring about change in any industry; we should be grateful that the film that became the medium's most popular offspring is one of such charm, innocence and all-round quality. The score is one of the greatest ever recorded, the effects are photo-real, the production design is timeless and the whole thing is stuck together with a masterly ability for storytelling.

For most of the generation lucky enough to discover *Star Wars* before its formula was imitated and diluted, it remains the shared, innocent and fantastical experience we remember from childhood, and nothing can change that.

SUPERMAN

Richard Donner, USA, 1978

A small boy is sent to Earth from a dying alien world. Blessed with superpowers, he becomes a crime-fighter in the city of Metropolis whilst his alter ego works as a newspaper reporter.

In 1973, 28-year-old Ilya Salkind pitched the idea of a Superman movie to his producer father Alexander. Although popular as cartoons, television shows and serials, comic books weren't considered suitable for feature-film adaptation, but the Salkinds were convinced it would work. Eventually gaining finance from Warners (who were to distribute but not produce), the film started shooting in March 1977 with Richard Donner (in demand after *The Omen*) at the helm. But a troubled preproduction (original director, *James Bond* legend Guy Hamilton, was forced to drop out at the last minute) rolled straight into a troubled shoot, with a titanic power struggle between the Salkinds and Donner. The European producers weren't interested in Superman the American icon, envisioning instead a campy, kitsch hero closer to the Batman series. Although Donner prevailed, his insistence on taking his time and doing it properly caused the abandonment of *Superman 2* (being shot simultaneously).

Donner's bullish perseverance would certainly pay dividends, his excellent judgement allowing for plenty of comedy without the loss of dignity. Reeve is superb as both Superman and alter ego Clark Kent, while the clever casting of Brando and Hackman adds a legitimacy to the film's claims of sophistication and sincerity. The success in realizing this claim is probably *Superman*'s most lasting influence – the comic-book adaptation golden rule: respect the characters at all costs.

CAST INCLUDES:
Christopher Reeve, Marlon Brando, Gene Hackman, Margot Kidder, Ned Beatty
SCREENPLAY:
Mario Puzo, David Newman, Leslie Newman, Robert Benton, Tom Mankiewicz, from Jerry Siegel & Joe Shuster's comic
CINEMATOGRAPHY:
Geoffrey Unsworth

ACADEMY AWARD
Special Achievement Award For Visual Effects:
Les Bowie, Colin Chilvers, Denys N. Coop, Roy Field, Derek Meddings, Zoran Perisic

ALIEN

Ridley Scott, GB, 1979

CAST INCLUDES:
Tom Skerritt, Sigourney Weaver, Harry Dean Stanton, John Hurt, Ian Holm, Yaphet Kotto
SCREENPLAY:
Dan O'Bannon, Ronald Shusett
CINEMATOGRAPHY:
Derek Vanlint

The deep-space mining ship *Nostromo* responds to a distress call from an uncharted planet. Some of the crew go aboard an ancient alien vessel on the surface, but after discovering the distress signal is actually a warning, they leave. However, one of them has already become host to a gestating alien. Ridley Scott's bold decision to focus on suspense and strong characterization was highly successful – tension between officers and engineers is exposed with great authenticity, as is the misogyny suffered by the film's superbly conceived and realized central character, Ellen Ripley (Weaver), whose perceived vulnerability makes her scenes of confrontation more interesting, even after her formidable character and superior endurance skills have become evident. The production design is breathtaking, and the alien itself is amongst the most memorable cinematic creations of its kind. The monster is terrifying, providing Scott with fantastic material on which to build the tension. The scenes of the crew searching the ship's cavernous chambers would have Alfred Hitchcock watching through his fingers.

MAD MAX 2: THE ROAD WARRIOR

George Miller, Australia, 1981

CAST INCLUDES:
Mel Gibson, Bruce Spence, Michael Preston, Max Phipps
SCREENPLAY:
Terry Hayes, George Miller, Brian Hannant
CINEMATOGRAPHY:
Dean Semler

After the death of his family in the first film, Max (Gibson) continues to roam the post-apocalyptic wastelands of Australia. Civilization has broken down still further, and fuel is now the most valuable commodity. After discovering an encampment under threat from a gang of thugs, he pledges to help the inhabitants. With the dark tone and brutal character of the eponymous antihero already established in the original film, returning co-writer/director George Miller is able to spend the first half of *Mad Max 2* illustrating the desperate situation in which society now finds itself. The desolate environment stifles all optimism, but Max is well equipped for life here – he is as much a part of the landscape as the opportunistic thieves and marauding gangs he encounters. But it's obvious a man like Max needs a mission, and the desert encampment he discovers provides him with one. The film's fantastic second half is essentially a protracted and violent car chase that sees Max attempt to drive a tanker truck, containing the only known fuel reserves, to safety. With a specific (and wonderfully simple) aim, Max and the film come alive. Shot and edited with a loose creativity that makes the audience really feel a part of the action, Miller is highly successful in wringing every last gruesome idea out of the simple concept.

SCANNERS

David Cronenberg, Canada, 1981

CAST INCLUDES:
Jennifer O'Neill, Stephen Lack, Patrick McGoohan, Lawrence Dane, Michael Ironside
SCREENPLAY:
David Cronenberg
CINEMATOGRAPHY:
Mark Irwin

A secret subculture of powerful telepaths led by Darryl Revok (*Ironside*) is intent on destroying society, whilst another wants to live in peace. Scientist Paul Ruth (McGoohan) hopes the unaffiliated telepath Cameron Vale (Lack) will infiltrate Revok's organization and help destroy it.

Cronenberg is on familiar territory in *Scanners*, arguably the best film to emerge from his late 1970s'/ early 1980s' obsession with disease and mutation. A concept that clearly inspired Bryan Singer's *X-Men*, the Scanners are presented as human mutants whose gifts have left them ostracized by society and, conversely, fought over by rival factions of their own subculture. As in *X-Men*, most have spent their lives as social outcasts with their new-found popularity bringing little comfort. But Cronenberg doesn't waste much time over the sociological aspects of his film; it is a sci-fi B-movie at heart and isn't ashamed to admit it. *Scanners* was one of those videos that was omnipresent during the 1980s' rental boom. Cronenberg would probably be proud to know that his film features (according to one survey) the 'most-paused moment' in the decade's prolific rental history – the shot of a Scanner's head exploding after going up against Revok in a psychic power struggle.

TIME BANDITS

Terry Gilliam, GB, 1981

CAST INCLUDES:
Craig Warnock, David Rappaport, Sean Connery, John Cleese, Michael Palin
SCREENPLAY:
Michael Palin, Terry Gilliam
CINEMATOGRAPHY:
Peter Biziou

A young boy is kidnapped by a gang of time-travelling dwarf thieves in possession of a stolen map showing gateways in time and reality. Pursued by the Supreme Being, the gang embark on a series of adventures, including meetings with Napoléon and an ogre. Terry Gilliam's only true children's movie is one of the most imaginative and daring fairy tales ever filmed. The director's insistence on casting all the lead roles with dwarves – with the exception of young Kevin (Warnock) – was a serious handicap in finding finance. Gilliam was expecting to be short of money from the start. He realized that he needed some star cameos if he was to get his hands on real money. Fortunately, Sean Connery happened to see the script and agreed to play the role of Agamemnon (and the fireman at the end of the film) for a cut rate, and with Gilliam cronies Cleese and Palin already on board, they were away. A triumph of imagination, Gilliam takes the opportunity to twist history around his own crazed sense of humour. The result is both bewitching and hilarious.

BLADE RUNNER

Ridley Scott, USA, 1982

CAST INCLUDES:
Harrison Ford, Rutger Hauer, Sean Young, Daryl Hannah, William Sanderson
SCREENPLAY:
Hampton Fancher, David Webb Peoples from Philip K. Dick's novel *Do Androids Dream of Electric Sheep?*
CINEMATOGRAPHY:
Jordan Cronenweth

Rick Deckard (Ford) is a retired police officer, once responsible for finding and killing renegade 'replicants' – man-made servants and soldiers almost indistinguishable from humans. A highly sophisticated and murderous gang led by the enigmatic Roy Batty (Hauer) is on the loose, and Deckard is persuaded to take the case. The first and possibly best Philip K. Dick adaptation, *Blade Runner* is an arresting triumph of design, atmosphere and storytelling. Ridley Scott's self-assured approach lends a convincing air to the year 2019, making the city's neon-lit streets seem as real as those walked by Deckard's spiritual grandfather, Philip Marlowe. In fact, the influence of Raymond Chandler is evident throughout Dick's novel and particularly the film. From character to narrative, to the shadowy visual style, *Blade Runner* is riddled with film noir references. Fortunately, powerful performances all round prevent the stylized aesthetic from swamping the story.

E.T. THE EXTRA-TERRESTRIAL

Steven Spielberg, USA, 1982

An alien botanist is befriended by a young boy when accidentally marooned on Earth. The pinnacle of Spielberg's filmmaking adolescence, *E.T.* is one of the best known and most beloved movies of all time. It represents an innocence all too often overlooked by modern family cinema, choosing to revel in innocuous sentimentality, successfully appealing to our imaginative and affectionate better nature. Perhaps it's a little too sentimental for some tastes, and over-exposure and excessive merchandizing in the 1980s certainly haven't helped the film's saccharine image, but even the most cynical moviegoer should give it another chance. After more than 20 years it can finally stand on its own, devoid of the hype, marketing and media saturation that made up as much of E.T.'s identity as the film itself; it's now just a simple, beautifully told story. It has been a long time since movies like this have been made with such skill, and it should be appreciated as the rare gem that it is.

CAST INCLUDES:
Henry Thomas, Dee Wallace-Stone, Robert MacNaughton, Drew Barrymore
SCREENPLAY:
Melissa Mathison
CINEMATOGRAPHY:
Allen Daviau

DID YOU KNOW?
E.T. won four Oscars at the 1983 Academy Awards.

STAR TREK: THE WRATH OF KHAN

Nicholas Meyer, USA, 1982

Khan (Montalban), an old adversary of Admiral James T. Kirk, seizes control of a federation starship and seeks revenge. Meanwhile, the mysterious Genesis project is also garnering attention. For the second movie featuring the original crew of the USS *Enterprise*, seasoned filmmaker Robert Wise *(West Side Story, The Sound of Music)* makes way for second-time director Nicholas Meyer, who turns in an exceptional sci-fi adventure, easily bettering his predecessor. As in virtually all the original *Star Trek* movies, Kirk and his crew are retired as the film starts, but a training mission (or similar excuse) requires them to be on board when some catastrophe calls the *Enterprise* into action. Montalban's gloriously extravagant performance and flamboyant dialogue prove to be amongst the film's best trump cards, but it's no one-man show. *The Wrath of Khan* is the most complete of the ten *Star Trek* movies. The sharp script successfully deals with the lead's age, providing plenty of banter between Kirk, Spock (Nimoy) and McCoy (Kelley). It also avoids the sort of action scenes that Roger Moore's James Bond was embarrassing himself with at about the same time.

CAST INCLUDES:
William Shatner, Leonard Nimoy, DeForest Kelley, Ricardo Montalban, Kirstie Alley, James Doohan,
SCREENPLAY:
Jack B. Sowards from a story by Harve Bennett & Jack B. Sowards, based on the television series by Gene Roddenberry
CINEMATOGRAPHY:
Gayne Rescher

TRON

Steven Lisberger, USA, 1982

CAST INCLUDES:
Jeff Bridges, Bruce Boxleitner, David Warner, Cindy Morgan, Barnard Hughes
SCREENPLAY:
Steven Lisberger, Bonnie MacBird
CINEMATOGRAPHY:
Bruce Logan

Computer hacker Kevin Flynn (Bridges) is turned into a software program by the malevolent computer of ENCOM, an abhorrent manufacturer of hugely successful video games for whom Flynn once worked. Meanwhile, an independent program, Tron (Boxleitner), is attempting to disable the Master Control Program (MCP) that runs the entire company. The hugely imaginative premise is based on the idea that every computer program is a conscious entity with the physical characteristics of its writer. The genius of the film is the incredible visual style developed for the software characters and their environment – where we spend about 80 per cent of the film's running time. Although it uses a combination of special effects techniques (including rotoscoping and compositing), the most striking achievement of *Tron* is the extent to which computer animation is used – unprecedented at the time. In fact, although *Tron* was Academy Award nominated for costume and sound, it was refused a nomination for special effects because the use of CGI was considered to be cheating.

GHOSTBUSTERS

Ivan Reitman, USA, 1984

A New York apartment building is subjected to a tidal wave of paranormal activity, and a ragtag group of eccentrics and losers must somehow defeat an ancient demon intent on destroying the world – what concept could better lend itself to the extravaganza of ideas, characters, special effects and one-liners thrown at it by the writers? Thought up by *Saturday Night Live* alumni Aykroyd and Ramis (who would play failed scientists Stantz and Spengler), the film took advantage of a new generation of more demanding and media-savvy kids. Aiming the comedy somewhere between their and their parents' sense of humour, the film was able to attract the children without deterring adults, making it the biggest-grossing comedy of all time. It also took advantage of the immense talents

of Bill Murray, the film's resident scene stealer. His Peter Venkman is a fantastically sardonic opportunist, just falling short of both sleazy and nasty (he spends half the film trying to get Weaver's Dana Barrett into bed, the other half victimizing Stantz and Spengler), but ultimately he's just lazy. The lethargic, laid-back manner with which he greets unimaginable confrontations provides some of the film's best scenes. It is brimming over with memorable moments and characters (the giant marshmallow man, the scary library ghost, Moranis's Louis Tully), but perhaps the film's most lasting gift to popular culture comes from theme-tune writer Ray Parker Jr. – now who you gonna call?

CAST INCLUDES:
Bill Murray, Dan Aykroyd, Sigourney Weaver, Harold Ramis, Rick Moranis
SCREENPLAY:
Dan Aykroyd, Harold Ramis
CINEMATOGRAPHY:
László Kovács

THE TERMINATOR

James Cameron, USA, 1984

CAST INCLUDES:
Arnold Schwarzenegger,
Michael Biehn, Linda
Hamilton, Paul Winfield,
Lance Henriksen
SCREENPLAY:
Harlan Ellison, James
Cameron, Gale Anne Hurd,
William Wisher
CINEMATOGRAPHY:
Adam Greenberg

A sophisticated android (Schwarzenegger) is sent from the future to kill Sarah Connor (Hamilton). Her only protector is the intense rebel soldier, Reese (Biehn), who followed the Terminator back in time.

Opening in a future scorched by nuclear holocaust, giant robots (or 'Hunter-Killers') pursue the scattered remnants of mankind through the desolate landscape. A subtitle reveals that 'The machines' war to exterminate mankind has raged for decades', then Brad Fiedel's dramatic score crashes in. So begins James Cameron's far from subtle debut for Cyberdine Systems model 101, better known as the Terminator, one of sci-fi's most iconic creations. Although impossible to imagine anyone else in the role, Schwarzenegger wasn't the first choice. Originally Lance Henriksen (who appears as police officer Vukovich, instead) was to play the part, but when Cameron saw the Austrian bodybuilder, he was convinced his stature would lend a more intimidating quality to his robotic killing machine. The film launched Schwarzenegger's career and the relentless android became his signature character.

Essentially a series of pursuits and shootouts, the film lacks the overblown scale and pomposity of its sequels and stays true to its B-movie roots. This more linear form better suits the clear concept and characters, most of whom have simple motivations and avoid stepping outside their remit. But the film still has an intelligent point to make, and its intention to highlight fears of dehumanization and the dangers of our reliance on machines is frighteningly successful.

BACK TO THE FUTURE

Robert Zemeckis, USA, 1985

CAST INCLUDES:
Michael J. Fox, Christopher
Lloyd, Lea Thompson,
Crispin Glover
SCREENPLAY:
Robert Zemeckis, Bob Gale
CINEMATOGRAPHY:
Dean Cundey

Teenager Marty McFly (Fox) inadvertently goes 30 years back in time and interrupts his mother and father's first meeting. To avoid jeopardizing his own existence he must convince his future parents that they're meant to be together. A staple for anybody who grew up in the '80s, *Back to the Future*'s mix of sci-fi, comedy and action proved a huge hit and turned its star into a household name. Directed and co-written by Robert Zemeckis and produced by Steven Spielberg, the film is a high point of the hugely successful cycle of glossy, high-concept kids' movies that were so prolific in the mid-1980s – *Ghostbusters*, *Inner Space*, *The Goonies*, etc. Like most of these, *Back to the Future*'s appeal lies partly in not talking down to its young audience, something which explains its longevity and popularity amongst adults. The immense charm Fox lends to lead character Marty is another success.

BRAZIL

Terry Gilliam, GB, 1985

CAST INCLUDES: Jonathan Pryce, Robert De Niro, Katherine Helmond, Ian Holm, Bob Hoskins, Michael Palin
SCREENPLAY: Terry Gilliam, Tom Stoppard, Charles McKeown
CINEMATOGRAPHY: Roger Pratt

In an officious future bureaucracy, a man is wrongly arrested and a browbeaten civil servant (Pryce) longs for a simple life with the woman from his dreams. When director Terry Gilliam completed *Brazil*, an attack on oppressive and stifling authority, he presented it to his backers at Universal who promptly told him to chop off half an hour and give it a happy ending. Bewildered by the irony of such an instruction, and with no intention of abiding by it, Gilliam went into battle. He took out adverts in trade papers, held secret screenings for US critics and generally made an absolute nuisance of himself until Universal eventually relented. But to call the film simply an attack on authority is an underestimation. Gilliam's frustration with all aspects of Western culture, politics and society are poured into this therapy session of a movie. Our obsession with vanity, the petty-minded officials who won't turn off a tap without the correct forms, the over-engineered appliances that never work, the mountains of paper that (quite literally) swamp people – everything the director finds abhorrent is roundly mocked and satirized. Gilliam's success in creating this depressing society is nicely tempered by his equally successful comic creations. The likes of Jim Broadbent (a bizarre plastic surgeon) and Michael Palin (an oily civil servant) are on hand, as is Robert De Niro, wonderful as Harry Buttle, a terrorist plumber who intercepts ignored maintenance requests and does the work himself. Orwell never created a better dystopian future, and he certainly wasn't this much fun.

ALIENS

James Cameron, GB, 1986

CAST INCLUDES: Sigourney Weaver, Carrie Henn, Michael Biehn, Lance Henriksen, Paul Reiser, Bill Paxton
SCREENPLAY: James Cameron, David Giler, Walter Hill
CINEMATOGRAPHY: Adrian Biddle

Ripley (Weaver), the sole survivor of the previous film, returns to Earth after 57 years in the suspended animation chamber of an escape pod. She discovers the planet that played host to the alien's eggs has been colonized, and contact with the pioneering families there has been lost. The sinister 'company' convinces Ripley to return as advisor to a detachment of marines. James Cameron cleverly changes direction for his sequel to Ridley Scott's 1979 masterpiece, *Alien*. Realizing there is no sense in attempting to re-create the subtleties and tension of the original, he opts for the gung ho approach and floods the screen with heavily armed space marines and literally dozens of aliens. On paper it sounds worryingly like the classic sequel to a classic film (a faster, bigger disappointment), but Cameron pulls it off. Where Scott seemed to sit behind you in the cinema audience and carefully massage your neck while cracking the occasional muscle, Cameron hits you over the head with a club and steals your seat. But that's not to say *Aliens* is dumb. Picking up on its predecessor's theme of motherhood, we are introduced to an orphaned girl, Newt (Henn), with whom Ripley forms an immediate bond (she lost a daughter on her journey back to Earth), and also the alien queen, allowing for a fantastic confrontation between two matriarchal figures. Ripley emerges as an even more densely layered character this time around. Tenacious, resourceful and sympathetic, Weaver plays the part with a mesmerizing conviction that helps establish Ripley as the genre's greatest female character.

ROBOCOP

Paul Verhoeven, USA, 1987

CAST INCLUDES:
Peter Weller, Nancy Allen, Dan O'Herlihy, Ronny Cox, Kurtwood Smith
SCREENPLAY:
Michael Miner, Edward Neumeier
CINEMATOGRAPHY:
Sol Negrin, Jost Vacano

In the near future, Detroit is gripped by a crime wave. OCP (a giant corporation now in charge of policing the city) initiates its RoboCop program, a radical new law-enforcement concept that will make a cyborg supercop of deceased police officer Alex Murphy (Weller). Paul Verhoeven's visceral, violent and excellent movie is truly a product of its time. It takes a shot at almost anything that moved in the Reagan 1980s: corporate business practice, a cynical media, vicious yuppies and law enforcement that verges on fascism. The Dutch director's image of America, as an outsider, allows for a more objective view, and with such an uncompromising visual and thematic style, it's no wonder *RoboCop* comes across as such an aggressive film. *RoboCop* has been described as 'fascism for liberals', a natural extension of the Reaganomics that inspire it. *RoboCop* is just as much a child of the era as the criminals he pursues, or the sinister corporation that created him. Don't write this one off as an exploitation flick; it's just too good.

DID YOU KNOW?

Batman was the highest-grossing movie of 1989.

BATMAN

Tim Burton, USA, 1989

A millionaire who, as a child, witnessed his parents' brutal slaying, turns his resources against the criminals of Gotham City, and in particular a sociopathic killer called The Joker.

Tim Burton's *Batman* is the first big-screen treatment to translate the comic's dark style and complicated hero intact, thankfully abstaining from the gaudy, camp approach of the television show (and later, the dire third and fourth films in the series). Keaton is brilliant in the title role, emotionally and physically convincing; his casting was originally controversial amongst fans but his performance still stands up today. Yet it's Nicholson's Joker that (perhaps unsurprisingly) steals the show. He struts outrageously through the part like a cross between Mick Jagger and his own Jack Torrence, turning in the most gleefully over the top performance of his career. The symbiotic relationship of the two characters, both suffering issues of duality in their personalities, lends the film great emotional depth. Such complicated characters had never before been seen in a comic-book adaptation (which at the time were usually relegated to serials or television). We can thank – or curse – *Batman*'s huge success for the wave of comic-book movies that have dominated the summer blockbuster season ever since. *Batman* was, and still is, their template.

CAST INCLUDES:
Michael Keaton, Jack Nicholson, Kim Basinger, Robert Wuhl, Pat Hingle
SCREENPLAY:
Bob Kane (Batman characters), Sam Hamm, Warren Skaaren
CINEMATOGRAPHY:
Roger Pratt

TOTAL RECALL

Paul Verhoeven, USA, 1990

CAST INCLUDES:
Arnold Schwarzenegger,
Rachel Ticotin, Sharon Stone,
Ronny Cox, Michael Ironside
SCREENPLAY:
Philip K. Dick (short story),
Ronald Shusett, Dan
O'Bannon, Jon Povill,
Gary Goldman
CINEMATOGRAPHY:
Jost Vacano

In the future, Douglas Quaid (Schwarzenegger) is a construction worker who dreams of visiting Mars. When he decides to have a holiday implanted directly into his brain by a specialist company, a whole host of memories start to resurface and he must follow a series of clues while evading various attempts on his life. Familiar territory for author Philip K. Dick (confused realities, ambiguous personalities, flawed technology) and director Verhoeven (twisty plot, fascist society), *Total Recall* is a successful combination of the two men's talents, just as much intelligent mystery thriller as it is crowd-pleasing blockbuster. Providing Schwarzenegger with one of the best and most demanding roles he's ever had, requiring a performance ranging in emotion and character due to Quaid's multiple personalities, is a pretty risky move. He pulls it off just fine, but this being a Verhoeven movie, everything is painted with huge, fat, brush strokes and subtle performances don't feature on the palette. In fact, subtlety has been dispensed with in all areas, allowing for a refreshingly simple and honest movie within a genre that has produced more than its fair share of pretentious films. At one point, cartoonish arch villain Cohaagen actually says, 'I'll blow this place up and be home in time for cornflakes!' You don't get one-liners like that in *Alien*.

CAST INCLUDES:
Sam Neill, Laura Dern,
Jeff Goldblum, Richard
Attenborough
SCREENPLAY:
Michael Crichton,
David Koepp
CINEMATOGRAPHY:
Dean Cundey

JURASSIC PARK

Steven Spielberg, USA, 1993

On a remote tropical island, an eccentric billionaire has built a safari park populated by genetically re-created dinosaurs. Not yet open for business, he invites palaeontologists Alan Grant (Neill) and Ellie Sattler (Dern), chaos theorist Ian Malcolm (Goldblum) and his grandchildren for a sneak preview. Unsurprisingly, things don't go smoothly. 'An adventure 65 million years in the making'; *Jurassic Park*'s tagline could refer to time spent developing technology for the monstrous hit that finally showed what CGI can do. Even if the story didn't work so well and the cast wasn't so good, it wouldn't have made any difference in 1993. After nearly a century of cartoons, miniatures and stop-motion, photo-real dinosaurs had hit the screens. Time has been surprisingly kind to *Jurassic Park*. The proliferation of CGI technology in modern cinema means the dinosaurs don't have quite the same impact, but considering their age, they stand up. The real revelation is the quality of everything else that, at the time, was overshadowed by the incredble dinosaurs.

TWELVE MONKEYS

Terry Gilliam, USA, 1995

By 2035 only 1 per cent of the population is still alive, the rest having been wiped out by an unknown virus. Convict James Cole (Willis) is sent back in time on a mission to discover the origins of the virus.

The most commercial film of Gilliam's career provides the auteur with a rare box-office hit that manages to retain a characteristic visual flair and offbeat narrative structure. The film sees both male leads grappling with madness. Cole's sanity is in question from the start. When he is selected for the mission it is unclear whether he is deemed insane by the authorities who have incarcerated him. He starts to wonder himself when locked up in a present-day asylum with 'crazy as a loon' Jeffrey Goines (Pitt). Gilliam enjoys keeping the state of both men's mental health ambiguous, twisting and turning the plot and timeline in order to confuse the viewer, even throwing in the odd red herring. Willis excels in one of the most layered and intelligent performances of his career, once again proving how good he can be when well cast by a competent director (*Pulp Fiction*, *The Sixth Sense*). He holds the film together but has the odd scene stolen by Pitt, clearly relishing the freedom inherent in the portrayal of a lunatic.

As original and interesting as his best work, *Twelve Monkeys* is a great 'entry level' Gilliam movie for those who are yet to be converted. More polished than *Brazil*, more coherent than *The Adventures of Baron Munchausen* and more mature than *Time Bandits*, it is an inventive and demanding addition to the Gilliam repertoire.

CAST INCLUDES:
Bruce Willis,
Madeleine Stowe, Brad Pitt,
Christopher Plummer
SCREENPLAY:
Chris Marker (film *La Jetee*),
David Webb Peoples,
Janet Peoples
CINEMATOGRAPHY:
Roger Pratt

DID YOU KNOW?
Most of the actors took a pay cut just so they could work with Terry Gilliam.

INDEPENDENCE DAY

Roland Emmerich, USA, 1996

CAST INCLUDES:
Bill Pullman, Jeff Goldblum,
Will Smith, Mary
McDonnall, Judd Hirsch,
Brent Spiner
SCREENPLAY:
Dean Devlin, Roland
Emmerich
CINEMATOGRAPHY:
Karl Walter Lindenlaub

ACADEMY AWARD
Best Effects, Visual Effects:
Volker Engel, Douglas Smith,
Clay Pinney, Joe Viskocil

Huge alien spaceships take up position above Earth's major cities, causing panic and confusion. After a period of silence it becomes clear that they intend to invade. Surfing a huge sci-fi tidal wave kicked up by the television tsunami that was *The X-Files*, *Independence Day* took great advantage of slick new visual effects and hoary old science-fiction themes to become one of the biggest-grossing films in history. Sticking surprisingly closely to H.G. Wells' *War of the Worlds,* co-writer/director Roland Emmerich crafts a good old-fashioned Cold War paranoia movie, with added bells and whistles. Choosing an ensemble cast rather than using a straightforward hero figure is a nice idea, allowing for a balance of serious and comedic characters that helps lighten the film without losing the dramatic impact. The cast come second to the effects, though. Finally able to destroy landmarks convincingly, one of the film's best moments is the very impressive obliteration of the White House. The plot may be full of holes, some of the dialogue might make your ears bleed, and the president's 'rousing' speech is sure to offend anyone brighter than a glass of water. But there is plenty of quality on show here, not to mention fun.

MEN IN BLACK

Barry Sonnenfeld, USA, 1997

CAST INCLUDES:
Tommy Lee Jones, Will Smith, Linda Fiorentino, Vincent D'Onofrio, Rip Torn
SCREENPLAY:
Ed Solomon from the comic by Lowell Cunningham
CINEMATOGRAPHY:
Donald Peterman

A wisecracking New York cop (Smith) is recruited to a secret agency responsible for keeping Earth's numerous extraterrestrial citizens in check. Partnered with a grouchy old-timer (Jones), together they must prevent an interplanetary diplomatic incident that could end the world. The tagline, 'Protecting the Earth from the scum of the universe', is a good indication of the film's simple, honest and unpretentious fun. Sonnenfeld relishes the creative opportunity, filling the film with quality gags, imaginative aliens and brilliantly conceived action scenarios. The teaming of Smith and Jones is an inspired piece of casting, their enjoyable chemistry lying at the heart of the film's appeal. Smith is repeatedly shocked, befuddled and rattled by his encounters with the bizarre alien communities that apparently exist right under our noses, while the deadpan Jones expresses a laconic lack of interest in them. Every creative and technical role on the film is carried out with professionalism, each contributor working in perfect harmony to create a super-slick, top-notch family movie.

THE MATRIX

Andy Wachowski, Larry Wachowski, USA, 1999

ACADEMY AWARDS
Best Editing: Zach Staenberg
Best Sound Effects Editing: Dane A. Davis
Best Visual Effects: John Gaeta, Janek Sirrs, Steve Courtley
Best Sound: John T. Reitz, Gregg Rudloff

CAST INCLUDES:
Keanu Reeves, Laurence Fishburne, Carrie-Anne Moss, Hugo Weaving
SCREENPLAY:
Andy Wachowski, Larry Wachowski
CINEMATOGRAPHY:
Bill Pope

A computer hacker, Anderson (Reeves), discovers mankind is actually held captive by alien machines that feed us an artificial, computer-created perception of reality while draining the electrical current produced by our brains. Some of the pseudo-religous concepts and philosophy contained within *The Matrix* may seem slightly misjudged, the excessive product placement is a valid gripe and the dreadful sequels have undoubtedly tainted the film's reputation – but none of that matters. In *The Matrix*, writer-director brothers Larry and Andy Wachowski created the most original and exciting action movie since *The Terminator*. Setting the film in a world where the rules of physics can be bent, or even broken, allows not only for spectacular visual effects (most obviously the much lauded 'bullet-time' which allows the camera to move around an object in three dimensions – and slow motion), but also imaginative, computer-game-like scenarios impossible in any normal environment.

X-MEN

Bryan Singer, USA, 2000

CAST INCLUDES: Hugh Jackman, Patrick Stewart, Ian McKellen, Famke Janssen, James Marsden
SCREENPLAY: Tom DeSanto, Bryan Singer, David Hayter
CINEMATOGRAPHY: Newton Thomas Sigel

In the near future, evolution has taken a massive step forward, creating tension between mutants and the world's normal citizens. Favouring integration between the two societies, Professor Charles Xavier (Stewart) and his followers must defend mankind from a band of more aggressive mutants. Bryan Singer's stylish comic-book adaptation is one of the most interesting and intelligent so far filmed. Though *Superman* successfully upped the ante by introducing a more developed and less camp tone than previous screen superheroes, it was arguably the troubled and ambiguous dual personality of Tim Burton's *Batman* that first applied 'serious' themes to the formula. With *X-Men*, the idea is expanded still further. The prevalent theme throughout the film is prejudice. Fear and distrust between the public and the mutants is expertly whipped up by self-serving politicians, in a manner reminiscent of 1950s' anti-Communist McCarthyism. This is a nice reference to (and indictment of) one of sci-fi's founding principles. No matter how talented the filmmakers, it's very difficult to pull off serious concepts in a movie with characters named Cyclops, Wolverine and Sabretooth. Singer's determination to cast the best actors possible is the film's masterstroke. The likes of Ian McKellen and Patrick Stewart lend an authoritative presence, whilst from the younger generation, Famke Janssen and Hugh Jackman are particularly impressive. *X-Men* is the most satisfying superhero movie since *Batman*, and like *Batman*, the sequel's up to scratch, too.

CAST INCLUDES:
Richard Harris, Robbie Coltrane, Daniel Radcliffe, Emma Watson, Rupert Grint, Alan Rickman
SCREENPLAY:
Steven Kloves from the novel by J.K. Rowling
CINEMATOGRAPHY:
John Seale

HARRY POTTER AND THE PHILOSOPHER'S STONE

Chris Columbus, GB/USA, 2001

Harry Potter (Radcliffe) is an orphaned 11-year-old boy living with his neglectful aunt and uncle. However, life soon takes an unexpected turn as he discovers he is a wizard. It was inevitable that the immense success of J.K. Rowling's books would bring Hollywood calling. Warner Brothers picked up the rights, and turned to safe pair of hands Chris Columbus *(Home Alone, Mrs Doubtfire)* to launch the franchise. Although unlikely to convert critics of the book, the first *Harry Potter* film is a lovingly produced feast for the eyes and ears. The production design of Stuart Craig and photography of John Seale are simply stunning, while John Williams turns in his best score since the *Indiana Jones* films. Harry and his friends Ron (Grint) and Hermione (Watson) are all adequate in their roles, but the assorted adult witches and wizards draw on an awesome pool of British acting talent. This film is essential viewing for more than just the kids and converted — any film fan should appreciate one of the greatest assortments of talent ever assembled.

SPIDER-MAN

Sam Raimi, USA, 2002

Troubled student Peter Parker (Maguire) is bitten by a spider and takes on some of the arachnid's characteristics. Deciding to use his new powers for good, he becomes a web-slinging, wall-walking superhero. The last major comic-book character to evade big-screen treatment, a potential Spider-Man movie was the subject of speculation and rumour for two decades before Sam Raimi (the *Evil Dead* trilogy) brought him to the cinema, raking in a massive $821 million in the process. The enormous financial success of *Spider-Man* is largely due to Raimi cleverly retaining enough of the comic's themes and style to satisfy its established fanbase, while coating the whole thing in box-office gloss to attract the multiplex crowd. But now the dust has settled, does all this mean the film's any good? Maguire is certainly impressive in the lead, believable as both nerdy schoolboy Parker and the eponymous hero. The rest of the cast are all spot-on, particularly Dunst as love interest Mary Jane Watson and Willem Dafoe as Spidey's schizophrenic nemesis, the Green Goblin, a scientist sent mad after using himself as guinea pig in a military experiment. Raimi keeps things light and swift, achieving unusual emotional diversity and depth for a blockbuster, and the technical aspects are all up to scratch, too.

CAST INCLUDES:
Tobey Maguire, Willem Dafoe, Kirsten Dunst, James Franco, Cliff Robertson, Rosemary Harris
SCREENPLAY:
David Koepp from the comic book by Stan Lee and Steve Ditko
CINEMATOGRAPHY:
Don Burgess

PAN'S LABYRINTH (EL LABERINTO DEL FAUNO)

Guillermo del Toro, Mexico, 2006

In the aftermath of the Spanish Civil War, Ofelia (Baquero) moves to live with her sickly mother, Carmen (Gil), and her new husband, the ruthless army captain Vidal (López). Ofelia soon meets a fairy who introduces her to a magical world full of bizarre creatures, one of whom informs her she is a princess with a series of strange tasks to complete. Watching *Pan's Labyrinth*, you get the feeling it's the film that director Guillermo del Toro has wanted to make for years – he has an unofficial deal with Hollywood that allows him to pursue personal projects so long as he delivers the occasional superhero sequel for the studios. This film draws all of del Toro's favourite themes together (orphaned children, supernatural worlds, magical beasts, big secrets) and absolutely nails each one.

CAST INCLUDES:
Ivana Baquero, Sergi López, Maribel Verdú, Doug Jones, Ariadna Gil
SCREENPLAY:
Guillermo del Toro
CINEMATOGRAPHY:
Guillermo Navarro

ACADEMY AWARDS
Best Art Direction: Eugenio Caballero, Pilar Revuelta
Best Cinematography: Guillermo Navarro
Best Makeup: David Martí

THE DARK KNIGHT

Christopher Nolan, USA, 2008

CAST INCLUDES:
Christian Bale, Heath Ledger, Aaron Eckhart, Maggie Gyllenhaal, Michael Caine, Gary Oldman, Morgan Freeman

SCREENPLAY:
Jonathan Nolan, Christopher Nolan, David S. Goyer

CINEMATOGRAPHY:
Wally Pfister

Batman (Bale) and Gotham District Attorney Harvey Dent (Eckhart) have such a stranglehold on the city's mob bosses that they must accept an uneasy alliance with unpredictable psychopath The Joker (Ledger). Writer/director Christopher Nolan blew cinemagoers away with his 2005 franchise starter, *Batman Begins*, but it's safe to say even the most dedicated fans can't have anticipated the unprecedented success of its sequel. The tragic death of Heath Ledger (who won a posthumous Oscar for the role) may have created a degree of morbid curiosity, but the universal acclaim and $1 billion international box office is down to much more. The film is stunningly complex and layered, but at the heart of the story is a simple conceit: the white knight who is to save Gotham's soul must be unimpeachable, so a dark knight is required to do the necessary dirty work. Batman himself must negotiate a complicated character arc which demands he transforms from a hero into a villain.

DISTRICT 9

Neill Blomkamp, USA, 2009

CAST INCLUDES:
Sharlto Copley, Jason Cope, Nathalie Boltt, Sylvaine Strike

SCREENPLAY:
Neill Blomkamp and Terri Tatchell

CINEMATOGRAPHY:
Trent Opaloch

In the near future Johannesburg is home to District 9, a sprawling ghetto used to house thousands of alien refugees known as 'Prawns'. Sinister corporation Multi-National United is charged with evicting the Prawns and place Wikus van der Merwe (Copley) in charge of the operation. But when van der Merwe is exposed to a strange alien chemical, he must overcome his prejudice and work with the Prawns to stay alive. Like the aliens themselves (substitutes for any oppressed human demographic you care to mention), *District 9* was treated very much as a curiosity upon its release. On the one hand it's a big, shiny, sci-fi movie bursting with visual effects, chase scenes and stunts, whilst on the other it's a brutal cinema vérité-style critique of apartheid and prejudice. It might sound incongruous but it works a treat. The hand-held camera provides a striking immediacy you simply don't expect in a film this big, whilst the bureaucratic van der Merwe is so incredibly ordinary it's easy to forget this is a faux documentary and not a real one (although the omnipresent eight-foot aliens help). Fortunately, first-time director Neill Blomkamp doesn't get so caught up in serious issues that he forgets the fun, and the film develops into a frantic chase movie as the tables are turned on van der Merwe. We may have seen some of it before, but we've never seen it done like this.

AVATAR

James Cameron, USA, 2009

CAST INCLUDES:
Sam Worthington, Zoe Saldana, Sigourney Weaver, Stephen Lang, Michelle Rodriguez, Giovanni Ribisi
SCREENPLAY:
James Cameron
CINEMATOGRAPHY:
Mauro Fiore

A corrupt mining corporation, aided by a gung ho military unit, attempts to drive the peace-loving Na'vi from the moon they call home. Against this backdrop, paraplegic soldier Jake Sully (Worthington) slowly comes to appreciate the Na'vi's majestic beauty and determines he must help to save them. After elaborating on someone else's interplanetary environments in 1986's *Aliens*, James Cameron finally got the chance to create his own in this outrageously successful sci-fi epic, and the results are staggering. The 12-year gap between *Avatar* and Cameron's previous dramatic outing (a little film called *Titanic*) was largely due to the innovative filmmaker taking time out to develop the 3-D technology he needed for the project. To realize his vision, everything from cameras to visual effects techniques needed to be developed from scratch, and the results are stunning. The extent to which the viewer feels a visceral connection to the three-metre-tall blue aliens is highly surprising, and we are transported to their home world of Pandora with such startling success it can be disorientating at times. A thinly disguised metaphor for threatened natural landscapes here on Earth, the aliens themselves are clearly designed to remind us of the numerous indigenous peoples of Earth whose homes have been annihilated by an industrialized invading force.

CAST INCLUDES:
Whitney Able, Scott McNairy
SCREENPLAY:
Gareth Edwards
CINEMATOGRAPHY:
Gareth Edwards

MONSTERS

Gareth Edwards, GB, 2010

After a NASA probe crash-lands in Central America, the entire region is rapidly overrun by an aggressive alien life form. When attempts to wipe out the invading monsters fail, a quarantine zone covering much of Mexico is established. Thrill-seeking American tourist Samantha (Able) finds herself trapped on the wrong side of the zone and must rely on photographer Andrew (McNairy) to reluctantly escort her home. Made for less than $800,000 with a crew of just two, writer-director Gareth Edwards' feature debut looks every bit the multmillion-dollar Hollywood blockbuster he clearly hoped it would. As a former visual effects artist, he at least had an idea of how to create the lavish CGI monsters without having to splash too much cash. As Samantha and Andrew overcome their initial impressions of each other and form a compelling bond, the danger inherent in their journey demands that they display a degree of unemotional objectivity, and this contributes greatly to the romantic tension. All of this makes for an interesting counterpoint to the sporadic exhilaration of monster attacks and the incredible unease Edwards manages to rustle up with his impressive grasp of suspense technique.

GRAVITY

Alfonso Cuarón, USA/GB, 2013

Dr Ryan Stone (Bullock) is a brilliant medical engineer on her first shuttle mission. She's travelling with veteran astronaut Matt Kowalsky (Clooney) in command of his last flight before retiring. But on a seemingly routine spacewalk, disaster strikes. The shuttle is destroyed, leaving Stone and Kowalsky completely alone – tethered to nothing but each other and spiralling out into the blackness. The deafening silence tells them they have lost any link to Earth and any chance for rescue. As fear turns to panic, every gulp of air eats away at what little oxygen is left. But the only way home may be to go further out into the terrifying expanse of space. Alfonso Cuarón's *Gravity* is an eerie, tense sci-fi thriller that's masterfully directed and visually stunning. Deciding they couldn't make the film they wanted using traditional methods, Cuarón, cinematographer Emmanuel Lubezki and visual effects supervisor Tim Webber decided to shoot the actors' faces and create everything else digitally. This created enormous challenges in terms of lighting, so Lubezki suggested folding an LED screen into a box, putting the actor inside, and using the light from the screen to light the actor. This 'light box' – the key to making the space-walk scenes realistic – was a nine-foot cube just big enough for one actor, who then had to memorize long combinations of precise movements to hit their marks at different points in the shot. Rewriting all the known rules of cinema, *Gravity* is an extraordinary film. Transcendently beautiful and visually astonishing, it's a white-knuckle ride of terror that engages every kind of dread and rivets you to the screen.

CAST INCLUDES:
Sandra Bullock, George Clooney, Ed Harris
SCREENPLAY:
Alfonso Cuarón, Jonás Cuarón
CINEMATOGRAPHY:
Emmanuel Lubezki

MYSTERY & THRILLER

LITTLE CAESAR

Mervyn LeRoy, USA, 1931

CAST INCLUDES:
Edward G. Robinson,
Douglas Fairbanks Jr.,
Glenda Farrell, William
Collier Jr., Sidney Blackmer
SCREENPLAY:
W.R. Burnett (novel),
Francis Edward
Faragoh, Robert N. Lee
CINEMATOGRAPHY:
Tony Gaudio

Little Caesar, often called the grandfather of the gangster movie, was produced at the beginning of the sound era, and while in some areas it shows its age, it is still an efficient and well-paced thriller. The film charts the rise of Rico (Robinson) from small-time crook up through the gangster hierarchy. His naked ambition and brutality enable him to supplant one crime boss after another, but he seems insatiable in his quest for power and the dubious respect of the demimonde. Robinson is convincing as the rising gangster boss with no humanity, only ruthless determination to climb to the top of the tree, no matter who he has to kill on the way. With his 'ugly mug', Robinson was an unlikely screen star, but in this film he found his forté as the short hood looking for respect and he gives an expressive and entertaining performance. Technically Little Caesar is quite basic by modern standards, but the fast-moving pace and gritty subject matter was new to audiences of the time. So much so that it effectively launched the gangster genre, even without the explicit violence and colourful slang that would later become such vital components. Despite the lack of on-screen violence there is no doubting how dangerous and amoral Rico actually is. This seminal mob flick is a must for all fans of gangster movies.

THE PUBLIC ENEMY

William A. Wellman, USA, 1931

CAST INCLUDES:
James Cagney, Edward
Woods, Jean Harlow, Joan
Blondell, Beryl Mercer
SCREENPLAY:
Harvey F. Thew from the
story by Kubec Glasmon
and John Bright
CINEMATOGRAPHY:
Devereaux Jennings

The public enemy of the title is Tom Powers (Cagney) and the film charts his rise from shoplifting street urchin to ruthless, bootlegging gangster boss. Similar in many respects to Little Caesar, which was released in the same year, The Public Enemy differs in that it is more concerned with exploring the social environment that creates criminals. Based on the real-life mobster Earl Weiss, it is the context of the film that makes it important. One of the first 'talkies', the gritty, violent themes were particularly suited to the Depression era; spoken dialogue and sound brought the gangster flick to life. The Production Code was not yet in force, and the opening of the film included a disclaimer from the studio that it was not trying to glamorize violence and criminal activity. Indeed, the Code was brought in as a direct response to films such as The Public Enemy. However, despite the disclaimer, violent it is. Cagney swaggers, spits and shoots and in the process creates a legend.

REBECCA

Alfred Hitchcock, USA, 1940

CAST INCLUDES:
Laurence Olivier,
Joan Fontaine, George
Sanders, Judith Anderson,
Gladys Cooper
SCREENPLAY:
Philip MacDonald, Michael
Hogan from the novel by
Daphne Du Maurier
CINEMATOGRAPHY:
George Barnes

Hitchcock's *Rebecca*, based on the novel of the same name by Daphne Du Maurier, is a brooding, melodramatic thriller. It follows the tale of a young woman (Fontaine) who is introduced to a rich widower, Maxim de Winter (Olivier). De Winter is travelling to get over the loss of his wife, Rebecca, whose tragic death continues to haunt him. They marry, and the previously unnamed young woman becomes 'the second Mrs de Winter', interestingly as the film is named after the dead and unseen first wife. Once the newlyweds return to Max's estate, however, it is clear that through Rebecca's memory, her grip on the staff and house has not diminished since her death. With a story by Du Maurier, direction by Hitchcock and starring Laurence Olivier, you know you are going to get something special. *Rebecca* does not disappoint; the story is enthralling, Hitchcock's camerawork is, as usual, flawless and Olivier's de Winter is by turns pitiable, charming and cold.

THE MALTESE FALCON

John Huston, USA, 1941

Sam Spade (Bogart) is a San Francisco private eye who becomes immersed in a violent mystery when he starts to investigate the murder of his partner. One strange character after another appears as he gets closer to solving the crime. Each character has one thing in common: a desire to get their hands on the golden, jewel-encrusted statue of the Maltese falcon. The falcon inspires greed, fear and violence, but in itself, however, it is relatively unimportant; it is merely the hook on which to hang the characters who are the substance of the film. Bogart's performance as Spade was to have an incredible impact on his career; the cold, tough guy with a world-weary grin would set him up for his classic roles in *Casablanca* and *The African Queen*. This film was also to be a turning point for its director John Huston. In this, his debut, he shows his obvious talent. The style of the movie has everything to do with making it a success. The plot and action are tight but the main attraction is the characters. The way in which the actors bring them to life is sublime to watch.

CAST INCLUDES: Humphrey Bogart, Mary Astor, Gladys George, Sydney Greenstreet, Peter Lorre, Barton MacLane
SCREENPLAY: Dashiell Hammett (novel), John Huston (screenplay)
CINEMATOGRAPHY: Arthur Edeson

DOUBLE INDEMNITY

Billy Wilder, USA, 1944

'I killed him for money – and for a woman. I didn't get the money. And I didn't get the woman.' So runs the opening line of this fascinating film as Walter Neff (MacMurray) begins his confession into a Dictaphone. Told in flashback with Neff narrating, we learn that he is an insurance rep who begins an affair with Phyllis (Stanwyck) when he visits her house to renew her husband's car insurance. They sign up her husband with a life policy, which has a double indemnity, and then murder him and make it look like an accident.

CAST INCLUDES:
Fred MacMurray, Barbara Stanwyck, Edward G. Robinson, Porter Hall, Jean Heather,
SCREENPLAY:
Billy Wilder, Raymond Chandler based on the novel by James M. Cain
CINEMATOGRAPHY:
John Seitz

The opening confession leads us nicely into the movie, but rather than being the end of the story it immediately follows the crime and so points towards a man who does not expect to escape justice. Stanwyck gives one of her best performances and casts the mould for the *femme fatale* character in many successive films. As befits the time, she is not overtly sexy, but her seductive manipulation of Neff is thoroughly believable. MacMurray plays Neff to perfection, but it is Robinson, as Barton Keyes the claims investigator, who sets the film alight.

The screenplay was based on a James M. Cain novel adapted by Raymond Chandler, who made the original material even more evocative and as sharp as broken glass. The dialogue gives the characters a smartness and presence on screen that is hugely entertaining. Billy Wilder's direction is precise and the way he combines elements of romance with cynicism, suspense with humour gives an interesting take on film noir.

THE BIG SLEEP

Howard Hawks, USA, 1946

CAST INCLUDES:
Humphrey Bogart, Lauren Bacall, John Ridgely, Martha Vickers, Dorothy Malone
SCREENPLAY:
William Faulkner, Jules Furthman, Leigh Bracket from the novel by Raymond Chandler
CINEMATOGRAPHY:
Sidney Hickox

An adaptation of a Raymond Chandler novel, this film is notoriously difficult to understand. This is not just because of the amazingly complex plot, but also because the author himself admitted that he did not know who had committed one of the seven murders in it. Philip Marlowe (Bogart) is the private detective hired by General Sternwood to investigate the blackmail of his younger daughter, Carmen (Vickers). This apparently straightforward case leads Marlowe into a maze of killers and blackmail, gamblers and sex, and ultimately into the arms of the general's other daughter, Vivian (Bacall). During filming, Bogart and Bacall were the talk of Hollywood due to their off-screen marriage and especially their age difference; he was 44 while she was only 20. On screen the two sparkled, and some of the highlights of the film are their shared scenes when they bring real chemistry into some fabulously flirty dialogue. This is Bogart at the top of his game.

KISS OF DEATH

Henry Hathaway, USA, 1947

CAST INCLUDES:
Victor Mature, Brian Donlevy, Coleen Gray, Richard Widmark, Taylor Holmes
SCREENPLAY:
Ben Hecht, Charles Lederer from the story by Eleazar Lipsky
CINEMATOGRAPHY:
Norbert Brodine

Kiss of Death is widely remembered for one scene in particular: when an old lady in a wheelchair is sent tumbling down the stairs. Shocking and senseless, it is a perfect illustration of the nature of the psycho-villain of the film, Tommy Udo (Widmark). Tommy has been betrayed by a former accomplice, Nick Bianco (Mature), who was captured when a robbery at a jewellery shop went awry. By turning in his partners in crime, Nick is paroled while they are imprisoned. When Tommy is released, he is out for revenge. Widmark was nominated for an Oscar for his debut role as the sadistic and psychotic Tommy. In an era when bad guys were rarely evil, his portrayal was interesting for its extremes; one moment mercilessly brutal and another manically giggling. Complementing this is Mature's performance, which is excellently balanced between stool pigeon and family man, his warmth creating sympathy. In Kiss of Death, Hathaway has created a classic film noir; his taut direction creates a moody, unrelenting pace. The black-and-white photography adds a fine tone to the film, and the use of light and shadows in the New York locations adds a sense of foreboding and tension. It is, however, Widmark's film; the warped humour and the terrifying brutality form the hook on which the rest of the movie hangs.

THE THIRD MAN

Carol Reed, GB, 1949

*T*he *Third Man* is set in post-war Vienna, a shattered city, divided between the allies and ruled by shady bureaucrats. Holly Martins (Cotton) arrives to take a job working for his friend Harry Lime (Welles), but when he gets to Vienna he discovers that Harry is dead. The death seems suspicious, so Holly begins to investigate. This film is cited by many as the best ever made, and whether you agree or not, it is difficult to criticize. Wonderful moments such as the chase in the sewers, the balloon seller, the cuckoo clock speech and Harry's entrance are all sublime. Harry himself is one of cinema's great characters; smooth and lethal, charming and repellent. The cinematography casts Vienna in a surreal light, a lopsided place full of unnatural angles as though the normal rules of perspective do not apply. This is completely in keeping with the action; the rubble and craters are a perfect backdrop to the intrigue of the politicians and black marketeers. Much of the credit must go to director Carol Reed. The vision, tone and pace of the film are superb; the result is a genuinely timeless classic.

CAST INCLUDES:
Joseph Cotton, Alida Valli, Orson Welles, Trevor Howard, Paul Hörbiger
SCREENPLAY:
Graham Greene from the story by Graham Greene and Alexander Korda
CINEMATOGRAPHY:
Robert Krasker

ACADEMY AWARD
Best Cinematography, Black-and-White:
Robert Krasker

STRANGERS ON A TRAIN

Alfred Hitchcock, USA, 1951

CAST INCLUDES:
Farley Granger, Ruth Roman, Robert Walker, Leo G. Carroll, Patricia Hitchcock
SCREENPLAY:
Raymond Chandler, Whitfield Cook, Czenzi Ormonde from the novel by Patricia Highsmith
CINEMATOGRAPHY:
Robert Burks

*B*ased on a novel by Patricia Highsmith, *Strangers on a Train* is a classic piece of Hitchcockian ingenuity. All the elements are there: an ordinary man caught in an impossible situation, some marvellous cinematic set pieces and the creeping, sinister build up of tension. Guy (Granger) is a professional tennis player whose marital problems have been well reported in the press. Bruno (Walker) meets Guy on a train and suggests that they help each other out; Bruno will murder Guy's wife if Guy will murder Bruno's father. With prior knowledge of the crime, both can establish an airtight alibi. So ends what Guy thinks is a harmless conversation, until his wife is murdered. Hitchcock's use of lighting and camera work is outstanding and adds to the atmosphere and suspense. Exhilarating and fast-moving, this is one of his best.

THE BIG HEAT

Fritz Lang, USA, 1953

DID YOU KNOW?
Bannion's wife, Katie, is played by Jocelyn Brando, older sister of Marlon.

CAST INCLUDES:
Glenn Ford, Gloria Grahame,
Jocelyn Brando, Alexander
Scourby, Lee Marvin
SCREENPLAY:
Sydney Boehm,
William P. McGivern
CINEMATOGRAPHY:
Charles Lang

On the surface, this film is a classic tale of one good cop and his search for justice and revenge in a corrupt town. Detective Bannion (Ford) is as straight as they come. A suicide investigation seems straightforward enough until the victim's mistress is murdered and Banion's boss orders him off the case. When he refuses, and starts shaking down the local gang boss, the response is quick, violent and ultimately tragic. Ford brings intensity to the film and shows what an excellent actor he is. However it is Lee Marvin and the female roles that bring an extra dimension to the film and it is this that makes *The Big Heat* much more than a regular revenge flick. Stone (Marvin) is a cold, menacing brute and the scene where he throws a coffee pot at Debby (Grahame) is truly shocking and probably the film's most famous moment. The director, Lang, also uses the female roles to hint at a darker side to the movie. In his determination to bring the criminals down, Bannion seems almost careless of the cost and, even worse, he actively involves and endangers those in his care. Three women murdered and one who is very scared are a high price for Bannion's revenge, although he seems oblivious to the fact. It is, however, the pace and tension that Lang has wrought from the tight script and excellent cast that make this gritty noir such a standout film. From an era before violence was commonplace in filmmaking, *The Big Heat* is an excellent example of how it can be used to add impact to a clever plot and depth to sharply drawn characters.

REAR WINDOW

Alfred Hitchcock, USA, 1954

This highly charged suspense classic from Hitchcock shows all his flair for original and intelligent storytelling. L.B. 'Jeff' Jeffries (Stewart) is a much-travelled photographer, confined to a wheelchair with his leg in a cast. The rear window of his apartment looks out into the courtyard that he shares with his neighbours. Jeff amuses himself by watching the comings and goings outside and uses his telephoto lens to see through the open windows into his neighbours' apartments. This innocent voyeurism takes a dark turn when Jeff becomes increasingly sure that one of his neighbours, Lars Thorwald (Burr), has murdered his wife.

CAST INCLUDES:
James Stewart,
Grace Kelly,
Wendell Corey,
Thelma Ritter,
Raymond Burr
SCREENPLAY:
John Michael Hayes,
Cornell Woolrich
CINEMATOGRAPHY:
Robert Burks

The theme of voyeurism is central to this film; we, the audience, impotently watch as Jeff helplessly watches the world through his window. Hitchcock places the audience in Jeff's shoes through his camerawork – all of the action takes place either in Jeff's apartment or is viewed from his wheelchair through the window. Whatever Jeff sees through the lens the audience also sees, and this breaks the need for much dialogue to tell the story; instead the plot unfolds visually.

Grace Kelly gives a fine performance as Jeff's girlfriend, Lisa, a daily visitor to the flat, and she becomes his legs when he sends her to investigate his suspicions. This highlights, once again, Jeff's impotence as he cannot go to her aid when she is in danger. This inability to move is another diabolical tool that Hitchcock uses to incessantly notch up the tension. And of course we, the audience, are as helpless as Jeff and must sit passively and wait for the gripping finale. We know it's coming, and we're right.

THE NIGHT OF THE HUNTER

Charles Laughton, USA, 1955

CAST INCLUDES:
Robert Mitchum, Shelley
Winters, Lillian Gish, James
Gleason, Evelyn Varden,
Peter Graves
SCREENPLAY:
James Agee, Davis Grubb
CINEMATOGRAPHY:
Stanley Cortez

Ben Harper (Graves) is in prison awaiting execution for murder. His cellmate, Rev. Powell (Mitchum), tries unsuccessfully to persuade him to reveal where he has stashed $10,000 – the fruits of his crime. When Powell is released from prison, he makes a beeline for Ben's home and the newly widowed Willa (Winters). Powell marries her for the money without realizing that her two children are the only ones who know the location of the cash. Robert Mitchum played one of the most memorable villains in cinema with his portrayal of the preacher and manages to get the perfect balance between oily charmer and walking nightmare. The cinematography is highly stylized and almost Gothic at times, and sets the theme of the film as a fable or bad dream. Both original and frightening, many of the techniques used here would later inspire other, more obvious horror flicks.

RIFIFI (DU RIFIFI CHEZ LES HOMMES)

Jules Dassin, France, 1955

Rififi was made in France after the director was blacklisted in the anti-Communist witchhunt in post-war Hollywood. This low-budget film noir went on to become a classic; the main robbery sequence has inspired many imitators, although few can match it for pace and tension. Tony (Servais) has just been released from a prison sentence and is bent on taking his revenge on his ex-girlfriend, who is now involved with a small-time police informer and night club boss. This film is beautifully shot; no set could ever match these streets, cafés and bars. The black-and-white photography creates a wonderful style and captures the moody, smoky Paris of the 1950s. The heist it features is a great piece of filmmaking; for almost 30 minutes the thieves work in silence. No music, dialogue or effects interrupt the on-screen visual feast; a creaking floorboard and dropped screwdriver are the only noises and simply add to the tension.

CAST INCLUDES: Jean Servais, Carl Möhner, Robert Manuel, Jules Dassin, Marie Sabouret
SCREENPLAY: Jules Dassin, René Wheeler from the novel by Auguste Le Breton
CINEMATOGRAPHY: Philippe Agostini

THE KILLING

Stanley Kubrick, USA, 1956

CAST INCLUDES:
Sterling Hayden, Coleen Gray, Vince Edwards, Jay C. Flippen, Marie Windsor
SCREENPLAY:
Stanley Kubrick, Jim Thompson from the novel by Lionel White
CINEMATOGRAPHY:
Lucien Ballard

The title here refers not to a death but rather to a big payday; in this case $2 million. When Johnny Clay (Hayden) is released from prison, he is planning one last big heist before he retires. He recruits a group of willing helpers to ensure that his complex plan can be pulled off without anyone getting hurt. However, he doesn't plan on one of his gang spilling the beans, a fact which leads to some unexpected results. This film was quite a breakthrough for Kubrick both in terms of budget, the class of the cast and the attention it received in Hollywood. The film itself is a testament to the quality of direction. At a time when nonlinear timelines were mainly seen in flashback alone, Kubrick shows a deft touch in editing the film, telling a version of the story from each character's perspective. This enables the story to be told both through flashbacks and in jumps forward and allows the various strands of the plot to be developed simultaneously. The black-and-white cinematography adds an extra dimension to this classic, gritty noir. While the cast all turn in great performances, Hayden is the standout actor. By having such an insight into each character, Kubrick exposes both the gangs' blind greed and their foibles; it is these weaknesses that will eventually lead to their downfall.

TOUCH OF EVIL

Orson Welles, USA, 1958

CAST INCLUDES:
Charlton Heston, Janet Leigh, Orson Welles, Joseph Calleia, Akim Tamiroff, Marlene Deitrich
SCREENPLAY:
Orson Welles from the novel by Whit Masterson
CINEMATOGRAPHY:
Russell Metty

A car explodes, witnessed by a couple on their honeymoon; he is Mike Vargas (Heston), Mexico's leading narcotics policeman, who puts the honeymoon on ice to help investigate the bombing and comes into conflict with the local police. Orson Welles plays Captain Quinlan, the huge, sweating, embittered chief of police, who regularly plants evidence to support his intuition. Mike's wife, Susan, played by Janet Leigh, is excellent as the innocent who gets dragged into the middle of the conflict. Heston is restrained and controlled as the principled Mexican cop, although his make-up does make him stand out from the 'Latino' actors rather than fit in with them. However, it is Welles who shines, both in front of and behind the camera as director. The cinematography and Welles' virtuoso camerawork make *Touch of Evil* a taut and well-paced thriller. This was Welles' last film as a director in Hollywood, and as one of the highlights of his career it is as unforgettable and spectacular as the climax of the film itself.

GOLDFINGER

Guy Hamilton, GB, 1964

CAST INCLUDES:
Sean Connery, Honor
Blackman, Gert Fröbe,
Shirley Eaton, Tania Mallet,
Harold Sakata
SCREENPLAY:
Richard Maibaum, Paul Dehn
from the novel by Ian Fleming
CINEMATOGRAPHY:
Ted Moore

Goldfinger, the third film in the Bond franchise, is considered by many aficionados to be the best of the lot. This time around, Bond (Connery), the suave, sophisticated, spy about town, has to foil Auric Goldfinger (Fröbe), who plans to contaminate the gold reserves at Fort Knox. This Bond film was the first to make those fantastic gadgets an integral part of the movie, and also introduced us to the Aston Martin DB5. Auric Goldfinger is a more low-key villain than many others, but his mute, hat-throwing henchman Oddjob (Sakata) must surely rate as one of the most memorable sidekicks in the series. Pussy Galore was one of the few Bond girls to really have much in the way of character and intelligence, thanks to Blackman's charm and some neat writing. Of course, the real draw is Bond himself. Connery is an outstanding and utterly convincing 007. With a twinkle in his eye and a fine chest of hair he manages to pull off that most difficult of balancing acts: fancied by women and cheered on by men.

BONNIE AND CLYDE

Arthur Penn, USA, 1967

Clyde Barrow (Beatty) is a small-time bank robber just out of prison, who hooks up with Bonnie Parker (Dunaway), a girl bored with her small-town life. Together they embark upon a string of violent bank robberies throughout the 1930s' midwest. This is a classic story loosely based on real-life exploits. In *Bonnie and Clyde*, Penn has created a film that is by turns funny, tragic, subtle and, for its time, extremely violent. At first the film almost has the feel of a caper as Bonnie and Clyde turn over banks, get into scrapes and then escape. This all changes, however, when Clyde accidentally kills someone during a getaway. The mood of the film becomes more serious, and although the robberies continue, the violence increases and the humour becomes darker. Beatty and Dunaway give wonderful performances as the lovers on the run, but it is the supporting cast members that really shine. The result is an interesting study of violence and celebrity, where the stunning cinematography makes the folk story into a legend.

ACADEMY AWARDS
Best Actress in a
Supporting Role:
Estelle Parsons
Best Cinematography:
Burnett Guffey

CAST INCLUDES:
Warren Beatty, Faye
Dunaway, Michael J. Pollard,
Gene Hackman,
Estelle Parsons
SCREENPLAY:
David Newman,
Robert Benton
CINEMATOGRAPHY:
Burnett Guffey

IN THE HEAT OF THE NIGHT

Norman Jewison, USA, 1967

This film, set in the Deep South of the 1960s, has been widely praised for its treatment of racism in the story of a black cop visiting a bigoted town. When the body of a wealthy industrialist is found, the local police think they have solved the murder when they arrest Tibbs (Poitier), a black man waiting at the nearby station. However, it becomes apparent that they have the wrong man when Tibbs is revealed as a hot-shot police investigator, in town to visit his mother. Tibbs agrees to stay on and help local Police Chief Gillespie (Steiger) and, with some fancy police work, shows the local cops how it's done. Director Jewison provides marvellous direction in this character study camouflaged as a thriller. Steiger truly deserved his Oscar for his role as the lazy, prejudiced cop who learns a grudging respect for Tibbs, and Poitier's customary dignity and quiet authority is a perfect counterpoint. The two make a fascinating pair and their quietly developing relationship is one of the central themes of the film. *In the Heat of the Night* can be seen as a forceful, social commentary or simply a classic murder mystery. Either way, it is a thoughtful and entertaining movie.

CAST INCLUDES:
Sidney Poitier, Rod Steiger, Warren Oates, Lee Grant, Larry Gates
SCREENPLAY:
Stirling Silliphant from the novel by John Ball
CINEMATOGRAPHY:
Haskell Wexler

POINT BLANK

John Boorman, USA, 1967

CAST INCLUDES:
Lee Marvin, Angie Dickinson, Keenan Wynn, Carroll O'Connor, Lloyd Bochner
SCREENPLAY:
Alexander Jacobs, David Newhouse, Rafe Newhouse from the novel by Donald E. Westlake
CINEMATOGRAPHY:
Philip H. Lathrop

After being double-crossed and left for dead, a mysterious man named Walker (Marvin) single-mindedly tries to retrieve the rather inconsequential sum of money that was stolen from him. There are many aspects to this movie that take it outside the realms of the standard revenge flick. Marvin excels as a cold-blooded ruthless man out for not so much revenge as his money, something he will do anything to secure. Boorman's dream-like direction is firmly rooted in the art house; combined with a number of flashbacks, the viewer is invited to consider whether what he watches unfolding is in fact happening at all. Is it all a dream? Is Walker actually dead? These questions become more compelling when one realizes that Walker does not kill anyone in the film. While various people do meet untimely ends when Walker appears, the deaths are not actually his doing. This is a compelling movie that has only dated a little, in no small part because of the soundtrack.

BULLITT

Peter Yates, USA, 1968

Frank Bullitt (McQueen) and two other cops are assigned the task of protecting a mob witness by a shady politician. Each policeman agrees to take a shift in the small room overlooking the freeway. During the second shift, gunmen shoot the witness and the guard, and the police discover that the door to the room had been opened to the gunmen. The witness is rushed to hospital and Bullitt asks that the fact of the shooting be covered up. A further attempt at a hit is made on the witness in the hospital, and the gunmen begin following Bullitt. After an explosive finale to a spectacular car chase, Bullitt discovers that the witness may not be who he seems.

Praised as one of the greatest police dramas of all time, much of *Bullitt*'s fame comes from 'that' car chase. It is remembered as one of the seminal early, perhaps first, examples of the craft, and the film won an Oscar for Best Editing. However, judged by today's standards of *Matrix*-style CGI fests, the sight of a couple of cars speeding around the steep hills of San Francisco does not perhaps hold the appeal it once did. Movie nerds can amuse themselves by counting the number of hubcaps falling off the same car and watching out for the number of times the cars pass the same VW. There are a few interesting early cameos to look out for, and the film is more intelligent than most of its genre. Car chase aside, however, the plot is slow and a little pedestrian, although McQueen shines as the rugged cop who will do whatever is necessary to find out the truth.

ACADEMY AWARD
Best Film Editing:
Frank P. Keller

CAST INCLUDES:
Steve McQueen, Robert Vaughn, Jacqueline Bisset, Don Gordon, Robert Duvall
SCREENPLAY:
Alan Trustman,
Harry Kleiner from the novel by Robert L. Fish
CINEMATOGRAPHY:
William A. Fraker

THE ITALIAN JOB

Peter Collinson, GB, 1969

CAST INCLUDES:
Michael Caine, Noel Coward,
Benny Hill, Raf Vallone,
Tony Beckley
SCREENPLAY:
Troy Kennedy-Martin
CINEMATOGRAPHY:
Douglas Slocombe

Charlie Croker (Caine) has just been released from prison, but far from going straight, he is planning his next big robbery. To finance the heist he approaches Mr Bridger (Coward), an aristocratic gang boss currently serving time himself. The planning of the robbery and the escape give car-chase fans plenty to get excited about, and some of the one-liners have passed into history – 'You're only supposed to blow the bloody doors off!' And no one can ever forget the ultimate cliffhanger of an ending. This was Michael Caine's second film and certainly helped to propel him to stardom. As the Cockney wide-boy criminal he displays a charisma and charm that fits in well with the cheeky chases through the streets of Turin. The film harks back to more innocent times, when criminals could pull off a heist with a cosh and a smart mouth. Adding to this sense of nostalgia is Noel Coward's brief performance as the crime lord Mr Bridger in this, his last, film. A small nod of recognition and a half-wave is all the response needed when he gets an enthusiastic ovation from his fellow inmates; this is a dignified curtain call to a distinguished career. Any review of this film would be incomplete without mention of Benny Hill, whose performance is simply a reprise of his television show. His humour is as quintessentially British as the Mini Cooper and he is perfectly cast as a professor with a liking for the larger lady.

DIRTY HARRY

Don Siegel, USA, 1971

CAST INCLUDES:
Clint Eastwood, Harry
Guardino, Reni Santoni, John
Vernon, Andrew Robinson
SCREENPLAY:
Harry Julian Fink, Rita M. Fink,
Dean Riesner
CINEMATOGRAPHY:
Bruce Surtees

'Ask yourself one question: do I feel lucky? Well, do ya punk?' So asks Inspector Harry Callaghan in one of Eastwood's most memorable roles and one of cinema's most memorable quotes. In this first film of the *Dirty Harry* series we are introduced to the dangerous and violent side of San Francisco that is Callaghan's workplace. After thwarting a bank robbery and a suicide attempt, Callaghan is faced with his main challenge – a deranged sharpshooter killing innocent civilians and holding the city to ransom. After success in westerns and war films, this was one of Eastwood's first major roles in a contemporary movie. Despite playing the part of a policeman, Callaghan is for Eastwood essentially a reprise of his role as the man with no name; a maverick solving his problems with a Colt. Callaghan is insensitive, unsociable, and any humanity is largely left unspoken. This role confirmed Eastwood as a major star and set him firmly on the path to Hollywood legend.

THE FRENCH CONNECTION

William Friedkin, USA, 1971

CAST INCLUDES:
Gene Hackman,
Fernando Rey, Roy Scheider,
Tony Lo Bianco,
Marcel Bozzuffi
SCREENPLAY:
Robin Moore (novel),
Ernest Tidyman (screenplay)
CINEMATOGRAPHY:
Owen Roizman

Popeye Doyle (Hackman) and Buddy Russon (Scheider) are two New York policemen on the trail of a large shipment of heroin from France. As the police close in, Alain Charnier (Rey), one of the importers, decides to kill the cops to give them time to complete the deal. Gene Hackman won an Oscar for his portrayal of Popeye Doyle and rightly so, for he gave us one of cinema's most enduring characters. Far from being a typical hero, Popeye is a quick-tempered, hard-drinking bigot and neither the screenplay nor Hackman try to make us have much sympathy for him. Primarily filmed on location in France and New York, the latter in particular is grimy and run-down, showing us a glimpse of the true dark side of the city. This film is a lesson in the use of quality actors and patient directing to build characters and then use them to tell the story with pace and tension.

THE GODFATHER

Francis Ford Coppola, USA, 1972

ACADEMY AWARDS
Best Actor in a Leading Role:
Marlon Brando
Best Picture: Albert S. Ruddy

At its simplest, *The Godfather* is a film about a conflict within the Mafia. However, this is simply the stage that Coppola uses to set out what he is really interested in: loyalty, family and, most importantly, power. Don Corleone (Brando) is the leader of a Mafia family, in dispute over a proposal to sell drugs. When he survives an assassination attempt, it sparks a gang war and brings his eldest son, Michael (Pacino), back into the family business. One of Coppola's neatest tricks is how he creates sympathy for the heroes and makes us care about them. No mean feat, given the nature of their business, but this is achieved through limiting the scope of the film, most of which takes place in a family setting. The whole cast is wonderful but Brando, in particular, is faultless – powerful and utterly compelling. Pacino is also at the top of his game here; Michael is quietly assured and confident, not necessarily liking what he does but never hesitating. Add to the mix a fine supporting cast and dark, rich cinematography and you have a film worthy of all the popular and critical acclaim.

CAST INCLUDES:
Marlon Brando, Al Pacino,
James Caan, Richard S.
Castellano, Robert Duvall
SCREENPLAY:
Francis Ford Coppola,
Mario Puzo from his novel
CINEMATOGRAPHY:
Gordon Willis

THE STING

George Roy Hill, USA, 1973

CAST INCLUDES:
Paul Newman, Robert
Redford, Robert Shaw,
Charles Durning, Ray Walston
SCREENPLAY:
David S. Ward
CINEMATOGRAPHY:
Robert Surtees

ACADEMY AWARDS
Best Art Direction-Set
Decoration: Henry Bumstead,
James W. Payne
Best Costume Design:
Edith Head
Best Director: George Roy Hill
Best Film Editing:
William Reynolds
Best Music, Scoring Original
Song Score
and/or Adaptation:
Marvin Hamlisch
Best Picture: Tony Bill,
Michael Phillips, Julia Phillips
Best Writing, Story and
Screenplay Based on Factual
Material or Material Not
Previously Published or
Produced: David S. Ward

Redford and Newman reprise their partnership from *Butch Cassidy and the Sundance Kid* as two Chicago con men brought together by the murder of a mutual friend. They plan revenge against the culprit, mob leader Lonnegan (Shaw), who is himself a master con man. Their revenge is the only type they are capable of – a sting. To carry out the sting, they set up a fake gambling den in which the unexpected climax takes place. However, it's not only Lonnegan they have to deal with; they also have the police breathing down their necks. It's an elaborate and tightly plotted film, full of so many twists and turns that we are barely able to keep up with them on first viewing.

A film as much remembered for the design and music as the plot, few who watch it forget Redford's red suit or the recurring piano theme of 'The Entertainer'. A real example of how 'they don't make them like they used to'; likeable, loveable rogues get their revenge on the gangland boss through a combination of quick talking, a certain cheeky charm and their cunning and guile. The movie swept the board at the Oscars, and has certainly stood the test of time, to the extent that almost every film about con men is inevitably and unfavourably compared to it. It's best not to talk about the disappointing and frankly pointless sequel ten years later, or the pale imitators.

MEAN STREETS

Martin Scorsese, USA, 1973

CAST INCLUDES:
Robert De Niro, Harvey Keitel, David Proval, Amy Robinson, Richard Romanus
SCREENPLAY:
Martin Scorsese, Mardik Martin
CINEMATOGRAPHY:
Kent L. Wakeford

In this, his debut, Scorsese demonstrates the depth and originality of his filmmaking that would go on to become his trademark. The mean streets in question are those of Little Italy, New York. Charlie (Keitel) is a small-time hood working for his uncle. His friend Johnny (De Niro) seems bent on self-destruction, running up debts, blowing up mail boxes and, more seriously, disrespecting the local Mafia. While not in quite the same league as *Taxi Driver*, *Mean Streets* is still an amazing first film. Keitel shines in his role of nice-guy hood, but the star of the film is undoubtedly De Niro in what was, for him, a real career breakthrough. Smart use of a cracking soundtrack is something that Scorsese always does well. Here he doesn't disappoint, and the bar fight with 'Hey Mr Postman' as a backing track is inspired. The result is a gritty movie that draws on all the Italian-American influences from Scorsese's early years, and sets De Niro on the path to superstardom. The use of hand-held cameras adds a sense of realism to the film, putting the action and the violence in the face of the viewer.

CHINATOWN

Roman Polanski, USA, 1974

ACADEMY AWARD
Best Writing. Original Screenplay: Robert Towne

CAST INCLUDES:
Jack Nicholson, Faye Dunaway, John Huston, Perry Lopez, John Hillerman
SCREENPLAY:
Robert Towne
CINEMATOGRAPHY:
John A. Alonzo

Robert Towne deservedly won an Oscar for his screenplay of this masterly, complex mystery. It all starts off on a familiar footing. Jake Gittes (Nicholson), a Los Angeles private eye, is hired by Evelyn Cross Mulwray (Dunaway) to investigate the adultery of her husband. From there Jake is led through a world of intrigue and corruption. Although the plot is convoluted, the quality of the script provides a clear path through the maze of events. Add in some wonderful dialogue and the journey is a fascinating one. Nicholson is magical: in Gittes we can see the superstar he will become. His wicked grin softens the world-weary cynicism and adds a sympathetic side to his hard, somewhat aloof character. Dunaway is enchanting as the enigmatic, classy blonde and Huston is the perfect foil as her disturbing and pitiless father. The gorgeous cinematography and varied score by Jerry Goldsmith add the final touches to a classic piece of filmmaking by Polanski. This was the first film Polanski made after the murder of his wife, Sharon Tate. This goes some way to explaining the tragic conclusion of the film and perhaps contributes to the feeling of despair it leaves you with.

THE CONVERSATION

Francis Ford Coppola, USA, 1974

CAST INCLUDES:
Gene Hackman, John Cazale, Allen Garfield, Frederic Forrest, Cindy Williams
SCREENPLAY:
Francis Ford Coppola
CINEMATOGRAPHY:
Bill Butler

Hackman plays Harry, a paranoid and reclusive professional surveillance man who is instructed to spy upon a young couple. After taping a crucial conversation, he suspects that his work may lead to their murder and becomes obsessed with finding out the truth. This film is a real gem, but one that is often overlooked in Coppola's canon, coming as it did between *Godfather*s *I* and *II,* and well before *Apocalypse Now*. However, both director and leading man are at their best in this taut, psychological thriller. The themes of surveillance, paranoia and eavesdropping were fresh in the minds of the American people when this film was released, shortly after the Watergate scandal broke. While the film has certainly dated, these themes are no less relevant today. However, this is far more than a sociological document; this is a character study of a reclusive loner who, over the course of the film, realizes that his job has real, and deadly, consequences for his subjects, and the ensuing crisis of conscience that this realization brings. Technically superb, it deserves loud home-cinema treatment, particularly in the opening sequence and in the scene where Harry attempts to decipher the all-important missing phrase from the recording. The same themes have been repeated often in films since, but no subsequent film has captured its brooding sense of paranoia and claustrophobia.

DOG DAY AFTERNOON

Sidney Lumet, USA, 1975

CAST INCLUDES:
Al Pacino, John Cazale, Charles Durning, James Broderick, Beulah Garrick
SCREENPLAY:
Frank Pierson from the articles by P.F. Kluge and Thomas Moore
CINEMATOGRAPHY:
Victor J. Kemper

Al Pacino plays Sonny, a man who hatches a plan to rob a bank. He bungles it, and the police and news crews are alerted when a siege ensues. Over the next 12 hours, Sonny finds himself at the centre of a media circus. Allegedly based on a true story, this film can be viewed as a biting satire on the media's infatuation with crime and criminals. Pacino's brilliant portrayal could not be further removed from his previous role, Michael Corleone, in the criminal food chain. It's perhaps a moot point now whether he or Nicholson was more deserving of the Oscar for Best Actor, which went to the latter for *One Flew Over The Cuckoo's Nest*. The direction of Sidney Lumet (who teamed up previously with Pacino for *Serpico*) and the cinematography contribute to the edgy atmosphere, as the golden hues make the viewer almost feel the sweltering heat of that long, sticky Brooklyn afternoon.

TAXI DRIVER

Martin Scorsese, USA, 1976

Travis Bickle (De Niro) drives his cab around the dingy streets of New York, witnessing the underbelly of the city and becoming consumed by it. We know it will only be a matter of time before it facilitates his downfall. Bickle flaunts his frustrated isolation like a fallen Good Samaritan, inflicting his loneliness on those around him in the shape of unwanted attention and overzealous help. The apparent salvation of a 12-year-old prostitute (Foster) is blinkered by the self-satisfaction that is obviously derived by Bickle from his far from altruistic act of kindness. This is a man crushed by the grim memories and experiences of the Vietnam War, a man with nothing in his life bar his sexist world-view of the helpless woman in need of liberation. Of course, Scorsese points out the obvious; Bickle is the one who searches for redemption, his actions reflecting his own deep-rooted belief in his own superfluous existence. *Taxi Driver* was, and still is, a seminal work that maintains a position of great importance in cinematic history. The internal struggle played out with such conviction by De Niro allows the audience to see one man's struggle with his tortured life. It's a character study unrivalled since, showing an actor at his peak and screenwriting and directing at their very best.

CAST INCLUDES:
Robert De Niro, Cybill Shepherd, Peter Boyle, Jodi Foster, Harvey Keitel
SCREENPLAY:
Paul Schrader
CINEMATOGRAPHY:
Michael Chapman

SCARFACE

Brian De Palma, USA, 1983

CAST INCLUDES:
Al Pacino, Steven Bauer,
Michelle Pfeiffer, Mary
Elizabeth Mastrantonio,
Robert Loggia
SCREENPLAY:
Oliver Stone
CINEMATOGRAPHY:
John A. Alonzo

Tony Montana (Pacino) is a Cuban refugee who tries to go straight on his arrival in the US. When that doesn't work out, he turns to crime and over time, comes to run the Miami cocaine underworld. What goes up must come down, however, and the film charts Tony's inevitable paranoid decline. Written by a young Oliver Stone and directed by Brian De Palma after a number of critical flops, *Scarface* has become an iconic gangster movie. So much so, many forget that it was itself a remake of the 1932 classic, which was perhaps as controversial at that time as this was when first released. Eschewing the poetic beauty and themes of family ties, honour and respect of the *Godfather* films, this is an altogether different beast; one where people meet their end by chainsaw and where the protagonist is clearly insane from the beginning. To that extent, it's what *Goodfellas* would have been had Scorcese concentrated on Pesci's character rather than Liotta's. Not a thinking-man's gangster movie, we feel little sympathy or attachment for Tony Montana during his rise to power and miserable descent. The destruction of Pfeiffer and Mastrantonio is certainly not pleasant, although in other respects the film is riotously enjoyable, full of '80s' excess and brutal, almost comic book, violence.

CAST INCLUDES:
Harrison Ford, Kelly McGillis,
Josef Sommer, Lukas Haas,
Jan Rubes, Danny Glover
SCREENPLAY:
William Kelley, Earl W.
Wallace, Pamela Wallace
CINEMATOGRAPHY:
John Seale

WITNESS

Peter Weir, USA, 1985

While travelling with his mother, Rachel (McGillis), Samuel, a young Amish boy, is witness to the men's room murder of an undercover cop. The killers are soon on his trail, forcing mother, son and hard-bitten cop John Book (Ford) to take refuge within the Amish community. Director Peter Weir does a wonderful job in turning a simple good-cop, bad-cop witness protection movie into something much more. He explores the conflicts of two opposite lifestyles coming into contact and how a good man, such as Book, can unintentionally bring violence into a previously peaceful world. On a different level, this is a simple and beautifully understated love story. The chemistry of Ford and McGillis virtually crackles and the tension that builds between them is a treat to watch. Both turn in career-high performances; McGillis is captivating as the young widow, and Ford is great in one of his first serious roles as the unassuming hero. The cinematography and use of music is outstanding, and the barn-raising scene, in particular, is a lesson in filmmaking.

THE UNTOUCHABLES

Brian De Palma, USA, 1987

Sean Connery won an Academy Award for his role as a veteran Chicago cop in this gangster movie set in the 1930s. Federal Agent Elliot Ness (Costner) is determined to bring down Chicago crime lord Al Capone (De Niro), despite the fact that Capone runs the city and controls the police force. To aid him, Ness recruits George Stone (Garcia), a rookie sharpshooter straight out of the academy, Malone (Connery), a tough, old-school, beat cop, and Oscar (Smith), a Treasury accountant. Together, this team takes the title role and sets about indicting Capone for tax evasion. What follows is a stylish cops-and-robbers movie with excellent camerawork from Burum and some remarkable set pieces. De Niro turns in an excellent, if short, performance as Capone. He faultlessly switches between showboating media star and brutal mobster – his baseball-themed 'pep talk' is classic stuff. Costner, in one of his best performances, gives a fine depiction of the initially honourable and innocent Ness. His performance perfectly captures the changes that Ness experiences as he faces the consequences of the increasingly dirty war that he is waging on Capone. It is Connery, however, who gives the outstanding performance of the film. His on-screen presence dominates his scenes and he is utterly believable as the grizzled, hard-talking, streetwise cop.

With *The Untouchables*, De Palma has created a wonderfully entertaining film that's stylish and directed with flair. The scene where Malone is murdered is a lesson to all filmmakers in how to build up tension. The climactic baby carriage scene at Union Station is a superb example of how the interaction of music, sound effects and slow motion can create one of cinema's greatest shoot-outs.

ACADEMY AWARD
Best Actor in a
Supporting Role:
Sean Connery

CAST INCLUDES: Kevin Costner, Sean Connery, Charles Martin Smith, Andy Garcia, Robert De Niro
SCREENPLAY: David Mamet from the novel by Oscar Fraley, Elliot Ness and Paul Robsky
CINEMATOGRAPHY: Stephen H. Burum

GOODFELLAS

Martin Scorsese, USA, 1990

Goodfellas is based on the true story of one man's life in the New York Mafia. Liotta plays Henry Hill, the central character of the film, with De Niro and Pesci making up the other 'Goodfellas'. As Hill grows up, he progresses from running errands for the local Mafia to become a fully fledged member of the gang. Henry is half-Italian, half-Irish and as such will never be accepted into the higher echelons, but this does not prevent him from living the good life; status, cars, cash and mistresses are all to be enjoyed. The story really gets interesting when the bonds and loyalty that tie the Goodfellas together start to unravel.

From the director that made such classics as *Taxi Driver* and *Raging Bull*, it is high praise to rate *Goodfellas* as one of Scorsese's finest films, but it is completely justified. Scorsese provides an insight into the mob but without losing the audience's sympathy with, and interest in, the

CAST INCLUDES: Robert De Niro, Ray Liotta, Joe Pesci, Lorraine Bracco, Paul Sorvino
SCREENPLAY: Martin Scorsese from the book *Wise Guy* by Nicholas Pileggi
CINEMATOGRAPHY: Michael Ballhaus

characters. Add to that some outstanding performances from actors such as De Niro, Liotta and especially Pesci, and you have a brilliant movie. There is a fair amount of violence, but more worthy of note is the tension that Scorsese builds. This film also has humour, and if that's not enough, there are a couple of great recipes – just remember to slice your garlic with a razor blade.

MILLER'S CROSSING

Joel Coen/Ethan Coen, USA, 1990

CAST INCLUDES:
Gabriel Byrne, Marcia Gay Harden, John Turturro, Jon Polito, Albert Finney
SCREENPLAY:
Joel Coen, Ethan Coen
CINEMATOGRAPHY:
Barry Sonnenfeld

For fans of gangster movies, the Coen brothers have produced a classic film, full of sharp-suited spivs, corrupt cops, long-suffering molls and the best use of hats in any movie. Tom Regan (Byrne) is the right-hand man of Leo (Finney), a big-time gangster during Prohibition. When Leo falls for Verna (Harden), he refuses to let rival boss Johnny Caspar (Polito) kill Verna's brother Berni (Turturro), a cheating, snivelling bookie. Confused? You will be: the plot twists and turns with double- and triple-crosses as the characters all work the angles. Keeping up with the shifting allegiances is not made any easier by the dialogue, which is pure Coen brothers; a blend of slang, obscure nicknames and 1930s' gangster rap. In addition to the snappy dialogue, the Coen stamp can be seen in the feel of the locations. The overall result is a complex but hugely entertaining pastiche of the gangster movie – watch it, then watch it again.

BASIC INSTINCT

Paul Verhoeven, USA, 1992

CAST INCLUDES:
Michael Douglas, Sharon Stone, George Dzundza, Jeanne Tripplehorn, Denis Arndt
SCREENPLAY:
Joe Eszterhas
CINEMATOGRAPHY:
Jan de Bont

Nick Curran (Douglas) is a wily San Francisco detective who gets out of his depth while investigating the murder of an ageing rocker. Already under investigation himself for being too handy with his gun, Curran finds himself relentlessly drawn into the world (and bed) of the prime suspect, Catherine Tramell (Stone). In *Basic Instinct*, Verhoeven succeeded in bringing a strong cast to what is essentially a high-quality erotic thriller, a genre in which you would not normally expect to see the Hollywood élite. In fact, the hype that surrounded the release was due more to the combination of violence, sex and, let's be honest, that leg-crossing scene than the sight of Michael Douglas (naked or otherwise). Sharon Stone is sexy as hell and Verhoeven allows her character, and not her not-insignificant charms, to dominate her scenes. Whether she is off camera or on, Stone is the centre of attention and this can be seen by the lust in the eyes of all those men (and women) around her. Interestingly, though, Stone is often directed straight to camera, a neat trick that further emphasizes her character's ability to manipulate those around her. *Basic Instinct* keeps you guessing all the way, and the action and style make this movie stand out from the crowd of cheaper and poorer imitations that it has spawned.

RESERVOIR DOGS

Quentin Tarantino, USA, 1992

CAST INCLUDES:
Harvey Keitel, Tim Roth,
Michael Madsen,
Steve Buscemi, Chris Penn
SCREENPLAY:
Roger Avary,
Quentin Tarantino
CINEMATOGRAPHY:
Andrzej Sekula

This amazing debut film came about when Quentin Tarantino, then one of LA's many struggling actor-writers, met Harvey Keitel's wife at a screenwriting class. She read the script, passed it to Harvey and the rest is cinematic history. Five strangers, known only by pseudonym colours, are recruited to rob a diamond merchant. When the heist goes bad, the suspicious dogs try to identify the rat in the pack. In what has become trademark Tarantino style, some wonderful writing and editing shows the action, not chronologically, but in flashbacks and cuts forward. This technique of simultaneously developing different strands of the plot makes what is actually a very simple story seem vastly more complex. Amid the accusations and increasingly violent recriminations that follow the heist, the tension builds to a wonderful standoff and shocking climax. Some critics vilified Tarantino for packaging as über-cool a film with so much sadism, bloodshed and depravity. However, while parts of the film are undeniably shocking, much of the gore is so over-stylized as to be unbelievable. A career-defining performance from Michael Madsen, alongside the talents of Harvey Keitel and Steve Buscemi, give this film a weight that most independent filmmakers can only dream of. The sharp dialogue and a too-cool-for-school soundtrack combine to give an originality and style that would inspire countless copies and set Tarantino on his way to becoming one of Hollywood's big players.

PULP FICTION

Quentin Tarantino, USA, 1994

CAST INCLUDES:
John Travolta,
Samuel L. Jackson,
Uma Thurman, Bruce Willis,
Ving Rhames, Tim Roth
SCREENPLAY:
Roger Avary (stories),
Quentin Tarantino
(screenplay)
CINEMATOGRAPHY:
Andrzej Sekula

Pulp Fiction is a skilful collection of interconnecting stories, with overlapping and interwoven plots, the main characters of which inhabit a world of drugs, crime and damage limitation. The main link in each story is Vincent Vega, brother of Mr Blonde from *Reservoir Dogs* and played by the once-again-cool John Travolta. Vincent and his partner, Jules (Jackson), are killers working for Marcellus Wallace (Rhames); the film tells the story of what happens when simple things like a date, a fixed fight, a diner robbery and returning your boss's dirty laundry do not go according to plan. There are so many aspects of *Pulp Fiction* that are worthy of praise. The screenplay is incredibly tight, making it a pleasure to watch the varied stories unfold. The all-star cast relishes the cracking dialogue – the Oscar-winning writing is extravagant and clever, and each character has a distinct personal style which leads to some wonderful scenes. *Pulp Fiction* is a fantastic film – quirky, funny and with (literally) heart-stopping moments.

LÉON

Luc Besson, France, 1994

CAST INCLUDES:
Jean Reno, Gary Oldman,
Natalie Portman,
Danny Aiello
SCREENPLAY:
Luc Besson
CINEMATOGRAPHY:
Thierry Arbogast

Léon tells the tale of Mathilda (Portman), a 12-year-old girl living in a family without love. Her father is involved in drug dealing for some bent cops led by the terrifying Agent Stansfield (Oldman). When Stansfield discovers he is being cheated by Mathilda's father, he takes revenge by executing the entire family apart from Mathilda, who escapes and seeks refuge in a neighbour's flat. When Mathilda discovers that the neighbour, Léon (Reno), is a contract killer, she begs him to teach her how to settle her own scores. Luc Besson, writer and director, puts together a stylish and riveting thriller, which doesn't take itself too seriously. The pace is fast-moving and the action sequences are enjoyable. Jean Reno gives a solid performance in the title role and manages to balance the conflicting elements of his character well. It is, however, Portman, as Mathilda, who steals the show with a combination of lost waif meets driven avenger. Oldman is excellent as the psychopathic cop, and if he overplays the part he can be forgiven as he is a pleasure to watch. Placing a 12-year-old girl so firmly in the centre of such a violent and adult-themed film was a brave move by Besson, and he was criticized for it. Some of the themes are similar to his earlier release, *La Femme Nikita* (1992), except that in that film the would-be assassin is a young woman and not a young girl. That aside, *Léon* is well directed, entertaining and has a dynamic visual flair.

SE7EN

David Fincher, USA, 1995

CAST INCLUDES: Morgan Freeman, Brad Pitt, Kevin Spacey, Gwyneth Paltrow
SCREENPLAY: Andrew Kevin Walker
CINEMATOGRAPHY: Darius Khondji, Harris Savides

Se7en was a turning point in director David Fincher's career; prior to this he made *Alien 3*, and after this he made *Fight Club*. In *Se7en*, Fincher has made a film that is original and stylish; add in Brad Pitt, Morgan Freeman and a fantastic twist and you have something definitely worth seeing. The plot is diabolically straightforward. Detectives Somerset (Freeman) and Mills (Pitt) are investigating a series of brutal murders where the killer (Spacey) is, quite literally, making the seven sins deadly. The style of the movie fits the subject; the lighting is dark, often torchlit at the crime scenes; outside the rain is almost constant and the atmosphere is depressing. Pitt and Freeman are convincing as the unlikely partners, and the script gives them enough space to stamp their not inconsiderable talents on the roles. Spacey, however, runs away with the film as the supremely arrogant and intelligent psycho – his final smile is perfection. Not for the faint-hearted, *Se7en* is uncompromising and at times stomach-churning, but the details of the crimes are entirely necessary to balance the simplicity of the plot. The violence is never gratuitous – Fincher displays a delicate, stylish touch that is all the more effective.

THE USUAL SUSPECTS

Bryan Singer, USA, 1995

Bryan Singer's *The Usual Suspects*, an entertaining take on the heist movie, received widespread acclaim and commercial success. Five criminals are pulled in by the cops for a line-up. Subsequently released, it becomes apparent that they were drawn together for a reason, when a spokesman for the elusive criminal mastermind Keyser Soze approaches them. Soze is a sinister and widely feared gangster who wants them to raid a ship containing a drug shipment, kill everyone on board and collect a large sum of cash. Told primarily through flashback, the mystery deepens and the tension builds to a surprising twist. It is this revelation that is the film's crowning glory, and its weakest point. The surprise is so unexpected that you could kick yourself for not seeing it coming, but there are few clues that would enable you to work it out and hence the effect is rather contrived. Spacey is especially effective and gives the most memorable performance of the film; the Academy obviously agreed. They also rewarded Christopher McQuarrie with an Oscar for the screenplay.

CAST INCLUDES: Stephen Baldwin, Gabriel Byrne, Benicio Del Toro, Kevin Pollak, Kevin Spacey
SCREENPLAY: Christopher McQuarrie
CINEMATOGRAPHY: Newton Thomas Sigel

FARGO

Joel Coen/Ethan Coen, USA, 1996

With wide-open scenery, snowy fields, and some really strange accents, surely this film is set in some far-flung corner of Scandinavia? No, the location is actually the Coen brothers' home state of Minnesota. William H. Macy stars as Jerry Lundegaard, a sleazy second-hand car dealer who hires a couple of hoods to kidnap his wife to get a ransom from her rich father-in-law. Unfortunately for them, Marge Gunderson (McDormand), a police chief from a sleepy town in the American midwest, picks up their trail, a task not made any easier by the fact that she is hugely pregnant. Like all of the Coen brothers' films, *Fargo* looks great and sounds better. The scenery and landscapes are bleak, but you sense that the Coens retain a fondness for their childhood home. McDormand's character and her pregnancy add a warmth and humanity to balance the brutality and violence of the kidnappers. However, the comedy is black and the irony is thick. The story is not the most original, but the storytelling is delightful.

CAST INCLUDES:
Frances McDormand, William H. Macy, Steve Buscemi, Harve Presnell, Peter Stormare
SCREENPLAY:
Ethan Coen, Joel Coen
CINEMATOGRAPHY:
Roger Deakins

ACADEMY AWARDS
Best Actress in a Leading Role: Frances McDormand
Best Writing, Screenplay Written Directly for the Screen: Ethan Coen, Joel Coen

L.A. CONFIDENTIAL

Curtis Hanson, USA, 1997

CAST INCLUDES:
Kevin Spacey, Russell Crowe, Guy Pearce, James Cromwell, Kim Basinger, Danny DeVito
SCREENPLAY:
Brian Helgeland, Curtis Hanson from the novel by James Ellroy
CINEMATOGRAPHY:
Dante Spinotti

The seedy side of 1950s' Los Angeles is the setting for this complex tale of Hollywood sleaze and police corruption. An investigation into a series of unexplained murders draws together three very different cops: straight-laced and honest Ed Exley (Pearce), urbane and suave Jack Vincennes (Spacey) and maverick Bud White (Crowe), with a brutal temper always simmering just below the surface. With such an array of stars as this film boasts, there is always the worry that the whole will not be equal to the sum of its parts. No need to doubt: all the cast are on wonderful form, and none more so than Basinger as the high-class hooker and 'ringer' for Veronica Lake. While *L.A. Confidential* is imbued with much of the mood and tradition of film noir, it doesn't have the feel of a period piece. Hanson weaves a tangled storyline, but razor-sharp characters and excellent timing mean that following the plot is a great ride. It is difficult not to be drawn into the lush sights and sounds of Ellroy's Los Angeles, at times cynical but always seductive.

MEMENTO

Christopher Nolan, USA, 2000

CAST INCLUDES:
Guy Pearce, Carrie-Anne
Moss, Joe Pantoliano, Mark
Boone Junior, Russ Fega
SCREENPLAY:
Christopher Nolan, Jonathan
Nolan (story)
CINEMATOGRAPHY:
Wally Pfister

In a cinematic world full of remakes, reimaginings and all out copies, it is rare to find a movie as original and thought-provoking as *Memento*. Guy Pearce plays Leonard Shelby, a man searching for the man who raped and murdered his wife. Shelby has a problem, however; since his wife's death, he suffers from a rare disorder that means that he cannot retain new memories. As a result, he must make copious notes, take photos of people he meets, and even tattoo his body with hints in order to keep track of the ongoing investigation. Christopher Nolan lays out what he has in store for us from the opening shot, when we see a Polaroid fading from fully developed to completely blank. Nolan plunges the viewer into Shelby's shoes with a neat trick; while each scene is played chronologically, they are ordered in reverse. Hence the film starts at the story's conclusion and fills in the gaps as it 'progresses' to the beginning. This makes watching the film a confusing experience and there is no neat payoff after the climax. All of the characters seem to have some level of duplicity and it is unclear who can be trusted; Shelby himself manipulates his own memories through the notes he makes. To write off the film as unfathomable, however, is to understate its intelligence and inventiveness. Solid performances by the cast as well as taut and stylish direction bring out the most from the rightly acclaimed screenplay. And if you are frustrated by the labyrinthine editing, the DVD of the film allows the scenes to be played chronologically.

CITY OF GOD (CIDADE DE DEUS)

Fernando Meirelles, Kátia Lund (co-director), Brazil, 2002

Shot using a hand-held camera, *City of God* is a vibrant and dynamic glimpse of life in the slums of Rio de Janeiro through the 1960s, '70s and '80s. The story is told from the point of view of Rocket (Rodrigues), a quiet boy with no intention of falling into the cesspit of petty crime, drugs and violence that surrounds him. Instead he takes photos of his surroundings in order to try and escape them. Li'l Ze (Firmino), however, grows up leading a gang and is a ruthless, cold-hearted killer who builds up an empire that controls the City of God. Shocking and violent, this film pulls no punches. Murder and robbery are everyday events for even the youngest child, and when gang warfare breaks out, everyone is pulled in. The opening shot of the film is wonderfully imaginative and a signal to the audience that they are in for a great ride. The inventive camerawork and use of fast editing give the film a vibrancy and energy like no other. In addition, some wonderful characters and a sprinkling of humour give the whole movie a balance that shows the filmmakers' compassion for their subject.

CAST INCLUDES:
Alexandre Rodrigues, Leandro Firmino, Phellipe Haagensen, Douglas Silva, Jonathan Haagensen
SCREENPLAY:
Bráulio Mantovani from the novel by Paulo Lins
CINEMATOGRAPHY:
César Charlone

OLDBOY

Chan-wook Park, Korea, 2003

CAST INCLUDES:
Min-sik Choi, Ji-tae Yu, Hye-jeong Kang, Dal-su Oh, Byeong-ok Kim
SCREENPLAY:
Jo-Yun Hwang, Chun-hyeong Lim, Chan-wook Park
CINEMATOGRAPHY:
Chung-hoon Chung

After a night out drinking, Korean everyman Dae-Su Oh (Min-sik Choi) disappears without trace. He awakes in a small cell where he remains for 15 years before being released just as suddenly and strangely as he was taken. Still with no idea who took him or why, Dae-Su is obsessed with finding out. If you like films that offer a glimpse at the extremities of taste and decency, this could be for you. Try and imagine the *Saw* movies as directed by Quentin Tarantino and you're approaching the boundless craziness of *Oldboy*, the second film in Chan-wook Park's 'vengeance trilogy' (the others being 2002's *Sympathy for Mr Vengeance* and 2005's *Lady Vengeance*). It's a film of extremes. The violence is visceral and unyielding; the single-take scene in which Dae-Su must battle through a dozen thugs whilst armed with a single claw hammer has already gone down in movie legend, as has the moment he enjoys his first meal after 15 years in captivity… a very wriggly octopus. But the dramatic structure and photography are both impeccable, and Choi gives a powerhouse performance.

CACHÉ (HIDDEN)

Michael Haneke, France, 2005

CAST INCLUDES:
Daniel Auteuil, Juliette
Binoche, Maurice Bénichou,
Lester Makedonsky
SCREENPLAY:
Michael Haneke
CINEMATOGRAPHY:
Christian Berger

Georges Laurent (Auteuil), the host of an upmarket TV talk show, starts receiving strange videos filmed outside his home. At first he and wife, Anne (Binoche), suspect friends of their son, Pierrot (Makedonsky), are playing a practical joke, but as clues are gradually revealed, Georges begins to suspect a much darker and more complicated reason for the mysterious events. Michael Haneke's most successful film to date is an unflinching examination of how repressed guilt can, given the right trigger, suddenly become so acute it destroys everything around it. Georges is a privileged and slightly arrogant literary expert and art lover who has surrounded himself with all the usual trappings of a successful intellectual. From inside his stylish Parisian home the social troubles tearing at his country seem quaintly irrelevant, merely another subject for discussion with like-minded highbrows. The film deals with what happens when someone finds a way through the imposing fences that crowd his home and manages to tease out a forgotten and shameful memory.

THE DEPARTED

Martin Scorsese, USA, 2006

DID YOU KNOW?
Martin Scorsese put the finishing touches on this film a week before its theatrical release.

CAST INCLUDES:
Leonardo DiCaprio, Matt Damon, Jack Nicholson, Mark Wahlberg, Martin Sheen, Ray Winstone, Vera Farmiga, Alec Baldwin
SCREENPLAY:
William Monahan
CINEMATOGRAPHY:
Michael Ballhaus

Billy Costigan (DiCaprio), a young police cadet, is placed undercover in a Boston crime organization run by gangster Frank Costello (Nicholson). But Costello has had the same idea and signed up promising young gangster Colin Sullivan (Damon) to the police force. At first glance *The Departed* looks like it could be little more than a strategic exercise for a legendary director in need of a commercial hit. The story is lifted from hit Hong Kong thriller *Infernal Affairs*, the cast is littered with some of the world's most popular movie stars and the style is modern and accessible. But Martin Scorsese never makes movies by numbers, and though at first glance he looks to be playing safe, *The Departed* is actually his most ambitious and accomplished film in years. A story with two characters who are diametrically opposed in their nature, but who must play against that nature, provides plenty of opportunity to examine what makes a bad person bad and a good person good. Scorsese doesn't miss a trick and is relentless when it comes to exposing the flaws and facets of human nature. His determination requires some serious heavy lifting from his two young stars, both of whom deliver the best performances of their careers so far. With the serious acting taken care of, the rest of the cast seem to be enjoying themselves immensely. Alec Baldwin and Mark Wahlberg are better than they've been in years, as is Jack Nicholson, who appears to relish working with Scorsese, an inaugural collaboration that must have been at the top of many a cinephile's wish list for decades.

THE BOURNE SUPREMACY

Paul Greengrass, USA, 2004

CAST INCLUDES:
Matt Damon, Joan Allen,
Julia Stiles, Paddy Considine,
Edgar Ramirez,
David Strathairn,
Scott Glenn, Albert Finney
SCREENPLAY:
Tony Gilroy,
Robert Ludlum (novel)
CINEMATOGRAPHY:
Oliver Wood

ACADEMY AWARDS
Best Achievement
in Editing:
Christopher Rouse
Best Achievement in Sound:
Scott Millan, David Parker,
Kirk Francis
Best Achievement in
Sound Editing:
Karen M. Baker,
Per Hallberg

The further adventures of Jason Bourne (Damon), a former CIA operative now suffering from partial amnesia and being hunted by his old colleagues. In this third film in the series, Bourne is brought out of hiding by an English journalist (Considine) who is seeking many of the answers Bourne himself needs in order to fit together the pieces of his former life.

The first instalment in this fantastically successful series, 2002's *The Bourne Identity*, laid down a marker for all subsequent action-thrillers and spy movies. Its success may have come largely out of the blue, but by the time the sequel, *The Bourne Supremacy*, rolled around two years later, audiences were savvy to its potential and turned out in droves. The glowing reviews and enthusiastic crowds must have seemed like a double-edged sword for Paul Greengrass when he signed on to direct: get it wrong and you're a pariah; get it right and you might just hit upon a masterpiece. Fortunately, Greengrass did an exceptional job of building on the accumulated strengths and qualities of the franchise, and needless to say it was a roaring success and has gone on to be considered the series' crowning glory. Matt Damon is back and as brilliant as ever as everyone's favourite amnesiac superspy, whilst the standout newcomer is undoubtedly the oily CIA honcho Noah Vosen (Strathairn), who is convinced Bourne is a liability that must be 'resolved'.

WAR

WINGS

William Wellman, USA, 1927

CAST INCLUDES:
Clara Bow, Charles 'Buddy' Rogers, Richard Arlen, Jobyna Ralston, Gary Cooper
SCREENPLAY:
Hope Loring, Louis D. Lighton from a story by John Monk Saunders
CINEMATOGRAPHY:
Harry Perry

Two pals, Jack Powell (Rogers) and David Armstrong (Arlen), are vying for the same girl, Sylvia Lewis (Ralston). Mary Preston (Bow) is the doting girl next door with her eye on Powell. After they join up as airmen when America enters the First World War, Mary joins the war effort as an ambulance driver in France. Dedicated 'to those young warriors of the sky whose wings are folded about them forever', *Wings* was the first winner of the Best Picture Oscar award, the only silent film to have that honour. With its superb pictorial qualities, and the spectacular dogfights balanced with a tender love triangle, it is one of the best flying films of any period. William Wellman's experiences as a much-decorated airman during the First World War, and later as a stunt pilot, lent authority to the breathtaking aerial sequences, all filmed without faking or process shots. This was done by mounting cameras on the front of the planes, the actors going aloft with the pilot, who would duck down as they struck the right heroic attitudes. The film was shot with the cooperation of the US government, which supplied thousands of soldiers, hundreds of planes, and pilots as extras. Paramount Studios was flooded with fan letters for a young Gary Cooper, who was offered a contract based on his 20-second appearance.

ALL QUIET ON THE WESTERN FRONT

Lewis Milestone, USA, 1930

CAST INCLUDES:
Lew Ayres, Louis Wolheim, John Wray, Raymond Griffith, Gerard Duval
SCREENPLAY:
Del Andrews, Maxwell Anderson, George Abbott
CINEMATOGRAPHY:
Arthur Edeson

In Germany, at the start of the First World War, a group of schoolboys is inspired to join up by their chauvinistic schoolmaster. The film then follows seven boys, full of patriotic fervour, who are thrown into the horror of trench warfare, mainly the initially enthusiastic recruit Paul Baumer (Ayres). One by one, his comrades are maimed or killed in action, and Paul gets more and more disillusioned by the futility of war, until he, too, when reaching for a butterfly, is fatally shot by a sniper's bullet. Based on Erich Maria Remarque's novel, this devastating film was a milestone in antiwar movies, particularly as it is an American movie seen from the German side. The penultimate scene, when the young soldier sees the beauty of a butterfly amidst the carnage, is justly celebrated. Particularly effective were the tracking shots of the soldiers attacking the enemy lines and the counterattacks, with death on both sides. So realistic were these sequences that they have often been used in documentary films of the war, and the film won three Oscars.

LA GRANDE ILLUSION
THE GRAND ILLUSION

Jean Renoir, France, 1937

During the First World War, three French soldiers, the working-class Maréchal (Gabin), the middle-class Jew Rosenthal (Dalio) and the aristocratic Boieldieu (Fresnay), after attempting to escape from various German POW camps, are held prisoner in a fortress run by the Commandant Von Rauffenstein (von Stroheim). Boieldieu dies so that Maréchal and Rosenthal can escape. They make their way to a farm, where a German war widow (Parlo) gives them refuge before they can get across the border to Switzerland. Jean Renoir's most popular film, based on a true story, is not only a moving antiwar statement (though none of the war is seen), but also a rich exploration of class loyalties and transcendent friendships. Von Rauffenstein believes he has more in common with Boieldieu than they have with their fellow countrymen because of class. The fluid deep-focus photography (Renoir tried to keep people in frame at the same time, giving them equal status), the set pieces like the singing of 'La Marseillaise' during theatricals by prisoners in drag, and the extraordinarily sensitive performances make *La Grande Illusion* one of cinema's most enduring masterpieces.

CAST INCLUDES:
Jean Gabin, Pierre Fresnay,
Erich von Stroheim,
Marcel Dalio,
Dita Parlo, Julien Carette
SCREENPLAY:
Charles Spaak, Jean Renoir
CINEMATOGRAPHY:
Christian Matras,
Claude Renoir

IN WHICH WE SERVE

David Lean/Noel Coward, GB, 1942

CAST INCLUDES:
Noel Coward, Michael
Wilding, John Mills, Bernard
Miles, Celia Johnson
SCREENPLAY:
Noel Coward
CINEMATOGRAPHY:
Ronald Neame

HMS *Torrin*, a Royal Navy destroyer, is dive-bombed during the Battle of Crete and sinks. The surviving crew members manage to reach a float. As they await rescue – or death – each of them remembers the events leading up to that moment, and the homes and families they have left behind. This 'story of a ship', mostly told in flashback, has Noel Coward giving a characteristically clipped performance as the captain based on Lord Louis Mountbatten, freely re-enacting his naval exploits. Coward won a special Oscar for his 'outstanding production achievement'. Permeating this moving wartime propaganda epic is the deep love for the ship which symbolizes the nation, without too many false heroics or flag-waving. The film is also significant in giving David Lean, who edited the film, his first chance to direct. Other first-timers were Celia Johnson, Richard Attenborough, Daniel Massey and an 11-week-old Juliet Mills.

FIVE GRAVES TO CAIRO

Billy Wilder, USA, 1943

A British tank commander (Tone), caught behind the lines during the North African Campaign, stumbles into a resort hotel at a desert oasis. While the hotel is occupied by the advancing Field-Marshall Rommel (von Stroheim), the soldier poses as a club-footed waiter in order to unravel the meaning of the mysterious 'Five Graves'. He is helped by a French maid (Baxter), with whom he falls in love. Although a comparatively minor Billy Wilder movie, it is hugely enjoyable, with the war mainly acted out inside an oasis hotel. The script manages to inject wit and humour into a tense cat-and-mouse war drama, played out by Tone and the magnificent von Stroheim, who would later appear in Wilder's *Sunset Boulevard* (1950). Here he plays Rommel as a brutal Hun, not the noble soldier as portrayed later by James Mason in *The Desert Fox* (1951). Also excellent is Fortunio Bonanova as an opera-loving Italian and Akim Tamiroff as the wily hotel owner.

CAST INCLUDES: Franchot Tone, Erich von Stroheim, Anne Baxter, Akim Tamiroff, Peter Van Eyck
SCREENPLAY: Charles Brackett, Billy Wilder
(from the play by Lajos Biró)
CINEMATOGRAPHY John F Seitz

THE LIFE AND DEATH OF COLONEL BLIMP

Michael Powell/Emeric Pressburger, GB, 1943

A portrait, over 40 years, of an archetypal British officer, Clive Wynne-Candy (Livesey), during the Boer War, the First World War and the beginning of the Second World War, when he is seen as an old has-been who still believes he can win any fight with honour and maintain 'gentlemanly conduct'. Throughout, he keeps his friendship with a 'good' German officer (Walbrook) with whom he had fought a duel in Berlin in 1902. It takes his old German friend to point out how much the rules have been changed when fighting the Nazis.

Winston Churchill ordered the film to be banned from export because he felt it gave the wrong impression of the British soldier. It also stressed, unusually for the times, Anglo-German friendship. However, Michael Powell and Emeric Pressburger tried to enshrine the ambiguity of the British national character in General Wynne-Candy (played with wit and sincerity by Roger Livesey, expertly ageing throughout the film). It was the first Technicolor film made by the brilliant British writing-directing team, and it is truly sumptuous. A very young Deborah Kerr plays three parts across the three eras, embodying Wynne-Candy's vision of feminine charms.

DID YOU KNOW?

Colonel Blimp was a British cartoon character in a then well-known strip.

CAST INCLUDES: Roger Livesey, Anton Walbrook, Deborah Kerr, Roland Culver
SCREENPLAY: Michael Powell, Emeric Pressburger from the cartoon character created by David Low
CINEMATOGRAPHY: Georges Périnal

ROMA, CITTÀ APERTA
ROME, OPEN CITY

Roberto Rossellini, Italy, 1945

CAST INCLUDES:
Anna Magnani, Aldo Fabrizi,
Marcello Pagliero,
Maria Michi, Harry Feist
SCREENPLAY:
Sergio Amidei,
Federico Fellini
CINEMATOGRAPHY:
Ubaldo Arata

In 1944, in the last days of the German occupation of Italy, Resistance leader Manfredi (Pagliero), fleeing the Gestapo, is given refuge by the pregnant Pina (Magnani). When she is shot, he takes shelter with a good-time girl (Michi), who betrays him. Manfredi and a priest (Fabrizi) are arrested. However, the film offers some hope for the future and victory. The film that brought the Italian Neo-Realist movement to fruition was concerned with capturing, as directly as possible, the experiences of ordinary people caught up in political events. Using a documentary approach and filming with minimal resources in the actual streets and apartments of Rome, Roberto Rossellini achieved an immediacy and intensity that audiences had never previously witnessed. Two of the few professionals in the cast, Magnani and Fabrizi, give extremely moving performances. Emerging from the ashes of the Second World War, *Rome, Open City* is one of Europe's first post-war masterpieces.

THEY WERE EXPENDABLE

John Ford, USA, 1945

CAST INCLUDES:
Robert Montgomery,
John Wayne, Donna Reed,
Jack Holt, Ward Bond
SCREENPLAY:
Frank W. Wead from the
book by William L. White
CINEMATOGRAPHY:
Joseph August

DID YOU KNOW?
In the credits, the rank
and service of every
cast and crew member who
served during the war is listed.

Just before the outbreak of the Second World War, Lieutenant John Brickley (Montgomery) is assigned to take his Motor Torpedo Boat Squadron to Manila Bay to assist in the defence against a possible Japanese attack in the Philippines. However, once there, he finds that the top brass has relegated the small PT craft to messenger duty. But when war breaks out, Brickley and his crew shoot down three Japanese planes during an attack on their base. Again, when the squadron is reassigned to Bataan, they are ordered to run messages, until they prove their worth and that of the PT boat.

An elegiac portrait of the American navy in the Philippines just before the islands fell to the Japanese in 1942, *They Were Expendable* was also a tribute to Lieutenant John D. Bulkeley (later Vice Admiral) who pioneered the use of the PT boat in combat, played under the different name of Lieutenant John Brickley by a superb Robert Montgomery. The conviction of Montgomery's performance can be partly put down to the fact that he had just completed four years as a naval officer. John Ford, too, had served in the navy, making several notable documentaries. This experience also added to the film's realism and poignancy, one of the finest of all Second World War movies.

BATTLEGROUND

William A. Wellman, USA, 1949

CAST INCLUDES:
Van Johnson, John Hodiak,
Ricardo Montalban, George
Murphy, Marshall Thompson,
James Whitmore
SCREENPLAY:
Robert Pirosh
CINEMATOGRAPHY:
Paul C. Vogel

ACADEMY AWARDS
Best Cinematography,
Black-and-White: Paul Vogel
Best Writing, Story and
Screenplay: Robert Pirosh

Members of the US Army infantry unit are trapped during the siege at the Belgian town of Bastogne in December 1944. Among the motley group are a skirt-chaser (Johnson), who falls for a local girl (Darcel); a small-town journalist (Hodiak); a young Mexican (Montalban); and a veteran (Murphy) waiting for his discharge. They hold their ground against the Nazis, despite being surrounded and outnumbered. When all seems lost, Allied tanks begin to move in to the area and save the battered group.

'The guts, gags and glory of a lot of wonderful guys' read the posters, without revealing that the film depicts the misery, agony and grief of soldiers, with no glorification of individual servicemen. Grimly honest, with a small amount of love interest to leaven the seriousness, it steered away from the usual romantic view of war. This may be because the director, Wellman, a former pilot during the First World War, knew what war was all about. Bastogne was brilliantly re-created on MGM's backlot.

SANDS OF IWO JIMA

Allan Dwan, USA, 1949

CAST INCLUDES:
John Wayne, John Agar,
Forrest Tucker, Arthur Franz,
Richard Jaekel, Adele Mara
SCREENPLAY:
James Edward Grant,
Harry Brown
CINEMATOGRAPHY:
Reggie Lanning

Tough Marine Sergeant John Stryker (Wayne) seems a martinet and a bully as he trains young Marines for combat in the Pacific. As he leads them into battle to capture the strategic island of Iwo Jima, held by the Japanese, the troops begin to appreciate the importance of trust and friendship, especially in dangerous situations. Filmed at Fort Pendleton with the full help of the Marines, this gung ho classic, nowadays offensive to Japanese sensibilities, is considered the John Wayne war movie, and was a huge hit. Wayne, who was never near a war, gives one of his most convincing performances. The use of authentic combat footage is striking, and the three surviving Marine veterans who raised the American flag on Mount Suribachi in the iconic gesture, repeated here, have small parts. The final battle on the island is excitingly realized, and the relationships between the men are well explored.

TWELVE O'CLOCK HIGH

Henry King, USA, 1949

At the height of the Second World War, a US bomber squadron based in England is demoralized having suffered many losses. Brigadier General Frank Savage (Peck) has taken over command from Colonel Keith Davenport (Merrill). The pilots resent the new man, but as they continue to fly dangerous missions over Germany, they develop mutual respect and admiration. The antiheroic, realistic approach to warfare was unusual so soon after the actual events. Although there are exciting aerial sequences, it is on the ground that the film really gets tense. Despite Gregory Peck standing out in one of his finest performances, the picture offers a splendid example of ensemble acting. The film's climax, in which the general waits patiently for his squad to return to base – painfully aware that they may not return at all – is one of the most subtle yet emotionally intense scenes of any Second World War drama.

CAST INCLUDES:
Gregory Peck, Dean Jagger,
Hugh Marlowe, Gary Merrill
SCREENPLAY:
Sy Bartlett, Beirne Lay Jr.
from their novel
CINEMATOGRAPHY:
Leon Shamroy

ACADEMY AWARDS
Best Actor in a Supporting
Role: Dean Jagger
Best Sound Recording:
20th Century Fox Sound
Department

THE DESERT FOX

Henry Hathaway, USA, 1951

Field Marshall Rommel, the Desert Fox, is the commander of the crack Afrika Korps, whose brilliant tactics have earned him the respect of both friend and foe. When the tide is turning at El Alamein, Rommel disobeys Hitler's orders and pulls his men out of battle. Returning to Germany, he is torn between loyalty to his country and his own better judgment. He is forced to take drastic measures to save his wife and son from possible danger. This is not only a war film but also the tragedy of a man who waited too long before acting on his better instincts. As interpreted by James Mason, Rommel is competent, self-assured, loyal and aggressive, and the movie treats him as a wonderful soldier who is, unfortunately, on the wrong side. Rommel's home life is expertly sketched, making his final action understandable. Many of the scenes are filmed in a quasi-documentary style by Henry Hathaway, avoiding romantic heroics and sentimentality, and California stands in brilliantly for the North African desert. Mason repeated his sensitive impersonation of Rommel again in *The Desert Rats* (1953).

CAST INCLUDES:
James Mason, Cedric Hardwicke, Jessica Tandy, Luther Adler, Everett Sloane, Leo G. Carroll, George Macready, Richard Boone, Eduard Franz
SCREENPLAY:
Nunnally Johnson from the biography by Brigadier Desmond Young
CINEMATOGRAPHY:
Norbert Brodine

THE RED BADGE OF COURAGE

John Huston, USA, 1951

CAST INCLUDES:
Audie Murphy, Bill Maudlin, Douglas Dick, Arthur Hunnicut, Royal Dano, Andy Devine
SCREENPLAY:
John Huston, Albert Band from the Stephen Crane novel
CINEMATOGRAPHY:
Harold Rosson

During the American Civil War, Henry (Murphy), a raw recruit, loses his illusions of heroism during his first skirmish, a baptism of fire that makes him desert prior to engaging the enemy for the second time. While spending an idyllic time in the forest, he witnesses his friend's death and receives a wound from a retreating soldier. Henry gradually comes to terms with the realities of warfare and emerges as a hero. Few films have pondered so acutely the feelings of anxiety and outright fear in a young man preparing for battle. John Huston has caught the feeling of fright and awe in Stephen Crane's classic war novel, using remarkable documentary-style photography, although the film is renowned for having been butchered by MGM. A narration delivered by James Whitmore fills in some of the gaps created by the studio's scissor-happy editors.

DID YOU KNOW?
The boat used in the film had already been scrapped by the time the film premiered.

THE CRUEL SEA

Charles Frend, GB, 1953

CAST INCLUDES:
Jack Hawkins, Donald Sinden, Denholm Elliott, Stanley Baker, Virginia McKenna
SCREENPLAY:
Eric Ambler from a novel by Nicholas Monsarrat
CINEMATOGRAPHY:
Gordon Dines

The story follows the Royal Navy Corvette *Compass Rose* and her Captain (Hawkins), who moulds an inexperienced crew into an effective and disciplined fighting force, from the dark days before Dunkirk through to final victory. Shortly after the outbreak of the Second World War, the *Compass Rose*, under Captain Ericson, leaves harbour for sea trials and three weeks of training for her inexperienced crew. This proves a baptism of fire, as they are battered by storms. They later encounter their first U-boat. As the war rages, the ship and crew succeed, with many losses of life, in helping to defeat the U-boat threat.

Eight years after the end of the Second World War, Michael Balcon's Ealing Studios brought Nicholas Monsarrat's best-selling novel *The Cruel Sea* to the screen, launching the careers of Donald Sinden, Denholm Elliott and Virginia McKenna and also establishing Jack Hawkins as a star. The screenplay doesn't avoid showing the futility of war, and emphasizes the emotional and psychological damage inflicted by it: several officers turn to drink, an officer has a breakdown, a rating calls the captain a 'Bloody murderer!', and Ericson himself cries when his decision to depth-charge a U-boat results in the death of British sailors. In fact, this was a rare reaction to the usual 'stiff-upper-lip' heroics of British war films. It is also a prime example of a documentary style lending authenticity to a fictional story.

FROM HERE TO ETERNITY

Fred Zinnemann, USA, 1953

On a Hawaiian military base just before Pearl Harbor, Private 'Prew' Prewitt (Clift) is a stubborn soldier who transfers into a new unit. He immediately makes enemies with the captain of the unit when he refuses to participate in the army boxing tournament. However, he finds comfort in the arms of a hooker (Reed). Prew's friend Private Maggio (Sinatra) is picked on by sadistic Fatso (Borgnine) and dies in a knife fight. Meanwhile, First Sergeant Warden (Lancaster) is carrying on an affair with the wife of the captain. Then, the bombing of Pearl Harbor changes everything. Based on James Jones' hefty 859-page novel of the same name, it was skilfully boiled down, and toned down, for American audiences of the early 1950s, while still tackling controversial subjects such as prostitution, adultery, military injustice, corruption and violence, alcohol abuse and murder. Shot with almost documentary realism, it was a huge success, winning eight Oscars. It was also notable for the casting against type of the usually ladylike Deborah Kerr as the adulterous wife – her sex scene with Burt Lancaster on the beach has become an anthology piece – and for reviving Sinatra's flagging career.

CAST INCLUDES:
Burt Lancaster, Deborah Kerr, Montgomery Clift, Frank Sinatra, Donna Reed, Ernest Borgnine
SCREENPLAY:
Daniel Taradash from the James Jones novel
CINEMATOGRAPHY:
Burnett Guffey

STALAG 17

Billy Wilder, USA, 1953

Stalag 17 is an unruly Second World War POW camp run by an arrogant and cruel camp commandant, Von Scherbach (Preminger), who advises the American officer inmates about the impossibility of escape. In fact, every time someone has attempted it, the Germans seem to be aware of it and they are caught. A feeling grows that there must be a spy among the prisoners and the suspicion falls on Sefton (Holden), a cynical, cocky loner whose only interest in their escape plans is laying bets on them. Stalag 17 is a rousing, biting depiction of the raw and tense conditions among American servicemen in a prisoner of war camp. It shows all the cruel ironies, the jousting and scheming and one-upmanship games, the temporary loyalties and feuds and the accumulated tensions of a group of men in confinement.

CAST INCLUDES:
William Holden, Don Taylor, Otto Preminger, Robert Strauss, Neville Brand, Peter Graves, Sig Rumann
SCREENPLAY:
Billy Wilder, Edwin Blum from the play by Donald Bevan and Edmund Trzcinski
CINEMATOGRAPHY:
Ernest Laszlo

ACADEMY AWARD
Best Actor in a Leading Role:
William Holden

MISTER ROBERTS

John Ford/Mervyn Leroy/Joshua Logan (uncredited), USA, 1955

On a small cargo ship, the USS *Reluctant* (a.k.a. 'the Bucket'), floating somewhere in the Pacific during the Second World War, Lieutenant Roberts (Fonda), the gentle cargo officer who fears he will miss seeing action before the war is over, mollifies a long-suffering crew, including the resourceful, lazy and boastful Ensign Pulver (Lemmon) and the world-weary doctor (Powell) against the machinations of their tyrannical captain (Cagney). After the crew wreaks havoc ashore, the captain inflicts a demanding work schedule on them. Driven beyond his breaking point, Mr Roberts avenges himself upon the hated symbol of the captain's authority, a jealously guarded and much-watered palm tree. Ensign Pulver also finds the strength to make his own stand against the captain's tyranny. There was a great deal of drama off-screen in the making of *Mister Roberts* when John Ford and Henry Fonda, re-creating his Broadway role, clashed, resulting in Ford walking off the picture. Ironically, Jack Warner wanted Marlon Brando or William Holden but Ford had held out for Fonda. Nevertheless, the film turned out to be a big box-office and critical hit, mainly because of the trenchant script and the performances of Fonda, returning to the screen after seven years, Cagney in one his most unsympathetic roles, Powell in his last screen appearance and Lemmon, whose Oscar-winning portrayal set the seal on the type of role he would soon be making his own. Although not a shot is fired in the film, it makes a strong statement about men at war.

CAST INCLUDES: Henry Fonda, James Cagney, William Powell, Jack Lemmon, Nick Adams
SCREENPLAY: Joshua Logan and Frank S. Nugent from the play by Logan and the novel by Thomas Heggen
CINEMATOGRAPHY: Winton C. Hoch

ACADEMY AWARD
Best Actor in a Supporting Role:
Jack Lemmon

ATTACK!

Robert Aldrich, USA, 1956

CAST INCLUDES:
Jack Palance, Eddie Albert,
Lee Marvin, Robert Strauss,
Buddy Ebsen
SCREENPLAY:
James Poe from the play
The Fragile Fox by
Norman Brooks
CINEMATOGRAPHY:
Joseph Biroc

During the Second World War's Battle of the Bulge, a cowardly captain (Albert) and a conniving colonel (Marvin), who ignores his inferior's mistakes, risk the lives of a platoon, diligently led by Lieutenant Costa (Palance), who suffers a smashed arm in the battle. The platoon has to fight its way back from the front line, where it has been stranded without cover. Costa then confronts the captain. Few punches are pulled in this chillingly ambiguous depiction of the attitude of certain officers during the Second World War, the main targets of the screenplay's scorn. No wonder the US Defense Department declined to cooperate on the production, a bold film to make during the Eisenhower era. The all-male cast, headed brilliantly by Jack Palance in one of his most demanding roles, demonstrate Robert Aldrich's central theme of 'man's efforts to prevail against impossible odds'. The powerful ending has Eddie Albert having a mental breakdown and Palance becoming an avenging monster.

THE BURMESE HARP BIRUMA NO TATEGOTO

Kon Ichikawa, Japan, 1956

By July 1945, the war was nearing its end for the Japanese forces in Burma. Among the many units crossing the mountains of Burma to escape into Thailand was one in which the men sang songs to the accompaniment of a strange handmade instrument resembling a Burmese harp. One of these soldier-musicians, the young Private Mizushima (Shoji Yasui), decides to become a Buddhist monk and attempts to bury as many bodies of Japanese soldiers as he can. Kon Ichikawa's first film on what he termed 'the pain of the age', is a non-naturalistic odyssey in visionary black-and-white images throbbing with the anguish that war brings. Adapted from Michio Takeyama's novel by the director's wife, it was one of the first of a number of Japanese films concerned with pacifist themes related to the defeat of Japan in 1945, and is almost an act of atonement made by the post-war Japanese film industry. It not only indicts militarism but is also a cry of anguish for those who suffered during the war. *The Burmese Harp* achieves its power and poignancy through the juxtaposition of the horror of war with the beauty of nature.

CAST INCLUDES:
Shôji Yasui, Rentaro Mikuni,
Tatsuya Mihashi, Taketoshi
Naîto, Jun Hamamura
SCREENPLAY:
Natto Wada based on the
novel by Michio Takeyama
CINEMATOGRAPHY:
Minoru Yokoyama

THE BRIDGE ON THE RIVER KWAI

David Lean, GB, 1957

British POWs in Burma are ordered to build a bridge across the River Kwai by camp commander Colonel Saito (Hayakawa), which will be used to transport Japanese munitions. Colonel Nicholson (Guinness) refuses, despite all the various 'persuasive' devices at Saito's disposal. Finally, Nicholson agrees, not so much to coooperate with his captor as to provide a morale-boosting project for the military engineers under his command. Meanwhile British and American intelligence officers, led by American Shears (Holden) and Major Warden (Hawkins), conspire to blow up the structure, but Nicholson has acquired a sense of pride in his creation and tries to foil their plans. *The Bridge on the River Kwai* was based on the best-selling novel by Pierre Boulle, out of which David Lean fashioned a spectacle of brilliant set pieces, at the same time forcing audiences to question their received ideas about individual courage and responsibility. Such is the film's cunning that we have been encouraged to identify with Guinness's character to the point that we, too, resist the demolition of the bridge, a structure that can only aid the enemy. Superbly cast, especially Guinness, who is the personification of courage and stubbornness, the film was distinguished by a narrative and visual sweep. It took a gruelling three months to shoot in Ceylon.

CAST INCLUDES: William Holden, Alec Guinness, Jack Hawkins, Sessue Hayakawa, Geoffrey Horne
SCREENPLAY: Carl Forman, Michael Wilson (Pierre Boulle credited for the blacklisted writers above) from the novel by Boulle
CINEMATOGRAPHY: Jack Hildyard

DID YOU KNOW?
The Bridge on the River Kwai won seven Oscars at the 1958 Academy Awards.

PATHS OF GLORY

Stanley Kubrick, USA, 1957

Based on an actual incident in the First World War that was hushed up by the French authorities at the time, *Paths of Glory* is set at the front, in France, in 1916. A general (Macready), with the complicity of another scheming general (Menjou), orders Colonel Dax (Douglas) to fire on his own troops because some of them refused to go over the top. Dax defies the orders, and three men are chosen at random and executed after a court martial. The furious colonel resigns his commission.

The antimilitarist stance of *Paths of Glory* was so powerful that the film was banned in parts of Europe (especially France) and in US military movie theatres for some years. It came opportunely in the aftermath of the Korean War and after Senator McCarthy's fall. The bitterly ironic and moving film established Stanley Kubrick as an important figure in American cinema. Much of the graphic description of trench warfare must be attributed to the camerawork of Georg Krause, but the crosscutting, the savage view of the officers and the harsh awareness of death were all Kubrick's. A particularly poignant scene is towards the end, when a young German woman (played by Kubrick's wife, Susanne Christian) stills a crowd of rowdy French veterans with a song in a café. It is perhaps significant that this outspoken movie never won a major award.

CAST INCLUDES:
Kirk Douglas, Ralph Meeker, Adolph Menjou, George Macready, Wayne Morris
SCREENPLAY:
Stanley Kubrick, James Thompson, Calder Willingham from the novel by Humphrey Cobb
CINEMATOGRAPHY:
Georg Krause

BALLAD OF A SOLDIER
BALLADA O SOLDATE

Grigori Chukhraj, USSR, 1959

CAST INCLUDES:
Vladimir Ivashov,
Zhanna Prokhorenko,
Antonina Maksimova,
Nikolai Kryuchkov
SCREENPLAY:
Grigori Chukhrai,
Valentin Yezhov
CINEMATOGRAPHY:
Vladimir Nikolayev,
Era Saveleya

A naïve young soldier refuses a medal and instead takes four days' leave from the front to visit his mother at the height of the Nazi invasion. En route, by train, truck and on foot, he meets various people affected by the war – a crippled veteran, a comic sentry, faithful and faithless wives, and a girl with whom he falls in love. We know from the outset that he will be killed in battle and buried by strangers, far from home, known to them only as 'a Russian soldier'.

This simple and moving view of everyday life in wartime Russia helped the move away from Soviet socialist realism towards a more humanistic cinema. With its ballad-like structure and unrhetorical style, the film drew on the director's own experiences of the misery and waste of war and the confusion of the aftermath. It continued the trickle of Soviet films welcomed in the West in the late 1950s. In fact, it was the first film from the USSR to enter an American film festival – in San Francisco – which it won.

THE GUNS OF NAVARONE

J. Lee Thompson, USA/GB, 1961

CAST INCLUDES:
Gregory Peck, David Niven,
Stanley Baker, Anthony
Quinn, Anthony Quayle,
Irene Papas, Gia Scala
SCREENPLAY:
Carl Foreman from the novel
by Alistair MacLean
CINEMATOGRAPHY:
Oswald Morris

A group of commandos, made up of Allied and Greek soldiers, each with a specialist talent, is assembled by British intelligence in an attempt to achieve the impossible – destroying the seemingly impregnable German artillery cannons concealed deep within solid rock on the Greek island of Navarone. A rip-roaring adventure yarn that includes bloody hand-to-hand conflicts between the good guys and the Nazis, an enormous tidal wave and our heroes scaling treacherously steep cliffs, most of it is spectacularly filmed on Rhodes. It was a tremendous box-office hit and it remains one of the best films of its type. The action spoke louder than words, although Carl Foreman's script had a great deal to say about the various loyalties and motivations of the characters, played by a terrific cast, with Niven almost stealing the show as a cynical, cowardly commando.

THE LONGEST DAY

Ken Annakin (British scenes), Andrew Marton (American scenes),
Bernhard Wicki (German scenes), USA , 1962

On 6 June 1944, the Allied invasion of France marked the end of Nazi domination over Europe. The attack involved 3,000,000 men, 11,000 planes and 4,000 ships. This epic re-creation is seen from the viewpoints of the French, English, German and American soldiers, and features an all-star cast, who speak in their own languages. The massive preparations, mistakes and random events that determined the outcome are shown and add to the realism. A three-hour epic, the film takes on the daunting task of covering that fateful day from all perspectives – from the German high command and front-line officers, to the French Resistance and all the key Allied participants. The screenplay by Cornelius Ryan, based on his own authoritative book, is as factually accurate as possible. The endless parade of stars (John Wayne, Sean Connery and Richard Burton, to name a few) makes for an astute mix of realism and Hollywood star-power.

CAST INCLUDES:
Richard Burton, Sean
Connery, Henry Fonda, Curt
Jurgens, Robert Mitchum,
Robert Ryan, John Wayne
SCREENPLAY:
Romain Gary, James Jones,
David Pursall, Jack Seddon,
Cornelius Ryan (from
his book)
CINEMATOGRAPHY:
Jean Bourgoin, Walter Wottitz

THE GREAT ESCAPE

John Sturges, USA, 1963

CAST INCLUDES:
Steve McQueen,
James Garner, Richard
Attenborough, James
Coburn, Charles Bronson,
Donald Pleasence,
James Donald
SCREENPLAY:
W.R. Burnett, James Clavell
from the book by Paul Brickhill
CINEMATOGRAPHY:
Daniel Fapp

In Stalag Luft III in Upper Silesia in March 1944, the German high command has selected a group of the most talented British, American and Canadian escape artists and placed them in a POW camp specifically designed to foil any attempts at escape. But as soon as they arrive, the prisoners, led by Steve McQueen as the rebellious Virgil Hilts, begin work on a series of tunnels under the direction of Roger 'Big X' Bartlett (Attenborough). More than 70 men get away, and the film then follows their attempts to get out of Germany. *The Great Escape* was the longest (173 minutes), most expensive and biggest money-making POW picture of all. Though the plot was similar to many other barbed-wire-tunnel-digging pictures, this was directed with greater gusto and offered some ingenious variations on the familiar theme. Filmed in Germany, the picture starts light-heartedly, and ends in a tragic but uplifting manner.

THE TRAIN

John Frankenheimer, France/Italy/USA, 1964

CAST INCLUDES:
Burt Lancaster, Paul Scofield,
Jeanne Moreau,
Michel Simon, Suzanne Flon
SCREENPLAY:
Franklin Coen, Frank Davis,
Walter Bernstein, Albert
Husson based on *Le Front de
l'Art* by Rose Valland
CINEMATOGRAPHY:
Jean Tournier, Walter Wottitz

During the last days of the German occupation of Paris, von Waldheim (Scofield), an art-obsessed German colonel, arranges to steal all of the city's great art treasures and send them on a train to Germany. When the French Resistance discovers the plan, Labiche (Lancaster), a French railway engineer, is ordered to stop the train. Not wishing to risk lives or the paintings, which are part of the French national heritage, Labiche concocts an elaborate scheme to keep the train in France. Both Labiche and von Waldheim become obsessed with their missions. *The Train* begins with a dedication 'to those French railway men, living and dead, whose magnificent spirit and whose courage inspired this story'. The film also seems a tribute to Burt Lancaster's athletic prowess. He leaps over walls and on and off trains. Even when he's shot in the leg, he moves faster than anyone else in the mostly genuine French cast. The fast-paced action is very well handled by John Frankenheimer. Real trains, not models, were used throughout, with multiple cameras capturing as much action in as few takes as possible. During one crash sequence, a locomotive came in too fast and destroyed six of the seven cameras in one blow. The film also raises the question whether any work of art is worth someone's life.

THE BEDFORD INCIDENT

James B. Harris, USA, 1965

CAST INCLUDES: Donald Sutherland, James MacArthur, Richard Widmark, Sidney Poitier, Martin Balsam
SCREENPLAY: James Poe based on a novel by Mark Rastovich
CINEMATOGRAPHY: Gilbert Taylor

The USS *Bedford*, on a routine NATO patrol, ends up in a showdown with a Russian submarine. Captain Eric Finlander (Widmark), the maniacal commander, obsessed with hunting down the sub, regardless of the risks involved, drives his tense crew to the brink of nervous exhaustion. Ben Munceford (Poitier), a photojournalist aboard, is assigned to record a 'typical' mission. His moral indignation is put to the test by the captain's obsession with forcing the sub to the surface. Several crew members are at their breaking points as Finlander continues his prowl. Especially affected is a former German U-boat commander (Portman), now aboard the *Bedford* as a NATO observer. The director, James B. Harris, managed to capture the claustrophobia of the confined setting, and maintained dramatic tension throughout. Although the cat-and-mouse chase is reminiscent of the earlier Second World War film with Robert Mitchum chasing a Nazi sub in *The Enemy Below* (1957) and the later *The Hunt For Red October* (1990), there is unspoken racism in Finlander's animosity towards Munceford, and the battle of wits on board the American destroyer reflects the battle outside it. It is also a reflection on the madness that could have ignited the Cold War into a hot one at any moment. In addition, it played on the public anxiety about nuclear war, as seen in other films such as *Dr Strangelove* (1964).

VON RYAN'S EXPRESS

Mark Robson, USA, 1965

An American Air Force pilot, Colonel Joseph Ryan (Sinatra), is shot down and placed in an Italian POW camp, mainly housing British troops. Because Ryan is now the highest-ranking officer, he takes over command from Major Eric Fincham (Howard), thus creating animosity between them. When Italy surrenders to the Allies, the Italian jailers desert and the prisoners are left on their own. Under Ryan's command, the prisoners escape from Italy by stealing a German prisoner of war train heading for a German concentration camp and divert it northwards to neutral Switzerland and freedom. When the Germans realize what has happened, the chase is on.

CAST INCLUDES:
Frank Sinatra, Trevor Howard, James Brolin, Raffaela Carra, Brad Dexter
SCREENPLAY:
Wendell Mayes, Joseph Landon from the novel by David Westheimer
CINEMATOGRAPHY:
William H. Daniels

Von Ryan's Express is a really rousing Second World War yarn, excellently handled by Mark Robson and his expert team. There are several exciting sequences, such as the escapees disguised in German uniforms trying to get past the checkpoints, an encounter with a double-dealing Gestapo agent, and an attack on the central railway control tower in Milan. The concluding battle, set in the Alps, has the prisoners attempting to clear the tracks while fighting off attacking German aircraft and also their oncoming German pursuers. It is as much fun as an old-fashioned serial.

DID YOU KNOW?
Michael Goodliffe, who plays Cpt Stein, was an actual PoW. He spent five years in a German camp.

THE DIRTY DOZEN

Robert Aldrich, USA/GB, 1967

CAST INCLUDES:
Lee Marvin, Ernest Borgnine, Charles Bronson, Jim Brown, John Cassavetes, Robert Ryan, Donald Sutherland
SCREENPLAY:
Lukas Heller, Nunnally Johnson from the novel by E.M. Nathanson
CINEMATOGRAPHY:
Edward Scaif

ACADEMY AWARD
Best Effects, Sound Effects: John Poyner

A group of 12 hardened American military prisoners – murderers, rapists, thieves and assorted misfits – most of whom are facing death sentences, are given the chance to redeem themselves by going on a suicide mission behind Nazi lines. They are whipped into a crack army unit by tough Major Reisman (Marvin), who initially uses them to best the troops of his by-the-book superior officer, Colonel Breed (Ryan), in war games. The 'dirty dozen' includes a sex pervert (Savalas), a psycho (Cassavetes) and a retarded killer (Sutherland). They then lead a perilous assault on a well-guarded chateau and kill the Nazi officials vacationing there, becoming somewhat dubious heroes. Robert Aldrich, who by the time of *The Dirty Dozen* had been delving into the darker side of life for more than a decade, scored a huge hit with this rousing thriller laced with a stinging cynicism perfectly in tune with the increasingly sceptical tenor of the times. Though condemned for its excessive violence, this much-imitated war movie was the most popular film of 1967. The ironic aspect is that these criminals are redeemed by committing acts that are more barbaric than the ones they were condemned for – because anything is acceptable in war. As in Aldrich's *Attack!*, it gives the impression that officers were hypocritical and stupid and only the ordinary soldier is worth anything.

WHERE EAGLES DARE

Brian G. Hutton, GB, 1968

In 1944, Major John Smith (Burton), a British agent, is in charge of a group of six Allied soldiers given the task of rescuing an American general — who is reportedly in possession of the plans for D-Day — from a seemingly impregnable German fortress located high in the Bavarian Alps. The general must be freed before being made to reveal Allied plans for an invasion of France. Assisting Smith is an American, Lieutenant Morris Schaffer (Eastwood), a fierce soldier with an array of deadly weapons. As the men penetrate the fortress, facing an endless supply of German soldiers, it becomes apparent that there are double and triple agents in the ranks of the rescue team.

Where Eagles Dare has all the elements of a stirring war adventure story, and makes spectacular use of the location high in the Alps for scenes such as the thrilling fight on top of a cable car. No need to ask for much deep characterization, although there is a sparky chemistry between the contrasting Richard Burton and Clint Eastwood, and there is the presence of one of the nastiest Nazis in the business, the sneering Anton Diffring. The plot, too, is more complex than many of the cliffhanging serials the film resembles.

CAST INCLUDES:
Clint Eastwood,
Richard Burton, Mary Ure,
Michael Horden,
Anton Diffring
SCREENPLAY:
Alistair MacLean from
his novel
CINEMATOGRAPHY:
Arthur Ibbetson

HELL IN THE PACIFIC

John Boorman, USA, 1968

CAST INCLUDES:
Lee Marvin, Toshirô Mifune
SCREENPLAY:
Alexander Jacobs,
Eric Bercovici
CINEMATOGRAPHY:
Conrad Hall

Set in the Pacific in 1944, the film focuses on two combatants stranded on the same barren atoll: a Japanese naval officer (Mifune) and a US Marine pilot (Marvin). At first the two men warily stalk each other, both revealing something by refusing to kill the other when the opportunity arises. As both men grasp the pointlessness of their behaviour, a truce develops between them. They soon become aware that coooperation would help speed their departure and increase their odds of survival. In what is virtually a silent film, Boorman invokes his recurring 'man against nature' theme, here seen as a plea for human solidarity. Marvin shows a psychological complexity rarely seen in his other work, while Mifune displays the kind of physical dynamism that brought him fame in the films of Akira Kurosawa. According to Marvin's widow, 'Of all the movies of Lee's career, *Hell in the Pacific* was undoubtedly the most important to him on a personal level. In it he was reliving, exploring and resolving his feelings about his war, and putting the results on the screen.' Conrad Hall's camerawork does justice to the spectacular beauty of the Micronesian islands where the film was shot. The drama of enemies forced to share their lives makes a powerful statement.

CAST INCLUDES:
Alan Arkin, Orson Welles,
Anthony Perkins, Martin
Balsam, Richard Benjamin,
Jon Voight
SCREENPLAY:
Buck Henry from the novel
by Joseph Heller
CINEMATOGRAPHY:
David Watkin

CATCH-22

Mike Nichols, USA, 1970

The film centres on a group of Second World War fliers in the Mediterranean and the insanity of war. The catch-22 of the title deals with a military snafu that results when a bombardier, the highly neurotic and paranoid Captain Yossarian (Arkin), attempts to get out of the military by feigning insanity — however, completing the paperwork for this proves him sane. No matter how crazily he behaves, the army Air Corps is crazier. His superiors and peers are all buffoons and maniacs. Indeed, the insanity of the war only seems to feed their personal aberrations. Eventually Yossarian is psychologically isolated. *Catch-22* is a funny, bizarre, satirical black comedy, and was still relevant nine years after the novel by Joseph Heller was published. It has a terrific all-star cast led by Arkin, whose deadpan performance refuses to provide Yossarian with any sentimentality. David Watkin's camerawork is brilliant, capturing the feel of the bright sunlight of the location, and Nichols' direction captures the paradoxes and surrealism that pervade military life.

TORA! TORA! TORA!

Richard Fleischer/Toshio Masuda/Kinji Fukasaku, USA/Japan, 1970

The bombing of Pearl Harbor is presented from the perspectives of both the Japanese and American sides. The first half shows the collapse of diplomacy between the nations as tension rises. While the Japanese military plans its attack on American military installations, the American forces, due to a series of blunders, leaves the naval and air forces sitting ducks for the impending attack. The second half is the devastating battle itself. Despite audiences knowing the result of the build-up towards Pearl Harbor, the tension that leads up to it is palpable and the climactic 30-minute battle, a massive feat of cinematic engineering, still excites as well as surprises. What makes this epic war film stand out from previous chronicles of the Second World War is that *Tora! Tora! Tora!* was an American–Japanese co-production giving an equitable view of the historic battle. Richard Fleisher oversaw the complicated production, having to work with two Japanese directors (after Akira Kurosawa withdrew from the film), turning the story, with dozens of characters, into a coherent whole.

CAST INCLUDES:
Martin Balsam,
Jason Robards, Sô Yamamura,
Joseph Cotton, E.G Marshall
SCREENPLAY:
Larry Forrester, Hideo Oguni,
Ryuzo Kikushima from
the books *Tora! Tora! Tora!*
by Gordon W. Prange and
*The Broken Seal:
Operation Magic and the
Secret Road to Pearl Harbor*
by Ladislas Farago
CINEMATOGRAPHY:
Charles F. Wheeler

ACADEMY AWARD
Best Effects,
Special Visual Effects:
L.B. Abbott, A.D. Flowers

M*A*S*H

Robert Altman, USA, 1970

CAST INCLUDES:
Donald Sutherland,
Elliott Gould, Tom Skerritt,
Sally Kellerman,
Robert Duvall
SCREENPLAY:
Ring Lardner Jr. from the
novel by Richard Hooker
CINEMATOGRAPHY:
Harold E. Stine

ACADEMY AWARD

Best Writing, Screenplay
Based on Material from
Another Medium:
Ring Lardner Jr.

This is life in a Mobile Army Surgical Hospital – a Korean War field hospital. Between gory operations to save soldiers' lives, anarchic medics Hawkeye (Sutherland) and Trapper John (Gould) play practical jokes and pursue nurses, under the nose of their nemesis, Major Burns (Duvall). When M*A*S*H appeared in 1970, audiences – caught up in rebellion generated by the civil rights movement, feminism, the drug culture and the demonstrations against the Vietnam War – revelled in the film's iconoclastic humour, its joyous deflation of patriotism, religion, heroism and other values cherished by the establishment. It wasn't lost on them that Korea was standing in for Vietnam. The outrageous black comedy became an immediate box-office success, and spawned a popular long-running TV series. It also was the first financial and critical success for Robert Altman, who said he was offered M*A*S*H because '14 more acceptable directors turned it down'. Altman's experimental use of sound is evident with simultaneous conversations and loudspeaker announcements.

PATTON

Franklin J. Schaffner, USA, 1970

This biopic follows the campaigns of US Commander General George S. Patton (Scott), from Tunis to the conquest of Sicily – where he slaps a fatigued soldier and is relieved of his command – later to England and to Normandy in charge of the Third Army. He lifts the siege of Bastogne during the Battle of the Bulge, then, pushing into Czechoslovakia and sniffing glorious victory, he is forced by Eisenhower to make way for Montgomery's northern front. After the war, Patton's forces occupy Bavaria, but his unconcealed resentment of the Russians and his refusal to dismiss Nazis from civil office lead to his downfall and bitter departure. One of the most intelligent war epics of its period, the film hinges on George C. Scott's gargantuan performance – conceived like a tragic Shakespearean hero. Scott, his head shaved, his craggy features cast in expressions of contempt or rage, took the role because Patton 'was a professional and I admire professionalism'. Yet Scott refused to pick up his Oscar, considering the award ceremony to be a 'meat market'. The script represents Patton as a huge, ebullient warlord – a driven man to whom war and victory are all – but also as an enigma of flawed humanity. Although there are only 11 minutes of battle scenes in the film, it illustrates much about modern warfare.

CAST INCLUDES:
George C. Scott,
Karl Malden, Stephen Young
SCREENPLAY:
Francis Ford Coppola
and Edmund H. North
from books by
Omar N. Bradley and
Ladislas Farago
CINEMATOGRAPHY:
Fred Koenekamp

DID YOU KNOW?

Patton won seven Oscars at the 1971 Academy Awards.

CROSS OF IRON

Sam Peckinpah, GB/West Germany, 1977

CAST INCLUDES:
James Coburn, Maximilian Schell, James Mason, David Warner
SCREENPLAY:
Julius Epstein, James Hamilton, Walter Kelley from the novel *The Willing Flesh* by Willi Heinrich
CINEMATOGRAPHY:
John Coquillon

Set in 1943, *Cross of Iron* focuses on Corporal Steiner (Coburn), an accomplished but war-weary combat veteran, leading a doomed German platoon facing annihilation on the Russian front. While the enemy attacks, Steiner's authority is undermined when Captain Stransky (Schell) takes over the command of his troops. A Prussian aristocrat, Stransky has one goal in mind: to win the coveted Iron Cross, Germany's highest medal, at any cost. There follows an intense battle of wills. 'Men on the front lines of Hell' screamed the posters for *Cross of Iron*, Sam Peckinpah's only war film, which proved to be just as disturbing and compelling as many of his westerns. *Variety* commented that 'pacifism, Peckinpah style, means mayhem is the message'. But the director's characteristic graphic style is wedded to the violence of the subject of war, seen from the German perspective. He presents a male ethos wherein moral certainty is collapsing. There's usually little room for women in Peckinpah's world, though an encounter with female guerillas shows them exacting revenge with dreadful results.

THE DEER HUNTER

Michael Cimino, USA, 1978

CAST INCLUDES:
Robert De Niro, John Cazale, John Savage, Christopher Walken, Meryl Streep
SCREENPLAY:
Michael Cimino, Deric Washburn, Louis Garfinkle, Quinn K. Redeker
CINEMATOGRAPHY:
Vilmos Zsigmond

The Deer Hunter explores the experiences shared by a group of young men growing up in a small Pennsylvania industrial town, whose lives are dominated by the gruelling labour in the steel mills. Mike (De Niro), Nick (Walken) and Stevie (Savage) are just about to depart for military training, having volunteered to go to Vietnam together. They are thrown into the hell of war, which affects their lives forever. This was the first major American movie about the Vietnam War, and one of the most controversial. The controversy derived from the harrowing sequence in which American POWs are forced to play Russian roulette by their captors, a device used here as a metaphor for the futility of the war itself. Also to be taken metaphorically is the untriumphal singing of 'God Bless America' at the end. The film's principal theme of friendship and the personal impact of war packs a devastating dramatic punch, and exactly caught the mood of the time. It won five Academy Awards, including Best Picture.

APOCALYPSE NOW

Francis Ford Coppola, USA, 1979

CAST INCLUDES:
Marlon Brando,
Martin Sheen, Robert Duvall,
Fred Forrest, Sam Bottoms,
Albert Hall, Dennis Hopper,
Larry Fishburne
SCREENPLAY:
John Milius, Francis Ford
Coppola loosely based on
Heart of Darkness
by Joseph Conrad
CINEMATOGRAPHY:
Vittorio Storaro

ACADEMY AWARDS
Best Cinematography:
Vittorio Storaro
Best Sound: Walter Murch,
Mark Berger, Richard Beggs,
Nathan Boxer.

Loosely based on *Heart of Darkness*, by Joseph Conrad, *Apocalypse Now* tells the story of Captain Willard (Sheen), a special agent sent into Cambodia to assassinate the renegade American Green Beret Colonel Kurtz (Brando), who has set himself up as a god to the local tribe. Willard is assigned a navy patrol boat operated by Chief (Hall) and three young 'rock-'n'-rollers with one foot in the grave' (Forrest, Bottoms and Fishburne). They are escorted on part of their journey by an air cavalry unit led by Lt Colonel Kilgore (Duvall), a gung ho commander, who carries out a helicopter bombing raid on a peasant village. When he reaches Colonel Kurtz's compound, a crazed photojournalist (Hopper) welcomes the crew, and Willard begins to question his orders to 'terminate the colonel's command'. The gruelling making of this film in the Filipino jungles is almost as famous as the film, as it led to vast budget overruns and physical and emotional breakdowns. *Apocalypse Now* assaults the senses with some extraordinary set pieces. Coppola certainly achieved his aim of wanting to give the audience the sense of 'the horror, the madness, the sensuousness and the moral dilemma of the Vietnam War'. The opening scene is a perfect illustration of how Coppola combines vision and sound when the sight of helicopter blades dissolves into those of an electric fan on the ceiling above Willard. The combined brilliance of the cinematography, editing and sound montage (Walter Murch) makes the bombing sequence one of the most celebrated in cinema history. After they have blasted the village to the sound of 'The Ride of the Valkyries', Duvall announces, 'I love the smell of napalm in the morning.' In 2001, *Apocalypse Now Redux*, a restored and updated version of the film, was released, including 49 minutes of never-before-seen footage.

THE BIG RED ONE

Sam Fuller, USA, 1980

CAST INCLUDES:
Lee Marvin, Mark Hamill,
Robert Carradine, Bobby
DiCicco, Kelly Ward Johnson
SCREENPLAY:
Samuel Fuller
CINEMATOGRAPHY:
Adam Greenberg

*T*he *Big Red One* follows the fortunes and misfortunes of a squad from the 1st US Infantry Division (The Big Red One) through the Second World War, from a beachhead assault on North Africa to France, Sicily, Belgium and on to the liberation of a concentration camp in Czechoslovakia. A nameless battle-hardened sergeant (Marvin) and four young recruits are the only members of the squad who survive the war. Director Sam Fuller had carried the story of *The Big Red One*, his first film in seven years, around in his head since his experiences as a GI in Europe during the Second World War. There are hardly any heroics – the final line is 'Survival is the only glory in war' – just a stark, yet poetic description of incidents. War is reduced to its bloody essentials in Fuller's direct, no-holds-barred method, and although his screenplay makes no effort to delve too deeply into the characters, through whose eyes a series of battles are seen, we gradually get to know their desires and fears. The film, shot almost entirely on location in Israel, was two years in the making.

DAS BOOT

Wolfgang Petersen, West Germany, 1981

CAST INCLUDES:
Jürgen Prochnow,
Herbert Grönemeyer,
Klaus Wennemann,
Hubertus Bengsch,
Martin Semmelrogge
SCREENPLAY:
Wolfgang Petersen from the
novel by Lothar G. Buchheim
CINEMATOGRAPHY:
Jost Vacano

*I*n 1941, the German submarine fleet is heavily engaged in the Battle of the Atlantic to harass and destroy English shipping. One such U-boat goes on a dangerous mission from La Rochelle to Spain and back, threatened by Allied depth charges and air raids. *Das Boot* (The Boat) is the most popular foreign-language film ever released in the United States. The film examines, in almost documentary detail, how these submariners maintained their professionalism, attempting to accomplish impossible missions while all the time attempting to understand and obey the ideology of the government under which they served. At $12 million, the most expensive German film to date is a compendium of every submarine movie ever made, with all the expected claustrophobic horrors. The main interest is not only in seeing the war from the German point of view, although most of the crew are 'good' Germans – there is only one despised Nazi on board – but also in the spectacular hand-held camerawork, accurately depicting conditions underwater. It lives up to the director's desire 'to show the gritty and terrible reality of war and to combine it with a highly entertaining story and fast-paced action style that would pull audiences into the experience of these young men'.

THE KILLING FIELDS

Roland Joffe, GB, 1984

CAST INCLUDES:
Sam Waterston, Haing S. Ngor, John Malkovich, Julian Sands, Craig T. Nelson, Spalding Gray, Bill Paterson, Athol Fugard
SCREENPLAY:
Bruce Robinson
CINEMATOGRAPHY:
Chris Menges

ACADEMY AWARDS

Best Actor in a Supporting Role: Haing S. Ngor
Best Cinematography: Chris Menges
Best Film Editing: Jim Clark

It is Year Zero when Pol Pot's Khmer Rouge entered the capital Phnom Penh, turned the population into serfs and slaughtered two million of them. The story is told from the perspective of Pulitzer Prize–winning American journalist Sidney Schanberg (Waterston), whose friendship with his interpreter, Dith Pran (Ngor), forms the basis of the film. Pran saves the lives of Schanberg and his fellow journalists, and is then left to save himself from the labour camps and certain death by obliterating all traces of his education. He escapes into Thailand and is finally reunited with Schanberg, who, in his turn, had been searching for him. *The Killing Fields* has a scale and humanity seldom seen these days, especially in British films, and the evocation of the suffering of the people, especially that of Dith Pran, has an unparalleled emotional force. The fact that he was portrayed by first-time actor Haing S. Ngor, a Cambodian gynaecologist whose own family had been wiped out by the Khmer Rouge, adds to the potency of the film. Unhappily, the Oscar-winning Dr Haing S. Ngor was brutally murdered by a street gang for no reason at all several years later. The whole atmosphere of the period is brilliantly captured by the camera of Chris Menges.

COME AND SEE (IDI I SMOTRI)

Elem Klimov, USSR, 1985

Teenaged Florya (Kravchenko) is taken off by a group of anti-German partisans, fighting in the woods of Byelorussia in 1943. They disappear and he is left to wander, gun in hand, until he rejoins them as a hardened and active participant as a result of the horrors he has witnessed. Drawn from three different books by Ales Adamovich, *Come and See* has been reconstructed as a surreal tragedy, described as 'an epic of derangement'. This sense of derangement is heightened by the film's soundtrack, most significantly when the bombing of a village damages Florya's hearing. Florya's ordeal, which turns his hair grey and wrinkles his young face, is undeniably moving. From the moment, early on in the film, when the boy discovers his village is destroyed and his family dead, the viewer joins him in witnessing an unbroken series of Nazi atrocities. Some of the images are unforgettable, such as the agonizing struggle through a swamp to reach an encampment of lamenting women, and the journey to find food, accompanied by a death's head effigy of Hitler.

CAST INCLUDES:
Aleksei Kravchenko,
Olga Mironova, Liubomiras
Lauciavicius,
Vladas Bagdonas
SCREENPLAY:
Ales Adamovich, Elem
Klimov based on the works
of Ales Adamovich
CINEMATOGRAPHY:
Aleksei Rodionov

PLATOON

Oliver Stone, USA, 1986

In Vietnam, Chris (Sheen), a raw recruit, or 'new meat', at first wonders whether he'll ever be able to survive in the jungle conditions. But he gradually adapts and, as time goes by, begins to see that the platoon is divided into two groups. On the one side is the evil, battle-scarred vet Sergeant Barnes (Berenger), who believes in total war, and on the other is the good, battle-weary veteran Sergeant Elias (Dafoe), who believes in compassion and humanity. After a lull of seven years since *Apocalypse Now*, the previous serious film to depict the Vietnam War directly, *Platoon* forcefully returned the war to the Hollywood agenda. It slammed the spectator with spectacular sights and sounds, portraying the mindless jingoism, the brutality, the torture and killing of Vietnamese peasants, and the dependency on booze and drugs of the average American soldier, or 'grunt'. Loosely autobiographical, the hell of Vietnam is made more real by Stone's own vivid memories of his time in Vietnam.

CAST INCLUDES:
Tom Berenger, Willem Dafoe, Charlie Sheen, Forest Whitaker, Francesco Quinn, Kevin Dillon, Reggie Johnson, Keith David, Johnny Depp
SCREENPLAY:
Oliver Stone
CINEMATOGRAPHY:
Robert Richardson

ACADEMY AWARDS
Best Picture: Arnold Kopelson
Best Director: Oliver Stone
Best Sound: John Wilkinson, Richard Rogers
Best Editing: Claire Simpson

FULL METAL JACKET

Stanley Kubrick, USA, 1987

Full Metal Jacket begins at Parris Island in South Carolina for one platoon's recruit training. We meet Sergeant Hartman (Ermey), the senior drill instructor, and several privates he decides to pick out and nickname. After boot camp, the new marines are shipped to Vietnam. Kubrick's penultimate film is a cynical, cold-as-steel, often stylized view of the Vietnam War, revealing the ritualized debasement of men in the name of patriotism in the first half, and the horrific results of this patriotism in the second. The boot-camp section goes further than any film before it in showing the sadistic brutality of the training, here in the person of Sergeant Hartman (brilliantly played by real-life drill sergeant R. Lee Ermey). The film is successful in personalizing war with the selective trials of soldiers, somewhere between the realism of *Platoon* and the surrealism of *Apocalypse Now*.

CAST INCLUDES:
Matthew Modine, R. Lee Ermey, Arliss Howard, Vince D'Onofrio, Adam Baldwin
SCREENPLAY:
Stanley Kubrick, Michael Herr and Gustav Hasford, based on the novel *The Short Timers* by Gustav Hasford
CINEMATOGRAPHY:
Douglas Milsome

GOOD MORNING, VIETNAM

Barry Levinson, USA, 1987

CAST INCLUDES:
Robin Williams,
Forest Whitaker, Tung Thanh
Tran, J.T. Walsh,
Robert Wuhl, Bruno Kirby
SCREENPLAY:
Mitch Markovich
CINEMATOGRAPHY:
Peter Sova

DID YOU KNOW?
Good Morning, Vietnam
was actually filmed
in Thailand.

Adrian Cronauer (Williams) is an airman disc jockey who is brought from Crete to Saigon in 1965 to entertain the troops and boost their morale. His morning programme on the Armed Forces Network is an inventive mix of outrageous comic routines, controversial political humour and loud rock music. While many at the station celebrate this breath of fresh air, his immediate superiors, including a straight-laced lieutenant and an uptight sergeant major, are angered by his unconventional and unpredictable behaviour. Based on the case of a US Armed Forces' DJ, the film, if one discounts *M*A*S*H* – ostensibly about the Korean War – was the first Vietnam comedy and one of the first to treat the Vietnamese as real people. Robin Williams gives what virtually amounts to an extremely funny virtuoso stand-up (though he's at the turntable) comedy solo. The broadcasts, all of which were ad-libbed by Williams, are what is mostly remembered about the film, but it also captures the tensions and misunderstandings of the war. Adrian's pursuit of a beautiful Vietnamese girl, and his friendship with her brother, eventually get him into deep trouble with those who see all Vietnamese as the enemy.

SCHINDLER'S LIST

Steven Spielberg, USA, 1993

At the start of the Second World War, Oskar Schindler (Neeson), a wealthy businessman who owns a munitions factory, is a member of the Nazi Party but quickly learns to manipulate the corrupt and cruel system to his own purposes. The drinking, gambling and womanizing Schindler becomes moved by the plight of the Jews, and he risks his own life and fortune by rescuing more than 1,000 of them from the gas chambers by employing them in his factory. This ambitious movie finally brought Steven Spielberg Best Picture and Best Director Oscars after trying for nearly 20 years. With an intelligent script and a superb cast, it has a documentary-style resonance achieved by shooting black-and-white hand-held camera footage. Filming in authentic locations in Poland, Spielberg came closer than most directors to capturing the impossible – the Holocaust. Possibly the most moving moment in the film is the epilogue (in colour) of the actual survivors and their families, including his widow, filing past Oskar Schindler's grave in Israel.

CAST INCLUDES:
Liam Neeson, Ralph Fiennes, Ben Kingsley, Caroline Goodall, Jonathan Sagalle
SCREENPLAY:
Steven Zaillian based on the novel *Schindler's Ark* by Thomas Keneally
CINEMATOGRAPHY:
Janusz Kaminski

DID YOU KNOW?
Schindler's List won seven Oscars at the 1994 Academy Awards.

SAVING PRIVATE RYAN

Steven Spielberg, USA, 1998

CAST INCLUDES:
Tom Hanks, Edward Burns, Tom Sizemore, Jeremy Davies, Van Diesel, Matt Damon
SCREENPLAY:
Robert Rodat
CINEMATOGRAPHY:
Janusz Kaminski

American soldiers land on Omaha Beach during the D-Day landings in the Second World War, with multiple deaths from enemy fire. An army captain (Hanks) has been assigned to take his squad of seven men into France to find Private Ryan (Damon), whose three brothers have been killed in combat, and get him home to his grieving mother. The film opens with some of the most devastating footage of combat ever committed to film. For 20 minutes the audience is assailed by sight and sound in an attempt to re-create the feeling of being in the midst of a battle. Much of this terrifying effect is due to the camerawork of Janusz Kaminski. Having established that war is hell, the film moves into a complex examination of heroism, much of it seen through the eyes of Corporal Upham (Davies), the frightened translator, who speaks excellent German and French, but is really a civilian and the audience's surrogate. The film won five Oscars.

DOWNFALL (DER UNTERGANG)

Oliver Hirschbiegel, Germany, 2004

CAST INCLUDES:
Bruno Ganz, Alexandra Maria Lara, Corinna Harfouch, Ulrich Matthes, Juliane Köhler, Heino Ferch
SCREENPLAY:
Bernd Eichinger (screenplay), Joachim Fest, Traudl Junge, Melissa Müller (books)
CINEMATOGRAPHY:
Rainer Klausmann

During the final days of the Second World War, Hitler is ensconced in his Berlin bunker becoming increasingly desperate and paranoid. Witness to everything is Traudl Junge (Lara), Hitler's young secretary. *Downfall* was greeted with equal measures of fascination and suspicion when it was released in 2004. Based largely on Junge's first-hand experience of life in Hitler's bunker, there was concern the filmmakers were giving undue credence to the memoirs of a former Nazi. In fact, Junge was simply a naïve young girl with no politics of her own and a headful of propaganda. Her factual accounts have proved mesmerizing to historians, and the film's balanced authenticity seems to flow from the objectivity with which she recalls her experiences (in both the 1989 book *Voices from the Bunker* and her 2002 autobiography, *Until the Final Hour*). *Downfall* is also noted for being something of a watershed for a German film industry which has, perhaps understandably, sought to avoid intelligent assessment of the war years. Hitler had never even appeared as a central character in a mainstream, post-war German film before Bruno Ganz took up the potentially poisoned chalice. Fortunately for all concerned, his performance is as nuanced and accomplished as the rest of the film. It doesn't matter if you find it to be a dramatic exercise, a melodrama of lost innocence or an historical document, *Downfall*'s claustrophobic brilliance is chilling and extremely compelling.

LETTERS FROM IWO JIMA

Clint Eastwood, USA, 2006

CAST INCLUDES:
Ken Watanabe, Kazunari Ninomiya, Tsuyoshi Ihara, Ryo Kase, Shido Nakamura
SCREENPLAY:
Iris Yamashita. Story by Iris Yamashita and Paul Haggis based on the book *Picture Letters from Commander in Chief* by Tadamichi Kuribayashi
CINEMATOGRAPHY:
Tom Stern

ACADEMY AWARD
Best Achievement in Sound Editing:
Alan Robert Murray, Bub Asman

Near the end of the Second World War we see the Battle for Iwo Jima from the perspective of two Japanese soldiers; unconventional General Kuribayashi (Watanabe) and conscripted baker Saigo (Ninomiya). The task of defending the island from the invading American forces is an impossible one, and whilst Kuribayashi insists on sacrificing everything, Saigo just wants to go home to his family.

When Clint Eastwood set out to tackle one of the more notorious battles of the Second World War, he was determined to show a fair hand to both sides. As a result he made two films, with the first, *Flags of Our Fathers*, released just a few months before *Letters from Iwo Jima* and telling the story from the American perspective. Not for the first time, a bit of distance between filmmaker and subject has produced an honest and incisive result, with *Letters from Iwo Jima* the more satisfying of the two films (even though its predecessor took almost twice as much money at the US box office). In spite of the bloody battle it's a calm and thoughtful film, with characters in sharp focus, their every decision and action held up for examination. The naturalistic performances of Watanabe and Ninomiya are devastating, and all the more powerful for their subtlety.

THE HURT LOCKER

Kathryn Bigelow, USA, 2009

CAST INCLUDES:
Jeremy Renner, Anthony Mackie, Brian Geraghty, Guy Pearce, Ralph Fiennes, David Morse
SCREENPLAY:
Mark Boal
CINEMATOGRAPHY:
Barry Ackroyd

ACADEMY AWARDS
Best Achievement in Directing: Kathryn Bigelow
Best Achievement in Editing: Bob Murawski, Chris Innis
Best Achievement in Sound: Paul N.J. Ottosson, Ray Beckett
Best Achievement in Sound Editing: Paul N.J. Ottosson
Best Motion Picture of the Year: Kathryn Bigelow, Mark Boal, Nicolas Chartier, Greg Shapiro
Best Writing, Screenplay Written Directly for the Screen: Mark Boal

Sergeant Will James (Renner) is the new team leader of a US Explosive Ordnance Disposal (EOD) unit in Iraq. Although his talent for diffusing bombs is of the highest order, his new comrades are troubled by an apparently reckless style. The slew of recent attempts to interpret the Iraq and Afganistan conflicts on film have been notable mainly for their failures. Most have suffered from a combination of highly politicized moralizing and generally underwhelming filmmaking, characteristics to which *The Hurt Locker* gives short shrift. Simple honesty, vibrancy and tension are the order of the day as we follow Sgt James and his two colleagues through the last weeks of their tour of duty. A typical job sees them enter into a known trap and attempt to diffuse an explosive device whilst insurgents take pot shots at them from the surrounding buildings. Such intense environments don't suit everyone, and the strain is clearly demonstrated through the unit's varying reactions and coping mechanisms. Alongside James, the confident and professional Sgt Sanborn (Mackie) struggles to maintain his calm façade, and the highly strung Specialist Eldridge (Geraghty) appears close to a complete nervous breakdown. Only James is equipped, designed even, to cope with life under such pressure, which is one of the film's more interesting points: how do you re-assimilate men who have become more at home crouching over explosives in an Iraqi marketplace than shopping for breakfast cereal in an American one?

AMERICAN SNIPER

Clint Eastwood, USA, 2015

CAST INCLUDES:
Bradley Cooper,
Sienna Miller, Kyle Gallner,
Luke Grimes, Ben Reed,
Elise Robertson
SCREENPLAY:
Jason Hall
CINEMATOGRAPHY:
Tom Stern

ACADEMY AWARD
Best Achievement in Sound
Editing: Alan Robert Murray,
Bub Asman

Chris Kyle (Cooper) is the most lethal sniper in US military history, but there is much more to this American hero than his skill with a rifle. He is sent to Iraq with only one mission: to protect his fellow soldiers. His pinpoint accuracy saves countless lives on the battlefield and, as stories of his courageous exploits spread, he earns the nickname 'Legend'. However, his reputation is also growing behind enemy lines, putting a price on his head and making him a prime target for insurgents. Despite the danger, as well as the toll on his family at home, Chris serves through four harrowing tours of duty in Iraq, racking up 160 confirmed kills, but upon returning home, he finds that he cannot leave the war behind.

Powered by Clint Eastwood's sure-handed direction and a gripping, career-best central performance from Bradley Cooper, *American Sniper* delivers a tense, vivid tribute to its real-life subject. Unafraid to show Kyle's dark side, it is a fascinating look at the cost of heroism. The film is based on Navy SEAL marksman Chris Kyle's best-selling memoir, and it is both a tribute to the warrior and a lament for war. Kyle approaches his work with steady nerves and a clear conscience, banishing the doubt and fatalism that afflict some of his comrades. In this world, violence is a moral necessity, albeit one that often exacts a cost from those who must wield it in the service of good. With impeccable action sequences that brilliantly convey the chaos of combat, this is Eastwood on top form. It was nominated for five Oscars at the 2015 Academy Awards, including Best Actor for Bradley Cooper and Best Picture, winning one for sound editing.

WESTERN

STAGECOACH

John Ford, USA, 1939

Nine people are making a coach trip through dangerous Indian territory: an outlaw under arrest called the Ringo Kid (Wayne), the marshal accompanying him (Bancroft), Dallas (Trevor), a woman of ill-repute, a timid liquor salesman (Meek), a shifty gambler (Carradine), an embezzling banker (Churchill), an alcoholic doctor (Mitchell), a pregnant woman (Platt) and the driver (Devine). En route, loves and hates develop among them, a baby is born, and there are deaths during an attack by Apaches at the climax.

Stagecoach was a landmark in the history of the western. It raised the genre to artistic status, bringing about a revival, stamped John Ford as one of the great Hollywood directors, and rocketed John Wayne from B-pictures to stardom. Beautifully shot in the now familiar Monument Valley, it was Ford's first western for 13 years. Much of the second unit work was directed by the legendary stuntman Yakima Canutt, who also played a cavalry scout. It is he who falls under the wagon wheels and horses' hooves and can be just glimpsed getting to his feet after the shot. While preparing for *Citizen Kane*, Orson Welles is said to have watched *Stagecoach* around 40 times, especially the scenes with a low-angle camera requiring the sets to have ceilings.

CAST INCLUDES:
John Wayne, Claire Trevor, Thomas Mitchell, John Carradine, Andy Devine, Donald Meek

SCREENPLAY:
Dudley Nichols from the Ernest Haycox story *Stage to Lordsburg*

CINEMATOGRAPHY:
Bert Glennon

ACADEMY AWARDS

Best Actor in a Supporting Role: Thomas Mitchell
Best Music, Scoring: Richard Hageman, Frank Harling, John Liepold, Leo Shuken

UNION PACIFIC

Cecil B. DeMille, USA, 1939

In 1862, in the midst of the American Civil War, two rival railroad companies decide to undertake the construction of an American transcontinental railroad that will stretch from the East to West Coasts. Engineer Jeff Butler (McCrea) is hired to ensure that the Union Pacific is completed and arrives at its destination on time. But financial opportunist Asa Barrows (Kolker) hopes to profit from obstructing it. Butler has his hands full fighting Barrows' agent, gambler Sid Campeau (Donlevy), and faces enormous odds, including derailments, an old Civil War army buddy (Preston) who is working for the bad guys, and hostile Indians.

The name of Cecil B. DeMille almost always guaranteed action on an epic scale, and this does not disappoint. The film includes an uncomplex, upright hero, an irredeemable villain, a spectacular train wreck, Indian attacks and a cavalry rescue. Like a few other DeMille movies of his best period (1937–1947), including *The Plainsman*, *North West Mounted Police* and *Unconquered*, it is an energetic, colourful, patriotic celebration of frontiersmen, extolling strength, perseverance and forthright manliness. Among all this shooting and fisticuffs, Barbara Stanwyck as a fiery Irish postmistress more than holds her own. DeMille effortlessly manages to alternate between studio soundstages and outdoor location work.

CAST INCLUDES:
Barbara Stanwyck, Joel McCrea, Robert Preston, Brian Donlevy, Akim Tamiroff, Anthony Quinn, Henry Kolker, George Bancroft, Berton Churchill, Louise Platt
SCREENPLAY:
Walter DeLeon, C. Gardner Sullivan, Jesse Lasky Jr. from the novel *Trouble Shooters* by Ernest Haycox
CINEMATOGRAPHY:
Victor Milner

THE OX-BOW INCIDENT

William Wellman, USA, 1943

Saddle tramps Gil Carter (Fonda) and Art Croft (Morgan) ride into a small Nevada town in 1885 just as an illegal posse gets up to track down the suspected killers of a popular rancher. Out for blood are the victim's best friend Jeff Farnley (Lawrence) and the bigoted local bigshot 'Major' Tetley (Conroy), who sees a vigilante killing as a way of imposing manliness on his cowardly son Gerald (Eythe). Carter goes along with the mob, partly to keep them from suspecting him. The mob arrests three drifters (Andrews, Quinn, Ford), tries them by a kangaroo court and lynches them. Carter, meanwhile, realizes too late that the men were innocent.

There have been few better examples of the dangers of mob hysteria than this powerful western directed with intensity and precision by William Wellman. It is even more remarkable for being released during the Second World War, when most Hollywood fare was of a patriotic nature. Henry Fonda's liberal persona is not overexploited, portraying him as an ordinary, good-hearted guy caught up in ugly events. By obscuring Fonda's eyes as he reads a final letter written by one of the victims, none of whom are presented as saints, Wellman allows the viewer to focus on the message instead of the personality.

CAST INCLUDES:
Henry Fonda, Dana Andrews, Anthony Quinn, Henry Morgan, Jane Darwell, Marc Lawrence, Frank Conroy, Francis Ford, William Eythe
SCREENPLAY:
Lamar Trotti from the novel by Walter Van Tilburg Clark
CINEMATOGRAPHY:
Arthur Miller

DUEL IN THE SUN

King Vidor, USA, 1946

Orphaned when her father is condemned for murdering his Indian wife and her lover, Pearl Chavez (Jones) goes to live with Texan Senator McCanles (Barrymore), his wife (Gish) and two sons. Both of the latter, upright Jesse (Cotten) – who is banished for contesting his father's opposition to the railroad – and arrogant and amoral Lewton (Peck), are attracted to her. After Lewton guns down her husband-to-be on the eve of the wedding and escapes into exile, Pearl joins him at Squaw's Head Rock, where the two engage in an agonized shoot-out before dying in a final embrace. This demented, delirious western of sibling rivalry for the love of a tempestuous half-breed is Hollywood high romanticism at its peak. Played mostly against blood-red skies, it was producer David O. Selznick's challenge to his own *Gone with the Wind*. He gave it one of the biggest publicity campaigns in US film history and it grossed around $17 million. Its eroticism, rare in a western and earning the movie the nickname 'Lust In The Dust', had it condemned by The Legion of Decency. It was denounced from the pulpit by Catholics and Protestants alike, and banned by some local councils. All this should be enough to tempt audiences to see this flamboyant and visually resplendent melodrama.

CAST INCLUDES:
Gregory Peck, Jennifer Jones, Joseph Cotten, Walter Huston, Herbert Marshall, Lionel Barrymore, Lillian Gish
SCREENPLAY:
David O. Selznick, Oliver Garrett from the novel by Niven Busch
CINEMATOGRAPHY:
Lee Garmes, Harold Rossen, Ray Rennahan

MY DARLING CLEMENTINE

John Ford, USA, 1946

CAST INCLUDES:
Henry Fonda, Linda Darnell, Victor Mature, Cathy Downs, Walter Brennan
SCREENPLAY:
Winston Miller, Samuel G. Engel from the story by Sam Hellman from the novel *Wyatt Earp, Frontier Marshal* by Stuart N. Lake
CINEMATOGRAPHY:
Joseph MacDonald

In 1882, Wyatt Earp (Fonda) and his brothers are driving their cattle towards California. Leaving James, the youngest brother, to guard the livestock, they go into town for some relaxation. On their return, they discover the cattle gone and James killed. Wyatt agrees to become marshal of Tombstone and makes his brothers his deputies. They suspect the Clanton clan headed by the ruthless patriarch Old Man Clanton (Brennan) and set about to prove their guilt, setting the stage for the celebrated gunfight at the OK Corral. Although rich in period detail, *My Darling Clementine* does not pretend to be realistic but is a mystic, poetic masterpiece, haunted by romantic imagery of paradise lost. The town of Tombstone was meticulously re-created in Monument Valley for the film and it provides some very striking images.

FORT APACHE

John Ford, USA, 1948

CAST INCLUDES:
John Wayne, Henry Fonda,
Shirley Temple,
John Agar, Ward Bond,
Victor MacLaglen
SCREENPLAY:
Frank S. Nugent from
the story *Massacre* by
James Warner Bellah
CINEMATOGRAPHY:
Archie Stout

Captain Kirby York (Wayne) knows the Indians well and seeks to make peace with the local tribes. Owen Thursday (Fonda), an arrogant lieutenant colonel from the east, takes command of the fort. His daughter, Philadelphia (Temple), is courted by the son (Agar) of the sergeant major (Bond), a liaison bitterly opposed by Thursday. Despising Indians and hoping to advance his career, he breaks York's agreement with Cochise, and launches a Custer-like charge that wipes out his entire force. York tells reporters that Thursday died gloriously.

This was the first of John Ford's magnificent cavalry trilogy (the others were *She Wore a Yellow Ribbon* and *Rio Grande*), made within two years, all starring John Wayne, all about the US cavalry's battles with the Indians and all beautifully filmed at Ford's favourite location – Monument Valley on the Arizona–Utah border. However, it is the life at the fort that is so vividly captured: the reunions and separations of loved ones, the waiting women, the carousing of the soldiers, the singing interludes, the formal dances including a Grand March at a non-commissioned officers' ball. Henry Fonda is superb as the unyielding commander, stiff in bearing and in behaviour, and John Wayne is the perfect contrast.

RED RIVER

Howard Hawks, USA, 1948

CAST INCLUDES:
John Wayne, Montgomery Clift, Joanne Dru, Walter Brennan, John Ireland
SCREENPLAY:
Borden Chase, Charles Schnee from the novel *The Chisholm Trail* by Borden Chase
CINEMATOGRAPHY:
Russell Harlan

The end of the Civil War finds Thomas Dunson (Wayne), master of a vast cattle domain in Texas, having to drive his livestock over the Chisholm Trail into Missouri, hoping to benefit from the huge market created by the new railroad. He falls out with his adopted son, Matthew Garth (Clift), and the picture ends with a showdown between father and son, using fists not guns, and a reconciliation. *Red River* is full of striking Fordian elements – silhouetted covered wagons, people posing against sunset skies, songs on the soundtrack – but it is purely Hawksian in its fascination with masculine by-play. The exploration of the Freudian subtext of the script – a dual character study in which the patriarchal John Wayne is faced with Montgomery Clift, fighting to prove his independence and 'kill the father' – gives the western an added depth. This succeeds brilliantly because of the contrast between Wayne's muscular macho security and Clift's nervy angularity, creating a special tension.

SHE WORE A YELLOW RIBBON

John Ford, USA, 1949

Captain Nathan Brittles (Wayne), a cavalry officer about to retire, must carry out one last mission: to escort two women to the safety of a military fort. This is the second of the three cavalry films with John Wayne and is the only one in colour. And what colour! The ochre hues of Monument Valley, the blue and gold uniforms, the saturated colours of wagons lit up during a spectacular storm, red sunsets on a desert cemetery where widower Wayne talks to his dead wife. Wayne, only 33 at the time, is marvellous as a man near retirement.

ACADEMY AWARD
Best Cinematography, Color:
Winton C. Hoch

CAST INCLUDES: John Wayne, Joanne Dru, John Agar, Ben Johnson, Harry Carey Jr., Victor McLaglen
SCREENPLAY: Frank S. Nugent, Laurence Stallings from the stories *War Party* and *The Big Hunt* by James Warner Bellah
CINEMATOGRAPHY: Winton C. Hoch

THE GUNFIGHTER

Henry King, USA, 1950

CAST INCLUDES:
Gregory Peck, Helen Westcott, Millard Mitchello, Karl Malden, Skip Homeier, Richard Jaeckel, B.G. Norman
SCREENPLAY:
William Bowers, William Sellers from a story by Bowers and André de Toth
CINEMATOGRAPHY:
Arthur Miller

DID YOU KNOW?
The western street in this film is the same one used in *The Ox-Bow Incident* (1943).

Ageing gunfighter Jimmy Ringo (Peck) regrets his criminal past, and is tired of travelling from town to town. But he finds there is no such thing as a retired gunslinger. Everywhere he goes he is regularly challenged by cocky young gunmen hoping to make names for themselves, such as Eddie (Jaeckel). Forced to shoot him, Ringo is now tailed by Eddie's three brothers. Ringo rides to yet another dusty western town to see the wife (Westcott) and young son Jimmie (Norman) he abandoned. Meanwhile, Eddie's brothers arrive in town. A local aspiring gunman (Homeier) also wants to kill Ringo, to establish his reputation. *The Gunfighter* is not a traditional western in that there is very little action, being more of a character study and morality play. It was also rare in painting an authentic picture of the late 19th-century West, suggesting the sepia photographs of the period. Sporting a heavy moustache for the first time, Peck brings gravitas to the role of a man who cannot escape his past. When the film failed at the box office, the studio moguls blamed the moustache. *The Gunfighter*, the second of six films that Peck made with director Henry King (the first being *Twelve O'Clock High*, 1949), has gained in critical appreciation over the years and is now considered one of the great westerns.

WINCHESTER '73

Anthony Mann, USA, 1953

Frontiersman Lin McAdam (Stewart) rides into town on the trail of Dutch Henry Brown (McNally), only to find himself in a Dodge City marksmanship contest. McAdam wins a precious Winchester model '73 rifle, but Dutch steals it and leaves town. McAdam is bent on tracking down his murderous antagonist, who happens to be his brother, while the rifle keeps changing hands. It passes to an Indian chief (Hudson), a gun trader (Drake), a bank robber (Duryea), back to Dutch, and finally, at a shoot-out on a rocky mountain precipice, into the hands of its rightful owner.

Winchester '73 is the film that established Anthony Mann as a western auteur, and the first of several collaborations with James Stewart and the writer Borden Chase. This 'story of a rifle' provided Mann with the possibility of covering many aspects of the genre: cavalry, Indians, settlers, badmen, etc. It also revealed a new Stewart, more bitter and uncompromising than had been seen before his collaboration with Mann. The scene where Stewart smashes Dan Duryea's head on the bar shows him to be an equal when it comes to sadism. Beautifully photographed by William Daniels, this exceptional western was responsible for a renewal of the genre.

CAST INCLUDES: James Stewart, Dan Duryea, Stephen McNally, Millard Mitchell, John McIntire, Shelley Winters, Charles Drake, Rock Hudson
SCREENPLAY: Robert L. Richards, Borden Chase from the story by Stuart N. Lake
CINEMATOGRAPHY: William Daniels

BEND OF THE RIVER

Anthony Mann, USA, 1952

CAST INCLUDES:
James Stewart, Arthur Kennedy, Julia Adams, Rock Hudson
SCREENPLAY:
Borden Chase from the novel *Bend of the Snake* by Bill Gulick
CINEMATOGRAPHY:
Irving Glassberg

Glyn McLyntock (Stewart), an ex-Missouri raider, now a reformed character trying to hide his criminal past, is working as a scout to a wagon train heading for farming land in Oregon. Along the way, he rescues former partner, Cole Garett (Kennedy), from hanging. At first Cole is a loyal companion and saves Glyn's life when the two men ambush a band of marauding Indians. Gradually, though, Cole's crooked instincts get the better of him, and it ends with a confrontation between the two men in the Snake River of the title, with the settlers' vital provisions at stake. This was the second of the five westerns director Anthony Mann made with James Stewart after *Winchester '73* (1950), which brought out a new, tougher Stewart than the drawling charmer of previous pictures. Here he is bitterly confronted with his past, personified by a corrupt Arthur Kennedy, who he must overcome. Stewart still bears the mark of the hangman's noose around his neck from which he escaped. The narrative spring is as tightly coiled as ever, moving with the inevitability of a Greek tragedy. There is also the conflict between the homesteaders and gold seekers that sets up the two sides of the Old West, the landscape of which is beautifully captured.

HIGH NOON

Fred Zinnemann, USA, 1952

CAST INCLUDES:
Gary Cooper, Grace Kelly, Thomas Mitchell, Lloyd Bridges, Katy Jurado
SCREENPLAY:
Carl Foreman from the story *The Tin Star* by John W. Cunningham
CINEMATOGRAPHY:
Floyd Crosby

Will Kane (Cooper) is about to marry a Quaker girl (Kelly) and retire as marshal of the small frontier town of Hadleyville when he is warned that the Miller gang, whose leader Kane had previously arrested, is arriving on the noon train to get him. As Tex Ritter famously sings 'Do Not Forsake Me Oh My Darlin' on the soundtrack, director Fred Zinnemann builds up the tension in masterly fashion, making this the high-water mark of his career. The pulsating action takes place in the same timescale as the 90-minute running time of the film, respecting the unity of time and place. Despite the intended analogy with McCarthyism, *High Noon* is a classic (and much imitated) western tale of a loner 'doing what a man has to do'. The townsfolk are well characterized, while Katy Jurado, dark and fiery, is contrasted vividly with Grace Kelly, blonde and cool. But it is 51-year-old Gary Cooper, still possessed of a mythic aura that he assumes with such easy masculine (though never aggressively macho) elegance, who gives his most soulful and agonizing performance. He rightly won an Oscar for the role.

THE NAKED SPUR

Anthony Mann, USA, 1953

Howard Kemp (Stewart), a bounty hunter trying to earn money to buy back land he unfairly lost while away at the Civil War, is on the trail of Ben Vandergroat (Ryan), who has a $5,000 price tag on his head. Kemp teams up with an old prospector, Jesse Torte (Mitchell), and a dishonorably discharged Union soldier, Roy Anderson (Meeker). They help capture Vandergroat, who is with his girlfriend, Lina Patch (Leigh), and decide to cut themselves in as partners for their share of the reward money. But the journey to the county jail is a hazardous one, especially as tension grows among the group.

The Naked Spur is another tough, intelligently written Anthony Mann-James Stewart western masterpiece, the only one of the five made for MGM. Aspiring to Greek tragic dimensions, the film is a study in greed, which is the spur of the title. Stewart, revealing a neurotic side, makes a spiritual journey at the same time as the physically arduous one through a varied landscape. Shot in the inspiring Rocky Mountains of Colorado – there are very few interiors – the characters are sometimes dwarfed by the vast landscape. Nevertheless, this action-packed western is not pretentious and the characterizations are vivid, with good James Stewart and evil Robert Ryan as worthy opponents.

CAST INCLUDES:
James Stewart, Janet Leigh, Robert Ryan, Ralph Meeker, Millard Mitchell
SCREENPLAY:
Sam Rolfe, Harold Jack Bloom
CINEMATOGRAPHY:
William C. Mellor

SHANE

George Stevens, USA, 1953

CAST INCLUDES:
Alan Ladd, Jean Arthur, Van Heflin, Brandon De Wilde, Jack Palance, Emile Meyer
SCREENPLAY:
A.B. Guthrie Jr., Jack Sher from the novel by Jack Schaefer
CINEMATOGRAPHY:
Loyal Griggs

Shane (Ladd), a lone rider, stops at the farm of homesteader Joe Starrett (Heflin), his wife, Marian (Arthur), and young son, Joey (De Wilde), just before Ryker (Meyer), a powerful and ruthless cattleman, arrives with his cronies to make the farmer a threatening offer for land that he intends to get by any means necessary. Told through the eyes of a young boy with disarming innocence and warmth, *Shane* has the mythic aura of an Arthurian legend. Alan Ladd in buckskins is at his most iconic: serene face, piercing eyes, tenderness behind the tough persona. We learn little of Shane's background – he comes from nowhere and returns to nowhere. He is first seen coming over the horizon between the antlers of a stag and, in the heartbreaking finale, Joey's voice echoes in the wilderness, 'Shane, come back. Come back, Shane.' One of the most beautifully composed of westerns, it was filmed in the lush landscapes of Wyoming.

THE SEARCHERS

John Ford, USA, 1956

CAST INCLUDES:
John Wayne, Jeffrey Hunter, Vera Miles, Ward Bond, Natalie Wood, John Qualen
SCREENPLAY:
Frank S. Nugent from the novel by Alan LeMay
CINEMATOGRAPHY:
Winton C. Hoch

Ex-confederate Ethan Edwards (Wayne) returns to his brother's house on the Texas frontier in 1868. After he leaves, the brother, wife and a son are killed by Comanches, who also abduct their two daughters. Joined by Martin Pawley (Hunter), an orphan with Cherokee blood adopted by the dead couple, Ethan finds the older girl dead and pursues the younger, Debbie (Wood), who he believes has married within the tribe. The two wander for five years until they discover that Debbie is a squaw of Chief Scar. The Indian-hating Ethan is determined to kill her, but relents when he catches her. 'Let's go home, Debbie,' he says finally. *The Searchers* is perhaps John Ford's masterpiece, and the last of the golden era of classical westerns begun with *Stagecoach* (1939). The western had matured and become less black and white (in both senses) since then, and so had John Wayne's character. Ethan, Ford's only real antihero, played by Wayne with complete conviction, is a complex, obsessive man. The five-year quest for Debbie is also a quest for himself, as well as Ford's exploration of his views on Native Americans. The film reiterates the director's reverence for family life from which Ethan is excluded. In the final, unforgettable image, Wayne clutches his arm in a gesture borrowed from Ford's first star Harry Carey, as the door closes on him, the symbol of the rejection of the homeless wanderer.

THE TALL T

Budd Boetticher, USA, 1956

CAST INCLUDES:
Randolph Scott, Richard Boone, Maureen O'Sullivan, Arthur Hunicutt, Henry Silva
SCREENPLAY:
Burt Kennedy from the story *The Captives* by Elmore Leonard
CINEMATOGRAPHY:
Charles Lawton Jr.

Having lost his horse in a bet, Pat Brennan (Scott) hitches a ride with a stagecoach carrying newlyweds, businessman Willard (Hubbard) and Doretta (O'Sullivan). At the next station the coach and its passengers fall into the hands of a trio of outlaws: Usher (Boone) and his two vicious underlings (Silva and Homeier). When Usher learns that Doretta is the daughter of a rich copper-mine owner, he decides to hold her for ransom. While tension builds over the next 24 hours as Usher awaits a response to his demands, and as a romantic attachment grows between Brennan and Doretta, a game of bluff and counter-bluff ensues. The second of seven B-westerns, directed by Budd Boetticher and starring Randolph Scott, *The Tall T* is as taut and laconic as its hero. In its concise way, running 78 minutes, made in a couple of weeks, and shot almost entirely outdoors, it says as much about dignity and courage than many longer, more expensive westerns. The classic plot is told with an unselfconscious narrative force, and each of the characters is finely etched. The distinctive psychopathy of the villains, particularly Richard Boone's unscrupulous but lonely, intelligent figure, is well contrasted with Scott's inherent decency.

CAST INCLUDES:
Glenn Ford, Van Heflin, Felicia Farr, Richard Jaeckel
SCREENPLAY:
Halsted Welles from the story by Elmore Leonard
CINEMATOGRAPHY:
Charles Lawton Jr.

3.10 TO YUMA

Delmer Daves, USA, 1957

The title refers to the time of the train on which rancher Dan Evans (Heflin) is to escort outlaw Ben Wade (Ford) to the state prison. Dan is a peace-loving rancher, devastated by drought, who, desperately in need of the reward money, has offered to take on the dangerous mission, knowing that Wade's friends will do anything to free their partner in crime. Tension mounts as the two men wait for the train in a hotel room in a small border town. At the climax, Evans has to face Wade's gang alone. *3.10 to Yuma,* like *High Noon*, deals with the psychological tensions of waiting, as well as exposing small-town complacency and cowardice. Relying more on suspense and sharp dialogue than physical action, the film brilliantly creates a claustrophobic atmosphere, confined as it is for much of the time to a hotel room. Delmer Daves creates this with an excellent use of close-ups and crane shots. At the heart of the film is the almost Faustian relationship between the wicked but persuasive Glenn Ford and the noble Van Heflin, trying to resist temptation. There is also a terrific theme song sung by Frankie Laine.

FORTY GUNS

Samuel Fuller, USA, 1957

Jessica Drummond (Stanwyck) more or less runs Cochise County, Arizona, where she makes her own law with a private posse of 40 cowboys. The wimpy sheriff (Jagger) cannot control her and an ex-gunslinger turned marshal (Sullivan) is sent for. His job is to bring law and order to the place. There is an immediate clash with Jessica, although the cattle queen finds herself falling for the lawman. But when her psychotic brother Brockie (Ericson) commits murder, the marshal is forced to kill Brockie, wounding Jessica in the process.

One of the westerns that strongly influenced Sergio Leone and later Clint Eastwood's *Unforgiven*, it strips the West of all its glamour, being raw and direct. To counterbalance this and to heighten the slightly off-beam drama, Fuller uses a breathtakingly bravura camera style. *Forty Guns* also stands among a number of westerns of the 1950s that sought to demythologize the cowboy and see the frontier with a modern sensibility, such as the myth of masculine power. Barbara Stanwyck is the 'high ridin' woman with a whip' and 'no man can tame her' of the film's theme song. In addition it has an ambivalent hero who resists using violence until the inevitable end. Fuller's comment on America's fascination with guns also includes some amusingly phallic lines. At one stage, when Stanwyck flirtatiously asks a gunfighter if she can feel his pistol, he warns her that it might go off in her face. Another character remarks that he would 'like to stay around long enough to clean her rifle'. At the stunning beginning, Stanwyck (clad in black leather) is seen riding at the head of her cavalry of 40 guns, snaking through the valleys and canyons; this scene sets the vibrant tone of the film.

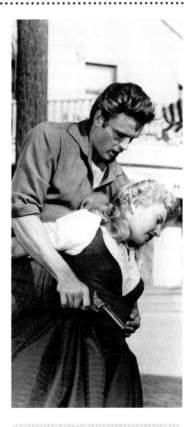

CAST INCLUDES:
Barbara Stanwyck,
Barry Sullivan, Dean Jagger,
Gene Barry, Eve Brent
SCREENPLAY:
Samuel Fuller
CINEMATOGRAPHY:
Joseph Biroc

THE BIG COUNTRY

ACADEMY AWARD
Best Actor in a Supporting
Role: Burl Ives

William Wyler, USA, 1958

CAST INCLUDES:
Gregory Peck, Charlton
Heston, Jean Simmons,
Charles Bickford, Burl Ives,
Carrol Baker
SCREENPLAY:
James R. Webb, Sy Bartlett,
Robert Wilder, Jessamyn
West (uncredited) from the
novel by Donald Hamilton
CINEMATOGRAPHY:
Franz Planer

Two enemy cattlemen, Major Henry Terrill (Bickford) and Rufus Hannassey (Ives), try to acquire the property of schoolteacher Julie Maragon (Simmons) because it has a well. James McKay (Peck) comes west to marry the major's spoiled daughter, Patricia (Baker), but falls foul of Steve Leech (Heston), the brutish foreman, who eventually wins Patricia while James marries the school ma'm after he's proved himself a real man. The two patriarchs kill each other, leaving room for peace. At the heart of this rousing epic western is a plea for pacifism, as represented by greenhorn Gregory Peck, something that could make it an anti-western. But, as in William Wyler's previous film, *Friendly Persuasion*, about a Quaker family, there comes a time when one must act to defend oneself. Thus, *The Big Country* had both sweep and substance, living up to its title on the wide Technirama screen. The film's highlights are the exciting opening sequence involving a carriage chase that recalls *Ben-Hur*, another Wyler picture, Peck's solitary attempts to master a wild stallion and the climactic shootout between Burl Ives and Charles Bickford in a giant canyon.

MAN OF THE WEST

Anthony Mann, USA, 1958

CAST INCLUDES:
Gary Cooper, Lee J. Cobb,
Julie London, Jack Lord, Royal
Dano, John Dehner
SCREENPLAY:
Reginald Rose from the novel
The Border Jumpers by
Will C. Brown
CINEMATOGRAPHY:
Ernest Haller

Link Jones (Cooper), a man of peace who gave up the life of a bank robber 20 years earlier, is faced with the need to use violence once more. The train on which he is travelling is ambushed and he, a cardsharp (O'Connell) and a schoolteacher turned dancehall singer (London) are stranded in the wilderness after being robbed. They come across the hideout of the gang of which Link was once a member. It is now led by a half-crazed outlaw (Cobb) who encourages his depraved crew in their sadism. Gradually, by talk and action, the hero overcomes them all and rides off with the girl. Although made in CinemaScope, most of the taut action of this strongly allegorical western is confined to the small space of the hideout where the characters interact. With a literate script by Reginald Rose (author of *Twelve Angry Men*), the movie is directed with intensity by western maestro Anthony Mann ('Mann of the West'), and Gary Cooper is at his anguished best in his last great role. He represents another one of Mann's deeply troubled heroes with a dark past that catches up with him. Generally dismissed on its first release, the film has since gained in reputation over the years.

LAST TRAIN FROM GUN HILL

John Sturges, USA, 1959

US Marshal Matt Morgan (Douglas) is determined to seek revenge on the man who raped and murdered his half-breed wife. The killers leave behind a saddle that he recognizes as the property of his friend Craig Belden (Quinn), a wealthy cattle rancher in the nearby town of Gun Hill. Realizing that Belden's son Rick (Holliman) is one of the killers, Morgan travels to Gun Hill to arrest him. Although sympathetic about the death of Morgan's wife, Belden predictably refuses to turn over his son when the marshal makes known the purpose of his visit, claiming that Morgan owes him for having once saved his life. Not only must Morgan locate and arrest Rick, but he has to do so before the last train leaves Gun Hill at 9pm.

This is a superior adult western from director John Sturges, a master of the genre. Rape was not often referred to so explicitly in Hollywood movies of the time, and this depiction is particularly disturbing given its idyllic woodland setting, its racial motivation and the fact that it is witnessed by the victim's young son. Kirk Douglas is at his most intense and uncompromising, never asking for sympathy, while Anthony Quinn matches him in passion. The splendid landscape is the perfect setting for the high-powered action, all the more effective for the gradual eruption.

CAST INCLUDES:
Kirk Douglas, Anthony Quinn, Carolyn Jones, Earl Holliman, Brad Dexter
SCREENPLAY:
James Poe based on the story *Showdown* by Les Crutchfield
CINEMATOGRAPHY:
Charles B. Lang Jr.

RIO BRAVO

Howard Hawks, USA, 1959

S heriff John T. Chance (Wayne) tries, with his three deputies – Stumpy, a limping old man (Brennan), the drunken Dude (Martin) and Colorado Ryan (Nelson), a trigger-happy youngster – to hold a murderer in jail for four days until the arrival of the US Marshal, despite the counter-efforts by the prisoner's wealthy brother. Chance also has the support of saloon gal Feathers (Dickinson), on the outside.

Howard Hawks purposely and magnificently abandons the wide-open spaces of the traditional western for the claustrophobic interiors of the prison, town bars and hotel rooms. It is also Hawks' riposte to *High Noon*, which both the director and Wayne disliked. John Wayne has his motley crew of supporters who may be too old and infirm, too young, too drunk and too female, but unlike Gary Cooper, he doesn't reject offers of help, wanting to be surrounded only by willing, loyal people. Dean Martin, giving his most profound performance, is touching as an alcoholic who redeems himself thanks to the cruel-to-be-kind efforts of Wayne. *Rio Bravo* is principally an affectionate, witty and sharply observed study of male camaraderie, with an exciting climax and a great score by Dimitri Tiomkin – plus a couple of songs warbled by crooner Martin and pop-star Nelson.

DID YOU KNOW?

The sets in Old Tucson are built to 7/8th scale, so the performers look larger than life.

CAST INCLUDES: John Wayne, Dean Martin, Walter Brennan, Angie Dickinson, Ricky Nelson, John Russell
SCREENPLAY: Jules Furthman, Leigh Brackett from a story by Barbara Hawks McCampbell
CINEMATOGRAPHY: Russell Harlan

THE MAGNIFICENT SEVEN

John Sturges, USA, 1960

CAST INCLUDES:
Yul Brynner, Steve McQueen,
Horst Buchholz,
Charles Bronson,
Robert Vaughn,
Brad Dexter,
James Coburn, Eli Wallach
SCREENPLAY:
William Roberts, Walter
Bernstein, Walter Newman
(uncredited)
CINEMATOGRAPHY:
Charles B. Lang Jr.

DID YOU KNOW?
Yul Brynner was married
on the set, and the
celebration used many
of the same props as the
fiesta scene.

Chris (Brynner) gathers together six other mercenaries to protect a Mexican mountain village from marauding bandits, led by the ruthless Calvera (Wallach). Having fortified the village and won hearts and minds by feeding the kids, they are let down by the peasants' lack of fighting spirit. However, the seven overcome the bandits in a climactic battle.

This wonderfully stirring, exciting and humorous western ingeniously transposes the traditional Japanese *jidai-geki* genre to the traditional American genre. It was perfectly logical that such a tale could have been adapted from Akira Kurosawa's *The Seven Samurai* given that the great Japanese director himself has acknowledged his debt to the Hollywood western. A further link with the earlier film was the casting of the oriental-looking Yul Brynner as the leader of the gang of seven. What fascinated director John Sturges was the different lethal skills of the seven, and the development of their self-sacrificial idealism. The pulsating action, the charisma of the cast and Elmer Bernstein's sweeping music score made it the huge hit it was. The movie boosted the careers of Steve McQueen, James Coburn and Charles Bronson, and led Eli Wallach to be cast as the heavy in spaghetti westerns a few years later. Three far from magnificent sequels followed.

LONELY ARE THE BRAVE

David Miller, USA, 1962

CAST INCLUDES:
Kirk Douglas, Gena
Rowlands, Walter Matthau,
George Kennedy
SCREENPLAY:
Dalton Trumbo from the
novel *Brave Cowboy* by
Edward Abbey
CINEMATOGRAPHY:
Philip Lathrop

Jack Burns (Douglas) is an itinerant cowboy who gets himself sent to prison in order to free a friend who has been sentenced for helping illegal immigrants from Mexico. However, his friend prefers to serve out his sentence, so he escapes alone and goes on the run. He is pursued relentlessly by the sheriff (Matthau) and his posse, who use helicopters and jeeps, making the power and speed of Jack's horse tragically irrelevant.

This poignant and pointed western, set in contemporary times, was Kirk Douglas's favourite film. It was he that convinced Universal to make it. 'It happens to be a point of view I love. This is what attracted me to the story – the difficulty of being an individual today.' Douglas convincingly plays an anachronism. The opening scene immediately sets up the theme when Douglas, dragging on a cigarette, looks up at the sky and watches the long trail of three streaking jet planes. But the film not only shows the way that the Old West, and some of its better values, are obliterated by the pervasive automobile and advancing technology, but also makes a statement about the inability of the USA to tolerate misfits. The lengthy mountain chase that is the climax of the film is enhanced with stunning black-and-white location photography.

THE MAN WHO SHOT LIBERTY VALANCE

John Ford, USA, 1962

CAST INCLUDES:
James Stewart, John Wayne,
Lee Marvin, Andy Devine,
Vera Miles, Edmond O'Brein
SCREENPLAY:
James Warner Bellah,
Willis Goldbeck from the
story by Dorothy M. Johnson
CINEMATOGRAPHY:
William H. Clothier

Senator Ransom Stoddard (Stewart) and his wife, Hallie (Miles), return to the small town of Shinbone for the funeral of his friend Tom Doniphon (Wayne) and talks to a journalist about the time he shot and killed violent outlaw Liberty Valance (Marvin). In flashback, we see what really happened. It was the unsung Tom who shot Valance from a hidden place. When the newspaper editor hears the truth, he refuses to print Stoddard's 'confession': 'When the legend becomes fact, then print the legend.' This sums up the plot of this nostalgic, melancholy and moving western by the 67-year-old John Ford. With his wonderful repertory of familiar actors, Ford seems to be summing up his whole career, showing his beloved populist West becoming eaten away by democracy, law and literacy (in the person of James Stewart). John Wayne represents this decline from the cocky hero in *Stagecoach* (1939), and even though he is defeated in the film, we know that he is a winner, as is the film in all its autumnal glory.

RIDE THE HIGH COUNTRY

Sam Peckinpah, USA, 1962

Ex-sheriff Steve Judd (McCrea) takes a job escorting a shipment of gold bullion down from the high Sierras to a bank, and is joined by former partner, Gil Westrum (Scott.) Along for the hazardous ride are Gil's rowdy young assistant, Heck Longtree (Starr), and Elsa Knudsen (Hartley), fleeing her zealously religious father to join her fiancé Billy Hammond (Drury) at the mining camp. After a grotesque marriage ceremony in the local brothel, Elsa has to be rescued from the brutal attentions of the five Hammond brothers. *Ride the High Country*, shot beautifully by Lucien Ballard, astoundingly in 26 days, is significant in being only Peckinpah's second film, but his first western. Here is established not only his unpretentious, affectionate nostalgia for the Old West but, by casting two icons of the genre, 59-year-old Randolph Scott in his last role and 57-year-old Joel McCrea in his last important role, Peckinpah also expresses his nostalgia for the old western.

CAST INCLUDES: Randolph Scott, Joel McCrea, Ronald Starr, Mariette Hartley, James Drury
SCREENPLAY: N.B. Stone Jr.
CINEMATOGRAPHY: Lucien Ballard

THE GOOD, THE BAD AND THE UGLY (IL BUONO, IL BRUTTO, IL CATTIVO)

Sergio Leone, Italy, 1966

CAST INCLUDES:
Clint Eastwood, Lee Van Cleef,
Eli Wallach, Aldo Giuffre
SCREENPLAY:
Luciano Vincenzoni, Sergio
Leone, Age Scarpelli
CINEMATOGRAPHY:
Tonino Delli Colli

Blondie (Eastwood) and Tuco (Wallach) operate a racket whereby Blondie captures Tuco, gets a reward, then rescues him from the rope at the last minute. But they keep double-crossing each other in the dangerous game. Along comes cold-blooded Setenza (Van Cleef) who thinks nothing of shooting a man's face through a pillow. He's after a box containing $200,000 of stolen money. This leads the three of them to a cemetery where it's buried, and a showdown. 'When you have to shoot, don't talk, shoot,' seemed to be the philosophy behind the film. The concluding part of the *Dollars* trilogy (after *A Fistful of Dollars* and *A Few Dollars More*) is more violent but it also has more depth and dark humour. Despite the title, none of the characters are good – all are monosyllabic, bad and ugly, except Clint 'Golden-haired Angel' Eastwood, who is monosyllabic, bad and handsome. The film has an amoral mythic grandeur along its bloody way to the gripping climax, the mother of all showdowns. Sergio Leone swings his camera around 180 degrees as the tricky trio face each other with long, lingering looks, while Ennio Morricone's pulsating music adds to the drama.

THE PROFESSIONALS

Richard Brooks, USA, 1966

The Mexican–US border, 1917. Four mercenaries – an explosives expert (Lancaster), a sharpshooter and tracker (Strode), a horse handler (Ryan) and one skilled in tactics and weaponry (Marvin) – are hired by a wealthy Texan oil baron (Bellamy) to rescue his wife (Cardinale) from a Mexican revolutionary hero (Palance) who has kidnapped her. They make their way across the treacherous landscape to Mexico and carry out the rescue, only to discover that she does not want to return. One of the most financially successful westerns of the 1960s, it was, despite its two-hour length, tightly directed and written by Richard Brooks. He also managed to integrate serious themes of loyalty and the need for personal ethics, with a great deal of slam-bang action and humour, while cynicism gives way to romance. The magnificent four – Lancaster, Ryan, Marvin and Strode – present us with four complex and flawed personalities. Conrad Hall's cinematography brilliantly evokes the mountains, the ochre-coloured desert and heat that our heroes have to conquer. The atmosphere, plot and setting obviously influenced Sam Peckinpah's *The Wild Bunch*, three years later.

CAST INCLUDES:
Burt Lancaster, Lee Marvin, Robert Ryan, Jack Palance, Ralph Bellamy, Claudia Cardinale, Woody Strode
SCREENPLAY:
Richard Brooks from the novel *A Mule For The Marquesa* by Frank O'Rourke
CINEMATOGRAPHY:
Conrad Hall

ONCE UPON A TIME IN THE WEST (C'ERA UNA VOLTA IL WEST)

Sergio Leone, Italy/USA, 1968

CAST INCLUDES:
Henry Fonda, Claudia Cardinale, Jason Robards, Charles Bronson, Gabriele Ferzetti
SCREENPLAY:
Sergio Leone, Sergio Donati, Bernardo Bertolucci
CINEMATOGRAPHY:
Tonino Delli Colli

Frank (Fonda), a cold-blooded, psychopathic gunman, suffers no guilt after annihilating an entire family (except the wife, who arrived after the slaughter) on the orders of a crazy, crippled railroad tycoon (Ferzetti) who wants the land. But now he must deal with the widow (Cardinale), a mysterious harmonica-playing cowboy (Bronson) and a half-breed outlaw (Robards) accused of the killings. A compendium of almost every western ever made, this amorality tale of epic grandeur is the apotheosis of the Sergio Leone style of long, lingering shots and meaningful close-ups. Skilfully using natural sound – waterdrops, footsteps, squeaky door hinges and a buzzing fly – the tension is immediately built up in the first 14 minutes. Much of the effect of this lyrical and bloody film comes from the music of Ennio Morricone, as important as any character, making the movie into a quasi-opera. Henry Fonda is inspiringly cast as a heavy, while Charles Bronson does more with silence than most of the actors with dialogue.

BUTCH CASSIDY AND THE SUNDANCE KID

George Roy Hill, USA, 1969

CAST INCLUDES:
Paul Newman, Robert Redford, Katherine Ross, Strother Martin
SCREENPLAY:
William Goldman
CINEMATOGRAPHY:
Conrad Hall

In the early 1900s, Butch Cassidy (Newman) and the Sundance Kid (Redford) are members of the 'Hole-in-the-Wall' gang. They rob banks and trains, but Butch's ambition is to go to Bolivia, which has silver, tin and gold mines. The two buddies are endlessly pursued by a remote and relentless posse forcing them into the hills. At one stage they are trapped and cornered by the posse on a ledge at the edge of a steep rock canyon with nowhere else to go. They are faced with a choice between a hopeless shoot-out and a near-suicidal leap. Although the Kid confesses he can't swim, they jump in tandem and the swift current carries them to safety. After a romantic interlude during which both men vie for schoolteacher Etta Place (Ross), they get to Bolivia, where the army catches up with them. This romanticized version of a true story is vastly entertaining and likeable. Newman is an independent, unconventional thinker, disrespectful of both the law and the establishment; Redford is more level-headed, the traditional western hero. Instead of the ultra-violence typical of other outlaw films of the day, the film, borrowing from *Jules et Jim* and *Bonnie and Clyde*, uses an ironic mixture of slapstick comedy and conventional western action to comment on the clichés of the cowboy genre. There is even the famous anachronistic (and Oscar-winning) song, 'Raindrops Keep Falling on My Head', which accompanies Newman doing tricks on a bicycle.

TRUE GRIT

Henry Hathaway, USA, 1969

CAST INCLUDES:
John Wayne, Glen Campbell,
Kim Darby, Robert Duvall,
Dennis Hopper
SCREENPLAY:
Marguerite Roberts
from the novel by
Charles Portis
CINEMATOGRAPHY:
Lucien Ballard

Rooster Cogburn (Wayne), a hulking, one-eyed, drunken, cantankerous old US Marshal, is hired by 14-year-old Mattie Ross (Darby) to find Tom Chaney (Corey), who killed her father. The headstrong Mattie has selected the ageing Cogburn because she believed he had 'true grit'. Also heading into Indian territory in search of Chaney is Texas ranger La Boeuf (Campbell), who wants to collect the reward placed on the fugitive's head for his earlier crimes. With him are three ruthless villains, Ned Pepper (Duvall), Quincy (Slate) and Moon (Hopper), who put both the lives of Cogburn and Mattie in danger. 'If I'd known, I'd have put the eye-patch on 35 years earlier,' the 62-year-old John Wayne quipped on receiving his first Best Actor Oscar for his 139th film. The award was not only long overdue but fully merited. What Wayne manages to do is create an ageing, uncouth, mean-tempered man, undoubtedly brave who, under the boorish exterior, conceals a tender heart without lapsing into mawkishness. The straight-shooting film, directed with supreme expertise by the 71-year-old Henry Hathaway, who had directed Wayne several times previously, had the refreshing presence of newcomer Kim Darby. In 1975, Wayne repeated his *True Grit* characterization opposite Katharine Hepburn in *Rooster Cogburn*, but the film failed to match its predecessor.

ACADEMY AWARD
Best Actor in a Leading Role:
John Wayne

THE WILD BUNCH

Sam Peckinpah, USA, 1969

Pike Bishop (Holden) is the leader of the Wild Bunch, a group of middle-aged, saddle-weary outlaws who find their way of life quickly growing obsolete in 1913. After surviving an ambush by bounty hunters, Pike realizes that the Wild Bunch cannot last forever and wants to plan one last job – 'doing' a railroad office near the Texas border – to make them wealthy before they ride off into the sunset. Deke Thornton (Ryan), the sixth member of the bunch, seeing no future in remaining with Bishop, has gone straight and is working as a bounty hunter determined to destroy his ex-cohorts. But death is not far away for the bunch.

CAST INCLUDES:
William Holden, Ernest Borgnine, Robert Ryan, Edmund O'Brein, Warren Oats, Ben Johnson, Jaime Sanchez
SCREENPLAY:
Walon Green, Sam Peckinpah
CINEMATOGRAPHY:
Lucien Ballard

Sam Peckinpah's bloody and meditative tale of the American West is considered by many to be the director's masterpiece. The western was a dying breed when Peckinpah, along with *Bonnie and Clyde*, two years earlier, ushered in a new breed of Hollywood film, depicting a harsh reality where lines between right and wrong became blurred. The film's sympathy is plainly with the outlaws who try to live from another age, although the scenes of carnage reflect the year the film was made. Many critics argued that the way Peckinpah filmed it made violence look good. Every killing was accentuated in slow motion, lending a distinctly lyrical touch as another gringo bit the dust. But it is clearly designed to show that violence doesn't pay. The film also deals with themes of ageing, friendship, loyalty, betrayal and deception. Peckinpah directed superbly with a sharp sense of characterization and atmosphere, making it into a moving elegy for the end of an era.

THE BALLAD OF CABLE HOGUE

Sam Peckinpah, USA, 1970

Cable Hogue (Robards), an itinerant prospector, is left to die in the desert by his two double-crossing partners until he miraculously discovers a water hole. It is in just the right spot for a much-needed rest stop on the local stagecoach line, and Hogue uses this to his advantage. He builds a house and makes money from the stagecoach passengers. Having made his fortune, and having gained the love of a gold-hearted hooker (Stevens), he is determined on revenge. Hogue has everything going his way until the advent of the automobile ends the era of the stagecoach. Sam Peckinpah's characteristic use of graphic violence was toned down somewhat in this gem of a western ballad, but his affectionate view of the Old West is very much in evidence throughout, as is his irony and edgy sense of humour. It could be considered the comic side of *The Wild Bunch,* the film's companion piece. In both films, the main characters' attempts to stem the advance of the new-style West end in death. Peckinpah described *The Ballad of Cable Hogue* as 'a new version of Sartre's *The Flies* and the *Keystone Kops*'. Jason Robards and Stella Stevens make a likeable couple, while David Warner is effective as a God-defying Luciferian preacher.

CAST INCLUDES:
Jason Robards, Stella Stevens, David Warner, Strother Martin
SCREENPLAY:
John Crawford, Edmund Penney
CINEMATOGRAPHY:
Lucien Ballard

LITTLE BIG MAN

Arthur Penn, USA, 1970

CAST INCLUDES:
Dustin Hoffman, Faye Dunaway, Martin Balsam, Chief Dan George, Richard Mulligan, Jeff Corey, Thayer David
SCREENPLAY:
Calder Willingham from the novel by Thomas Berger.
CINEMATOGRAPHY:
Harry Stradling

Jack Crabb (Hoffman) is a 121-year-old survivor of Custer's Last Stand, who reminisces over his long and eventful life. In 1859, as a 10-year-old abandoned orphan, he is adopted by the Cheyenne and made a brave called Little Big Man. Aged 16, he rides into battle against white soldiers but is captured and taken in by a reverend (David) and his wife (Dunaway). In his mid-20s, he joins Custer (Mulligan), determines to kill him, then offers himself to the general as an Indian scout. At the last battle, Crabb is saved by a Cheyenne. Director Arthur Penn manages astutely to veer from broad comedy to making serious comments about Indian culture – the Cheyennes are presented as an ideal alternative to the white world – and analogies between their treatment by the whites and the Vietnam War. It was not the first attempt to redress the balance in favour of the Native Americans, but it began a new trend in which the western was appropriated by directors in order to express their liberal views.

McCABE AND MRS MILLER

Robert Altman, USA, 1971

In the northwestern zinc-mining town of Presbyterian Church at the turn of the century, McCabe (Beatty), a bumbling small-time gambler, in the guise of a notorious gunslinger, becomes a business partner in a bordello run by the tougher, more sophisticated, opium-smoking Mrs Miller (Christie). They fall in love and he dreams of building a city out of the muddy frontier settlement, but he has to face gunmen sent by a powerful mining company to kill him.

In a way, Robert Altman's first film of this genre (like his only other one, *Buffalo Bill and the Indians*) could be considered an anti-western, exposing the myth of the heroic westerner and replacing it with an almost Marxist view of the westerner as an opportunistic financier, spreading capitalism and corruption. Awash with contemporary allusions, this personal film is very much enhanced by Vilmos Zsigmond's atmospheric photography – especially the memorable closing sequence in the snow – and the convincing creation of a mythical American town. Warren Beatty, glowering handsomely, makes McCabe an unheroic, uneducated figure, who doesn't wear a gun. On the soundtrack, commenting on the action, are Leonard Cohen songs that conjure up the spirit of the 1970s.

CAST INCLUDES:
Warren Beatty, Julie Christie, René Auberjonois, John Schuck, Bert Remsen, Keith Carradine
SCREENPLAY:
Robert Altman, Brian McKay from the novel *McCabe* by Edmund Naughton
CINEMATOGRAPHY:
Vilmos Zsigmond

BAD COMPANY

Robert Benton, USA, 1972

Two young deserters from the Union army, con man Jake Rumsey (Bridges) and the God-fearing Drew Dixon (Brown), join up while fleeing the American Civil War. They first meet when Drew is mugged by Jake. With two other draft dodgers, Loney (Savage) and Arthur (Houser), they set off towards the Mississippi and the West, becoming outlaws while dodging a professional criminal (Huddleston), cut-throats, sheriffs and recruiting officers. This was the first feature directed by Robert Benton who, with David Newman, wrote the sensational *Bonnie and Clyde*. The same team's *Bad Company* shares the same black humour, amorality and loving concern for the feel of the period. As the earlier film demythologized the gangster movie, this one does the same with the western. Here, survival depends on crime, the only activity that pays. Wonderfully photographed by Gordon Willis (*The Godfather*) in a variety of autumnal browns, this is an unjustly neglected masterpiece of the 1970s. Because of the Vietnam War, this episodic tale of deserters and draft dodgers had a resonance with young audiences.

THE LIFE AND TIMES OF JUDGE ROY BEAN
John Huston, USA, 1972

After being run out of the outlaw town of Vinegaroon, the robber and rapist Roy Bean (Newman) is left for dead. But Bean returns to take his revenge. He sets himself up as a judge and has an affair with Maria Elena (Principal), a local Mexican girl who saved Bean's life. The town prospers under his own brand of frontier justice, robbing or killing anyone who tries to make their way through it. The town is renamed Langtry, in honour of the actress Lily Langtry (Gardner), his feminine ideal. Gradually the town achieves respectability, and Bean loses his power. So he leaves, only to return 20 years later to seek revenge again, but he finds it full of automobiles and oil derricks.

CAST INCLUDES:
Paul Newman, Victoria Principal, Anthony Perkins, Tab Hunter, Ava Gardner
SCREENPLAY:
John Milius
CINEMATOGRAPHY:
Richard Moore

Shot in Mexico, this episodic and somewhat surreal tale of the famous 'hanging judge' obsessed with actress Lily Langtry is a bizarre mixture of drama and comedy, romanticism and cynicism. The same story, though far less wide-ranging, was told in William Wyler's *The Westerner* (1940), in which Bean was a villain portrayed by Walter Brennan. As played here by Paul Newman, he is more of a misunderstood antihero, who is seen differently by a variety of well-cast characters, including Anthony Perkins as an itinerant preacher resembling a black crow, who comes to bury Bean's victims. The director, John Huston, who also has a cameo role, seems to have enjoyed himself making it, an enjoyment communicated to audiences.

ULZANA'S RAID

Robert Aldrich, USA, 1972

Angered at their mistreatment by whites, a group of renegade Apaches led by Ulzana (Martinez) escape from their reservation and embark on a rampage of murder, rape and destruction. A small detachment of troops under the inexperienced DeBuin (Davison), accompanied by two army scouts, the veteran McIntosh (Lancaster) and an Apache (Luke), are assigned to track down the Indians. As DeBuin, McIntosh and their party venture into the unfriendly landscape, issues start to surface about the morality of their mission. Soon the white men are fighting amongst themselves, divided over the task at hand. Meanwhile, their efforts to stop Ulzana's raid seem fruitless. Robert Aldrich's intelligent, edgy and graphic film contains many of the features one expects from the director: characters verging on insanity, eruptions into violence, told in a style full of overhead shots, vast close-ups and shock-cuts. The film attempts to draw parallels with contemporary society. While the cavalry, like the US troops in Vietnam, try to fight conventionally, the Indians use guerrilla tactics like the Vietcong. The veteran soldiers behave almost as savagely as the Indians, much as some soldiers did in the Vietnam conflict. At the film's centre is Burt Lancaster's mature and calming presence, while Joseph Biroc's magnificent cinematography evokes the scorching heat of the barren desert.

CAST INCLUDES:
Burt Lancaster,
Bruce Davison, Jorge Luke,
Richard Jaeckel,
Joaquin Martinez
SCREENPLAY:
Alan Sharp
CINEMATOGRAPHY:
Joseph Biroc

HIGH PLAINS DRIFTER

Clint Eastwood, USA, 1973

CAST INCLUDES:
Clint Eastwood, Verna Bloom,
Marianna Hill, Mitchell Ryan,
Jack Ging
SCREENPLAY:
Ernest Tidyman
CINEMATOGRAPHY:
Bruce Surtees

A stranger (Eastwood), mysteriously materializes out of the desert heat, riding into the small town of Lago. He seems to have returned from the dead to exact revenge on the townsfolk of Lago, who once stood by and watched him, their sheriff, whipped to 'death' by a trio of hired gunmen. He requires the inhabitants to literally paint the town red and change its name to Hell. The townspeople are scared of him, and the three gunmen try, unsuccessfully, to kill him again. Clint Eastwood's second film as star and director, and his first western, is a stylish revenge drama that pays tribute to Clint's mentors Sergio Leone and Don Siegel. (Among the graves in the cemetery are those of 'Donald Siegel' and 'S. Leone'.) But it is more allegorical and offbeat than even their pictures, with an added eerie, supernatural element, emphasized by Bruce Surtees' almost surreal camerawork. This is counterbalanced by realistic images of a tougher West, cold and gritty, peopled with unshaven men and plain women. Universal wanted the film to be shot on the studio lot but, instead, Clint had a whole town built (and burned to the ground) in the desert near Lake Mono in the California Sierras.

THE OUTLAW JOSEY WALES

Clint Eastwood, USA, 1976

Josey Wales (Eastwood) is a peaceful Missouri farmer whose wife and children are brutally murdered by a band of marauding Unionist guerillas. He joins a Confederate gang and exacts bloody revenge on the Unionists. When the war ends, as an outlaw with a price on his head, he makes a journey to Texas, picking up various companions along the way and eventually setting up a commune where, gradually, his thoughts return from killing to farming. This inspired epic of great scope, structured as a series of brilliant set pieces, was originally to have been directed by Clint Eastwood's co-scenarist Phil Kaufman, but the former took over after shooting had already begun because of a disagreement as to the nature of the eponymous character. In the event, it turned out to be one of Eastwood's finest achievements both as actor and director. The lyrical landscape photography of Bruce Surtees, Jerry Fielding's fine score and some of the relationships make this a tender film despite the violence, necessary in this picture of a harsh existence. Chief Dan George as an old Cherokee brave lends the film light relief.

CAST INCLUDES:
Clint Eastwood, Chief Dan George, Sondra Locke, Bill McKinney, John Vernon
SCREENPLAY:
Phil Kaufman, Sonia Chernus from the novel *Gone To Texas* by Forrest Carter
CINEMATOGRAPHY:
Bruce Surtees

THE SHOOTIST

Don Siegel, USA, 1976

After J.B. Books (Wayne), a retired gunfighter, learns that he's dying of stomach cancer and has no more than two months to live, he moves into a boarding house in Carson City run by prim widow Bond Rogers (Bacall) and her impressionable son, Gillom (Howard), to die quietly. But when word gets around that the old 'shootist' is in town, there are those who contemplate a showdown with the legend. Annoyed by the attention and realizing that if he waits long enough, he'll die in great pain, Books decides to seek out his enemies and go down with guns blazing. In the finale, he kills three local villains, but he manages to persuade Gillom to foreswear the life of violence he's led. This graceful valediction to a great star opens with a moving black-and-white montage from John Wayne's earlier westerns, which is offered as a backstory to the J.B. Books character. Wayne, like Books, was dying of cancer as the film was being shot. This makes the parallels between fiction and reality all the more poignant.

CAST INCLUDES:
John Wayne, Lauren Bacall, Ron Howard, James Stewart, John Carradine, Richard Boone, Hugh O'Brian
SCREENPLAY:
Miles Hood Swarthout, Scott Hale from the novel by Glendon Swarthout
CINEMATOGRAPHY:
Bruce Surtees

THE LONG RIDERS

Walter Hill, USA, 1990

CAST INCLUDES:
James Keach, Stacy Keach, David Carradine, Keith Carradine, Robert Carradine, Dennis Quaid, Randy Quaid, Christopher Guest, Nicholas Guest
SCREENPLAY:
Bill Bryden, Steven P. Smith, Stacy and James Keach
CINEMATOGRAPHY:
Ric Waite

Cole, Jim and Bob Younger (the Carradine brothers), Frank and Jesse James (the Keach brothers), Ed and Clell Miller (the Quaid brothers) and Charlie and Bob Ford (the Guest brothers), a loosely knit gang of bank and train robbers, are relentlessly pursued by the Pinkerton Detective Agency. However, they are fiercely protected by their neighbours and relatives while the gang goes robbing. Occasionally they go their own ways, only to come together again, despite the tensions among them. The spectacular but disastrous Northfield Minnesota Raid, followed by the murder of Jesse by the treacherous Ford brothers, ends the criminal careers of the legendary outlaws. 'We started robbing banks and we just kept going,' was the main motivation given by the notorious James gang, but there is far more to Walter Hill's visually poetic but gritty and violent western. The film firmly places the gang within the rural folk culture of post–Civil War Missouri, stressing the tight family relationships and the social rituals. The same subject was treated in *The Great Northfield Minnesota Raid* (1971), but Hill's use of slow motion, flashbacks, distorted sound, and the extremely unusual but effective casting of four sets of brothers in the main roles injected new life into old material.

YOUNG GUNS

Christopher Cain, USA, 1988

CAST INCLUDES:
Emilio Estevez, Kiefer Sutherland, Lou Diamond Phillips, Charlie Sheen, Terence Stamp, Jack Palance
SCREENPLAY:
John Fusco
CINEMATOGRAPHY:
Dean Semler

British ranch owner John Tunstall (Stamp) hires six young men to help him tend and guard his ranch. In addition, he teaches them to read and to be civilized. When Tunstall refuses to sell his land to corrupt and ruthless ranch owner Lawrence Murphy (Palance), he is brutally murdered by Murphy's men. The six 'young guns' are then made lawmen named the Regulators, and have sworn to bring the murderers to justice. But, one of their number, William H. Bonney, later Billy the Kid (Estevez), has his own plans for the men who killed their father-figure – gun them down, one by one. Due to Billy's actions, the Regulators are soon branded outlaws, wanted dead or alive. This oft-repeated tale of Billy the Kid has been adapted in every era to suit the climate and audiences of the time. Since the first full-scale screen version, King Vidor's *Billy The Kid* (1930), there have been dozens of features, the notorious young outlaw being played by, among others, Robert Taylor (30), Paul Newman (32) and Kris Kristofferson (37). Christopher Cain's good-humoured 'modern' take on the story – the dialogue contains expressions like 'kiss my ass' – certainly appealed to young audiences and followers of the Brat Pack. Emilio Estevez (26) and the other Regulators are closer to the right age of the outlaws, and Jack Palance features for those older spectators who prefer the more classical westerns. A sequel, *Young Guns II* (1990) was inevitable.

DANCES WITH WOLVES

Kevin Costner, USA, 1990

CAST INCLUDES:
Kevin Costner,
Mary McDonnell,
Graham Greene,
Rodney A. Grant,
Floyd 'Red Crow' Westerman
SCREENPLAY:
Michael Blake from his novel
CINEMATOGRAPHY:
Dean Semler

Lieutenant John J. Dunbar (Costner), a Unionist officer decorated for bravery, asks to be posted to the western frontier. Living alone at the mysteriously abandoned Fort Sedgewick, he befriends members of the Sioux tribe. He earns their trust and they rename him Dances with Wolves. He falls in love with Stands With a Fist (McDonnell), a white woman adopted by the Sioux when she was a girl, and marries her. Captured by the newly arrived cavalry, he is brutally treated as a turncoat. As a debut director, Kevin Costner displayed extraordinary confidence, also succeeding in getting unstereotypical performances from his Native American actors who speak their own languages with subtitles. He proved himself more than worthy of the Best Director Oscar (the film won seven overall) and breathed new life into what was considered a dying genre.

UNFORGIVEN

Clint Eastwood, USA, 1992

CAST INCLUDES:
Clint Eastwood, Gene
Hackman, Morgan Freeman,
Richard Harris, Frances
Fisher, Saul Rubinek
SCREENPLAY:
David Webb Peoples
CINEMATOGRAPHY:
Jack N. Green

When Little Bill Daggett (Hackman), a sadistic, dictatorial sheriff of a small frontier town, denies justice to the prostitutes of the local brothel, one of whom has been viciously slashed by two clients, the women hire Bill Munny (Eastwood), a retired, once-ruthless gunfighter, now a gentle widower and hog farmer, to shoot the culprits. He accepts the job to help support his two motherless children, and is joined by his former partner (Freeman) and a cocky greenhorn. However, Munny must contend with his new moral code in the face of revisiting the life he left behind. Dedicated 'to Sergio and Don', the two directors, Leone and Siegel, who served as his most important mentors, *Unforgiven*, according to Clint Eastwood, 'summarized everything I feel about the western. The moral is the concern with gunplay.' Eastwood's tenth western is also his crowning achievement in the genre in which he made his name. He had acquired the script some ten years earlier, but he had wanted to 'age' into it. At 62, he was ready to play the role to perfection. This 'revisionist' western, exploring the darker side of the myths of the Old West, gave the kiss of life to the genre. It is striking in its willingness to confront the effects of violence on both those who commit it and those who suffer it, and for the sense of the characters' realization of their own mortality.

THE LAST OF THE MOHICANS

Michael Mann, USA, 1992

CAST INCLUDES:
Daniel Day-Lewis,
Madeleine Stowe,
Russell Means, Jodhi May,
Eric Schweig, Maurice
Roëves, Patrice Chéreau,
Wes Studi
SCREENPLAY:
Michael Mann,
Christopher Crowe
CINEMATOGRAPHY:
Dante Spinotti

ACADEMY AWARD
Best Sound:
Chris Jenkins, Doug Hemphill,
Mark Smith, Simon Kaye

Hawkeye (Day-Lewis) is a European-born adopted son of Chingachgook (American Indian Movement leader Russell Means), a patrician Mohican. Hawkeye, a fur trapper, gets caught between two cultures when he falls for Cora Munro (Stowe), a British army officer's daughter, whom he had rescued from a Huron war party. Hawkeye serves as a guide for the British at Fort William Henry (reconstructed exactly from historical documents) until it falls to the French (and their Indian allies), with Colonel Munro (Roëves) surrendering to General Montcalm (Chéreau). The third Hollywood version of the James Fenimore Cooper classic adventure yarn is also the most wildly romantic, the most exciting, the most attractive (it is beautifully lit and photographed) and the most violent – the scalpings are pretty graphic. Daniel Day-Lewis, with flowing mane and heaving muscles, makes a virile but sensitive hero. Director Michael Mann brilliantly captures the essence of the era (the 1750s) – the hand-to-hand battles, the harsh life in the wilderness. The film was shot on location in North Carolina's Smoky Mountains and the old-growth forests stand in spectacularly for the New York State of Cooper's novel.

BROKEBACK MOUNTAIN

Ang Lee, USA, 2005

In the isolated Wyoming mountain ranges, a strong bond develops between Ennis (Ledger) and Jack (Gyllenhaal), two young ranch hands hired to tend sheep. After parting ways at the end of the season, they each begin to understand their feelings a little better and eventually reunite and begin a love affair that lasts, in one way or another, for 19 years. Director Ang Lee has never stuck to a specific genre, or even style, since making his breakthrough with the 1994 romantic comedy, *Eat Drink Man Woman*. In a career that has seen him flit effortlessly between Hollywood, Britain, Hong Kong and his native Taiwan, his films seem to be just as diverse as the places in which he makes them. From *Sense and Sensibility* (1995) to *Hulk* (2003) is quite a leap, but eyebrows were still raised when it was announced that his latest project would be a 'gay cowboy movie'. If there is a thread of any sort running through his previous work, it must be a fascination with emotional control. *Brokeback Mountain* is a natural extension and represents the pinnacle of this theme. In Lee's hands this is an extraordinarily moving story.

CAST INCLUDES:
Jake Gyllenhaal, Heath Ledger, Michelle Williams, Anne Hathaway, Randy Quaid
CINEMATOGRAPHY:
Rodrigo Prieto
SCREENPLAY:
Larry McMurtry, Diana Ossana, Annie Proulx (short story)

ACADEMY AWARDS
Best Achievement in Directing: Ang Lee
Best Achievement in Music Written for Motion Pictures, Original Score: Gustavo Santaolalla
Best Writing, Adapted Screenplay: Larry McMurtry, Diana Ossana

THE PROPOSITION

John Hillcoat, Australia, 2005

CAST INCLUDES:
Guy Pearce, Ray Winstone,
Richard Wilson,
Danny Huston, Emily Watson
SCREENPLAY:
Nick Cave
CINEMATOGRAPHY:
Benoît Delhomme

In the late 19th-century Australian wilderness, Captain Stanley (Winstone) fights a desperate war with the outlaw gangs who run wild. After capturing Charlie (Pearce) and Mike Burns (Wilson), brothers of notorious outlaw Arthur (Huston), Stanley makes Charlie an offer: find and kill Arthur or their beloved baby brother Mike will hang. The pedigree wasn't all that promising for *The Proposition*. Director John Hillcoat had only a couple of forgotten thrillers to his name, and although Nick Cave is a respected musician, he was an untested screenwriter when their film got the green light. Together they surprised the whole industry with a brooding and bloody modern classic that seemed to single-handedly reinvigorate Australian cinema. Although there's much thematic depth, it is essentially a character study; an examination of what men are capable of when given no choice in the matter. Pearce offers up his best performance since *L.A. Confidential* and Huston is magnetic during his limited screen time, but it's Winstone you'll probably remember. He plays Stanley as a deeply contradictory figure who, in his determination to 'civilize' his adopted homeland, has ended up using determinedly uncivilized methods. His inspiration is undoubtedly beloved wife, Martha (Watson), a fragile English rose he will do anything to guard from the harsh realities of their world. In fact, so much effort is expended on her protection that it soon seems inevitable that her husband's professional life will eventually intrude, and the prospect looms ominously over everything.

DID YOU KNOW?
Nick Cave's score for the film was written before the film was shot.

THE ASSASSINATION OF JESSE JAMES BY THE COWARD ROBERT FORD

Andrew Dominik, USA, 2007

During the winter of 1882, Jesse James (Pitt) is increasingly paranoid and depressed after the retirement of his older brother and the collapse of his gang. Bob Ford (Affleck), a young outlaw who idolizes James, talks his way into his hero's inner circle only to turn against him.

CAST INCLUDES:
Brad Pitt, Casey Affleck, Sam Shepard, Jeremy Renner, Sam Rockwell, Mary-Louise Parker
SCREENPLAY:
Andrew Dominik, Ron Hansen (novel)
CINEMATOGRAPHY:
Roger Deakins

It's not unusual for westerns to be elegiac or to revel in the mythologizing of an antihero, but *The Assassination* pushes these themes to the limit. In spite of his reputation as a Robin Hood–type hero of the poor, Jesse James was undeniably rotten, stealing indiscriminately and killing anyone deemed a threat. Considering such historical inconveniences, one of the film's greatest accomplishments lies in the successful presentation of James as a sympathetic antihero. Casting Brad Pitt was always going to help, but it's the other character in the eponymous title – Robert Ford – who does the most to make sense of this contradictory outlaw. We see James through an enigmatic lens with perfect lighting and dramatic music, the same romanticized and surreal figure Robert Ford pictured when reading the paperback chronicles of the James gang so beloved from his youth. Bitterness and resentment grow from a perceived lack of respect and Ford becomes ever more paranoid. By the time the action in the title is carried out, Ford may see James as a fraud and a threat but we, the audience, are still watching the legend.

THERE WILL BE BLOOD

Paul Thomas Anderson, USA, 2007

Daniel Plainview (Day-Lewis) is a ruthless oil prospector leaving a trail of broken promises and conned farmers wherever he goes. When his search for oil brings him to the Californian community of Little Boston, local preacher Eli Sunday (Dano) becomes determined to at first understand, and later stop, the tyrannical Plainview.

Although anticipated for a rare performance by frequently retired acting legend Daniel Day-Lewis, this dark drama seemed to sneak up on audiences largely unawares. An instant classic of powerhouse cinema the film may be, but the importance of Day-Lewis in the central role cannot be underestimated. Plainview is a monster of stupendous proportions and utterly dominates the film, appearing in almost every scene. On the odd occasion he isn't on screen, his spectre looms large over those who are, seemingly encouraging them to whisper their admonishments for fear of him overhearing from another scene. With his adopted son the supposed evidence of his being a good 'family man', Plainview wheels from town to town conning poor locals out of oil-rich land in return for empty promises and broken dreams. In Eli Sunday he finally comes up against someone who is prepared to challenge him, but the preacher proves unable to overcome such a powerful man (in spite of peddling his own neat line in hypocrisy and hogwash). As antagonist to Plainview, Dano has one of the toughest jobs in recent cinema in bringing Sunday to life. His BAFTA nomination demonstrates the exceptional job he did, although Day-Lewis went one better and won the Academy Award.

CAST INCLUDES:
Daniel Day-Lewis, Paul Dano,
Barry Del Sherman,
Matthew Braden Stringer
SCREENPLAY:
Paul Thomas Anderson,
based on the novel by
Upton Sinclair
CINEMATOGRAPHY:
Robert Elswit

NO COUNTRY FOR OLD MEN

Ethan Coen/Joel Coen, USA, 2007

In rural Texas, working man Llewellyn Moss (Brolin) stumbles across a case of cash at the scene of a drug deal gone wrong. At first he doesn't realize that both local sheriff Ed Tom Bell (Jones) and psychopathic hit man Anton Chigurh (Bardem) are both on his trail. After a couple of rather bloated and disappointing offerings (*Intolerable Cruelty* and *The Ladykillers*) the Coen brothers stripped everything down to basics and, in *No Country for Old Men*, have given us the sort of smart and focused classic we'd become used to. Styled as film noir, it largely avoids the absurdity that is a common feature of the Coens' writing. Bardem is mesmerizing as Chigurh; his unnerving performance dominates the film with the sort of menace other bad guys can only dream of. With his weapon of choice (a compressed-air cattle gun) and implacable approach, he is inevitably always two steps ahead of Sheriff Bell, who is exasperated by just how unpleasant people can be to each other. Brolin also excels in a role he was born to play. Quick thinking but not all that bright, Moss takes a while to realize the trouble he's in, but once he does you wouldn't want to bet against him.

ACADEMY AWARDS

Best Achievement
in Directing:
Ethan Coen, Joel Coen
Best Motion Picture
of the Year: Scott Rudin,
Ethan Coen, Joel Coen
Best Performance by an
Actor in a Supporting Role:
Javier Bardem
Best Writing, Screenplay
Based on Material Previously
Produced or Published:
Joel Coen, Ethan Coen

CAST INCLUDES: Tommy Lee Jones, Javier Bardem, Josh Brolin, Woody Harrelson, Kelly Macdonald, Garrett Dillahunt, Tess Harper
SCREENPLAY: Joel Coen and Ethan Coen
CINEMATOGRAPHY: Roger Deakins

INDEX

INDEX

PICTURE CREDITS